THE OFFICIAL PRICE GUIDE TO

CHRISTMAS

and Other Holiday Collectibles

Dawn Reno Langley

House of Collectibles

New York Toronto London Sydney Auckland

House of Collectibles and colophon are registered
trademarks of Random House, Inc.

RANDOM HOUSE is a registered trademark of Random House, Inc.

This book is available at special discounts for bulk purchases for sales promotions or premiums. Special editions, including personalized covers, excerpts of existing books, and corporate imprints, can be cre-ated in large quantities for special needs. For more information, write to Special Markets/Premium Sales, 1745 Broadway, MD 6-2, New York, NY 10019 or e-mail specialmarkets@randomhouse.com.

Please address inquiries about electronic licensing of any products for use on a network, in software, or on CD-ROM to the Subsidiary Rights Department, Random House Information Group, fax 212-572-6003.

Visit the House of Collectibles Web site: www.houseofcollectibles.com

Printed in the United States of America

10 9 8 7 6 5 4 3 2 1

ISBN-13: 978-0-375-72128-1

ISBN-10: 0-375-72128-2

*For my husband,
Norris, with loving thanks for
taking care of everything
while I worked on this book!*

CONTENTS

July

August

September

October

November

December

INTRODUCTION

Books like these are not written without the cooperation of many people, and the first thing I want to do is to acknowledge the collectors, dealers, artists, museums, antique shops, auction houses, family members, and friends who offered their time, expertise, photographs, and research to help bring this book to fruition. Many a weekend phone call answered questions about collectibles, and many an e-mail brought new insight to this researcher. The field of holiday collectibles is immense, but, thankfully, the hearts of those who love the items produced for annual holidays is even larger. An enormous "thank you" goes to all of you! As they say, you know who you are.

How to Use This Book

After much deliberation, my editors and I decided that a book on holiday collectibles needed to be divided by month, and though I thought that most of the items produced would fall into less than half a dozen categories, I was wrong. In every month of the year, we found holidays, and for each of those holidays, there are items produced that are considered collectible. Yes, some holidays are more popular than others (Christmas is still the undisputed king), but for some, the hunt for the elusive article is much more enticing than competing with thousands of other aficionados for the same piece. Even the most "uncelebrated" holiday has been recognized at some point or another, and collectors pursue whatever items were created as a result of that recognition.

This book is designed to be an overview of all the holidays, with emphasis on those that are most popular (Christmas, Easter, Halloween, Valentine's Day, Thanksgiving, July 4th). I have offered a history of the holiday, how it is celebrated, and the items created for those celebrations. In addition, in-depth information about the companies that made the festive items is included, and, whenever applicable, information about the artists responsible for illustrating the collectibles is also offered.

Prices are listed to give the collector a general idea of what those pieces might be worth. A caveat must be offered here: During the years I've been writing books on collecting, the one constant is that prices are *never* written in stone. What your composition Santa Claus figure is worth in a flea market in New York might not match the price on the same figure in an antique store in Los Angeles. The values are meant to give you a general ballpark figure, not an amount to be entered on an insurance claim. Use this book as a guide and remember that, depending upon how many people want the same item you do, prices can escalate quite rapidly and can often be incredibly mercurial.

Thousands of items flood the various holiday markets, providing a plethora of fun objects to adorn trees, decorate tables, enhance walls, and delight customers. A collector could accumulate items for a holiday collection and keep busy until the end of time. Every category of "stuff" expands as a balloon does when filled with air, but the balloon gets larger and larger, offering incredible opportunities for everyone.

Each collector will find it easier to add to his or her collection if a certain set of parameters is applied. Some will want to collect items from just one holiday, while others want to collect books attributed to holidays in general, or postcards illustrated by a certain artist, or Gurley candles in any shape or size. My only advice is that you keep it specific and buy the best you can afford. No one can promise you that your pieces will increase in value as the years go by, but if you simply buy what you love, it won't matter. Just enjoy them!

Should you want additional information on any particular collectible, the extensive bibliography at the end of this book will give you some ideas to begin your research. There are also a number of collector organizations that bring people together to talk about the items they collect, and many of these organizations produce newsletters that present valuable insights about particular objects. Online bulletin boards and chat rooms that focus on your particular area of interest can provide much help—with information as well as buying and selling opportunities. For example, eBay has discussion boards, chat rooms, groups, and an answer center to help you discover more and more about the collectibles you want to add to your treasure trove. Take advantage of them!

Another decision that I made when constructing this book was to include holiday items from various periods, from the antique to the reproduction, from the mass-produced to the one-of-a-kind pieces of art. Just as people choose to collect items from one type of holiday, they might also choose to collect items from a particular era. One collector of Santas concentrates her hunt on only wooden Santas, while another wants only German Santas from the Victorian era. The artists included in this volume produce work eagerly awaited by their fans, and their artwork often represents a new vision of the holiday they are interpreting. Some purists believe that building a collection means having to focus on items produced before a certain decade, but since elegant, unusual and beautiful holiday items appear every season, why not add them to your cache? In most cases, these festive *objets d'art* are available for only a limited time anyway.

One of the most important tips I can offer the beginning collector is to pay attention to condition when adding bits and pieces to your collection. Specifically, if you might be interested in selling parts of your accumulation in years to come, you should concentrate on finding articles in perfect condition, or as close to perfect condition as you can find. Since most holiday items have some fragility, you run the risk of damaging them anytime they are brought out for display. If you find an item you simply cannot live without, but it is slightly damaged, chances are very good that the damage will increase with time. Not only is a damaged piece worth far less, you might lose it entirely if it's handled incorrectly.

It's fun to search out treasures, to feel your heart beat fast when you win a piece at auction or find the missing item in a set. Nothing else is quite as satisfying as decorating a home for the holidays and bringing out tangible memories of days gone by. Enjoy your little piece of festivity!

What's Hot and What's Not

It goes without saying that Christmas items are always hot, even in July. EBay reports its top-selling categories on a regular basis, and ornaments, Santas, and angels are consistently at the top of the list. Through the years, Kris Kringle has been a staple in the holiday collecting field, and I expect Christmas stuff will always be at the top of the list.

Until the 1980s, Halloween items were largely ignored. Then collectors started realizing that these generally disposable items were not only attractive and fun, but provided a bit of the chase that turns collectors on. Dealers reported an increase in sales of Halloween items that they used to have to lure people to buy. Yard sale experts and flea market aficionados saw a spike in the amount of money they had to pay for cardboard skeleton figurines, composition Jack-O'-Lanterns, and accordion witch centerpieces. Wise collectors started compiling anything created in the shape of a Halloween icon, and before long, prices had rocketed out of sight. A hot collectible category had been born. Nowadays, you're lucky to uncover a Halloween decoration at a yard sale for a reasonable price; usually, smart collectors and dealers arrive early at those yard sales!

Valentine's and Easter items have the same history as the Halloween goodies just mentioned. There are very few Victorian Valentine cards left that haven't been around the market time and again. And Easter bunnies, chicks, baskets, and eggs are also in short supply. So, what does the new collector look for?

Mardi Gras necklaces, masks, and party-related stuff is gaining in popularity. They can still be had for pocket change, but the items that are dated, like party invitations, are worth more. It's a fun holiday, but unfortunately, the items tend to be mass-produced and cheaply made. The collector who wants to find the truly unique or one-of-a-kind item will need to pay the price.

Thanksgiving platters, serving dishes, salt and pepper shakers, table and wall decorations, and Thanksgiving icon figures are still reasonably priced and easy to find. The beauty of collecting Thanksgiving objects is that you can use them over and over again, so your investment doesn't go to waste. Prices have not yet risen to a point that prohibits the buyer from adding these collectibles to their shelves.

Buyers looking for July 4th, Memorial Day, Presidents' Day, Veterans' Day, and Patriots' Day collectibles often bump heads with people who hunt for political or presidential items. That can produce some frustration, not to mention some incredibly high priced ephemera.

One of the hottest collecting areas is Day of the Dead figures, boxes, and pottery. They are still reasonably priced, usually original works of art, and lots of fun to collect. Some collectors have started amassing fair-sized assortments of these colorful and funky representations of the dead, but they are produced every year, so you have plenty of choices. Now's the time to get on this bandwagon!

Other holiday collectibles that are still reasonably priced and readily accessible include New Year's, Saint Patrick's Day, Mother's and Father's Day (as well as Sisters' Day, Grandparents' Day, Bosses' Day, and all the other Hallmark-inspired holidays), Martin Luther King, Jr., Day, and a number of other holidays. There's plenty to go around, so why aren't you out there shopping? Let me know what you find! You can always e-mail me with your thoughts at dawnelainelangley@hotmail.com.

– 1 –
JANUARY

New Year's (January 1)
The Holiday

The first holiday of the year is appropriately scheduled on the first day of the year—or more precisely, on the *eve* of the first day of the year. Though different cultures celebrate New Year's differently—and the year begins at different points on the calendar, depending on the culture—one thing remains constant: it is a time for rejoicing, a time of new beginnings, and a time to make noise. The earliest recorded instance of celebrating the new year began thousands of years ago when Babylonians celebrated the advent of spring as the beginning of the fertile period. This holiday was the beginning of their year, celebrated in the first month, which at that time was March/April (called *Nisannu*), not January. Ancient citizens of the world were concerned with when to plant their crops, since those crops represented life to them. When the New Moon (the crescent moon) showed in the sky, Babylonians began their celebrations, which lasted eleven days. The whole holiday, called *Akitu*, was celebrated to honor the supreme god Marduk, his crown prince Nabû, and other gods.

The holiday was not celebrated on January 1 until much later. The Romans continued celebrating the New Year's festival in March, as had the Babylonians. However, their calendar started changing as emperors took the liberty of synchronizing the calendar with the sun itself. The calendar became known as the Julian calendar (named after Julius Caesar) when it was permanently decided in 46 B.C. that January would be the first month of the year. The Gregorian calendar, used everywhere in the world, was first used in 1582. There is a difference of approximately three days between the Julian calendar and the Gregorian.

The Romans celebrated their New Year in January, the time closest to the winter solstice, until the church decided, during the Middle Ages, that the festivities were too pagan. The church opposed the holiday, and the only celebration of January 1 recognized by the church was the Festival of Christ's Circumcision.

In German culture, the holiday that we now know as New Year's Eve started out as the Tradition of Sylvester, a night of fools and fun. This was in honor of Pope Sylvester I (pope from 314 to 335), the man who, according to legend, baptized Roman Emperor Constantine I the Great and cured him of leprosy. Everyone celebrates with a Sylvester Ball where people eat, drink, and make merry. Near the stroke of midnight, glasses are filled with champagne or another kind of drink, and Germans wish each other *ein gutes neues Jahr* (a good new year).

Surprisingly, the Western world has only been celebrating the New Year holiday for approximately four hundred years. The first celebrations of the holiday began approximately four thousand years ago in ancient Egypt and Babylonia, where residents of the area celebrated the beginning of their planting and harvest cycle. The king traditionally left the area for a while, the residents had parties for eleven days while he was gone, and then he returned in all his finery for a parade. At that time, the residents settled down and began the new year. The tradition of making New Year's resolutions, however, is much older. Babylonians made them more than four thousand years ago (during their "partying time"), and it is said that the most popular resolution was to return borrowed farm equipment.

Today, the countries that use the Gregorian calendar are the ones where New Year's Eve or New Year's Day celebrations are most common. In addition to North and South America, Australia, the United Kingdom, Europe, Scandinavia, and Russia celebrate the holiday.

The Symbols

The New Year's Baby

Another New Year's icon (the baby) began long ago. The first time a baby was used to signify the New Year was in Greece around 400–600 B.C. where a baby in a basket was paraded around to celebrate fertility and the rebirth of the god Dionysus. Some sources say that the symbol of the baby came from Hermes or Cupid, the most ancient of the child gods. As stated before, the celebration was tied in to the beginning of the planting season, and for the Greeks, March was originally the first of their year. Egyptians also used a baby to symbolize rebirth.

Eventually, the baby came to represent the baby Jesus, which finally convinced the church to accept the holiday. The baby became identified with the nativity of Jesus, and the image of a newborn was used to symbolize the beginning of the year. Though most cultures have incorporated the image of the baby into the New Year's celebration in some way, the most common image, and the one most often depicted on greeting cards and postcards, is that of the New Year's baby holding a banner, which originated in fourteenth-century Germany.

Through the years, the child became accepted as the symbol of the New Year, but it is the writer George McDonald who, in his novella *The Golden Key*, identified the baby as the oldest being of all. In the story, the child was asked, "Where did you come from Baby my dear?" and the child answered, "Out of the everywhere into the here." Though the symbolic baby appeared on greeting cards throughout the 1800s, comic strip artist Winsor

McKay, famous for creating the *Little Nemo* comic strip, drew the image we most recognize as the New Year's baby for a New Year's story in 1806.

Parades

In the United States, the first Tournament of Roses parade to celebrate New Year's Day took place in 1890. The Pasadena Valley Hunt Club held a festival to "tell the world about our paradise," as Professor Charles Holder suggested at one of the club's meetings. After the first parade, the event grew in popularity and games were added to the schedule of events. In 1902 a football game became part of the festivities, and the rest, as they say, is history.

Noisemaking

Noisemaking at midnight is a tradition that has endured since ancient New Year's festivals. People thought that if they made enough noise, they would scare off evil spirits. Though most New Year's Eve partygoers still maintain this tradition, there are differences, depending upon the country's beliefs. For instance, Denmark revelers bring the New Year in with a "smash" by banging on friends' doors and throwing pottery against the sides of their houses. Quite a few countries also bring in the New Year by shooting off fireworks, originally part of Chinese New Year's celebrations.

Auld Lang Syne

The traditional New Year's song, "Auld Lang Syne," originated in the British Isles in the seventeenth century when groups of party guests stood in a circle and sang the song. The lyrics were written by the Scottish poet Robert Burns in 1788.

Times Square

In more recent times, New Year's Eve celebrations in New York City's Times Square—later to become the most well-known American New Year's tradition—began in 1904, the same year the neon light was invented. *New York Times* owner Alfred Ochs wanted to commemorate the opening of the newspaper's new offices in the Times Tower in what had originally been known as Longacre Square, which Ochs successfully lobbied to rename Times Square. The first party was actually an all-day street festival that culminated with fireworks at the end of the night, enjoyed by more than 200,000 people. Three years later, when the city banned the fireworks display, Ochs "arranged to have a large, illuminated seven-hundred-pound iron and wood ball lowered from the tower flagpole precisely at midnight to signal the end of 1907 and the beginning of 1908" (Times Square Alliance). Since then, the ball has fallen every year (except during World War II's dim-out years 1942 and 1943), but has changed in composition from the original iron and wood to aluminum (1955), then to the "Star of Hope," a Waterford crystal ball created for the millennium celebration. Quite a few other cities are now dropping some kind of ball to commemorate New Year's Eve. For instance, Atlanta drops a giant peach and Raleigh, North Carolina, drops an acorn.

Champagne

Typically, when midnight rolls around, celebrants pop the cork of a champagne bottle to welcome in the New Year. Twenty-five percent of the year's sales of champagne occur during the week between Christmas and New Year's. According to *WineIntro.com*, the tradition of clinking one's glass comes from the Middle Ages. "To prove that his wine was safe, the host would pour a bit of his guest's wine into his own glass and drink it first. If the guest trusted his host, however, he would merely clink his flagon against that of his host's when his host offered his cup for the sample. The 'clink' (or perhaps 'clunk' back then, since wood or metal was more common for drinking vessels) was a sign of trust and honesty." From its creation, champagne has been used for celebrations, but the bubbles were an accidental side product. Dom Pérignon, a Benedictine monk, was charged with getting rid of the bubbles, because the sparkling wines would often explode their bottles, causing wineries to lose a major part of their stock. However, he did not succeed. He was not the original maker of champagne, as many believe, but he did have quite an influence on what makes champagne what it is today: a blend of wines from different vineyards.

The Collectibles

With all the New Year's parties and revelers, you would imagine that the wealth of collectibles would be enormous. Unfortunately, most of the items are quickly discarded, either the night of the party or shortly afterward. However, noisemakers, champagne flutes, and other items that are not ephemera can be found. Since New Year's collectibles aren't the hottest holiday items, they are generally quite affordable.

Champagne flutes

Commemorative champagne glasses are typical of New Year's celebrations, and one of the most popular companies to make them is Waterford. First established in 1793 in the town of Waterford in southeastern Ireland, the company's goal was to "create the finest quality crystal for drinking vessels and objects of beauty for the home."

Another of the companies that creates flutes is Christofle, which has been in business since 1830 when Charles Christofle, the original owner, began supplying French royalty with silver plate. Since that time, this French company has equipped the Ritz Hotel, the Orient Express, and major ocean liners with dinner services, glassware, and silverware. Their New Year's champagne flutes are often supplied to large hotels that are known for their holiday celebrations.

Decorations

By the Victorian period (Queen Victoria ruled 1837–1901), New Year's parties were another reason for celebration, and the people of the era, who needed no other excuse to celebrate, put their considerable talents to decorating their ostentatious homes for the event. Open house parties celebrated the season with extensive menus including eggnog, punch, cakes, and hot puddings. Originally, the decorations were largely made from lace and other fine materials, but later the Victorians began producing cardboard candy containers, silver and foil signs proclaiming the New Year, and greeting cards to celebrate the occasion. Handkerchiefs imprinted with greetings of the season and Happy New Year's mottoes in "Berlin work" (a type of needlework that had become the rage in the 1800s), were produced.

Centerpieces, ornaments, and fine crystal and dinnerware decorated Victorian tables. Families and friends gathered for the celebrations, which became increasingly festive as the years went by. By the 1900s, New Year's decorations included honeycomb paper balls, often embossed with the date of the New Year.

Because paper items are extremely fragile, decorations of this type are rare.

Dinnerware, Plates, and Holiday Serving Pieces

Once New Year's parties became part of the holiday year, food serving pieces were produced specifically for the occasion. In the late nineteenth century, sterling silver teaspoons were produced with the greeting "Happy New Year's." Punch bowls and cups were made to serve the traditional eggnog, and Victorians used their best sets of dinnerware to serve the New Year meal. Most of the major dinnerware producers have at least one set of New Year dinnerware to their credit.

Greeting Cards

The Victorians were responsible for making greeting cards part of the holiday celebrations. It started in England with John Horsley, who designed the cards that were printed by Joseph Cundall and sold in England for a shilling in 1843.

Some of the companies responsible for the cards given for New Year's include Robert Canton, Benjamin Sulman, Eyre & Spottiswoode, Raphael Tuck & Sons, Hildesheimer & Faulkner, Louis Prang, Augustus Thierry, H. Rothe, and W. Hagelberg.

Canton, who was in business during the latter part of the nineteenth century, is well known for valentines. His Christmas and New Year's greeting cards resemble the ones he produced for Valentine's Day, with pierced and embossed edges and chromolithograph illustrations.

Another maker of valentines, Benjamin Sulman, also produced other holiday greeting cards. His trademark, an S with a bee centered on it, graced the back of all of his cards. The company was in business only between the 1860s and 1870s.

Eyre & Spottiswoode, known for their elegance and good taste, produced cards at the end of the nineteenth century for "Her Majesty's Stationery Office 1875."

In 1871 Raphael Tuck & Sons applied their considerable chromolithographic skills to producing greeting cards for New Year's. Their nationwide competition for artistic designs unearthed some of the best illustrations ever displayed on greeting cards. Until their factory was destroyed during World War II, the Tuck greeting card was the one to receive.

Hildesheimer & Faulkner was known primarily for printing trade cards in their New York office. Their designs were produced during the latter part of the nineteenth century and were said to be "distinguished by a delicacy and refinement of taste" by the *Bristol Mercury and Daily Post*.

Hats

Throughout history, people have worn laurel wreaths, crowns, and other types of headgear with a circular shape, symbolizing the world or the never-ending circle of life and power. Traditionally, hats are worn at New Year's celebrations around the world to symbolize a full year filled with blessings and good luck. Quite a few cultures celebrate the holiday by wearing new clothes, and hats tend to be part of the New Year's outfit. Even several Native American tribes marked the New Year by wearing new clothing.

The Victorians, the first to create paper hats for their party guests, often featured hat-wearing partygoers on their postcards and greeting cards to celebrate the holidays. The top hat, worn by men, and the crown, worn by women, were typical parts of Victorian dress for New Year's Eve parties and balls, and the custom continues today with disposable versions.

The hundred-year-old versions are often difficult to find, but they are fairly easy to spot. Their decorative accents are distinctly Victorian and they are sometimes accessorized with ribbon and lace of the period.

Noisemakers

In ancient days, people made noise to scare away evil spirits on New Year's Eve, usually by banging on a pot or drum. As the years went by and people began to celebrate the holiday with parties, noisemakers such as whistles, bells, and horns were used.

After the turn of the century, companies began making tin and wood noisemakers, slappers, horns, clickers, and shakers. Companies in Japan and Germany also made (and continue to make) metal toys for this holiday. America started importing German party favors at the beginning of the twentieth century. Collectors who pride themselves on noisemaker collections often start their collections after World War I, when German imports were halted and American companies took over the bulk of the manufacturing. Some of the companies known for noisemakers are T. Cohn, a manufacturer of metal toys; Kirchof; U.S. Metal Toy Mfg. Co.; and J. Chien.

After World War II, some companies began manufacturing plastic noisemakers and other New Year's party favors.

Postcards

Historically, postcards are sent to commemorate holidays. The ones sent for New Year's were often embellished with symbols of the celebration. Some of these symbols include old Father Time and the New Year's baby; symbols of prosperity such as four-leaf clovers, pigs, goats, chimney sweeps, and stars; symbols of the season like snowmen, elves, gnomes, and dwarves; and symbols of the year such as the date or items that are indicative of the era.

Two of the most popular postcard producers are Raphael Tuck & Sons and the George C. Whitney Company. There are far too many companies, both European and American, to give a complete listing here. For more advanced collectors, we suggest you find a reference book for deltiologists (postcard collectors). Many European artists created illustrations that adorned postcards during the Victorian era and throughout the 1920s. German, Scandinavian, and English postcards were extremely popular and were often sent by family members to those who had immigrated to the United States.

The George C. Whitney Company started in 1866 when Sumner Whitney opened a stationery store in Worcester, Massachusetts. George and his brother Edward eventually

Postcard, A Bright and Happy New Year. Postmarked 1926. *Courtesy of Cocoa Village Antique Mall.*
$10–15.

joined the company and worked together. George later took over the company and helped it grow by buying out ten major producers of valentines. By the end of the century, he was creating embossed papers, full-color ornaments, valentines, and postcards. In 1910 a fire destroyed his factory, but Whitney moved to a new building in Worcester and continued production. The early cards, produced before the fire, had a red "W" imprinted on the back. After the fire, the cards were marked "Whitney Made/Worcester, Mass." The company closed in 1942 when World War II caused massive paper shortages.

Raphael Tuck & Sons began in 1866 as a small husband-and-wife shop in London, but they soon became the premier name in postcard publishing. Their sons joined the company in 1871, the same year they published their first Christmas card. Within ten years, they were holding contests for artists who wanted to illustrate their cards. As a result, many of the cards were signed by the artists who submitted their work to the company. The contest was one of many gimmicks the Tucks used to sell their cards and postcards. By 1900 they founded a New York office for the company, invited American artists to create designs for the cards, and became a success in the printing business. Unfortunately, the Tuck family and its company became victims of Nazi warplanes during the London Blitz in 1940 and lost the artwork, machines, lithographs, and paper necessary to run their business. However, there were plenty of cards in circulation, all with the distinctive trademark: "Art Publishers to Their Majesties the King and Queen." Purnell and Sons took over the company and continued to produce postcards until 1953.

Snow Globes
Snow globes (also called shakers, snowstorms, water balls, water domes, or globes) first appeared for sale in the mid-1800s and were created by French artisans. Not surprisingly, some of the early snow globes incorporated miniature versions of the Eiffel Tower inside the globe and were sold at the Paris Universal Exhibition of 1878. They were originally used as paperweights and were filled with flaked minerals, like glass, bone flakes, china chips, or meerschaum. Water filled the earliest versions, but later a light oil or glycerin was used to

Postcard, Wishing You a Happy New Year. Circa 1920s. *Courtesy of Cocoa Village Antique Mall.* $8–10.

Postcard, A Happy New Year. Postmarked 1934. *Courtesy of Cocoa Village Antique Mall.* $6–8.

slow the descent of the flakes. This change makes it easier for the collector to determine the age of a particular snow globe.

During the Victorian era, snow globes became extremely popular and artisans throughout Europe and America created them as paperweights, toys, and souvenirs. Those early examples were both artistic and expensive. But in 1927 an entrepreneur named Joseph Garaja filed a patent for an idea that enabled him to mass-produce the globes. Soon, they were inexpensively produced by the millions.

Snow globes come in various shapes and sizes, including figurals. Those made of glass with ceramic or wood bases are more valuable than the plastic ones. One word of caution: Snow globes should not be displayed in direct sunlight.

PRICE LIST: NEW YEAR'S EVE COLLECTIBLES

Candy Container, Pig. Papier-mâché. 3¾" high. German. Circa 1930. Made by Erzgebirge. Has a money-sack between his front legs. Brings luck for the New Year. Excellent condition. **$30–35**

Champagne Glasses. Pair of Waterford Crystal Millennium Collection toasting flutes. Description on box tag is "Happiness Toasting Flute Pair." New, mint in package condition. **$80–100**

Clickers. USA (Newark, NJ). Approximately 4¼" long. Decorated with dancers and balloons. Good condition. **$15–25**

Cup and Saucer. Millennium Presentation Gift. Czech Republic "Year 2000" Presentation Cup and Saucer complete with certificate of authenticity and original display case. Given by the president of the Czech Republic to Western businessmen. Made and designed by the Thun Studio in the Czech Republic. In felt lined display case. Mint condition. **$10–20**

Decorations, New Year's. Circa 1940s–1950s. Paper. U.S. Drip-proof coasters, 20 napkins, table cover, centerpiece, 8 matching place cards, and working clock (14" tall). Marked $1.25. Made by House of Paper. All in original packaging.   **$20–30**

Dessert Set. Millennium 9-piece dessert set for New Year's festivities. Includes 11" cake plate and eight 7¾" dessert plates. Made by Lynns. Dated 2000. Mint condition.   **$25–40**

Doll, New Year's Eve Alex. 2001 Madame Alexander Fashion Doll Collection (model #28445). Limited edition doll (#0262 of 2,200 pieces). Alex has brown hair, green eyes, and wears a moss green gown overlaid with iridescent bronze net. Accessories include appliqued evening sandals, dangling bronze earrings, and sequined bracelet. 16" tall. Mint in box condition.   **$130–150**

Eggnog Set, Hazel Atlas, Tom and Jerry. Seven-piece Tom and Jerry Set by Hazel Atlas. Some of the words and music to Auld Lang Syne printed on the set in red and green. Bowl is 9" in diameter and 4½" tall. Mugs are 3" tall and 2⅞" in diameter. Excellent condition with no chips or cracks.   **$35–45**

Eyeglasses, 2004 New Year's Celebration, Times Square. One pair "2004" glasses (in gold or red, white, and blue). Mint condition.   **$5–7**

Glasses, Champagne Flutes. Given to invited guests who attended a New Year's Eve Party at Harrah's. A peacock (their 2005 party theme) is etched on each of these flutes. Marked "New Year's Eve 2005 Party." Mint condition.   **$15–18 each**

Glasses, Champagne Glass. Waterford Crystal Holiday Heirloom Collection, *New Year's Toast*, Champagne Glass 2001–2002. New in box, Model #118444. Mint condition.   **$50–60**

Glasses, Ten Champagne Flutes. Crystal by Christofle. Mint condition.   **$1,900–2,000**

Glasses, Glow in Dark. 1992 spelled out on glasses. Plastic. Mint in package.   **$4-6**

Glasses, Water Goblet. Waterford Clarendon, Amethyst Hock Wine Goblet. Set of 2. "Auld Lang Syne" printed on the glasses. Mint condition.   **$40–50**

Greeting Card, New Year's. Victorian antique chromolithograph New Year's greeting card. Circa 1800s. 5" × 7". Shows brown dog stepping out of a doorway into snow. At lower right: "The New Year brings you / Happiness, Health and Peace!" Below that is printed in small dark red letters: "Helena Maguire." Good condition.   **$15–20**

Hand Towel, New Year's Martini Glass. Patience Brewster Krinkles New Year's Cheers Martini Glass Linen Hand Towel. Features a martini glass man. Dept 56 Krinkles. 22" × 14". Cotton ramie blend that is machine washable. Excellent condition.   **$10–15**

Hat, 2004 Celebration Times Square. Paper. Made by Duane Reade. Mint condition. **$2–3**

Hat, New Year's. Sterling silver. Tiffany & Company. 2004 Times Square Celebration. Mint condition.   **$225–250**

Hats, New Year's Top Hats. Packed by the box, 36 hats (assorted colors) per box.
                                                                        $47–50 per box

Hats, Paper. Set of three New Year's hats: one 1942 crown with some wear; one crepe paper with severe damage; and one plastic foil red, silver, and gold hat with tag that says "Compliments of Harold Holberg Adjusters N.Y. 370." Good condition. **$4–6**

Horns, Eight. Collection of Happy New Year's horns. Made in Japan. Paper and cardboard. Various colors and decorations. Circa 1950s. Very good condition. **$12–18**

Necktie, Millennium, New Year's 2001. Made by Salvatore Ferragamo in Italy. 100% silk. Depicts popping champagne bottles and glasses with bubbles. 01-01-01 coming out of the tops of some bottles. Blue ground. 3⅝" × 60". Mint condition. **$25–30**

Noisemaker, Circular. Decorated with bald man dressed in tux, popping balloon. Lithograph very colorful and in excellent condition. Circa 1950s. **$10–12**

Noisemaker, Clown. Tin with wood handle. Circa 1920s–1940s. Marked "TC Made in USA." Clowns encircle the noisemaker, all in different positions. Excellent condition. **$10–12**

Noisemaker, Ratchet. Decorated with "bobby soxer" dancers. Tin with wood handle. Circa 1950s. Marked "Made in USA." Very good condition. **$8–10**

Noisemaker, Ratchet. Decorated with clowns. Tin with wood handle. Circa 1920s–1940s. Marked "TC Made in USA." Excellent condition. **$10–12**

Noisemaker, Ratchet. Decorated with flapper girl and young man dressed for "partying" on front. Patented date of Nov. 27, 1928. Made by Kirchof, Newark, N.J. Good condition. **$10–15**

Noisemaker, Rolling. Decorated with clowns on one side and dancers on the other. Tin with wood handle. Circa 1920s–1940s. Marked "TC Made in USA." Excellent condition. **$10–12**

Noisemaker, Tin. Lithographed with woman in flamenco costume. Made by Kirchof, Newark, N.J. 8½" × 3". Dual clacker. Circa 1950s. Excellent condition. **$10–15**

Noisemakers, Lot of 10 Vintage (circa 1960s) Noisemakers for New Year's Eve. Metal. Several with round smiley faces and party scenes with streamers, as well as people wearing party hats. Several are bell-like with clappers. Some spin around as they make noise. Horn has musical sounds. Very good condition. **$20–30**

Noisemakers, Pair. Circa 1950 Kirchof wooden-handled noisemakers featuring clown graphics. Diameter 3". Minor wear. Good condition. **$12–18**

Noisemakers, Seven. Group of noisemakers, some with Black Americana decoration. Tin. Circa 1920s–1950s. Excellent condition. **$30–50**

Ornament, Barbie. Hallmark Keepsake Ornament. Barbie, as the Princess Millennium, attends the Gala 1999 New Year's Eve Ball. Wears an elegant formal gown of midnight blue, accented by jewelry and a sparkling crown. Carries a crystal ball that symbolizes the beginning of a new year. Mint condition. **$45–55**

Ornament, Millennium Lady. Blown glass, handpainted and decorated. 9" long. Holds glittery sign that says "Happy New Millennium." From Kurt Adler. Mint condition. **$15–20**

Ornament, New Year's 2000. Gorham crystal. U.S. Depicts champagne bottle and bucket, marked "2000." Mint in box condition. **$8–10**

Ornament, New Year's in Times Square. Handpainted. Glass. Michael Storrings's painting of New Year's in Times Square. Mint, new condition. **$72–80**

Paper Plates, New Year's. Made in 1950s by Reed. Originally marked 25 cents. Eight in the original package. Vintage graphics with a New Year's baby. 8½" diameter. Near mint.**$3–5**

Party Supplies, Hats and Noisemakers. Lot of paper and metal party supplies, includes cone-shaped hats, expandable horns, and tin noisemakers. Mint condition. **$12–18**

Pin, Millennium 2000 Dove. Crystal dove made of pavé set with Swarovksi crystals. Wings polished 14 karat gold plate. Tiny emerald-colored crystal in eye. Tac pin. Mint condition. **$10–14**

Pin, New Year's Eve Champagne Glass. Clear rhinestones surround a large emerald-colored rhinestone in a 14 karat gold setting. Mint condition. **$10–14**

Pin, New Year's Eve Martini Glass. Polished platinum and Swarovski crystals. Set in gold plate. Mint condition. **$10–14**

Plate, New Year's Eve Celebration Plate from Flamingo Laughlin (Flamingo Hotel, Laughlin, Nevada). 2001: A Space Adventure. Features characters from "Star Wars." Dinner plate size. Marked for 2000 New Year's celebration. Brand new in box. Mint condition. **$10–20**

Plate, Wedgwood. 7¼" blue Wedgwood jasperware or jasperware plate, dated 2001, issued for New Year's series. White applied jasperware floral garland, cherubs, and a central classical motif. Wedgwood mark on back. Very good condition. **$46–50**

Porcelain Champagne Bucket Keepsake. Lenox, Korbel & America china box that states "May your past live on as treasured memories and your future unfold as dreams fulfilled." Measures 3½" × 2¼", including the handles of the bucket. Cutout design; attached is a gold tassel for hanging on the tree. Mint condition. **$10–15**

Postcard, 1908, Wishing You a Happy New Year. Message written on the back but it was not posted. Good condition. **$2–3**

Postcard, 1909, A Happy New Year. Embossed New Year's Day postcard. Mailed January 2, 1909. Printed in Germany. Depicts fairies ringing in the New Year. Excellent condition. **$7–10**

Postcard, A Bright and Happy New Year. Snowy road with fir and pine cones. Postmarked 1926. Excellent condition. **$10–15**

Postcard, A Happy New Year. Bells and flowers. Postmarked 1934. Excellent condition. **$6–8**

Postcard, Boy and Girl. Circa 1800s card, originally glued into a scrapbook from 1895. The card says "Joyous and Blest Be Thy New Year" on the scroll the boy is holding. Good condition. Excellent condition. **$25–45**

Postcard, New Year's. Colorful elves making snowballs and riding sleighs. Circa 1908. Postmarked. Very good condition. **$6–8**

Postcard, Wishing You a Happy New Year. Bluebirds in the snow. No writing on back. Circa 1920s. Excellent condition. **$8–10**

Postcards, Lot of Fifteen. New Year's postcards from turn of the century. Quite a few have babies on them. Some have Father Time images. Most in very good or good condition. **$20–30**

Printer's Block, Father Time. Approximately 2½". Shows Father Time talking to young boy. Marked 1931. Excellent condition. **$10–15**

Record, U2's "New Year's Day." Circa 1983. 12" 45 RPM promotional copy. Island Records (DMD 604). Rare. Excellent condition. **$5–7**

Sign, New Year's. Hallmark Cards, circa 1960s. New Year's baby in diaper and hat, blowing horn. Approximately 8" × 34". Shows some storage wear. Never used. Excellent condition. **$10–15**

Snowglobe, "Mr. Christmas." Happy New Year Automated Snow Globe Millennium Edition (2000). Snow continuously falls as "Auld Lang Syne" plays. Globe does not have to be turned over. Uses four AA Batteries. Mint in box condition. **$15–25**

Spoon. Marked "New Year's Spiel 1939." Canada. Made of sterling silver. Approximately 5½" long. Good condition. **$20–30**

Stuffed Animal, Macy's Snoopy Limited Edition Millennium. Wears a crown; when his left paw is pressed, he plays Auld Lang Syne. He counts down the hours on his noisemaker, a key chain with a working countdown clock and dancing lights. Can be set for each year. Mint condition. **$10–15**

Stuffed Animal, Snowman. "Welcome to the year 2000 Snow Man." Approx. 6" × 12". Runs on batteries (included); when his hand is pressed, he counts backward from 10 then says, "Welcome to the year 2000." He then giggles and his body wiggles. Original package with all original labels. Near mint condition. **$4–6**

Toy, Noisemaker Dancing Girls. Lithographed. Kirchof, Newark, N.J. Marked along the side with "Made in USA." Metal toy with lithographed design of 1930s-style dancing girls around the top outside. Solid yellow on the inside. Handle is red painted wood. 3⅜" × 2½". Excellent condition. **$12–15**

Toys, Noisemakers, Pair. Made by U.S. Metal Toy Mfg. Co. Each is marked with the U.S. Metal Toy logo in the lower right corner. Each has a clown's face decorating the front with a white background. Each has a red plastic handle on back. Approximately 3½" in diameter. Very good condition. **$20–30 (pair)**

Trade Card, New Year's. Victorian Era trade card. Used by companies and merchants in the mid- to late 1800s to advertise their products and services to the public. New Year's greeting written inside a horseshoe shape. Taken from original collection pasted in book, circa 1895. Good condition. **$10–15**

Chinese New Year

The Chinese New Year celebrations usually start in mid-January or mid-February (depending on the arrival of the second new moon after the winter solstice); the celebrations last approximately fifteen days. The holiday is an occasion for cleaning homes and gathering for a feast. People believe that cleaning the home will maintain good luck. Windows and doors are sealed and fireworks are set off to ward away evil spirits.

The Festival of Lanterns is held on New Year's Day to bring in the New Year. People fill the streets, carrying lanterns and forming a line behind a brightly colored dragon. As with other holidays, Chinese New Year is a time when people share small gifts and dress in their best clothes for the festivities.

PRICE LIST: CHINESE NEW YEAR COLLECTIBLES

Artist Proof First Day Cover. Hand-drawn and painted KAH cachet First day of issue 8" × 10" artist proof on heavy card stock paper. Excellent condition.   **$25–30**

Bracelet, Chinese Coin, Panda 2000. 14 karat gold. 15 mm diameter, 9.6 grams. 7" long. Rope design circling, hand diamond cut. Mint condition.   **$115–125**

Coins, Hollywood Park Chinese New Year Series. Gold plated and limited to 888 pieces. Mint condition.   **$100–125**

Costume, Child's, Chinese New Year Lion Dance Costume. Handpainted and detailed head. Lion design. 10" × 10" × 10". Child's size. Excellent condition.   **$30–40**

Decorations, Children. Happy little boy and girl in traditional red and gold. Wall hanging decoration, professionally mounted and framed under glass with deep red wood with gold trim by Jinpra Frame Company in New York City. 19½" × 14½". Excellent condition.

$20–25

Doll Clothes, American Girl, Chinese New Year Outfit. Made in China for Pleasant Company, 1996. Included are pants, jacket, black shoes, red undershirt, hair ribbons, and floral clips. Excellent condition.   **$65–75**

Dolls, Set of Three. 8" Chinese New Year dolls by Madame Alexander, 1997. Made for just one year and hard to find. Dressed in red Chinese pants outfits. Mint in box condition.

$175–200

Dress, Mandarin, New Year's. Child's size. Elegant red and black design with sash. Excellent condition.   **$10–15**

Fan, Needlework, Chinese New Year. Created by T. C. Chiu for STAPCO. Counted cross-stitch kit from Design Works, called Chinese Fan. 13" × 22" finished size. Excellent condition.   **$25–35**

Hat, Antique. Made in China. Silk with elaborate embroidery and hand stitching. Guanyin, the goddess of mercy, depicted on the back. Gold leaf underlay with a pagoda, lotus tree, boy, and bird on the back. Connective piece of a large dragonfly. The front top piece has gold underlay and gods or sages, such as Qin Qiong and Yuchi Gong, to bring wealth for the New Year. Measures approximately 7" × 4". Very good condition.

$160–175

Masks and Outfits, Chinese New Year Girl and Boy. Used during Chinese New Year festivities; called *Da Tou Wa Wa* (Big Head Doll). Mint condition.   **$30–40 pair**

Painting, "Chinese New Year." Original oil painting, 24" × 36". Shows figures of what appear to be family members, group of women in front holding flowers, smiling at each other; in rear, an elderly gentleman looking into the distance. Excellent condition.   **$30–50**

Record, New Year Song, Teresa Teng. PLP-2001. Near mint condition.   **$39–45**

Stamps, Chinese New Year. Full set of 12 sheets. Mint, new condition.   **$100–125**

Japanese New Year (January 1)

The Japanese celebrate their New Year (*Shogatsu*) on January 1, as many Western traditions do. However, their holiday is for the most part a religious celebration. Families gather together for several days and endeavor to leave the old year behind as they welcome in the new one. For the Japanese, New Year's is the most important holiday, since they see each year as distinct and different from every other. Every year symbolizes a new start. It is a time of prayers and solemn greetings, a time to spend cleaning out both your home and your life, a time to spend with family, and a time for Buddhist and Shinto families to worship as they see fit.

Homes are traditionally decorated with ornaments made with bamboo, plum trees, and pine. Like the Chinese, Japanese families clean their homes to bring in the New Year. They also have a traditional meal that includes soba noodles, which are a symbol of longevity. Other foods consumed during the holiday festivities include "*osechi ryori*, *otoso* (sweetened rice wine) and *ozoni* (a soup with *mochi*)" (*Japan Guide*).

Those who follow the Shinto religion visit shrines and temples during this special holiday. At midnight, large temple bells are rung to signal that the New Year has commenced. Throughout the holiday, people try to spread joy, to keep everything clean, and to refrain from working. The three day holiday celebration fills the temples throughout the country with worshippers dressed in their best kimonos or Western clothes. They pray for good luck, then go on to visit family members and friends, greeting them with New Year wishes, a custom called *Nenshi*.

The second day of the holiday is a time for two special ceremonies: *Hatsuni* and *Kaizome*. During Hatsuni, the first goods of the year are stocked in commercial establishments. Kaizome is the celebration of the first calligraphic writing with a brush. The first dream of the new year (*Hatsu-Yume)* is also celebrated on this day.

On the third day, *Genshisai*, an ancient ritual, is performed in the Imperial Court, and *Gagaku*, an ancient and rare dance and music art form, is also performed. Throughout the three days, people relax and enjoy games and other amusements. Japanese badminton, card games, and kite flying are leisure activities associated with this holiday. People usually send each other cards, marked to be delivered on January 1, to celebrate the occasion.

PRICE LIST: JAPANESE NEW YEAR COLLECTIBLES

Art, Limited Edition Print, The Shiba Shrine on New Year Day. By Utagawa Kunisada. Circa 1844. Depicts three elegant young ladies of the merchant class dressed in gorgeous robes for the festival stroll during the New Year holiday outside the Myojin shrine at Shiba. Hand titled and numbered. Authentic, handcrafted *washi* (traditional Japanese paper). Measures 2' × 1.5'. Excellent condition. **$100–150**

Art, Woodblock Reprint. By Eishi (1756–1829). Depicts the Yoshiwara on the New Year's Day. Created in 1930s. 14¼" × 10". Excellent condition. **$55–75**

Calendar, New Year's Day. Pine and Crane, first through fifth issue in the "Japanese Floral Calendar"; created exclusively for The Hamilton Collection. Twelve works inspired by the natural motifs of the Japanese Floral Calendar, and created by Chokin artist Shuho and calligrapher Senkin Kage. Each plate has a certificate of authenticity. Mint condition. **$100–125**

Doll, Happy New Year Barbie, Japanese Kimono. Circa 1996–1997. Dressed in *Furisode*-type kimono in *Sakura* (cherry) pattern. Japanese symbol for "Happy New Year" on box. Mint condition. **$60–75**

Pinball Machine, Japanese New Year. Official pachinko machine used in an international casino. Ultra-smooth finish on playboard. High definition LCD screen allows you to watch movie. Spectacular light show and stereo sound effects. Face is a beautiful finish, with wood trim. Mint condition. **$90–125**

Martin Luther King, Jr., Day (Third Monday in January)

In 1983 President Ronald Reagan signed into legislation the designation of the third Monday in January as Martin Luther King, Jr., Day. At first there was some resistance to this holiday, and several southern states instituted holidays for Confederate generals on that day, but it has come to be known nationally as a day commemorating the great civil rights leader who was born January 15, 1929, and was assassinated in 1968. Typically, celebrations include parades, songfests, speeches, dinners, and peaceful gatherings.

Collectibles for this holiday range from photographs and posters to T-shirts, postcards, and greeting cards.

PRICE LIST: MARTIN LUTHER KING, JR., DAY COLLECTIBLES

Art, Wood Engraving, "Martin Luther King." By Ben Shahn and Stefan Martin. 1966. 634 × 512 mm; 20¾" × 20", full margins. Signed, numbered 213/300 and inscribed "sc" in pencil by Martin, lower margin. Signed in brown ink by Shahn, lower right. With Shahn's red ink signature stamp, lower right. Published by the International Graphics Arts Society, New York. Excellent condition. **$1,000–1,200**

Book, Children's, *Celebrating Martin Luther King Jr. Day: Dreaming of Change.* By Joel Kupperstein and illustrated by Fred Willingham. One line of text per page. Suitable for a child grade K–2. 16 pages. Published by Creative Teaching Press as an early "read to learn" book. Excellent condition. **$8–12**

Book, *Judgment Days.* By Nick Kotz. Proof/Advance reading copy. Marked to be published in January 2005, 40th anniversary of Civil Rights Act of 1965. Martin Luther King, Jr., and Lyndon Johnson on cover, leaning toward each other. Excellent condition. **$30–40**

Button/Pin, Martin Luther King "I Have A Dream." Commemorates the anniversary of Martin Luther King, Jr.'s death in 1968. Mint condition. **$50–60**

Pamphlet, "*Pacem In Terris* Peace and Freedom Award." Martin Luther King, Jr. (1929–1968). Signed by Martin Luther King, Jr. Excellent condition. **$3,400–3,600**

Pin, Martin Luther King, Jr., Day. The American Red Cross. Excellent condition. **$3–5**

Program, Funeral of Martin Luther King, Jr. From the Ebenezer Baptist Church in Atlanta, Georgia, dated April 9, 1968. Gives a brief history of his life and major accomplishments. Provides a schedule for the service. Identifies speakers at the service, including the mayor of Atlanta, Rosa Parks, and other high-profile activists of the day. Pallbearers of note are listed, including Jesse Jackson. Very good condition. **$225–250**

Screenprint, "Martin Luther King—Mountain Top." By Romare Bearden. Color screenprint, 1968. 760 × 495 mm; 29⅞" × 19½", full margins. Proof, aside from the edition of 68. Signed and dedicated "To Harry and Bea" in pencil, lower left. Excellent condition.
$4,200–4,500

Stamp, First Day Art Cover. Postmarked on Martin Luther King, Jr. Day. Original artwork, executed in pen, ink, and pencil. Excellent condition. **$8–10**

Stamp, First Day Cover, Martin Luther King Stamp Cachet 1979. Official First Day of Issue 15 cent stamp and artcraft cachet envelope honoring Martin Luther King, Jr., distinguished civil rights leader and recipient of the Nobel Peace Prize, 1929–1968. Black Heritage USA series. Dated January 13, 1979, and postmarked Atlanta, Georgia, 30304. Excellent condition. **$2–4**

Stamp, First Day Cover. Robert F. Kennedy and Martin Luther King, Jr. Dual First Day artcraft cachet. Excellent condition. **$3–4**

– 2 –
FEBRUARY

Valentine's Day (February 14)
The Holiday

Collectors revel in the amount of items produced for this holiday, especially since quite a few items have stood the test of time. During Valentine's Day, lovers and those who want to be lovers convey their feelings through cards, flowers, chocolates, jewelry, and other trinkets, providing a boon for the greeting card business and jewelry stores. Valentine's Day is the second most popular card-giving holiday, after Christmas. The Greeting Card Association of America states that 25 percent of all the cards sent every year are Valentines—and 85 percent of the people who send them are women. Florists consider Valentine's Day their busiest business day of the year, and the holiday generates over a billion dollars annually for the candy industry. For collectors, that's a glorious number, since all of those items come in some kind of wrapper or container that will ultimately be collectible. Yet, although thousands celebrate and spend money on this "lover's holiday" every year, very few actually know the history behind the festivities, or the reason we celebrate it on February 14.

As with many other holidays, Valentine's Day has both ancient pagan and Christian elements in its history. The festival of Lupercalia, celebrated on February 15, was held in ancient Rome as a fertility holiday and a way of welcoming the return of springtime. Faunus, the Roman god of animal husbandry and secrets of nature, was at the center of the celebration. According to legend, Faunus's cave was where the twins Romulus and Remus, the fabled founders of Rome, were raised by a wolf.

The festival began near that cave when priests of the Luperci (young men of noble birth who celebrated this annual festival) gathered to sacrifice a goat (for fertility) or a dog (for purification). The people of Rome would begin the festival by purifying (or sweeping out) their houses, then sprinkling salt and a type of wheat throughout the interiors. The most important part of the fertility festival, though, was conducted in the streets of Rome when young

Postcard, To My Valentine. Circa 1920. *Courtesy of Cocoa Village Antique Mall.* $12–15.

boys took strips of goat hide and chased young Roman girls, slapping them with the strips. The girls welcomed the slaps because they believed it would make them more fertile in the year to come. After the chase, all single women reportedly placed their names in an urn, and the boys would each choose one. Marriage often resulted from these "blind" matches.

Three saints named Valentine are recognized by the Catholic Church, but the one whose legendary card to his lover sparked the sending of Valentine's Day cards was a priest who served under Roman Emperor Claudius II in the third century A.D. According to legend, the emperor had decided that single soldiers were better at their job than married ones, so he decreed that no young men could get married. You can imagine that was not a popular edict! The priest Valentinius defied the order and continued to perform secretive marriage ceremonies for young lovers.

Claudius, upset with Valentinius's bold insubordination, jailed the priest and sentenced him to death by beheading. Valentinius ironically fell in love with the jailer's blind daughter and used his powers of healing to restore her sight. Before he was beheaded on February 14 in the year 270, he sent a farewell note to his lover signed "from your Valentinius."

In 498 Pope Gelasius recognized the Valentine's Day holiday and noted it would be celebrated on February 14, but he outlawed the Roman "lottery system" of marriage that had been part of the festival of Lupercalia.

Though the details of this legend are rather blurry, it is clear that Valentinius (or Valentine) became synonymous with sentimentality, romance, and heroism, all characteristics that made him a popular saint during the Middle Ages. It is not surprising that the most romantic figures of that time, the knights, created their code of chivalry based on the same aspects, and that "courtly love" celebrated the epistolary romance that Valentinius began with his note to his beloved in the third century. In the Middle Ages, it was believed that birds began their mating season in mid-February, and thus the idea of celebrating romance at that time became even more ingrained in the public view.

Geoffrey Chaucer, well known for his *Canterbury Tales*, is the first writer to mention the holiday in his poem "Parliament of Fowls" with this line:

> For this was on St. Valentine's Day,
> When every fowl cometh there to choose his mate.

The poem, probably written between 1372 and 1386, was composed to honor Richard II's engagement to Anne of Bohemia, and it was the first written work to link Valentine's Day with the birds' mating season.

In the early 15th century, Charles, Duke of Orléans, sent a poem to his wife as he was being held prisoner in the Tower of London after being captured at the battle of Agincourt. This poem, said to be the oldest Valentine's Day card in existence, is held in the manuscript collection at the British Library in London.

The holiday became popular in Great Britain during the seventeenth century, with the exchange of mottoes or cards. Early cards were handmade—some simple, some elaborate—and were delivered to the doors of maidens by their admirers. Most of the phrases or sentiments included were poetic in nature and were written by the giver of the card, but as the holiday grew more popular, card-givers began copying phrases from other writers. In fact, books known as "valentine writers" were produced specifically for this purpose.

By the eighteenth century, lace-bordered and beribboned hearts had become the norm, and the card-giving practice spread to America. Small tokens of the giver's affection often accompanied the hearts, cupids, and birds (often doves) now seen as symbols of the holiday. Cupid, the ancient Roman god of love, became symbolic because his arrow could pierce the heart of the romancer's object of desire. Birds, due to the medieval belief that mating season began in mid-February, continued to appear as one of the most popular illustrations on Valentine's Day cards. Flowers, symbolic of romance, became powerful symbols, as well—particularly roses and violets.

Some of the tokens that accompanied those early handmade cards included lace handkerchiefs or small bouquets of flowers, especially posies (also known as nosegays). The handwritten notes and letters were detailed and decorated in various styles, including pinprick (similar to the doilies that are sometimes used today for valentine decorations) and cutouts. Sometimes the cards were decorated with petals from real flowers, scraps of material, bits of thread, lace, bark, or locks of hair. Even small precious stones or jewels might make their way into a design. Some of the cards were puzzles, while others were decoupaged or handpainted. There are examples of valentines decorated with crewelwork and embroidery in museum collections, as well. When valentines were sent, the giver sealed the card or envelope with wax, which was then imprinted with the sender's seal or initial.

By the 1700s, printed cards were produced for the retail market in England, and by the end of the century, note papers with embossed and decorative borders were added. These European valentines were very expensive, but they opened the doors to manufacturers who saw their popularity and capitalized on it. The cards, decorated with handpainted floral motifs, cherubs, hearts, and lacy designs, expanded the paper market. These earliest versions are

Postcard, To My Valentine. Circa 1910s. *Courtesy of Cocoa Village Antique Mall.* $8–12.

not often available for collectors but have made their way into museums. The de Grummond Children's Literature Collection, in the University of Southern Mississippi Libraries, holds more than 650 valentines collected over fifty years by graphic arts specialist Richard August Neubert. The de Grummond Collection includes foldouts, cobweb designs, shadow boxes, mechanicals, and every type of card made from 1838 to the 1980s. In addition to the valentines, the museum also holds a number of valentine writer books including *Cupid's Annual Charter, The New Quizzical Valentine Writer, Richardson's New London Fashionable Gentleman's Valentine Writer*, and *Cupid's Album*. The following verse from *The True Lovers' Budget* provides a sentimental example:

> I lost my heart when last we met, and tis my firm belief
> Twas you, my chosen Valentine, twas you that was the thief.
> I do not wish it back again, provided you'll agree
> That your bright jewel of a heart may be purloined by me.
> And that we mutually keep each other's heart for life,
> Holding possession upon terms of husband and of wife.

Other museums that hold various valentine card collections include the British Museum, the Henry Ford Museum, the Shelburne Museum, the Smithsonian Institution, and many more.

The Collectibles

Valentines and Cards

Handmade valentines, often considered folk art today, date from the early 1600s in Europe. Some of the most popular styles of handmade cards include *fraktur* (or fracture), *wycinanki, scherenschnitte*, rebus, cutout, acrostic, theorem, beehive, and pin pricking. Collectors of these types of cards often look for more than just valentines—they look for technique and design, in other words, a work of art.

German cardmakers originated the design called *fraktur*, a type of calligraphy in which the letters appear to be broken horizontally. This ornamental lettering mimicked the illuminated manuscripts of the Middle Ages. Often, collectors will discover Pennsylvania Dutch examples of *fraktur* with borders decorated with birds, mermaids, hearts, and angels. Some of the *fraktur* artists had distinctive styles and color palettes, so those versed in the art can often look at valentines and tell which artist created them. During the late sixteenth century and through the eighteenth century, *fraktur* artists employed style books from other countries in Europe.

Wycinanki paper cutting (also known as Polish paper-cutting) designs were created by Polish peasants for the holidays. The designs were symmetrical and frequently used layers and colors to complete their design. They displayed their work on windows and walls during religious events.

The German paper-cutting style (each country or region appears to have developed its own paper-cutting techniques) is called *scherenschnitte*. The true artists of this discipline delight in using as many different colored papers as possible in their work. Pennsylvania Germans still practice this form of folk art, particularly in Amish villages. *Scherenschnitte* valentines incorporate people, animals, and scenes in their designs, and they are carefully assembled like jigsaw puzzles to create their intricate tableaux. Contemporary designs are created today by artists like Sharyn Sowell, who does her delicate work with a very sharp pair of Swiss scissors.

Valentines designed in the rebus style use a symbol or picture instead of a word, for example, an eye for "I" or a heart for the word "love." Rebus books are still created for children.

Cutout designs were used to create valentines and are still utilized by schoolchildren today. To make a cutout, a piece of paper is folded over several times, and then, using scissors, a design is cut into the paper. When the paper is unfolded, the design becomes evident. Usually, the card is pasted onto a piece of colored paper so the cutout shows up more clearly.

People who wrote their own poetry for valentines often employed a style called acrostic, in which the person's name is spelled out vertically down the left hand side of the page, and each letter in the name is used to start a new line of poetry.

Theorem (sometimes called *poonah*) style is achieved by painting a design through a stencil cut in oil paper. The technique originated in Poonah, a Bombay province in India. Once the painting is finished, the artist brushes gum arabic over it to preserve the design.

The beehive, or cobweb card, originally used in the early nineteenth century, is one of the most desirable valentines because of its intricate design. Popular in England, the card was made by snipping a square or circle of paper into threads. By lifting the center thread, the whole design would lift, creating a "beehive" or "cobweb." Underneath the design, the maker would paint flowers or some other valentine token. Sometimes a lock of hair would be included. Naturally, these cards were extremely delicate, so collectors consider them valuable.

Scherenschnitte Art, Choose Your Love, Love Your Choice. Made of pieces from a book about Ohio's Agricultural Statistics, 1854–1855. Over the top of it, a woman had pasted quotes, poems and articles from newspapers and magazines of the day. *Photo and Copyright © Sharyn Sowell. All rights reserved.* $295–325.

The pinprick design, attained by simply pricking a piece of paper with a pin for the desired effect, was duplicated later by machinery, but in the early days of valentines, different size pins or needles were used. After the pinpricked design was created, the card maker sometimes colored the design.

The first valentine company of note was Dobbs & Company, a producer of paper in London which, according to some sources, began printing valentines as early as 1803. Dobbs utilized silk and satin backings in its cards. Decorative accents included flowers and cupids, as well as hand-painted figures. Usually, the maker's mark was imprinted near the border of this company's greeting cards. Collectors love these cards for their intricate embossing and detailing, as well as decorative lacy frills, often applied in layers. Even though the company was based in England, Dobbs sold quite a bit to the American market and incorporated American symbols and motifs into their designs.

By the 1830s, other companies in London, such as Joseph Addenbrooke, Thomas De La Rue, Joseph Mansell, J. T. Wood, George Meek, and Mullord Brothers, imitated the Dobbs design and began producing their own lines of greeting cards.

In 1835 Pope Gregory XVI gave what is believed to be the remains of Valentinius to Father John Spratt of Ireland, and the black and gold casket is put on display every Valentine's Day at the Whitefriar Street Church in Dublin. However, in 1969, the Catholic Church removed all mention of the feasts of saints whose origins were questionable from their religious texts. Because there had been three priests named Valentinius who were alive at the time the legendary Valentinius was said to have been imprisoned, the feast of Saint Valentine was questionable, and so his celebration was removed from the church calendar.

The Industrial Revolution helped contribute to the mass production of valentines by making machinery for the process. Commercial valentines, printed and lithographed by prominent paper manufacturers, replaced handmade versions in the first quarter of the nineteenth century. At first, the lithographed designs were hand-colored and often left space for the giver's signature or personal message. Sometimes the card would include a pocket, in which a smaller note, a lock of hair, or a tiny token might be tucked.

Even the island nations have been responsible for creating their own type of valentines. Natives of Barbados and other islands created sailors' valentines, popular from approximately 1830 to 1880, and sold them to English and American sailors who sent them home to mothers, sisters, wives, and lovers. Some of the earliest examples are held by museums, but collectors can still find some for sale in today's antique market, though they are relatively expensive. Usually, the valentines are actually boxes, and the design is created with seashells. The shells created both designs and words, depending on the artist's ability. Today, some artists, such as Linda Susan Hennigan, recreate those valentines and sell them to collectors.

The negative side of valentine giving was evident in the 1840s by the production of "comic valentines," which were often quite cruel in their sentiments. The caricatures designed for this type of card insulted certain professions (e.g., schoolteachers), or body types (thin or fat), or made fun of a person's bad habits (e.g., drinking). These cards were often sent anonymously. Though some of these comic cards were lithographed, most were of woodblock design and were not as pretty as their romantic counterparts.

The American public began giving Valentine's Day cards in earnest during the 1850s when Esther A. Howland began mass-producing valentines. She was a Mount Holyoke graduate and a Worcester, Massachusetts, native. By importing lace papers and floral decorations from England, she began an assembly-line production of the cards with what is reputed to be the first all-female production line. Her business grossed $10,000 annually until she retired in 1881. The business she built, the New England Valentine Company, marked its cards with a small red "H" stamped in the corner of the back page or a white heart glued on the back page (or a label) with a stamped "H." Later versions of the cards were embossed "N.E.V.Co." She sold the company to the George C. Whitney Company, her rival, who continued the production of greeting cards and contributed to the immense popularity of the holiday.

Whitney started producing valentines in the 1860s and marked his cards with a stamped "W" on the back. His store started in Worcester, Massachusetts, as a stationery store, but he began purchasing machinery to make embossing and lace designs after seeing the popularity of those designs produced in England. When he bought out Howland's company, he became the leader in valentine manufacturing for many years. His company was in business from 1866 to 1942.

Eugene Rimmel produced a different type of valentine during the 1860s: a perfumed sachet valentine. The company had offices in New York, London, and Paris. Though primarily known as a perfumer, Rimmel chose to include his renowned scents in sachets of cotton wool that were packed in exquisitely decorated envelopes made of silver or gold embossed and decorated paper. He employed lithographers, painters, silk workers, filigree artists, and lacquerists to create his gorgeous tokens of love. A decade later, Rimmel branched out even further and employed Brazilian nuns to create flowers made from the feathers of rain forest birds, like hummingbirds and parrots.

Other U.S. companies that made these popular greeting cards during the latter part of the nineteenth century (and some into the twentieth) included Jonathan King, George Kershaw & Son, Turner and Fisher, and David Mossman. Some children's book publishers were also known for their valentines, including Dean & Son, Louis Prang, Ernest Nister, McLoughlin Brothers, and Raphael Tuck & Sons.

During the Civil War, a special type of valentine produced for soldiers and their loved ones was a bit simpler in design than its European counterparts, but the sentiment was the same. Often a lock of hair was attached to the card itself, and if the soldier were lucky enough to return home from the war, the valentine's card was one of the items he considered most precious.

The cost of stamps made a difference in how valentines were produced in the mid-nineteenth century. By that time, the United States and England had instituted regular postal rates that were determined by weight. Up until that point, greeting cards were made without the accompanying envelopes we are used to seeing today. Prior to this time, cards folded up, and the corners of the card folded inside to form its own envelope, which would be sealed with a drop of wax. Once people became used to mailing their cards rather than delivering them personally, valentines had to have their own matching envelopes. Instead of delivering cards only to family members or loved ones and friends, the public began sending valentines to a larger circle of friends and acquaintances.

Cards designed as foldouts or that stood up on a base were especially popular from about 1895 to 1915. Honeycombed inserts or foldouts graced embossed and lithographed cards. Most of the designs originated in Germany, although some American companies did produce cards with honeycomb accents. Many of the cards featured ribbons, swags, cherubs, children, flowers, lace, birds with fluttering wings, butterflies, carriages with windows that opened, houses with doors or windows that opened, ships, hot air balloons, and almost anything else that was fanciful and romantic. The movable parts make this type of card popular with collectors. Since they are easy to rip or tear, most have made it into some sort of frame where their beauty can be enjoyed but not destroyed.

Hallmark Cards, the company most recognizable for today's greeting cards, began in 1910 when eighteen-year-old Joyce Clyde Hall started selling postcards. The company became known as Hall Brothers (after Joyce and his brothers) in 1911. In 1912 they started selling greeting cards. Hall and his brother, Rollie, are credited with inventing modern wrapping paper in 1917 when they ran out of traditional colored tissue paper. In 1925 the company adopted the name "Hallmark" after the symbol used by goldsmiths in London in the fourteenth century, but it was not until 1928 that they began printing the name on the back of every card and promoting it in advertising campaigns, a practice the company continues to the present day. In 1944 Hallmark's current slogan, "When you care enough to send the very best" was adopted and used for the first time. Hallmark is credited with introducing many new holidays to the American public, as well as lines of cards for specific segments of the population (e.g., Mahogany cards for African Americans and Tree of Life cards for Jewish consumers).

Another important American greeting card company is American Greetings, founded in 1906 by Jacob Sapirstein. He sold cards from a horse-drawn cart, and his family continued working in the company. His son, Irving, followed in his father's footsteps and ran the company until 1987, when he passed the reins to his son-in-law, Morry Weiss. Some of their licensed characters include Strawberry Shortcake, the Care Bears, The Get-Along Gang, and Holly Hobbie. They also hold an exclusive license for Nickelodeon characters.

Other Collectibles

In addition to cards, love tokens are traditionally given on Valentine's Day. During the 1870s, those gifts included hairpins, jewelry (brooches, watches, rings, lockets), music boxes, silk neckties, tussie-mussies (flower holders), embroidered slippers, fans, gloves, handkerchiefs (embroidered and beribboned), and love spoons.

Many other Valentine's Day items are available for the collector, including party decorations, figurines, candy containers, candy molds, dolls, and toys.

Hair Combs

Hair combs have been worn by women for centuries and are often difficult to date; however, the combs given for Valentine's Day during the Victorian era were often made of tortoiseshell or sterling silver. During the art deco period (about 1925 to the late 1930s), combs were made of bakelite or celluloid. Watch for combs with typical Valentine's Day symbols like hearts, doves, or cupids.

Jewelry

To this day, it is typical for a lover to give a ring or another type of jewelry to his or her valentine. Rings have symbolically been used as a pledge of love because their circular shape symbolizes completeness, fulfillment, and eternity. The tradition of wearing a wedding or engagement ring on the left ring finger came from ancient Rome. Ancient Egyptian physicians believed that the vein to the heart came directly through that finger. Rings were considered payment or barter for a bride, and stones were not added to rings until much later. It wasn't until Archduke Maximilian of Austria included a diamond in his engagement ring for Mary of Burgundy (betrothed in 1476, married in 1477) that the tradition of the diamond engagement ring began.

Tussie-Mussies

Tussie-mussies, in fashion during Queen Victoria's era, brought the language of flowers to life. The tussie-mussie was the ornate holder in which a sprig of flowers was carried. Surprisingly, though, the original reason for carrying flowers encased in tussie-mussies was not romantic at all. During the Victorian Era, small poseys or tussie-mussies were carried close to the nose to ward off the stench in the streets and of the plague, and were composed primarily of scented herbs such as rosemary, thyme, and rue.

But a tussie-mussie held more than just a sweetly scented small bouquet or posy. It also carried a type of code for messengers of love. If a suitor was shy, he could let the flowers speak the words he could not say. A red rose means love, a yellow one signifies jealousy, and white means "I am worthy of you." A single pink carnation symbolizes pure love while a variegated pink carnation means refusal. A nosegay of pansies means "I'm thinking of you," and lilies of the valley indicate a return of happiness. Pity the poor man who did not learn the language of flowers, because he might be saying the exact opposite of what he intended.

Tussie-mussies were elegantly designed, and were courting tools in their own right. Considered a type of jewelry, they were carved out of whalebone or fashioned out of sterling silver, accented with mother-of-pearl, miniature portraits, or precious stones. Some were even made of paper. Today, tussie-mussies are often used in weddings. A note about collecting tussie-mussies, however: There are reproductions of tussie-mussies all over the marketplace. Newer versions might be nickel-plate, glass, or tin. Old versions are rare, heavier, and more expensive.

Fans

Hand-held fans were another token of love given on Valentine's Day. The language of the fan was one spoken by women to men, another way of sending subtle messages of love without speaking. For instance, if a woman dropped her fan, it was her unspoken message that she belonged to the man at whom she was looking. If she fanned herself quickly, it meant "I love you so much." When she rested the fan on her lips, she was saying, "I don't trust you." If she wanted to talk to the gentleman, she ran her fingers along the ribs of the fan. The earlier the fan, the more likely it is to have been made of a delicate fabric, like silk or satin, and to be handpainted, embroidered, or decorated with sequins. The sticks, leafs, and guards of the fan were made of sandalwood, teak, bone, or ivory. Sometimes the paintings on fans are signed, but more often they are not. The value of a fan is largely determined by the material with which it was made, as well as the beauty of its decorative elements. Fan cards were made throughout the Victorian era for Valentine's Day and other holidays. These paper fans were often embellished with symbols of the holiday, such as various flowers, birds, butterflies, hearts, and cupids.

Gloves and Handkerchiefs

The gift of ladies' gloves to a lover for Valentine's Day began in the days of knights. Typically, a knight would keep his lady's glove in his helmet for luck and would fight with his life to keep that glove. Gloves were extremely popular during the latter 1700s and are often depicted on valentines.

Throughout history, handkerchiefs were thought to have spiritual or healing powers. In literature, handkerchiefs are mentioned as intimate pieces of a woman's wardrobe, and even in the Bible, a handkerchief is said to have healed the woman who touched it. Shakespeare used handkerchiefs in his plays as indicators of love or power (e.g., Desdemona's handkerchief and the power it had over Othello), and lovers have held their partner's scented handkerchiefs throughout the years. According to some reports, the first fancy handkerchief was created by a Venetian woman in the seventeenth century, a piece of flax she decorated with lace. Supposedly, when she showed it to her friends and demonstrated how she used it for wiping, they all wanted one. Until that point, handkerchiefs were like napkins—useful, but not pretty. From Italy, the handkerchief trend spread throughout Europe, and the more it was adapted by aristocrats, the fancier it became. When Marie Antoinette mentioned one day that she would like a handkerchief that was square, King Louis XVI actually issued a decree which stated that from that day forward, all handkerchiefs would be made in a length equal to their width.

During the plague, handkerchiefs were heavily scented and held to the nose so that the stench of illness and decaying bodies would be less offensive. As time went on, the handkerchief took on a more romantic meaning, and the signals used by someone with a handkerchief mimicked those used by a woman with a fan. For instance, if a woman drew her hanky across her cheek, she was saying "I love you," but if she drew it through her hands, it meant the opposite. To lay her handkerchief on the right cheek meant "yes," but on the left meant "no." Twirling it in either hand was not a good signal; in the left, it meant "I wish to be rid of you," and in the right, "I love another."

The more lace on a handkerchief's edge, the better. If the lace is long and intricate, the kerchief's value rises—but condition is paramount. Today's collector doesn't mind collecting hankies with monograms on them, largely because the quality of the cloth is usually better. Valentine hankies are still being sold today and are usually made of linen or a high count cotton.

Love Spoons

Love spoons, dating back to the sixteenth century, were given to one's betrothed and were often hand-carved from a single piece of wood. In Wales, a man would present this gift to the girl he was to marry; often the spoons were carved with symbols of love. Makers continued to create spoons after that time and throughout the years, in various sizes and shapes. For instance, a nineteenth-century sailor might create one out of a whalebone, while others might be made from silver and decorated with hearts and flowers. Some examples have figures carved into their ivory handles. Symbols depicted on love spoons might include a key or keyhole (home, security), chain (linking of lives), ball in cage (captivation), heart-shaped bowl (bountiful life), horseshoe (luck), bell (wedding or anniversary), leaves and flowers (nature), or a vine or twisted stem (lives entwined).

Party Decorations

Valentine's Day party decorations came into fashion in the nineteenth century. Homes were decorated with paper streamers, doilies, place cards, napkins, cups, and invitations. Companies designed honeycomb hearts, cherubs, flowers, and doves to hang from doorways or ceilings. Ribbons, streamers, and crepe paper trailed across dining room tables, over arched doorways, and around mantles and staircases. Most decorations were red and white, but pink was also used.

Candy and Candy Containers

The same American and German companies that made Valentine's Day party decorations also created nut and candy containers for those parties. Eventually, those containers were sold in supermarkets and candy stores. Cardboard heart-shaped boxes were created and filled with chocolate goodies. By the middle of the twentieth century, sentimental sayings covered the boxes. Throughout the United States, schoolchildren celebrated the holiday by exchanging small gifts of candy and miniature valentines decorated with die cuts, paper lace, and ribbons. Some of the containers created for the adult market were tin or plastic, but all were decorated with the same iconic symbols of the day.

Candy makers, both commercial and household, needed molds to create their goodies; thus chocolate and ice cream molds in the shape of hearts and cupids are available for the enterprising collector. During the mid-twentieth century, primarily before World War II, aluminum and iron molds were popular.

Several candy makers are known for their Valentine's Day offerings and the candy containers they made to hold them. The chocolate candy industry uses about four billion pounds of milk a year to create the confections that melt in your mouth (Do you know why chocolate melts in your mouth? Because the melting point is just below human body temperature!). Schrafft's, Whitman's, and Necco are three of the most popular makers of Valentine's Day candies.

Schrafft's candy was a staple in the Valentine's Day candy business from the turn of the twentieth century until it ceased its candy operations in Charlestown, Massachusetts, in the early 1980s. As a Bostonian, I distinctly remember having a sundae with my grandmother when Christmas shopping. The sundae was literally dripping its hot sauce all over the table, but that was acceptable because it was Schrafft's—and watching the chocolate overflow was part of the experience. Valentine's Day was extra special if you received a heart-shaped box of Schrafft's chocolates. These candy containers were pressed cardboard, decorated in silks or satins, often topped with a large bow. Many of them still exist and are fairly inexpensive for today's collector.

Whitman's Samplers are made in all sizes and are still available for the chocolate-giver for today's Valentine's Day celebrations. Stephen Whitman opened his confectionary and candy shop on the streets of Philadelphia in 1842 and became the first to market packaged chocolate. He was known for advertising his candy, paying the stars who posed for print ads for Whitman's Chocolates. By 1912 the company produced its first Whitman's Sampler in a box decorated with a cross-stitch design. That same box was sent to troops during World War II, as well as after the terrorist attacks in 2001, with handwritten notes of encouragement from the people who packaged the boxes. It is difficult to tell the age of Whitman's Sampler boxes because the design has not changed over the years.

NECCO, the New England Confectionary Company, is responsible for creating the candy hearts with clever little sayings on them that schoolchildren distribute (and munch by the dozens) on Valentine's Day. They sell more than eight billion conversation hearts every year. The company began in 1847 when Oliver R. Chase of Boston invented the first candy lozenge cutter. In 1866 the company started producing "Conversation Candies," and grew from there. Through the years, the company has acquired other candy companies, expanding from the simple sugar lozenge candy to candy bars, chocolate bars, and other trademarked candies. One of its candy companies, Mary Jane bars, originally occupied the house where Paul Revere grew up and lived with his family. In 2003 the company moved to a much larger plant in Revere, Massachusetts, where it still manufactures its trademarked Conversation Candies.

In addition to the paper or pressed cardboard candy containers, certain companies, like The E. Rosen Candy Company of Pawtucket, Rhode Island, made hard plastic containers for candy. E. Rosen started his business in 1911 and bought a factory (Rosbro Plastics) that made novelty styrene toys during the 1940s and 1950s. In 1946 Rosen bought the Tico Toys Novelty Company and sold unmarked toys to major department stores and other businesses throughout New England. Rosen produced heart-shaped candy containers in all materials and varied decorative accents. In addition, some of their candy containers are recognizable cartoon characters like Bugs Bunny, Frosty the Snowman, and Rudolph the Red Nosed Reindeer.

Dolls

Dollmakers have created many Valentine's Day dolls through the years, and collectors should be familiar with the makers of these dolls. There are many more than can be mentioned here, so this discussion will focus on a few of the major ones. There were many candy container dolls (e.g., Marcie and Dutchess dolls) made of hard plastic in the 1940s and 1950s that had full ballroom skirts. Some were seated atop candy boxes, while others were the candy container itself. These dolls are often collected by those interested in Valentine memorabilia, and might not be marked with a manufacturer's name, date, or place of production.

In 1924 Madame Alexander began producing their trademark dolls by Madame Beatrice Alexander Behrman, the daughter of Russian immigrants. Since the 1920s, the company has produced dolls for just about every holiday, including many that epitomize the Valentine's Day tradition. Each year new bow-mouthed beauties are created, new dresses are made, and holidays celebrated with new editions of the Madame Alexander doll line.

Mattel's line of Barbie dolls began in 1959 when Ruth Handler decided her daughter needed a three-dimensional grown-up doll to play with, rather than the paper versions she'd been using. The dolls burst onto the scene and grew in popularity so quickly through the 1960s and into the 1970s that a convention was begun in 1980, and collecting Barbies became an earnest hobby for many Americans, as well as other collectors throughout the world. During the 1980s, the Happy Holidays series began and since that time, Valentine's Day Barbies have been created every year.

Suffice it to say that the Valentine's Day collector has many, many choices in the variety of objects available for consumers. Whether you choose to collect fragile, intricately designed valentines or you would rather hunt for aluminum chocolate molds, you have a wealth of items from which to choose.

PRICE LIST: VALENTINE'S DAY COLLECTIBLES

Bell, Multilingual Vintage Valentine Girl Bell. Lady in a green hat and shirt with a skirt decorated with raised hearts and "I love you" in seven languages: English, German, Italian, Chinese, Spanish, French, and Swedish. Very good condition. $22–25

Book, *Necco Sweethearts Be My Valentine.* By Barbara McGrath and Frank Mazzola. Excellent condition. **$5–7**

Buttons, Four Red and White Heart-Shaped Valentine. Glass. The buttons measure slightly more than ½" in width and height. Excellent condition. **$6–8**

Calendar, Valentine Girl. Angel from calendar has a tree with hearts and is holding a valentine. Circa 1910. 4½" × 4". Excellent condition. **$80–100**

Candlesticks, Hearts. Brass candlesticks with center heart design. 9½" × 4" × 3" diameter. Made in 1970. Very good condition. **$12–15**

Candy Box, Schrafft's Vintage Valentine Candy Box. Heart measures 8¼" × 8". The bottom of the cardboard heart is red with white lace. Very good condition. **$7–10**

Candy Box, Schrafft's Vintage Two-pound Candy Box. Heart shaped with ruffled trim. Lavender orchids and lilacs decorating the box have fallen off, but are included with box. 18" × 18". Excellent condition. **$8–12**

Candy Containers, Fannie Farmer Man and Woman Celluloid Valentine Lollipop Holders. Circa 1940s–1950s. Very good condition. **$32–40**

Cards, Three Cards used in 1940s–1950s. The kind a school child would give to a classmate. Good condition. **$7–10**

Doll, Be My Valentine. Created by Michele Girard-Kassis. Doll holds construction paper, markers, lace doily, and is dressed in her fanciest dress, getting ready to give away her card. Porcelain, 12" tall, with stand. Mint in box. **$55–75**

Doll, Juliet Raggedy Ann Doll. Wears a Renaissance-style dress with a heart locket and bow. Limited edition. 16" tall. Raggedy Ann™. ©Johnny Gruelle. All rights reserved. Mint condition. **$28–35**

Doll, Lee Middleton "Sweet Hearts." Limited Edition of only 1,000. Vinyl. Wears white satin dress with red embroidered hearts and heart-shaped trim, white satin panties with matching trim, lacy socks, and white shoes with tiny bows. Holds bright red satin heart pillow. Mint condition. **$140–150**

Fan, Valentine. Circa 1910 Valentine open-up fan, Winsch Schmucker angels. Opens to 13" wide. Marked "A Token Of Love" and "Germany." All roses, hearts, and angels are embossed. Each piece connected to the next with pink ribbon that stops the pieces from extending too far and limits possible damage. Excellent condition. **$75–90**

Figurine, Charming Tails "Bee My Honey." Created by artist Dean Griff. Mouse dressed as bee surrounded by flowers. Mint in box condition. **$19–24**

Figurine, Charming Tails "Showered In Love." Created by artist Dean Griff. Cuddling mice with bright red umbrella and heart shaped raindrops. Mint in box condition. **$19–24**

Figurine, Charming Tails "Whole Bushel." Created by artist Dean Griff. "Heartwarmers" from Fitz and Floyd®. Basket is full of bright red and pink hearts, flying all about on flexible wires. Mint in box condition. **$19–24**

Figurine, Charming Tails "You Really Spice Up My Life." Created by artist Dean Griff in artist's resin and vivid yet natural color palette. Mouse with large red chili peppers. Mint in box condition. **$19–24**

Figurine, Charming Tails "I'm Sending All My Love." Approximately 5" tall. Mouse getting ready to send messages of love. Ceramic. Mint condition. **$20–22**

Figurine, Charming Tails "Kiss Me." Approximately 5" tall. Ceramic. Mouse with pretty pink bows. Mint condition. **$20–22**

Figurine, Mary's Moo Moos® "I Bull-ieve This Belongs to You." Mary's Moo Moos® "Adora-bull" collectible cow figurine. Mint in box condition. **$15–18**

Figurine, Precious Moments® "Give with a Grateful Heart." Limited edition. Girl with kitten in a basket figurine. Mint condition. **$30–40**

Figurine, Precious Moments® "I Love You More Every Day." #114032. Girl with Calendar. Mint condition. **$36–40**

Figurine, Precious Moments® "Overflowing with Love." #108523. Girl surrounded by hearts. Mint condition. **$26–30**

Figurine, Precious Moments® "Your Love Means The World to Me." For the Hamilton Collection. Little angel figurine with a gleaming halo atop his head and expressive teardrop eyes looking heavenward. Mint in box condition. **$40–48**

Figurine, Valentine Boy or Girl Cupid Angel Figurine. Cupid wears a white robe with gold accents (also on wings) and is holding a bow and arrow, as well as a heart. Very good condition. **$18–22**

Greeting Card, 3-D Die Cut. Cupids Playing Tennis. Circa early 1900s. Approx. 3" × 4". Folds up to read "To My Valentine." Excellent condition. **$60–70**

Greeting Card, Beehive. Circa 1830s. White rising beehive design. Handpainted pansies and roses underneath the beehive. Approximately 4" × 6". Very good condition. **$350–500**

Greeting Card, Biedermeier Movable Card. Circa 1810. Depicts a water mill. Published in Germany or Austria. 4⅛" × 3⅜". Beautiful colors and detail. Works perfectly. Excellent condition. **$450–475**

Greeting Card, Biedermeier Type Movable Card. Circa 1810. France. Card has a pull tab mechanism. When the tab is pulled the gentleman takes a bow. 3" × 4". Works perfectly. Excellent condition. **$370–400**

Greeting Card, Cupid Driving Car. Circa 1920s. Depicts a blue car with cupid driving a couple. Approximately 16" × 9". Great details and graphics, as well as outstanding colorations. Poem included. Includes a picture frame-like stand. Very good condition. **$46–52**

Greeting Card, Cupid with Honeycomb. 5" high. Marked "Made in USA." Red honeycomb is a little faded. Very good condition. **$12–15**

Greeting Card, Fraktur. Circa 1830s. Heart shaped with ribbons. Approximately 6" × 6". **$1,000–1,200**

Greeting Card, Heart with Honeycomb. 8¼" high. Good condition.   **$12–15**

Greeting Card, Kewpie. Circa 1918. Card and envelope depicts Kewpie dolls hugging under an umbrella. Stamp is postmarked Denver, Colorado, Feb. 14, 1918. Very good condition.   **$32–38**

Greeting Card, Mechanical Fan Valentine, Little Girl with Curls. Circa 1930s. Size: 4" × 6". Very good condition.   **$11–15**

Greeting Card, Mickey Mouse. Circa 1939. Hallmark copyright 1939. Inside is picture of Mickey and Pluto. Closed card measures 4" × 6". Good condition.   **$26–30**

Greeting Card, Pop-up in Shadow Box. 3-D card reads "To my Valentine. Roses sweet I often see, But you're the sweetest Rose for me." Frame: 11" × 13". Card: 7½" × 9". Excellent condition.   **$75–85**

Greeting Card, Raphael Tuck & Sons, Ltd. Printed in Germany. Valentine. Depicts hot air balloon with ribbon, attached to basket holding two children. Heavily embossed die-cut thick paper. Front states "Nobody's Looking but the Owl and the Moon." Some damage, but good for such a fragile card. Good condition.   **$90–110**

Greeting Card, Standing Boat. Boat named Cupid with a "Message of Love" on a small pretty girl. Two additional girls on the boat holding Japanese style lanterns and a parchment or vellum-type sail. These two girls, the "Message of Love" girl, and the sail are all pop-up or 3-D. Approx. 12" × 8½". Near mint condition.   **$80–90**

Greeting Card, Standing. Circa early 1900s. Paper doily heart with a satin cameo-style print of a woman looking at a love letter with Cupid over her shoulder. Stand is also 3-D. The satin heart shape pops out from the card itself. Approximately 13½" × 8¼". Message is "With All Good Wishes." Excellent condition.   **$35–48**

Greeting Card, Valentine, Southern Belle Little Girl with Fold-Out Skirt. Germany. Circa 1920s. Back marked "Florence from Mama 1925." Very good condition.   **$50–60**

Greeting Card, Wizard of Oz Valentine. Circa 1941. Greeting on back of card says "from Duane." Maker's mark: Licensed by Loew's Incorporated from Motion Picture "Wizard of Oz" A.C. Co 151. Very good condition.   **$35–40**

Greeting Cards, Box of 1960s Hallmark Batman Valentines. All twelve Valentines are unused, three each of the four designs. Cards open and say "I'm falling for you Valentine," "I'm out to get you Valentine," "Valentine you really pack a wallop," and "You're just my speed Valentine."   **$45–55**

Greeting Cards, Display of Ten Vintage Valentines. Mounted on red paper and framed in black frame. Overall size of frame 16¼" × 21". All Valentines in good condition.   **$40–50**

Greeting Cards, Lot of 158 Vintage Cards. Majority are die-cut, only a few "square" Valentine cards. A few date from the 1940s. A few mechanical, a few moveable "large eyes," stand-ups, pop-ups, early "Scarecrow," two oversized mechanicals, a few homemade cards, puppies, some "googlie-eyes" cards, ships, hearts, cupids, three or four circus, cats and dogs, teddy bears, and more. All cards are complete. Excellent condition.   **$105–155**

Handkerchief, Valentine. A gentleman plights his troth with a lady in the center, surrounded by white scrollwork and a chain of hearts. Circa 1920. Hand-rolled. Burmel original. 14" × 14". Excellent condition. **$38–45**

Handkerchief, Valentine. Little birds bringing Valentine greetings. Circa 1930s. Hand rolled. 13 × 13½". Very good condition. **$22–25**

Handkerchief, Valentine. "L'Amour Toujours" (Love always) repeated twice. Circa 1920s. Hand rolled hem. 12 × 12½". Very good condition. **$36–40**

Jewelry Box, Cherub. Measures just under 2" × ⅝". Excellent condition. **$18–22**

Jewelry Box. Jeweled, hinged enamel heart box accented with Swarovski crystals. 2" × 2". Mint condition. **$35–40**

Jewelry, Bracelet. Puffy heart bracelet with thirteen hearts. Circa 1960s. All but one heart is sterling. Some hearts have inscriptions: Helen (twice), Annie, H. H., Aunt Molly, and J. D. Hearts include "I Love U," "Forget Me Not," wishbone, three-leaf clovers, two wonderful Art Nouveau hearts including a beautiful lady with flowing hair. The wishbone heart is sterling and all the others are marked. The sterling bracelet has alternating etched and smooth links and is a little less than 8" long. Very good condition. **$400–425**

Jewelry, Bracelet. Wide black cuff bracelet with embedded clear rhinestone heart. 1¾" wide. Excellent condition. **$48–54**

Jewelry, Bracelet. Sterling puffy heart bracelet marked on the clasp and on one heart even though all hearts test sterling. Fourteen hearts and three of them have duplicates. Sterling bracelet is a pretty twisted rope design and measures 6⅞" long. None of the hearts are engraved with initials. Excellent condition. **$400–425**

Jewelry, Charm Bracelet. Faux coins and plastic hearts swirled with white. Measures 8" × 1". Very good condition. **$33–38**

Jewelry, Earrings and Necklace. Heart-shaped purple amethysts on genuine gold chain with lobster claw clasp. 2.3 grams; carat weight: 1.13 cttw; 10K yellow gold. Mint condition. **$260–275**

Jewelry, Earrings. Dangling cupid earrings for pierced ears measure 2¾" long. Excellent condition. **$14–18**

Jewelry, Heart Brooch. Circa 1930s feathered brooch. Measures 8" long with "egret" feathers. Clear and emerald rhinestone heart brooch has a clamp at the bottom back that holds these original white feathers. Excellent condition. **$52–60**

Jewelry, Key Pin. Circa 1960s sterling key pin with dangling puffy heart. Measures 2¼" wide. Marked "Sterling" and an unidentifiable maker's mark. Very good condition. **$52–60**

Jewelry, Locket. Six garnets set into large sterling Nouveau locket that measures 1¼" long, not including the jump ring. Locket is 1⅜" wide when closed. Marked "925." Very good condition. **$225–250**

Jewelry, Necklace. Solid sterling replica of a chocolate kiss from Hershey's. 19½" long chain. Excellent condition. **$40–45**

Jewelry, Pendant. Thomas Kinkade heart-shaped diamond jewelry pendant from Ashton-Drake. Inspired by Kinkade's painting "A Perfect Red Rose." Measures 1-³⁄₁₆" × 1". Hand-crafted, single diamond set into a sterling silver heart plated with 24K gold and suspended within a second heart formed of sterling silver roses and gold-plated ribbons. Inscribed on back, "Always in My Heart." 18" gold-plated rope chain. Includes certificate of authenticity. Mint condition. **$99–110**

Jewelry, Pendant. Sterling chain with rhodium-plated filigree heart pendant. Circa 1960s. Dainty but strong chain is 15" long. Heart is prong set with crystal clear rhinestones. Mint condition. **$30–35**

Jewelry, Pin. Heart pin of gold tone raised stripes and fuchsia, dark pink, heavy enamel. Circa 1975. 1¼" wide. Excellent condition. **$20–25**

Jewelry, Pin. Heart pin, made of plastic, hangs on brass from a jaunty red bow. 2⅛" long overall; the heart is 1½" wide. Unmarked. Excellent condition. **$14–18**

Jewelry, Pin. Mustard seed pin. Circa 1950. Coro design. Bow pin measures 1" wide; the pin dangles 1⅜" long. Excellent condition. **$15–18**

Jewlery, Pin. "Be Mine" valentine heart pin. Circa 1970s. 1⅜" long. Excellent condition. **$18–20**

Magazine, *The Rural Repository*, Hudson, New York, February 14, 1846. Shows a view of the Hudson River at top. Includes article on Saint Valentine's Day. Magazine size: 9" × 11.5". Eight pages. Very good condition. **$35–40**

Mechanical Valentine. Designed by Frances Brundage. Circa 1890s–1910. Depicts little girl carrying roses. Her heart opens to reveal heart. 12" × 7". Excellent condition. **$225–250**

Mousepad, Vintage Valentines. Images circa early twentieth century. 9¼" × 7¾" × ¼" cloth top mousepad. Mint condition. **$15–18**

Music Box, Heart Full of Love. Created by artist Lena Liu for Ardleigh Elliott. Limited edition. Heart-shaped porcelain collectible music box. Mint in box condition. **$15–18**

Ornament, American Heart Association Ornaments. "Matters of the Heart" mouth-blown, hand-painted glass ornaments. Red dress ornament and heart and angels ornament. A portion of the proceeds from the sale of the ornaments goes to the American Heart Association. Mint condition. **$50–55 each**

Planter, Relpo Valentine Heart. Samson Import, dated 1960. Heart-shaped openwork around the edge. Very good condition. **$28–32**

Postcard, Children in Fur Coats with Verse. Illustrated by International Art postcard artist Heinmuller with two children dressed in Edwardian fashion fur coats and hats. The card has a divided back and is postmarked 1916 with a one cent stamp attached. Good condition. **$8–12**

Postcard, "To My Love, My Valentine." Front reads: "Dearest you can never guess half of the love and tenderness that I hold both fond and true, Deeply in my heart for you." Postmarked February 12, 1910, Manasquan, N.J. Very good condition. **$4–6**

Postcard, Cupid Traffic Cop Valentine. Circa early 1900s. Features Kewpie traffic cop with a Valentine remembrance: "Here at my heart he'd bid you stop, If Cupid were a Traffic Cop." Never mailed. Very good condition. **$10–15**

Postcard, Mechanical. Cupid brings Valentine gifts to Georgian beauty. Embossed, mechanical. 1910 Winsch copyright. Printed in Germany. Very good condition. **$17–20**

Postcard, To My Valentine. Two cherubs with heart. Embossed. Circa 1920. Very good condition. **$12–15**

Postcard, To My Valentine. Embossed. Circa 1910s. Very good condition. **$8–12**

Postcard, Tuck Valentine Cupid Series. Raphael Tuck & Sons postcard "Sportive Cupids" series of Valentine postcards, no. 21. Depicts a blond cupid with blond curls singing and holding a sheet of music that says "Love's Grand Sweet Song!" Marked in back with pencil. Maker's mark: "Art Publishers to Their Majesties the King and Queen." Never postmarked. Very good condition. **$25–30**

Postcard, Valentine. Antique embossed gilded ASB postcard, solitary tree under moon, hearts, forget-me-nots, 1909. Divided card, no postmark, but inked mailing address to Baltimore, Maryland, and a message that includes a date of February 14, 1909. Made in Germany and carries the ASB (Arthur Schurer, Berlin) trademark and # 267. Very good condition. **$10–12**

Postcard, Victorian Woman in Feather Hat. Circa early 1900s. "To My Valentine" in gold under the heart and roses. Very good condition. **$6–8**

Postcards, Six Bonte Fantasy Veggie Post Cards. Series 400 of the Fantasy Valentine series of vegetable fruit people. Includes Messrs Onion, Apricot, Celery and Rhubarb, Kernel Walnut and Misses Grape, Miss Parsnip and Green Pepper, Mr. Blackberry. Good condition. **$25–35**

Postcards, Renaissance Troubadours. Pair of antique embossed Alsop postcards. Neither card used. Each has a one-cent stamp space. "Post Card" banner is that of George N. Alsop, Va. Very good condition. **$40–50**

Purse, "Roses Are Red." Made by Mary Frances from the Motif collection. Embellished with beads, trims, opalescent rice pearls and beaded fringe, and accented with micro-glitter. Three small roses on the front of the bag along with a clear faceted heart bauble. Back of the bag is lavender with more micro-glitter and another faceted heart. Mint condition.
$146–156

Scherenschnitte Art, "Choose Your Love, Love Your Choice." Original artwork. Created by artist Sharyn Sowell. Made of pieces from a book about Ohio's Agricultural Statistics 1854–1855. Over the top of it, a woman had pasted quotes, poems, and articles from newspapers and magazines of the day. These pieces adorn this unusual piece. The words "choose your love, love your choice" were printed in the artist's studio using vintage type printed on

Scherenschnitte Art, I Love You More Than Heart Can Tell. *Photo and Copyright © Sharyn Sowell. All rights reserved.* $295–325.

the empty pages of the journal. It measures 12" × 12", no mat. Photo and Copyright © Sharyn Sowell. All rights reserved. Mint and original condition. **$295–325**

Scherenschnitte Art, "I Love You More Than Heart Can Tell." Incredibly detailed piece, black heart on white paper. Photo and Copyright © Sharyn Sowell. All rights reserved. Mint and original condition. **$295–325**

Toy, Candy Container. Be Mine Valentine's Day cowboy. Circa 1950s. Made by E. Rosen. Excellent condition. **$50–60**

Toy, Teddy Bear, Boyds Adora U Teddy Bear. Bright white plush fur and luscious red ribbon bow. Holds a red felt pillow that spells out "LOVE." Mint condition. **$15–18**

Toy, Teddy Bear, Hugs N. Kisses. Mocha and mixed gold plush bears from Boyds are attached at the lips. Hubby holds rose bouquet in his hand. Each is 6" high. Mint condition. **$20–25**

Toy, Teddy Bear, Sir Hugsalot. Boyds Bear, Collectible Teddy Bear. White chenille plush and bean-filled, features white velvet paw pads, red heart-print foot pads, and a red heart-print pillow. Mint condition. **$25–30**

Toy, Teddy Bears, Valentine's Day Red and White Teddy Bear Set. Made by Boyds Bears. Made of lush fur and full of beans. Mint condition. **$25–30**

Toys, Teddy Bears, Lovey and Dovey Teddy Bears. Made by Boyds. Pair of teddy bears cuddles close, holding a felt banner that says, "We may not have it all together, but together we have it all!" Mint condition. **$15–18**

Tussie-Mussie, Silver. Circa twentieth century. Heavy silver work done in a beautiful style with a large sterling bow holding the stem of the bouquet holder. Marked "Tishum Art, 925." 2¾" in diameter × 3⅜" tall; the bow is 1¼" across. Mint condition. **$100–115**

Vase, Valentine Day Vase Cupids and Heart. Circa 1963. Made by Inaro of Japan in 1963. Bottom of vase reads; "Inarco Copyright 1963, Cleveland, Ohio E-1560." Excellent condition. **$75–100**

Wreath, Annalee Cupids. Wreath has two Annalee cupids inside the heart. Vintage Annalee design. Excellent condition. **$65–75**

Presidents' Day (Third Monday in February)

This holiday is one that is intrinsically American. George Washington, the first president of the United States (1789–1797), was designated the "Father" of the country. He is credited with winning independence for the new nation, as commander in chief of the colonial armies in the American Revolution, and came to represent everything the country strived for during its earliest years.

The original holiday began during the last full year of Washington's presidency (1796) to celebrate his birthday, February 22 (1732). Americans celebrated Washington's birthday with balls, parties, speeches, and receptions. As the holiday grew, stories about his childhood (cutting down the cherry tree) and his other accomplishments took on legendary status. The holiday was celebrated with magazine covers, student parties in school, postcards, commemorative coins, and many other types of collectible items.

When President Lincoln later became a beloved icon, his birthday, February 12, was also celebrated by American citizens. The holiday began in 1866, the year after his assassination. That first commemoration was a small event held in Washington, D.C. For a long time, some southern states did not join in this celebration. Items created to celebrate Lincoln's birthday include cutouts of his now-famous profile and the log cabin that symbolized his humble upbringing. Postcards, coins, candy containers in the shape of log cabins, figurines, busts, statues, handkerchiefs, and sterling silver spoons, as well as many other items, have been included in personal collections.

Most states celebrated each of the presidential birthdays separately, in spite of the fact that they were so close together in date. In 1968 the holiday was switched to the third Monday in February, as a result of H.R. 15951, a law enacted to simplify the list of yearly holidays. There was a fair amount of controversy regarding this decision, and although the suggestion to rename the holiday came up, most did not agree with calling the day Presidents' Day, largely because not all presidents were held in such high esteem as Washington and Lincoln. The states themselves chose to either continue celebrating Washington's Birthday or to switch to the newly designated Presidents' Day.

Separate celebrations continue for both presidents. For instance, the George Washington Birthplace National Monument in Virginia celebrates Washington's birthday with activities during the day, while Lincoln's birthday is celebrated with events that include a February 12th wreath-laying ceremony at the Abraham Lincoln Birthplace National Historic Site in Hodgenville, Kentucky.

For those who want to celebrate all the presidents, there are celebrations organized by the National Park Service (*www.nps.gov*).

Today, Presidents' Day is celebrated with the usual pomp and circumstance, but it is also a day of special sales by department stores and other businesses, as well as events like races and marathons.

PRICE LIST: PRESIDENTS' DAY COLLECTIBLES

Car Sticker, Presidents' Day Eagle. Vinyl. 3" × 8". Various colors. Mint condition. **$3.50–4**

Coins, Three 10th Anniversary Presidents' Day Coins. Dated 1989–1999. Charleston Mint Company. Mint in box condition. **$100–115**

Cover, Presidents' Day 2005. Holiday took place on February 21st. Cover postmarked on board the carrier USS *Ronald Reagan* that day. The ship's postal clerk stamped the cover with the USS *Ronald Reagan*'s crest on the lower left side. Additional computer-generated images of the Presidential Seal and President Reagan's signature, above the crest. Postage stamp one of the five Old Glory Booklet issues of 2003. Mint condition. **$2–3**

Handbill, Grateful Dead—Abe Lincoln's Birthday Party Handbill (Bill Graham Presents, 1967). 9" × 11". No posters or postcards made for this event, just handbills. Joining the Dead on this bill were Moby Grape, Sly and the Family Stone, and the New Salvation Army Band. Excellent condition. **$5–8**

Invitation, President Lincoln's Birthday. Held on the S.S. *Caledonia*. Picture of Lincoln on front and says "Birthday Invitation." At bottom of invitation in gold lettering it says "Frank C Clark Cruise"; inside menu says "S.S. *Caledonia*." Rope is red, white, and blue. 9½" by 6¾". Dated 1928. Good condition. **$10–15**

Medal, Commemorative. Made for the GAR (Grand Army of the Republic) to commemorate Lincoln's 100th birthday. 3" diameter, made of brass. Circa 1909. Front: Lincoln's bust and the words, "With Malice Towards None, With Charity for All," and dates 1809 and 1909. Back: "This Medal Was Struck for the Grand Army of the Republic in Commemoration of the 100th Anniversary of the Birth of Abraham Lincoln." Maker's mark on the bottom part of Lincoln's shoulder reads, "Copyright Davisons Sons Phila." Words encased in wreath. Very good condition. **$30–40**

Pamphlet, Commemorative, Washington's Birthday. Congressional Banquet in Honor of George Washington, and the Principles of Washington. February 22, 1852. Reported and published by William Hincks and F. H. Smith. Boston. 57 pages. Printed by Dutten Wentworth 1852. Good condition. **$18–22**

Pin, 2004 Hollywood Presidents' Day Pin. Features a girl holding an ax in front of cherry tree. Limited edition of 300. Mint in box condition. **$18–20**

Pin, Mickey Mouse and Goofy. Limited edition dangle pin. Mickey and Goofy as former Presidents. The dangle reads "Presidents Day 2005 Walt Disney World®." The U.S. Capitol is in the background. Mickey resembles George Washington, complete with white wig. Goofy, dressed like Abe Lincoln, is on the right with his arm on Mickey's shoulder. Mint condition. **$12–15**

Postcard, Lincoln, 1809–1865. His portrait in oval, framed by flag. Postmark 1911. Good condition. **$15–25**

Postcard, Lincoln's Address at Gettysburg. Postmark 1910. Very good condition. **$15–25**

Postcard, Lincoln's Birthday. Centennial postcard, copyright 1908 by E. Nash. Not mailed. Words "Prudential Post Card & Novelty Co." stamped on card. Embossed decorative accents. Divided back. Very good condition. **$4.50–6**

Postcard, Lincoln, 1809–1865. Postmark 1911. *Courtesy of Cocoa Village Antique Mall.* $15–25.

Postcard, Lincoln's Address at Gettysburg. Postmark 1910. *Courtesy of Cocoa Village Antique Mall.* $15–25.

Postcard, Presidents' Day. Postmarked 1914. Little boy with a flag draped over a picture of George Washington. It says "Liberty and Union Now and Forever." Good condition.

$5–7

Postcard, Theodore Roosevelt. Card marked: "Theodore Roosevelt, President's Day, Keokuk, Iowa, 1907." Black and white photo of TR against a photo of the Capitol. Addressed on split back. Good condition.

$10–15

Postcards, Two Washington's Birthday. Embossed postcards published by Raphael Tuck. Series # 156. First shows "Washington's Inauguration As President." Second shows "Washington at the Battle of Princeton." Postmarked 1909. Both cards have writing on reverse. Good condition.

$7–9

Stencil, Tupperware Holiday Stencil, Presidents' Day. Stencils are of log cabin, Abraham Lincoln, George Washington, and cherry tree. 6" × 6" aqua plastic. For children's arts and crafts projects. Mint condition.

$6–8

Mardi Gras

The beginning of Mardi Gras (also known as Carnival, or Shrove Tuesday) in the United States dates back to 1699 when explorers of New Orleans celebrated their French heritage with the holiday. They established *krewes*, organizations that hosted parades and balls. The celebrations begin forty-seven days before Easter and end on the day before Ash Wednesday. Mardi Gras is always held forty-seven days before Easter, sometimes falling on a Tuesday, which coincides with the meaning of the words "Mardi Gras" (Fat Tuesday). (Although the holiday usually falls in February—hence its inclusion in this chapter—it sometimes falls in early March.) Christians traditionally chose to celebrate this holiday to mark the last time they could enjoy themselves before the forty days of Lent, when they would fast and generally lead a much more restricted life. Actually, the word "carnival" comes from an old Italian word *carnevale* ("farewell to [things of] the flesh"). Thus, the three days before Ash Wednesday is Shrovetide, an old English word that means "to repent." Lent itself isn't mentioned in the Bible; the word comes from a Middle English word (*lente*), which means springtime, and it was during that season (spring) that meat became forbidden during the weeks preceding Easter.

Some sources state that the citizens of New Orleans and surrounding areas were holding masked balls from 1718 until the Spanish government took over and banned the balls. Finally, in 1827, masked balls were restored and elegant parties were held among the city's elite until the 1850s, when rioting in the streets threatened to ruin the city's traditions. The Mystick Krewe of Comus, aware that the parties would not continue without organization, was started in 1857 and planned a themed parade to celebrate the holiday. In 1872 the newly named "king of Carnival," Rex, chose the official colors for the holiday: purple, green, and gold, with purple representing justice, green representing faith, and gold representing power. During that year's celebration, the Krewe of Rex was formed, specifically to honor the visiting Grand Duke Alexis Romanoff of Russia. Because the Krewe didn't have existing royalty to welcome the Grand Duke, they appointed a "king of Mardi Gras" for the day. Since that time, the mockery has continued and a new king is appointed every year, the identity of which is a secret until the day of the parade.

The parades and the krewes have been known to thinly disguise their parade celebrants to criticize the political views of the day. They also mock themselves, and New Orleans's African American population joins in the mockery with their own parade to bring to light the snobbishness of the parade and its celebrants. The oldest African American parade, on Mardi Gras morning, is organized by the Zulu Social Aid and Pleasure Club, a group that first marched in 1901 and became known as Zulu in 1909. Mocking the traditional krewes' self-importance, Zulu's first king, William Story, wore a lard can as a crown and carried a banana stalk as a scepter. By 1991, it was no longer legal for certain clubs to discriminate by marching in the Zulu parade (e.g., Momus, Comus, and Proteus).

Some of the many collectibles available to Mardi Gras celebrants, as well as those who prefer to collect from the privacy of their own homes, are beads, masks, posters, works of art, invitations to balls, favors from balls, postcards, stamps, and items made by the various bars and restaurants throughout the New Orleans metropolitan area. Due to the devastating effects of Katrina, the price of Mardi Gras collectibles from New Orleans is expected to rise, particularly those collectibles produced in the year following the hurricane (2006). It will be a matter of time before it is clear whether Mardi Gras collectibles from other years will be affected by Hurricane Katrina, but I believe it's safe to say that Mardi Gras collectibles will be more precious to those who have a soft spot for New Orleans and its traditions.

PRICE LIST: MARDI GRAS COLLECTIBLES

Beads, Czechoslovakian Glass. Circa 1950. 16½" long. Multiple colors, shapes, and sizes. Tag "Made in Czechoslovakia" still intact. Excellent condition.   **$60–75**

Beads, Glass. Vintage beads. Set of two with original paper. Excellent condition. **$185–210**

Beads. Hundreds of Mardi Gras float bead throws. Mint condition.   **$75–85**

Costume, Pocahontas Costume. Designed by a professional costumer from New Orleans for the 1999 millennium Mardi Gras parade by the Corps of Napoleon Crew. Headdress built on a harness. Costume contains many sequins, feathers, and appliques, and is fairly light for its tremendous volume. Size 4. Measurements: Bust 33.5", waist 25.5", length 55". Excellent condition.   **$2000–2500**

Dance Card, Krewe of Proteus, 1903. 5" × 3". Very good condition.   **$78–90**

Dance Card, Krewe of Proteus, 1904. 5" × 6". Hard to find item. Good condition.

$110–125

Doll, Abigail, 1780 Masquerade. Retired. From the Cameo Girls 2002 collection. Approximately 7" × 4". Handcrafted, hand painted, cold cast. Limited edition of 1,500. Individually numbered on the bottom. Paperwork states: "On the wrought-iron balcony of her Bourbon St. pied-à-terre, Abigail bewitches the gents who loiter on the cobblestones below as they wait for a glimpse of the magical mademoiselle. Her royal colors mark the season for revelry. The masque of peafowl plumage hides her lovely face but nothing can conceal that very interesting come-hither look. Powdered wig stolen from Marie Antoinette." Mint in box condition.   **$60–75**

Favor, Comus Ball. Silver-plated footed tray, given to a lady with request for a dance with a masked and unidentified Krewe member. Measures 7¼" × 5¼". Engraved "MKC" and dated 1948. Maker: Adler's Jewelers on Canal Street in New Orleans. Made especially for Comus for that year. Excellent condition.   **$60–75**

Favor, Comus Ball. Round Dish. 5" diameter × 1¼" high × ¾" deep. Thick glass. Weighs 1 lb. 12 oz. Crown has three plumes in it. Given by a krewe member to one of the few ladies invited to the ball. From Adler's Jewelers on Canal Street. Excellent condition.   **$100–125**

Frame, Ceramic, with Mardi Gras Masks. New. 5" × 7". Mint condition.   **$8–10**

Frame, Ceramic. Large jester on left and smaller on right. Brightly colored. 3.75" × 5.75". Mint condition.   **$4–6**

Invitation. 1899 "Krewe of Nereus" Mardi Gras Invitation. "French Opera House, Monday January 30th, 1899." Graphics depict the god of the sea (Nereus in Greek mythology was god of the sea). The title of the Tableau Ball was "A Visit to the North Pole." Reverse: Queen with winged cherubs in attendance, adorning her chariot/sleigh with roses. She holds the reins as butterflies, dragonflies, and bees lead the way. A nymph, perhaps one of Nereus's fifty daughters, sits in the upper right corner. Measures 6⅝" × 9" and was the krewe's fourth presentation. Good condition.   **$450–500**

Invitation. 1906 Proteus invitation for the krewe's silver anniversary. Invitation is actually a large booklet, bound with a silver cord, that opens up to reveal a detailed representation of the previous twenty-four invitations. Excellent condition. **$170–200**

Jewelry, Pin. Circa 1968. Brooch pin favor from Krewe of Proteus Ball. Proteus riding waves. Silver. Approximately 3" diameter. Excellent condition. **$75–100**

Jewelry, Pin. Sterling silver with gold wash. Shape of a heart (basket-weave) with enameled flowers and leaves in pink, blue, and green. Signed on the back as follows: "Proteus, –1915, Sterling." Pin given to the members of the Krewe of Proteus at the 1915 Mardi Gras Ball in New Orleans. Measures 1¾" × 1½". Excellent condition. **$465–500**

Mask, Carnival, Pizzazzz-Green. Mint condition. **$45–55**

Mask, Carnival, Trim Adorable. Mint condition. **$25–30**

Mask, Comedy/Tragedy Mini Tile. Mint condition. **$35–40**

Mask, Comedy/Tragedy Pedestal Mask. Mint condition. **$30–40**

Mask, Desireé. Tall, plush plumes extending over and below the mask's sleek ivory face. Mint condition. **$75–90**

Mask, Feather. Beautiful real feathers; long black ones (14"–16") are coque (rooster feathers), and the shorter ones (4"–6") are called hackle. Both kinds luxurious to the touch and eye-catching. Face mask covered with matching sequins and extremely well-made. Padded underside elastic strap for securing to head. Mint condition. **$95–115**

Mask, Fleur de Lis. Colors of Mardi Gras encircle eyeslits. Mint condition. **$30–40**

Mask, French Quarter Poirot. Famous face of New Orleans and master of hedonistic activities, decorated appropriately. Mint condition. **$30–40**

Mask, Mardi Gras Madness Marionette. Mint condition. **$90–110**

Mask, Mardi Gras Masquerader. Mint condition. **$75–100**

Mask, Mardi Gras Sideshow Jester. Mint condition. **$100–120**

Mask, Mardi Gras Vamp. Painted in traditional Mardi Gras colors. Mint condition. **$25–35**

Mask, Mardi Gras. Full face, maroon feathers, gold face, purple and gold mask. Ceramic and measures 14" × 14". Excellent condition. **$55–65**

Mask, Mardi Gras, Late 1800s. Handmade, punched copper, canvas backing, handpainted. 16" × 11". Features chin rest with eye slits and nose holes. Originally from Krewe of Proteus. Very good condition. **$100–125**

Mask, Charades Sophisticate. Tall plume. Mint condition. **$45–55**

Mask, Papier-mâché. Full face in a bright teal-colored finish. Butterfly design in gold leaf on cheeks and forehead, and embellished with pink and red paillettes, and glass cabochon jewels. 8½" × 5½". Excellent condition. **$75–125**

Mask, Shooting Star. Handpainted in traditional Mardi Gras colors with stars cascading down face. Mint condition. **$35–45**

Mask, Stick Mask. Gold. Mint condition. $20–30

Mask, Stick Mask. Purple. Mint condition. $20–30

Mask, The Classic Half-Mask. Embellished with red, green, sky blue, gold, black, purple, or white feathers, and gilded with coordinating sequin trim and beads. Mint condition.
$25–35

Mask, The Jester-Aire Head Series. Limited Edition. Mint condition. $600–650

Medals, Four, Krewe of Venus. Four different medals, pure .999 silver. Silver-dollar-sized Krewe of Venus, New Orleans Mardi Gras medals, dating from 1969 to 1973. Each medal is a special proof striking, with light contact marks. Excellent condition. $50–60

Poster, 1988 Mardi Gras Art Poster, Hugh Ricks. Hugh Ricks is known for his Louisiana World Expo Art Poster, his Albuquerque International Ballon Fiesta Official Posters (1985, 1989, 1990, and 1991), his New Orleans Jazz and Heritage Festival art posters (1983, 1987), and his Mardi Gras fine art posters from 1985, 1986, 1988, 1989, 1991, 1992, and 1994. This is a signed and numbered artist's proof. Number 47 of 100 printed, signed "Hugh Ricks to Ken Smith." Framed by Falcon Galleries in Louisville, Kentucky. Measures 22" × 30", framed. Poster originally released by ProCreations in an open edition of 5,000, a signed and numbered edition of 750, and the artist's proof edition of 100. Near mint condition.
$135–175

Poster, Mardi Gras, New Orleans, 1995. Artist: Andrea Mistretta. 24" × 32". Mint condition.
$18–22

Poster, Mardi Gras, New Orleans, 1996. Artist: Andrea Mistretta. 24" × 32". Mint condition.
$20–25

Poster, Mardi Gras, New Orleans, 1997. Artist: Andrea Mistretta. 24" × 32". Mint condition.
$18–22

Poster, Mardi Gras, New Orleans, 1998. Artist: Andrea Mistretta. 24" × 32". Mint condition.
$18–22

Poster, Mardi Gras, New Orleans, 1999. Artist: Andrea Mistretta. 24" × 32". Mint condition.
$18–22

Poster, Mardi Gras, New Orleans, 2001. Artist: Andrea Mistretta. 24" × 29". Mint condition.
$36–40

Poster, New Orleans, Mardi Gras, 2003. Artist: Andrea Mistretta. 24" × 32". Mint condition.
$20–25

Poster, New Orleans, Mardi Gras, 2005. Artist: Andrea Mistretta. 24" × 32". Mint condition.
$20–25

Poster, New Orleans, Mardi Gras Mambo, 2002. Artist: Andrea Mistretta. 24" × 32". Mint condition.
$18–22

Poster, Mardi Gras, 1980. Robert Gordy. Limited edition of 3,000. 22" × 32½". Published by ProCreations. Mint condition. **$150–200**

Shot Glass, Mardi Gras Masks. Made of glass with painted decoration. Approximately 3" tall. New. Mint condition. **$5–7**

Snow Globe, Mardi Gras. Globe is marked "New Orleans" and is filled with Mardi Gras masks. New. Mint condition. **$6–10**

T-Shirt, Mardi Gras. Marked "Party like it's 1999" with Mardi Gras Party brands sponsored T-Shirt. Good condition. **$5–7**

– 3 –
MARCH

International Women's Day (March 8)

March 8 is the day when women around the world commemorate the long struggle to attain justice, freedom, equality, peace and development—and the right to vote. The United Nations also recognizes this day as important to humankind in general. Though the international holiday began in Denmark in 1911, the National Women's Day holiday began in America with the Socialist Party of America on February 28, 1908. Throughout that decade, more and more women in countries all over the world took up the cause and added the holiday to their annual celebrations. Women in the United States won the right to vote in 1920 with passage of the Nineteenth Amendment.

Some of the collectibles that commemorate this holiday include postage stamps from all over the world, coins, posters, magazines, pinbacks, banners, T-shirts, and photos.

PRICE LIST: INTERNATIONAL WOMEN'S DAY COLLECTIBLES

First day cover, El Salvador 1990 International Women's Day Issue. Central/Latin America. Mint condition. $3–5

Pin/Pinback, International Women's Day. Wording on face: "Fight for Unemployment Insurance, International Women's Day, March 8." Stamped printed label inside: "Local No. 4 Chicago, Amalgamated Lithographers of America, Union Label" and "Union Label." Two stamped labels in excellent condition. ⅞" diameter pin. Red and white with white lettering. Older woman on left side center and a young woman right side center. Good condition.
                                                                                       $27–35

Stamp and First Day Cover, The International Women's Year 1975. Cover stamped with the first day of issue showing as August 26, 1975, in Seneca Falls, New York. Comes with a narrative card that tells about the event. Excellent condition. $2–3

Stamps, People's Republic of China, 1973 International Women's Day. Scott #1114-1116 International Women's Day. Mint condition. **$8–10**

Saint Joseph's Day (March 19)

Often overshadowed by Saint Patrick's Day, Saint Joseph's holiday is celebrated on March 19 by Catholics who believe Joseph, the husband of Mary, the mother of Jesus, was a man who lived according to the laws of God. Though he is said to be in the line of the House of David, and thus a member of royalty, he was poor and had moved to Galilee to become a builder. Matthew wrote about him during the announcement of Mary's conception, their visit with the Magi, the flight to Egypt, and their return to Nazareth. Because Joseph is not included in the stories of Jesus's ministry or the Passion, most scholars believe he had already died by that point.

Pope Pius IX (reigned 1846–1878) proclaimed that Joseph was the patron of the Universal Church and that his birthday would be celebrated on March 19. The Feast of Saint Joseph is celebrated in Italian communities; it is a holiday when a feast of meatless dishes is created and served to people who stand in for Jesus, Mary, and Joseph. Anything that is left over is given to the poor.

New York, Boston, and New Orleans have large Saint Joseph's Feasts, and it is said that the famous swallows of Capistrano in California return to their roosts on Saint Joseph's Day. According to the web site for the Mission San Juan Capistrano, "Acú, a descendent of the Juaneño Indians, was the Mission's bell ringer until his death in 1924, and . . . [o]ne of Acú's most colorful tales was that of the swallows (or *las golondrinas* as he called them). Acú believed that the swallows flew over the Atlantic Ocean to Jerusalem each winter. In their beaks they carried little twigs, on which they could rest on water when tired."

PRICE LIST: SAINT JOSEPH'S DAY COLLECTIBLES

Bottle, Saint Joseph's Medicine. 5½" × 2½" × ½". Clear glass. Centered on front: St. Joseph's ASSURES PURITY. Centered at the bottom: "2." Very good condition. **$2–4**

Cookbook, *Book of Feasts Cookbook, Recipes and Stories from America's Celebrations.* Written by Kay Goldstein, Liza Nelson; photography by Al Clayton. Copyright 1993. 163 pages, color photographs. Signed by both authors. Includes 20-page section on the Feast of Saint Joseph's Day in New Orleans, Louisiana. Excellent condition. **$10–12**

Figure, Lilliput Lane Saint Joseph's Church. Issued February 1993, retired September 1997. Excellent condition. **$25–30**

Pin, Saint Joseph's Hospital Service. ¾" wide enamel on bronze tone metal. Ball hinge and circular locking clasp. Very good condition. **$2–4**

Plate, Belleek, Saint Joseph's Hospital Centennial, 1887–1987. Plate issued in a limited edition of 500 and given only to staff members of hospital in Houston, Texas. Three images of the hospital, portrayed by artist Robert Brickhouse, depict the original Saint Joseph Infirmary (1887), the first building on the current site (1895), and the medical center complex as seen in 1987. 8¼" diameter plate is #30 of the 500. Excellent condition. **$100–115**

Portrait, Saint Joseph Holding Christ Child. Oil on canvas. Shows Saint Joseph with his staff of lilies, signifying his purity. Holds baby Jesus in other arm. Portrait framed in hammered gold gilt metal frame with wood backing. Excellent condition. **$550–600**

Postcard, Saint Joseph's Old Spanish Cathedral, Saint Augustine. Not postmarked. Unused. Standard Size. Good condition. **$4–6**

Tin, Saint Joseph's Aspirin. 3" × 3", contained thirty-six 5-grain tablets. Lithographed, colorful. Very good condition. **$8–10**

Saint Patrick's Day (March 17)

Credited with being the person who drove the snakes from Ireland, Saint Patrick's legend is a long, complicated one. He was born in 387 A.D. in Kilpatrick, Scotland, and he died on March 17, 461 (some sources date his death as 493, some as 460). His parents were of Roman heritage and held positions of high rank. When he was a teenager, Patrick was kidnapped and sold into slavery to a chieftain in Ireland, where he kept his master's sheep for six years. He fled captivity and traveled to Britain, where he devoted his life to serving God. He studied under Saint Germain, who took the young apostle under his wing and helped him become a priest. Once Patrick took his vows, he felt the call of Ireland and returned there with the blessing of Pope Celestine I.

It is said that Patrick arrived on the shores of Ireland in 433 and immediately met opposition from the Druid priests, in spite of the fact that he understood their ways (he had learned about their traditions during his enslavement). Attempts to stop Saint Patrick from converting the populace were fruitless, and people soon became convinced that his meek demeanor was a mere scrim to hide the larger miracle he would attain.

According to legend, on Easter Day, the Druids and magicians of the area joined their considerable strength in an attempt to sway the Irish people. They caused a dense fog to fall over the land, but Saint Patrick kept praying and the fog lifted to let the sun shine through. Then, though the king of the chieftains had said that none should show the strangers any respect, one did raise himself to honor Saint Patrick, then another. At that time, Patrick plucked a shamrock leaf and used it to explain the Blessed Trinity. On that day, Patrick received permission to preach the Christian faith throughout Ireland.

He spent his life working with the faithful, teaching others about God, and often putting his own life into jeopardy. Though the legends say he rid the country of snakes, the Catholic Church states that Patrick was actually responsible for vanquishing demons from the country.

Though some sources state that Saint Patrick's birthday was celebrated from the time of his death, others say that it's not clear when the holiday began. However, we do know that the Charitable Irish Society of Boston began celebrating Saint Patrick's Day on March 17, 1737. To this day, the parade in Boston for that holiday is one of the main events of the year. It is usually followed by a traditional boiled dinner (before or after Mass), and a roaring good time at one of the local pubs. However, the trip to the pub is largely an Ameri-

47

can tradition. In Ireland, prior to the 1970s, all drinking was done at home because Irish laws mandated that pubs close on the holiday because it was considered a religious day.

New York City held its first Saint Patrick's Day parade on March 17, 1762, when Irish soldiers serving in the English military marched through downtown. The music they generated excited national pride in those of Irish descent and began a long history of parades in areas throughout the United States where Irish Americans lived.

By the middle of the nineteenth century, the Irish encountered ethnic prejudices (typical signs on business windows read: "No Irish Need Apply"). Whether welcome or not, thousands more Irish poured into the country after the potato famines in their homeland (the Great Potato Famine lasted from 1845 to 1849). The difficulties they faced made the Irish community come together and organize in a way no immigrant group had before. They became a political force, and in time the parades became an event that all politicians wanted to attend.

Saint Patrick's Day collectibles include cardboard or papier-mâché candy containers and favors, decorative accents, jewelry, clothing, figurines, postcards, greeting cards, and all kinds of party decorations. Most of the items created are in the form of Saint Patrick's Day icons like four-leaf clovers, kelly-green top hats, Paddy's pig, or leprechauns (a mischievous elf who is reputed to have a secret treasure). Except for the four-leaf clover, the symbols of Saint Patrick's Day appear related more to Ireland than to the saint himself.

PRICE LIST: SAINT PATRICK'S DAY COLLECTIBLES

Art, Painting, "Saint Patrick's Blessing." 54" × 18". "May the Irish hills caress you. May her lakes and rivers bless you. May the luck of the Irish enfold you. May the blessing of Saint Patrick behold you. Ancient Irish Blessing." Vibrant colors. Excellent condition. **$600–750**

Basket, Longaberger 1999, Saint Patrick's Day Basket with Lid. Mint condition.   **$42–48**

Bears, Fenton Bear Set. Saint Patrick's Day, Shamrocks. Special order for Collector's Showcase in 2003. Factory decorated. Opal satin glass, and sprayed with a light green paint. Decorated with a bow tie and shamrocks. Both have a four-leaf clover on their backside. Only 100 sets were made. Bottom reads, "Exclusively for Collector's Showcase," signed by the artist. Mint in box condition.   **$80–90**

Cover, Linto, USS *Hatfield*, Saint Patrick's Day, 1941. Cacheted cover cancelled USS *Hatfield*, March 17, 1941. Cover number 74 of 93 on reverse. Excellent condition.   **$10–15**

Doll, 2004 Madame Alexander Saint Patrick's Day Doll. "Step Dancing Sweetheart" with gleaming red hair. Limited to one year of production. Embroidered classic Irish symbols on velveteen dress and cape. Hand-detailed face, open/close green eyes, posable head, arms, and legs. 8" tall. Mint condition.   **$50–60**

Figure, Wade Betty Boop Collection. Saint Patrick's Day Figure commissioned by C & S Collectables and produced by Wade in a limited edition of 750 in 2001. Approximately 7" tall. Good condition.   **$200–225**

Figurine, "I'm Yours." Wee Fores Folk M-806. Limited Edition. 2005 Saint Patrick's Day. Mint condition. **$60–70**

Figurines, Irish Dancing Boy and Girl. Lefton Porcelain. Dressed in Saint Patrick's Day clothing. Lefton tag on bottom. Excellent condition. **$10–15**

Inflatable, Saint Patrick's Day Figure. 6' tall. Excellent condition. **$35–40**

Jersey, Red Sox, 2005. Majestic Red Sox Green Saint Patrick's Day Jersey. Officially Licensed. Size XL. 100% polyester mesh. Very good condition. **$100–110**

Jersey, Saint Louis Cardinals, '04 BERGER. Worn "Saint Patrick's Day" Jersey of #53 Brandon Berger. Green mesh with logo sewn on the front. Made by Majestic, Size 48, tagged in the tail. Very good condition. **$170–190**

Magazine, LIFE Magazine, March 7, 1907. St. Patrick's Day Issue K278. Very good condition. **$20–25**

Pen Blanks, Ancient Irish Bog Oak. Five blanks from wood that has been radiocarbon dated to be 1,532–1,533 years old. Tree grew during Saint Patrick's time in Ireland. Size varies in thickness from ½" to ¾"; all are 5¼" long. Very good condition. **$35–50**

Plate, Belleek, 1985. Saint Patrick's Day plate l, "Slemish Mountain." First of series. Created by artist Fergus Cleary and cast onto Belleek's own Parian China. Sprigs of shamrock frame the scene. Measures approximately 8½" in diameter. Excellent condition. **$40–50**

Postcard, HBG Griggs Saint Patrick's Day. Embossed. Circa early 1900s. Caption reads: "Let Erin Remember The Days Of Old." L. & E. Series 2269. No postmark. Divided back. Very good condition. **$20–25**

Postcard, Saint Patrick's Day Greetings from Waterford. Circa 1910. Unknown publisher. Very good condition. **$15–20**

Postcard, Saint Patrick's Day. Circa 1915. Made by Raphael Tuck & Sons, Saint Patrick's Day Post Cards, Series No. 106. Shows man kissing woman on the cheek. Excellent condition. **$13–15**

Postcards, Sixteen Irish and Saint Patrick's Day. Circa 1910s–1920s. All in good condition. **$20–25 for lot**

Print, "Saint Patrick's Day 1863." By Bradley Schmehl. Hand signed and numbered limited edition print. Civil War Saint Patrick's Day at Camp Falmouth, Virginia, 1863. Image size: 25½" × 17". Print number: 84/850. Excellent condition. **$10–15**

Stein, Hamm's Beer 1974, Saint Patrick's Day. Wording on stein reads "O'Hamm's Salutes the Irish!" Illustrations of the Hamm's Beer Bear, leprechauns, and a variety of partygoers. Glazed porcelain beer stein by Ceramarte of Brazil, numbered 008613. 6" in height. Very good condition. **$10–15**

Sword, Franklin Mint, Saint Patrick's Sword. Comes in display case. Excellent condition. **$400–450**

Toy, Stuffed Animal, Bear. Build a Bear-BABW-Saint Patrick's Day Bear-McBearish. 14" tall. Available 2001 and second in the series. Shamrock patch on its paw. Excellent condition. **$15–20**

T-shirt, Guinness and Harp. Circa 1989 Saint Patrick's Day, Guinness and Harp shirt. Screenstars, XL, 50/50. 27" mid-collar to bottom hem, and 7¼" sleeves. Very good condition. **$15–18**

− 4 −
APRIL

All Fool's Day/April Fool's Day (April 1)

All Fool's Day, or April Fool's Day, resulted from a change in calendar dates. Originally, by the Roman calendar, the end of New Year's Week, which led into the new year was celebrated on April 1, but in 1582, Pope Gregory XIII replaced the original calendar with the Gregorian calendar and declared that January 1 would be the date the new year would begin. People who continued to celebrate the original ending of New Year's Week as April 1 were considered fools. The French had adopted the new calendar right away, so they are largely responsible for pulling pranks on those who had not, calling them "fool's errands." They called April 1 *Poisson d'Avril*, or April Fish. To this day, French schoolchildren tape a picture of a fish on the back of a schoolmate, yell *"Poisson d'Avril!"* and run away.

Great Britain finally caught up with the Gregorian calendar in 1752, and American colonists (still British subjects at that time) began celebrating the New Year on January 1 around the same time. Pranks continued to be played on unsuspecting people on April 1. Traditionally, it's not a good idea to play an April Fool's joke on someone before noon, because that causes the bad luck to be returned to the perpetrator of the trick. It's also said that a man who gets married on April 1 will be ruled by his wife for the life of their marriage.

In England, if you are the recipient of a trick, you are called a "noodle." In Scotland, the holiday, called Gowkie Day (after the gowk, or cuckoo, a traditional symbol of a fool and cuckold) is forty-eight hours long. The first half is called "April Gowk." The second day is called "Taily Day," and all jokes are aimed at the buttocks (the infamous "kick me" signs came from this Scottish celebration).

Collectibles for this holiday include postcards and greeting cards (some with the symbolic fish), games, and puzzles.

PRICE LIST: ALL FOOL'S/APRIL FOOL'S DAY COLLECTIBLES

DVD, Movie "April Fool's Day." Circa 1986. Mint condition. $10–12

Flyer, "April Fool's Dance Concert and Costume Ball" with Sparrow, Santana Bluz, Outcasts. 3/30–31/67, at California Hall, San Francisco. Approximately 8½" × 11". Near mint condition. $50–60

Pin, Disney's Goofy, 2002. From the Disney Store "12 months of Magic" collection. Mint condition. $7–10

Poker Chip, Hard Rock Casino. $5 Poker Chip, limited edition, celebrating April Fool's Day, 2001. Las Vegas, Nevada. Uncirculated, mint condition. $35–45

Postcard, Embossed Fishes and Seahorses. French postcard for April Fool's Day with gold fish and seahorses. Circa 1900–1910s. Standard size. Very good condition. $15–20

Soft Drink Tray, Norman Rockwell. Limited Edition 1976 Norman Rockwell tray entitled "April Fool's Day." Picture on the tray was purposely made with mistakes. It asks on the front "How many errors can you find in this original April Fool cover used on the Saturday Evening Post of April 3, 1948?" Very good condition. $10–15

Passover (15th day of the Hebrew month Nissan)

This Jewish holiday, also called Pesach, lasts for eight days and is celebrated with special foods, songs, and customs. It is the time to commemorate the freedom and exodus of the Israelites who left Egypt during the reign of Ramses II in the thirteenth century B.C.E. . The holiday starts on the fifteenth day of the Hebrew month of Nissan, which is usually sometime in April. The festivities begin at sundown and celebrants begin the holiday with a special meal, called a *seder*, which includes unleavened bread, bitter herbs, and various other symbolic foods. There is a definitive schedule of events for the *seder*, which includes the retelling of the Biblical exodus, with family members each taking turns to tell the tale. Traditionally, even the seating at the table is significant, as well as a ritual hand washing, candle lighting, and wine drinking. During the *seder*, stories are told about the original reason for the celebration, and traditional songs are sung. For the eight days of Passover, no one eats leavened bread or anything that is made with flour or leavening; matzo, an unleavened bread, is eaten.

Items that collectors might choose for their Passover collection would include Passover trays, silver items made especially for the holiday, books, cookbooks, tablecloths, specially marked food tins, *seder* plates, photos, matzo covers, pins, dinner plates, signs, record albums, candy molds, and candle holders.

PRICE LIST: PASSOVER COLLECTIBLES

Art, Handmade Haggadah. Created by Israeli artist C. Dadi. Dadi took two years to make this 72-page book, written on scroll. Many illustrations. Buffalo leather cover. Measures approx. 12" × 14". Excellent condition. $20,000–25,000

Baby Bib. White with blue lettering "Kosher for Passover." Excellent condition.   **$6–8**

Book, Haggadah Passover Seder Service. Copyright 1939 by General Foods, compliments of Maxwell House Coffee. Good condition.   **$9–12**

Cap, Coca-Cola. Marked "Approved for Passover—Rabbi H. Kohn." Fair condition.   **$12–15**

Cookbooks, Passover. Lot of Eleven Jewish/Passover cookbooks. Circa 1977–1997. Good condition.   **$25–35**

Cups, Three. Silver Kiddush/Passover Cups. Continental, Polish, and American. All three are inscribed or have embossed decorations. The largest has a plain background with an inscribed figure (Moses?) holding what appear to be the Commandments. Another of the three is embossed with flowers, and the third has embossed figures on the lower two-thirds of the cup and Hebrew writing around the rim. All three in good condition.   **$600–650**

Matzo Cover. Satin. 16½" × 13¾". Very good condition.   **$7–9**

Nutcracker, Wooden. Miniature. Made for Passover by Polish artist, circa nineteenth century. Body is round barrel. Pressure is created by turning the screw. Very good condition.   **$150–160**

Passover Haggadah. Commentary Halel Nirtza by Rabbi Moshe Ben Amram Grunwald from Chust. Printed in Beregsas (Beregovo) in the Czech Republic in 1922. The only Haggadah that was printed in Beregsas. 128 pages. First edition. Good condition.   **$110–115**

Passover Haggadah. Printed in Egypt with translations in Arabic and Hebrew. Printed Bersano & Elimelech, Egypt. Circa 1800s. Good condition.   **$150–160**

Passover Plate, Brass. Circa 1950. Israel. Embossed flowers along rim. Center has six circular symbols and one larger one. All have Hebrew writing within them. Good condition.   **$475–525**

Plaque, Royal Doulton. Limited edition of 7,500. Marked No. 2493. Depicts a family at the Passover dinner table. Very good condition.   **$75–85**

Plate, Matzo. Spode design in blue and white. Based on Jewish manuscripts of 1880s. Excellent condition.   **$40–45**

Plate, Passover Service. Ridgway 10" dinner service plate in black and white for Passover. Back is marked with manufacturer's mark stating: "Bardiger, London; Tepper, London." Inside circle: Manufactured by Ridgway England, Reg. No. 699855. Excellent condition.   **$130–140**

Plate, Passover. Pewter. Circa seventeenth–eighteenth century. With architectural and foliate engraved decoration, the rim inscribed in Hebrew. Diam: 9" Very good condition.   **$1,300–1,500**

Print, Jewish Passover. Circa 1950. Rich colors. Matting has yellowed some with age. Measures approx. 12½" × 10½". Good condition.   **$15–20**

Earth Day (April 22 or March 21)

There are two conflicting stories about the founder of Earth Day, as well as the date on which it is celebrated, so here are both.

Some sources say that Wisconsin Senator Gaylord Nelson founded Earth Day and made it a part of the holidays celebrated all over the world on March 21, 1970 (later, it was changed to April 22). He had begun thinking about the possibility in 1962, then convinced President John F. Kennedy to support the idea. In 1963 they brought the attention of the American people to the importance of conserving our precious natural resources, but the politicians in charge weren't interested in putting it on their agenda (though American citizens were). In 1995 President Clinton awarded Nelson the Presidential Medal of Freedom on the twenty-fifth anniversary of the first Earth Day holiday.

Other sources say that John McConnell declared the holiday in 1970, stating that March 21 would be Earth Day. He created the holiday because of his interest in "Space exploration and awareness of the March Equinox, nature's primary day of global equilibrium." His declaration was signed by important international persons, such as U.N. Secretary General U Thant, author Margaret Mead, and many others.

Both reports state that the United Nations and countries all over the world celebrate an International Earth Day, whether it's on March 21 or April 22.

The holiday has generated commemorative posters, books, T-shirts, knapsacks, grocery bags, greeting cards, stickers, magnets, cups, and mugs.

PRICE LIST: EARTH DAY COLLECTIBLES

Comic, "Superman for Earth Day." Forty-six-piece Comic Production Art Set. One-shot Superman story, Earth Day. Mint condition. **$500–550**

Grocery Tote, Earth Day. Khaki colored with white logo on front. Mint condition. **$18–20**

Invitation, "Every Day Is Earth Day." Created by Peter Max for opening of major exhibit of his work to benefit the Sierra Club. June 8–July 1, 1990. Hanson Galleries in San Francisco and Carmel, California. Measures 8½" × 11" when open. Near mint condition.
$20–25

Mug, Earth Day Network. White barrel mug imprinted with the logo for 2005. Mint condition. **$6–7**

Pin, Disney. "Jiminy Cricket" Earth Day 2003 Promotional Pin. 2" × 3", with colorful glossy illustration of Jiminy Cricket with colorful background "Environmentality Begins With You—Earth Day 2003." Mint condition. **$2–3**

Poster, Thirtieth Anniversary of Earth Day. Earth Day 2000. Limited edition event poster. 14" × 24". Unframed. Limited edition of 300 prints. Hand signed by Bob Masse and "Earth Day Founder" Denis Hayes. Numbered 235/300. Excellent condition. **$100–125**

Poster, Earth Day Network, 2005. Mint condition. **$9–10**

Poster, Robert Rauschenberg Earth Day Poster. Dated 1990 and signed. 40" × 60". Not mounted or framed. Excellent condition. **$200–225**

Toy, Mouse. Annalee trademarked Earth Day Mouse. Mouse is digging into the ground and sign on his spade reads "Earth Day 1999, Plant a Tree." 7" tall. Mint condition. **$15–20**

T-shirt, Earth Day Network, 2005. Various sizes. Mint condition. **$20–22**

Saint George's Day (April 23)

England celebrates the birthday of its patron saint on April 23. Saint George is one of the most popular of the Christian saints, and best known for his legendary act of slaying a dragon, an event with no historical facts surrounding it.

There is, however, much evidence of his martyrdom at Lydda in Judea (now Lod in present-day Israel) before his death in 307 A.D. George, an officer in the Roman army, reputedly refused to offer sacrifices to the Roman gods, preferring instead to give to the poor and to tell all of his belief in the Christian god. For those beliefs, he was tortured for seven years, then beheaded.

In the fifth century, believers built a monastery in his name in Jerusalem. Several stories exist about whether his remains stayed in Lydda or were moved to Cairo, Egypt.

Though it isn't clear how he became the patron saint of England, it appears that the story of his battle and his life was translated into Anglo-Saxon by Abbot Aelfric in the early 1000s, and a church was dedicated in his name in Donaster in 1061. King Edward III first utilized the battle cry "Saint George for England" in 1348. Ironically, Saint George never set foot in England.

Saint George's emblem (a white background and red cross) became England's flag and part of Britain's flag, the well-known Union Jack. On his holiday, English people wear a red rose in their buttonholes. Although some areas celebrate the holiday with parades or other activities, the celebrations do not echo what other countries do for their own national holidays (for example, July). Instead, it appears that Saint George is the unsung patron saint about whom few schoolchildren know.

One event named after the saint is the Saint George's Cup, a golf tournament. On this day, England's greatest playwright, William Shakespeare, was born; ironically, it was also the day he died, so there are festivals and events to celebrate his birth. There are also parades, concerts, festivals, and the like for Saint George's Day.

Collectibles include jewelry, toys, dinnerware, posters, and flags.

PRICE LIST: SAINT GEORGE'S DAY COLLECTIBLES

Figurine, Saint George and Dragon. Made by Hummel. 6½" × 6" × 3". Weighs 1.5 lbs. Made of porcelain. Hummel/Goebel figurine. Signed "M. I. Hummel" on base. Artist dated on bottom. Excellent condition. **$80–100**

Figurine, Saint George and the Dragon. Made by Royal Doulton Co. 16" × 15¼" × 7¼". Depicts the Christian soldier and martyr, Saint George, on his horse and ready to do battle. Wears armor and carries a sword and shield. Horse is draped with robe with medieval griffins on it. Mark on bottom reads "Saint George, Potted by Doulton & Co. Limited, HN 2067." Excellent condition. **$175–200**

Jewelry, Brooch. Shell cameo. Depicts Saint George slaying the Dragon; mounted in a fine gilt frame. Very finely carved. Dated mid-nineteenth century. Combines the style of the period together with the workmanship of the cameo carvers. Excellent condition. **$355–375**

Jewelry, Ring. 22K Saint George gold coin ring. Circa 1919. Depicts Saint George on a horse with a sword in his hand. Very heavy. Excellent condition. **$675–700**

Lithograph, Print. Signed Salvador Dali lithograph titled "Saint George and the Dragon." Measures 15" × 22½" on 21½" × 30" Arches paper. Signed and numbered in pencil from an edition of 225. Unframed. Excellent condition. **$175–200**

Medal, Russian. Order of Saint George, 3rd class. Given for bravery in the battlefield. Ribbon probably was added later, but genuine medal, with an original suspension ring. Excellent condition. **$1,400–1,500**

Toby Mug, Saint George. Made by Royal Doulton. 7" tall. Pattern D6618, 1967. Four registration marks. Excellent condition. **$250–300**

Easter
The Holiday

The holiest of Christian holidays, Easter is the day when Christians celebrate Christ's resurrection into eternal life, thereby giving all Christians the hope of life after death. Before 325 A.D., the Easter holiday was celebrated on various days of the week, but the Roman Emperor Constantine (288?–337) decreed that Easter would be celebrated on the first Sunday after the full moon following the vernal equinox. Citizens of the era donned new clothes and headgear, then paraded through the streets, relishing the new beginning that the spring season brought to the Earth. This was the beginning of the Easter parade. Constantine was also responsible for declaring the cross to be the symbol of Christianity.

The Venerable Bede (673?–735), a monk who wrote the first history of England, is said to have been the person who defined the word "Easter" as coming from the Scandinavian word *Ostra* and the Teutonic *Ostern* or *Eastre*. The celebration in Anglo-Saxon days was a ribald festival to celebrate the coming of spring. The pagan elements of the holiday come from these two names, which are goddesses connected with fertility or springtime. Festivals were held to honor these fertility goddesses, which is probably why Easter is associated with eggs. Because this holiday usually happens in early spring, it has become the time when people celebrate the birth of all new life. Baby chicks and lambs also are characteristic of the Easter season and represent the rebirth of spring. When Christians introduced their holidays to these early pagan cultures, they tried to blend the old festivals with the new Christian holidays as seamlessly as possible.

Because early Christians were often Jews, some saw this new holiday as an extension of their Passover celebrations. In fact, some Eastern countries still celebrate this holiday as part of Passover. For Christians, Easter comes at the end of Lent, the forty-six-day period that begins on Ash Wednesday (the day after Mardi Gras).

The goddess Eastre, symbolized by a rabbit, was worshipped by the pagans, and it is thought that her animal symbol gave birth to our recognition of the Easter bunny. That tradition was extended to the Christian faith and to modern celebrants of the holiday when Germans brought the symbol to America, and Pennsylvanian Germans introduced it to their new American communities in the early eighteenth century. Children of that era were led to believe that bunnies would hide in the grass and leave bonnets on the doorstep that were filled with colored eggs. Gradually, this tradition led to the one most children believe in today, but the eggs are candies, the grass is cellophane, and the bunnies are chocolate!

The Collectibles

Easter Eggs

The Easter egg tradition has been part of this holiday for thousands of years. The Passover seder uses a hardboiled egg as a symbol of new life, and it's possible that this is where the tradition of the Easter egg begins. However, there are many other stories of how eggs came to symbolize this holiday. Eggs were considered meat in Western civilizations, so eating eggs at the end of Lent was akin to eating meat to celebrate the end of the Lenten season.

Certain cultures that exchange eggs use colors to symbolize the religious importance of the holiday. For example, Greeks exchange red eggs, symbolizing the blood of Christ. Germans and Austrians use green on their eggs and give them on Maundy Thursday (the Thursday before Easter Sunday), while Slavic peoples decorate their eggs in silver and gold. Armenians decorate hollow eggs with pictures of the Virgin Mary, Jesus Christ, and other religious figures and designs.

Slavic countries have a folk tradition of decorating eggs in a batik-like decorating process known as *pisanka* or *pysanki* (which means "to design" or "to write"). This process is accomplished by dipping the egg in beeswax, then in a varying number of dye baths. After each dye is applied, wax is painted over the area, until colors and designs emerge.

The Easter egg tradition extends to a wide range of games, including Easter egg hunts and rolls. Though Easter egg hunts began long ago, with Romans holding races on an oval track and awarding the winners with eggs, the hunts continue today with children excitedly combing through their front lawns or church vestries looking for gaily-colored foil eggs. Rolling an Easter egg down a hill symbolized the stone being rolled away from Christ's tomb. The English became known for taking the symbolic game and transporting it to the world of children. Nowadays, the Easter egg roll is even practiced on the lawn of the White House.

Like other cultures, Russians celebrate Easter by giving eggs—and three kisses—to each other. When Czarina Maria received an egg from her husband in 1884, she loved it so much that the maker, Peter Carl Fabergé, was given the assignment of making one every year for

Easter Carrots. 4.5" Grungy Mini Carrots. *Courtesy of Jamieson Studios.* $2.50 each, or $24 for a dozen.

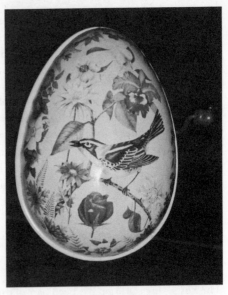

Wind-up Egg Music Box, Mattel. *Courtesy of Holly Knight.* $18–24.

her. Fabergé took egg decorating to new heights by using precious metals, enamels, and jewels. He had inherited his family's jewelry business in 1872, and began managing it while continuing to improve on his talents. Soon he had a staff of jewelry makers and goldsmiths working for him. Fabergé created his designs by imitating historical works he had seen in his travels or at the Hermitage, the state art museum in Saint Petersburg. Sometimes the eggs depicted important events in Russian history, such as coronations and anniversaries. Their designs were always a secret before they were presented. Fifty-six Imperial eggs were presented, but only forty-four of them have been found. However, a dozen more were commissioned by Alexander Ferdinandovich Kelch, a Siberian gold mine owner. After the revolution, the availability of precious jewels and metals decreased, affecting Fabergé's business. But more importantly, the country was in chaos as the Russian Revolution unfolded. In 1917, Fabergé fled Russia, and he died in 1920 in Lausanne, Switzerland. The company was restarted in Paris in 1924, and is still one of the most respected jewelry and fine gift makers in the world. Fabergé created its first new egg in 1991 and presented it to Russian premier Mikhail Gorbachev at the awards ceremony for the Nobel Peace Prize.

Lilies

Another symbol of Easter is the Easter lily. Mentioned often in the Bible, the lily is connected with Jesus's Sermon on the Mount, in which he asked listeners to "consider the lilies of the field." Legend has it that after Christ's death, lilies grew in the Garden of Gethsemane where drops of his sweat had fallen to the earth during his time of great despair.

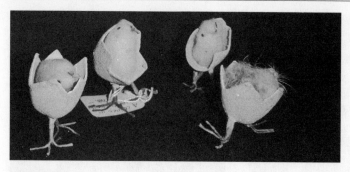

Mica Egg Cups. Circa 1930s. Wire feet, fuzzy chicks.
Courtesy of Holly Knight. $28–35 for all four.

Churches cover their altars with Easter lilies during the season to symbolize the remembrance of the wages Jesus paid for Christians' sins. Lilies often decorate collectible Easter items.

Other less expensive collectibles are also available for those collectors who want to fill their homes with Easter-related items. For instance, spoons in the shape of lilies or crosses were created in the late 1800s, and some dinnerware or fine porcelain firms made pieces for the Easter table.

Candy Containers

In the early 1900s, imports included German cardboard candy containers, made in the shape of Easter rabbits, chicks, and eggs, which were filled with candy and distributed to children as gifts of the season. Some were clothed and had glass eyes. Some were adorned with a removable ribbon around their necks. The papier-mâché versions were made from approximately 1900 to 1940. Most had removable heads. If the figure has a cart or basket, it is more valuable.

During the 1940s and 1950s, Japanese versions of tin candy containers were made, some with movable parts. Most of these are reasonably priced. Often, these figurines were mechanical or wind-ups and were attached to wagons, horses, or cars. Tin egg containers made in the same colorful tradition are also available. Some even have music boxes inside.

Party Decorations

Easter decorations produced for parties or family dinners include rabbit and chick figures, often made of cotton batting and fake fur, as well as cardboard or papier-mâché. During the twentieth century, figures of tin, plastic, molded glass, and porcelain were created. Nut cups, table coverings, baskets, napkins, plates, cups, and centerpieces are all available for the Easter table. Some of the centerpieces are truly works of art, incorporating wire bases, honeycomb eggs, lithographed eggs, bunnies, tulips, and other Easter icons.

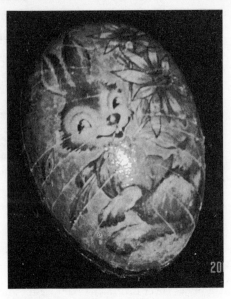

Easter Egg Ornaments. From ¾" to 1¼". Circa 1970s. *Courtesy of Holly Knight.* $3–5 each.

Paper Egg. Approximately 2" long. Circa 1950s. Marked "Western Germany" on inside. *Courtesy of Holly Knight.* $8–10.

Special foods made for these celebrations included foods made in molds, such as cakes, gelatin products, and chocolate. The molds themselves are highly collectible and can range from very small versions to molds that are several feet in height. They are often eggs, bunnies, chicks, and Easter lilies. Both tin and pewter molds were made, some by the same chocolate factories famous for producing candy for Valentine's Day (see chapter 2 for more information about those manufacturers).

Cards

As with other holidays, Easter celebrants exchanged greeting cards or postcards to pass along loving messages. Though most of the greetings are decorated with the icons already mentioned, there are other examples that include figures like the Palmer Cox Brownies, Kewpies, Campbell's Soup Kids, and (in more contemporary times) figures created by designer Mary Engelbreit. The same companies famous for making greeting cards for other holidays also made Easter cards. (Some of those companies are mentioned in the section on Valentine's Day.)

Easter Art and Artwork

More contemporary collectibles also include limited edition plates made by such manufacturers as Avon and Franklin Mint; plastic baskets complete with eggs, bunnies, and chicks; candy boxes; figurines and "villages" for those figures; and stuffed animals. Some of the

Candy Containers. Blue is 6", yellow is 7½", pink is 9". Circa 1940s. *Courtesy of Cocoa Village Antique Mall.* $50–100 each.

Papier-mâché Bunny. Approximately 6" tall. Circa 1950s. *Courtesy of Holly Knight.* $18–22.

Papier-mâché Bunny. Approximately 8" tall. Circa 1940s. *Courtesy of Cocoa Village Antique Mall.* $65–80.

Bunny Chocolate Mold, tin. 7" tall. Circa 1930s. *Courtesy of Cocoa Village Antique Mall.* $65–100.

Bunny Chocolate Molds. From 3" to 11". German, circa 1920s–1940s. *Courtesy of Trout Creek Folk Art, Napa, Calif.* $175–600.

Bunny & Peep Make–Do. Small mohair bunny sits atop a hand dyed wool "make–do" pin cushion. Wool appliqué and featherstitching adorn the ball. Bunny holds a tiny mohair peep. *Baker & Co. Original design.* $245–275.

Carrot Riding Rabbit. 6" tall. Papier-mâché. 2004. *Original folk art by Trout Creek Folk Art, Napa, Calif.* $85–115.

most interesting Easter artwork and collectibles are being made by today's folk artists and ornament manufacturers, including Ginny Betourne/Trout Creek Folk Art, Lori Ann Baker–Corelis/Baker & Company Designs, Christopher Radko, Bethany Lowe Designs, and Jamieson Studios. These artists have kindly given permission for their work to be included in this book on holiday collectibles. There is more information, and examples of their art, throughout the book, particularly in the Halloween and Christmas sections.

Ginny Betourne/Trout Creek Folk Art creates sculpted and painted vegetable figures that she calls "all things absurd and sometimes wicked." She sells her figures on her web site *www.troutcreekfolkart.com*, as well as at various shows throughout the West. All of her artwork is one of a kind and valued highly by holiday collectors.

Lori Ann Baker–Corelis/Baker & Company Designs makes teddy bears and rabbits, dressing them in designs inspired by vintage toys, and has been doing so since 1989. She considers fabric her medium and learned her sculptural skills at Kenyon College. Her animals are crafted from the finest German and English mohair, the eyes are made of hand-blown glass or vintage buttons, and she uses 100-percent wool for paw pads. As she states on her web site *www.bakercompanydesigns.com*, some of her creations "are dressed in fine wool flannels, antique fabrics or wool vests . . . accessorized with antique bits of trim, buttons, holiday decorations or small toys. . . . Many characters are open editions or limited production, and others may be one of a kinds."

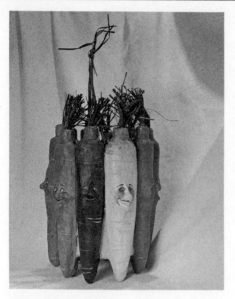

Carrot Bucket. Papier-mâché. 11" tall. 2005. *Original folk art by Trout Creek Folk Art, Napa, Calif.* $145–175.

Rabbit with Terrified Carrots. Papier-mâché. 11" tall. 2003. *Original folk art by Trout Creek Folk Art, Napa, Calif.* $115–130.

In 1986 glass artist Christopher Radko produced sixty-five European glass mouth-blown Christmas ornaments. Since that time, he has created over ten thousand designs for Christmas and other occasions (see the Christmas section for more information). The Radko company employs European glassblowers to produce the ornaments, and each one takes seven days to create. His ornaments are available on his web site, *www.christopherradko.com*, as well as through licensed retailers.

Bethany Lowe Designs began in 1985 with original vintage folk art and holiday designs. She went international in 1997 when she decided to travel abroad to see whether she could reproduce her designs while maintaining quality, and she has succeeded in combining original design and affordability. Materials used in Bethany Lowe Designs include papier-mâché, paper pulp, resin, tin, hand-dyed and appliquéd wool, cotton batting, mercury glass, pottery, wood, and vintage reproduction papers. In 2004 the White House commissioned some of her designs. Bethany Lowe's work is available through her web site, *www.bethanylowe.com*, as well as through licensed retailers.

John W. Jamieson (Jamieson Studios) creates affordable holiday reproductions and uses original molds from the 1930s and 1940s to create papier-mâché and molded paper pulp decorative holiday items. Jamieson Studios produces items for all of the major holidays and has been featured in national magazines, on television shows, and in museum shops. Jamieson sells his items on his web site, *www.jamiesonstudios.com*, as well as through licensed retailers.

Mr. Pinks. 17" mohair bunny wearing a wool felt coat and vest. Collar is made from part of a vintage coat. *Courtesy of Baker & Co. Designs.* $395–425.

Ballerina Bunny and Easter Clown Bunny. 16" × 11" and 19" × 11". 2005. Paper pulp heads and felt wired bodies. *Courtesy of Bethany Lowe Designs, Inc.* $52.95–60.

PRICE LIST: EASTER COLLECTIBLES

Accordion Basket, Cardboard. Easter bunny and eggs. Circa 1940s. Approximately 8" tall. Good condition. $12–15

Basket, Filled with Plush Easter Bunnies, Cotton Chicks, and Eggs. Bunnies and chicks, circa 1920s. Very good condition. $175–225

Box, Oval, Keepsake. An Easter egg that is trimmed in lavender and painted in spring colors. Little bunnies and chicks dancing around the edges. Glazed coating. 4½" × 4" × 3¾" tall. Mint condition. $9–11

Bunnies, Papier-mâché, Two. Pair are approximately 4½" tall. Circa 1940s. One has green highlights and the other has yellow. Very good condition. $20–30

Bunny Candle, Wax. Made by Gurley. Approximately 3" tall. Circa 1950s. Very good condition. $15–20

Bunny Pull Toy, Wooden. Painted in pink, yellow, and purple. Circa 1950s. Very good condition. $45–65

Bunny, Chalkware. White with carrot in hands. Handpainted face. Approximately 6" tall. Circa 1940s. Very good condition. $12–20

Bunny, Chocolate Mold, Tin. Seated bunny. 7" tall. Circa 1930s. Excellent condition. $65–100

Candy Containers, chenille. 9" tall. Made from vintage molds. *Courtesy of Jamieson Studios.* $59.95/set.

Candy Containers, chalkware. Reproduced from vintage originals. *Courtesy of Jamieson Studios.* $38–42.

Candy Containers. 6" high. *Courtesy of Jamieson Studios.* $18–20.

Basket. Filled with plush Easter bunnies, cotton chicks, and eggs. Bunnies and chicks circa 1920s. *Courtesy of Cocoa Village Antique Mall.* $175–225.

Bunny, Papier-mâché. Easter bunny has basket on back with two small chalkware bunnies in tow. Approximately 6" tall. Circa 1940s. Very good condition. **$40–80**

Bunny, Papier-mâché. Pink and white. Approximately 6" tall. Circa 1950s. Very good condition. **$18–22**

Bunny, Papier-mâché. Seated bunny has glass eyes. Approximately 8" tall. Yellow ribbon around neck. Circa 1940s. Excellent condition. **$65–80**

Bunny, Papier-mâché. Seated bunny with painted eyes. Approximately 4½" tall. Yellow accents. Circa 1940s. Very good condition. **$35–55**

Candy Container, Bunny with Baskets on Back. Highlighted with yellow, pink, and blue. Circa 1940s. (Blue is most valuable). Blue: 6". Yellow: 7½". Pink: 9". Excellent condition. **$50–100 each**

Candy Container, Bunny with Cart Filled with Eggs, Pressed Cardboard. Circa 1940s. Approximately 8" × 6½". Excellent condition. **$45–55**.

Candy Container, Chick. Spring-neck chick candy container. 6½" tall. Reproduced from Vintage Originals. Courtesy of Jamieson Studios. New. Mint condition. **$23–25**.

Candy Container, Rabbit. Papier-mâché German candy container. Rabbit with glass eyes dressed in cloth clothes with a basket on his back. 7½" tall. Jointed arms and legs. Excellent condition. **$450–550**.

Candy Container, Rabbit. Spring-eared rabbit container. 7½" high × 4½" long. Reproduced from Vintage Originals. Courtesy of Jamieson Studios. New. Mint condition. **$25–30**.

Candy Container, Standing Rabbit. Rabbit stands on four wooden legs, his body is papier-mâché and his eyes are glass. Head is removable for candy. Approximately 7½" long and stands about 7¾" tall. Very good condition. **$200–225**.

Candy Containers and Ornaments, Birds. Set of six (each item). Candy containers are 3½" long (heads are removable). Reproduced from Vintage Originals. Mint condition. **$30–35**.

Candy Containers, Set of Six Bird Candy Containers. 3.5" long (head is removable). Reproduced from Vintage Originals. Mint condition. **$30–35**.

Candy Containers, Chenille Rabbit. Two containers. 9" high. Reproduced from Vintage Originals. Courtesy of Jamieson Studios. Mint condition. **$60–70/set**.

Candy Containers, Rabbits. Three chalkware rabbits. Parents 7" high; children 4¼" high. Reproduced from Vintage Originals. Courtesy of Jamieson Studios. Mint condition. **$38–45**.

Candy Dish, Easter Treats. By Christopher Radko. Depicts two Easter bunnies holding a basket on their backs. Pastel colors. 5¼" × 3¼". Mint condition. **$30–40**.

Card, Accordion Easter Basket with Male and Female Bunny and Flowers. 9" × 7½". One bunny is missing an ear. Circa 1920s. Marked "Made in USA/Beistle Co." Fair condition. **$25–30**.

Chicken, Chalkware. Approximately 4" tall. Circa 1930s. Excellent condition. **$30–40**.

Chicken, Plaster-type Material, Metal Feet (?). Approximately 3½" tall. Marked "Japan." Circa 1930s. Very good condition. **$25–35**.

Chicks (Five), Chenille. Some are yellow and some are pink. Flowers on their heads. Approximately 1" to 3" tall. Circa 1940s. Very good condition. **$12–18 each**.

Chicks in Basket, Cotton. Two in colorful small Easter basket. Marked made in Japan. Circa 1940s. Very good condition. **$40–50/set**.

Chicks in Basket, Cotton. 3" tall. Made in Japan. Very good condition. **$30–40**.

Chicks on a Swing. Three chicks, cotton, on wood and wire swing, with silk bow. Circa 1920s. Very good condition. **$65–80**.

Chicks with Parasols and Hats, Plush with Feathers. Approximately 4" tall. Circa 1940s. Very good condition. **$50–60/pair**.

Card, Accordion Easter Basket. 9" × 7½". Circa 1920s. *Courtesy of Cocoa Village Antique Mall.* $25–30.

Chicks on a Swing. Chicks are cotton, swing is wood and wire, bow is silk. Circa 1920s. *Courtesy of Cocoa Village Antique Mall.* $65–80.

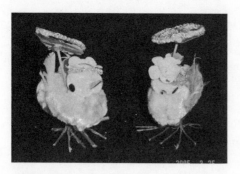

Chicks with Parasols and Hats. Approximately 4" tall. Plush with feathers. Circa 1940s. *Courtesy of Cocoa Village Antique Mall.* $50–60/pair.

Ducks. Pipecleaners and chenille. Occupied Japan, circa 1950s. *Courtesy of Cocoa Village Antique Mall.* $15–20.

Cutout Easter Bunnies, Paper. Made in Germany. Lithographed bunnies, originally in one long strip. Approximately 4" tall. Circa 1900s. Very good condition. **$10–15**

Cutout Easter Bunnies, Paper. Made in Germany. Marked "PZB." Gentlemen bunnies in their "Easter finest" are chromolithographed in bright colors and stand approximately 7" tall. A strip of three from an originally longer piece. Very good condition. **$12–16**

Ducks (Three) with Hats. Pipecleaners and chenille. Occupied Japan. Circa 1950s. Very good condition. **$15–20 each**

Easter Basket with Chicks. Approximately 4" tall. Marked on bottom of basket "Made in Occupied Japan." Very good condition. **$45–55**

Easter Box, Wood. Circular box with removable top depicts Easter bunnies dancing in a circle. Two other tops (no bottoms). All made in Italy or Germany. Circa 1940s. Good condition. **$25–35 for group**

Easter Bunny, Porcelain. Reclining bunny in pink with handpainted decorative accents. Approximately 3" long. Circa 1970s. Very good condition.   **$10–15**

Easter Egg, Metal. Decorated with chick and spring flowers. Marked "Swiss made." Circa 1970s. Good condition.   **$6–8**

Easter Grass. Green, lavender, yellow, pink, and light blue. Courtesy of Jamieson Studios. New. Mint condition.   **$2–3 per bag**

Egg Cups, Mica. Four chicks in mica egg cups. Wire feet, fuzzy chicks. Circa 1930s. Good condition.   **$28–35 for all four**

Egg, Chocolate Mold, Tin. Circa 1930s. Approximately 6" tall. Very good condition.
$45–65

Egg, Paper. Bunny in garden with colored eggs. Approximately 2" long. Marked "Western Germany" on inside. Circa 1950s. Very good condition.   **$8–10**

Egg, Paper. Chicks in a garden, sitting on large colored eggs. Approximately 2" long. Marked "Western Germany" on inside. Circa 1950s. Very good condition.   **$8–10**

Egg, Paper. Duck in rain gear with duckling on back. Approximately 5" long. Marked "Made in Western Germany" on inside. Dated on outside rim 1984. Very good condition.
$10–15

Egg, Paper. Gold decorated with bunnies, ducks, little girls, eggs, and houses. Approximately 4" long. Marked "Made in Western Germany" on inside of egg. Circa 1950s. Very good condition.   **$10–15**

Egg, Paper. Large egg with cartoon-like duck family at a picnic on outside. Approximately 12" long. Circa 1970s. Very good condition.   **$25–35**

Fabergé Egg. 14½" emerald cut crystal Fabergé egg. 19" diameter. Clear crystal stem and base. Base has "Fabergé" engraved on top ledge; bottom has a starburst design. Lid is removable with a 4½" opening. Total weight is 6 lb. 4.2 oz. Excellent to mint condition.
$200–225

Figure, Ballerina Bunny and Easter Clown Bunny. Ballerina: dressed in pink tutu and has pink ruffled collar. She holds string of pastel colored ornaments. 16" × 11". Paper pulp head; felt wired body. © Bethany Lowe. Introduced in 2005. Mint condition.   **$44.95–50**

Figure, Chalkware, Vaillancourt Folk Art. Fantasy cabin with Easter Bunny reaching for door handle. Vaillancourt Folk Art studio in Sutton, Mass., makes chalkware figures using old chocolate molds. Piece is hand-painted, numbered, and dated 1992. 6" tall. Excellent condition.   **$225–250**

Figure, Easter Clown. Bunny dressed in green and pink clown costume and holding an egg basket. 19" × 11". Paper pulp head and felt wired body. © Bethany Lowe. Introduced 2005. Mint condition.   **$52.95–60**

Folk Art, Angry Chick. Chalkware and papier-mâché figure. Circa 2001. 3" tall. Original folk art by Trout Creek Folk Art, Napa, Calif. New. Mint condition.   **$45–65**

Angry Chick. Chalkware and papier-mâché. 3" tall. 2001. *Original folk art by Trout Creek Folk Art, Napa, Calif.* $45–65.

Bunnykins. 8½" tall. Papier-mâché. ©*Lori C. Mitchell 2005.* $245–275.

Folk Art, Bunnykins. 8½" tall. Papier-mâché. ©Lori C. Mitchell, 2005. Mint condition.
$245–275

Folk Art, Candy Container, Peek-a-boo Bunny. 9¾" tall. Papier-mâché. ©Lori C. Mitchell, 2005. Mint condition.
$375–400

Folk Art, Carrot Bucket. Ten cooperative carrots form a carrot bucket. Papier-mâché. 11" tall. Original folk art by Trout Creek Folk Art, Napa, Calif., 2005. New. Mint condition.
$145–175

Folk Art, Carrot Riding Rabbit. Papier-mâché. 6" tall. Original folk art by Trout Creek Folk Art, Napa, Calif., 2004. New. Mint condition.
$85–115

Folk Art, Flopsy. 7½" tall. Papier-mâché. ©Lori C. Mitchell, 2005. Mint condition.
$230–250

Folk Art, Goblin Enjoying Ice Cream. Papier-mâché and wire. 6" tall. Original folk art by Trout Creek Folk Art, Napa, Calif., 2005. New. Mint condition.
$145–200

Folk Art, Rabbit with Terrified Carrots. Papier-mâché figure. 11" tall. Original folk art by Trout Creek Folk Art, Napa, Calif., 2003. New. Mint condition.
$115–130

Folk Art, Turnip Bucket. Papier-mâché. 5" tall. Original folk art by Trout Creek Folk Art, Napa, Calif., 2004. New. Mint condition.
$55–75

Folk Art, Uncle Bigelow. 7½" tall. Papier-mâché. ©Lori C. Mitchell, 2003. Mint condition.
$225–250

Peek–a–boo Bunny. 9¾" tall. Papier-mâché. ©*Lori C. Mitchell* 2005. $375–400.

Flopsy Bunny. 7½" tall. Papier-mâché. ©*Lori C. Mitchell* 2005. $230–250.

Lithograph, Bunnies. Six bunnies and Mama. Signed by Louise Benoort. Circa 1960s. Approximately 16" × 10". Unframed. Excellent condition.   **$55–75**

Molds, Chocolate, Bunnies. Assorted bunny molds, ranging from 3" to 11". German. Circa 1920s–1940s. Very good condition.   **$175–600**

Ornament, Bunny Bonnet Gem. Made by Christopher Radko. 2½" tall. Bunny's face wearing ornately decorated top hat. Contemporary. Excellent condition.   **$33–40**

Ornament, Carrot Coaster. Made by Christopher Radko. 5" long. Bunny driving a red drag-style coaster (styled like carrot). Contemporary. Excellent condition.   **$38–48**

Ornament, Cock a Doodle Cottontail. Made by Christopher Radko. 4½" tall. Colorful ornament of finely dressed rabbit riding a rooster. Contemporary. Excellent condition.   **$40–50**

Ornament, Golden Fluff. Made by Christopher Radko. Tiny chick holding pastel-colored Easter egg. 4" tall. Contemporary. Excellent condition.   **$36–40**

Ornaments, Easter Eggs. All decorated differently. Sizes range from ¾" to 1¼". Circa 1970s. Excellent condition.   **$3–5 each**

Ornaments, Egg-like Ornaments Decorated with Flowers. Made by Christopher Radko. 4½" long. Each is decorated in pastel colors. Excellent condition.   **$36–40**

Avon Plate, "Springtime Stroll." 4¾" diameter. 1991. *Photo Courtesy of Nancy's Collectibles.* $15–20.

Avon Plate, "Colorful Moments." 5" diameter. 1992. Porcelain trimmed in 22k gold. $15–20.

Plate, All Dressed Up, Avon. Family of bunnies getting dressed in their Easter finery. Trimmed in gold. The mark reads "All Dressed Up, 1994 Easter Plate, Porcelain Trimmed 22k gold, Avon Collectibles." 5" in diameter. Excellent condition. **$15–20**

Plate, Avon, 1991. "Springtime Stroll." Depicts bunny family strolling for Easter. 4¾" plate. Great condition. **$15–20**

Plate, Easter Bouquet, Avon. Pictures two bunnies in a field of various flowers and butterflies, gathering a bouquet of flowers. Trimmed in gold; 5" diameter. The plate is marked "Easter Bouquet, 1996 Easter Plate, from an original painting by the noted American artist Ann Wilson, Porcelain trimmed in 22k gold, Avon Collectibles, 1996." Mint in box condition. **$15–20**

Plate, Easter Parade, Avon. Girl bunny carrying a potted tulip, a boy bunny carrying a basket of eggs, and a squirrel carrying a tulip. A duck wearing a top hat and carrying a cane leads the parade. Trimmed in gold. The mark reads "Easter Parade, 1993 Easter Plate, Porcelain trimmed in 22k gold, Avon 1993." Excellent condition. **$15–20**

Plate, My Easter Bonnet, Avon. Bunny peeking out from under a large decorated Easter bonnet. Trimmed in gold, 5" diameter. The mark is "My Easter Bonnet, 1995 Easter Plate, Porcelain trimmed in 22k gold, Avon Collectibles, 1995." Mint in box condition. **$15–20**

Postcard, A Happy Easter to You. Circa 1910. Very good condition. **$10–18**

Postcard, Easter Greetings. Chicks in egg baskets. Circa 1910. Very good condition. **$10–15**

Postcard, Easter Greetings. Postmarked 1917. Very good condition. **$10–18**

Postcard, Easter Joys. Bunny and artistic rabbit. Embossed. Postmarked 1910. Very good condition. **$15–20**

Postcard, Happy Easter Morning. Marked 1912 (postmark). Very good condition. **$10–18**

Pull Toy, Chick. Tin with wood wheels. 4" × 3½". Circa 1920s. Good condition. **$15–20**

Postcard, Easter Joys. Postmarked 1910. *Courtesy of Cocoa Village Antique Mall.* $15–20.

Postcard, Easter Greetings. Circa 1910. *Courtesy of Cocoa Village Antique Mall.* $10–15.

Rabbit with Cart, Tin. 9" × 2¼". Reproduced from Vintage Originals. Courtesy of Jamieson Studios. New. Mint condition. **$25–30**

Rabbit, Candy Container. Paperboard. Brown or Gray. 6½" × 5½". Reproduced from Vintage Originals. Courtesy of Jamieson Studios. New. Mint condition. **$20–24**

Rabbit, Composition. Paper pulp composition rabbit with back basket. Blue or Pink. 11". Reproduced from Vintage Originals. Courtesy of Jamieson Studios. New. Mint condition. **$33–35 each**

Rabbit, Lop-eared. Yellow or lavender. 6". Reproduced from Vintage Originals. Courtesy of Jamieson Studios. New. Mint condition. **$18–20**

Roosters (Two). Chenille and pipecleaners. Occupied Japan. Circa 1950s. Excellent condition. **$15–18 each**

Roosters. Pipecleaners and chenille. Made in Japan. One has carrot; two have tennis rackets. Circa 1940s. Very good condition. **$15–18 each**

Stuffed Animal, Rabbit, Pickford Bears, Ltd. "Flora" is dressed in a dress with white and yellow gingham background with orange carrots. In the pocket is a stuffed carrot. She has a straw hat with a silver button. 11" tall (to top of ears). The tag reads "Pickford Bears Ltd., 'Flora,' Hare of Serenity, The Brass Button Collectables." Excellent condition. **$12–15**

Tin, England. Group of bunnies on cover. Oval shaped. Circa 1930s. 5¾" × 2½" tall. Near mint condition. **$15–20**

Chick Pull Toy. 4" × 3½". Tin with wood wheels. Circa 1920s. *Courtesy of Cocoa Village Antique Mall.* $15–20.

Rabbit with Cart. 9" × 2¼". Tin, reproduced from vintage originals. *Courtesy of Jamieson Studios.*

Candy Container Rabbit. 6½" × 5½". Paperboard, reproduced from vintage originals. *Courtesy of Jamieson Studios.* $20–24.

Composition Rabbits. 11" tall. Paper pulp. *Courtesy of Jamieson Studios.* $33–35.

Chenille and Pipecleaner Roosters. Occupied Japan. Circa 1950s. *Courtesy of Cocoa Village Antique Mall.* $15–18.

Toy, Bunny Driving Car. Car is made of loofah; bunny made of felt and wood with cloth clothes. Egg in back of car made of pressed cardboard and marked "Germany" with scenes of bunnies and trains. Car and bunny unmarked, but thought to be German. Circa 1910. Car: 8" × 3½" × 3". Bunny is 5½" tall, missing one ear. Good condition. **$950–1100**

Toy, Celluloid Easter Chick in Boat. Measures 4" long. Very colorful and marked "USA" with a "V" and "C" and "O" on side canoe. Probably made by Viscoloid. Circa 1920s. Very good condition. **$160–190**

Toy, Mechanical Bunny. Dressed in sailor's outfit made of felt with silver rivet buttons and white braid trim. Carries original basket on back. Red and white stripes inside floppy ears, glass eyes, metal legs and feet, composition hands. Mohair covering, original painted features. When wound, will move back and forth in walking motion. Circa 1920s. Very good condition. **$225–275**

Toy, Metal Easter Bunny Truck. 11½" two-piece pull toy. Signed "A Walt Reach Toy by Courtland." Metal sides show scene with Easter eggs, chicks, and bunnies. Circa 1950s. Excellent condition. **$225–250**

Toy, Stuffed Bunny. "Blue Boy." 17" beige free-standing bunny with lop ears. Wears a coat and vest of wool felt. Collar is cut from a vintage one and he carries wool carrots. Original folk art creation by Baker & Co. Designs Ltd. New. Mint condition. **$395–425**

Toy, Stuffed Bunny. "Bess." Beige mohair 17" free-standing bunny. She wears a straw hat adorned with vintage ribbons. She carries a basket with her pink mohair bird friend. Original folk art creation by Baker & Co. Designs Ltd. New. Mint condition. **$365–400**

Toy, Stuffed Bunny. "Bunny & Peep Make-Do." Small beige mohair bunny sits atop a hand dyed wool "make-do" pincushion. Wool appliqué and feather stitching adorn the ball. Bunny holds a tiny mohair peep. Original folk art creation by Baker & Co. Designs Ltd. New. Mint condition. **$245–290**

Toy, Stuffed Bunny. "Bunny Make-Do in Pink." Small beige mohair bunny atop a hand dyed wool "make-do" pincushion. Feather stitching and beading adorn the ball. Bunny holds a wool flower. Original folk art creation by Baker & Co. Designs Ltd. New. Mint condition. **$245–290**

Toy, Stuffed Bunny. "Bunny on a Tuffet." 10" beige mohair bunny sitting atop a hand dyed wool tuffet pincushion. Feather stitching and beading decorate the tuffet and she holds a wool strawberry. Original folk art creation by Baker & Co. Designs Ltd. New. Mint condition. **$265–300**

Toy, Stuffed Bunny. "Mr. Pinks 1." 17" mohair free-standing bunny wearing a wool felt coat and vest with tiny buttons all round. Collar is made from part of a vintage one. Carries a watch. Original folk art creation by Baker & Co. Designs Ltd. New. Mint condition. **$395–425**

Toy, Stuffed Bunny. "Spot." 15" beige mohair bunny with big feet. Spots are hand appliquéd. He carries wool carrots. Original folk art creation by Baker & Co. Designs Ltd. New. Mint condition. **$275–325**

Bess. 17" tall. Mohair, stuffed, wearing a straw hat adorned with vintage ribbons. *Original folk art creation by Baker & Co. Designs Ltd.* $365–400.

Bunny & Peep Make–Do. Small beige mohair bunny sits atop a hand dyed wool "make–do" pincushion. Wool appliqué and featherstitching adorn the ball. Bunny holds a tiny mohair peep. *Original folk art creation by Baker & Co. Designs Ltd.* $245–290.

Bunny on a Tuffet. 10" tall. Beige mohair bunny sits atop a hand dyed wool tuffet pincushion. Feather stitching and beading decorate the tuffet. Bunny holds a wool strawberry. *Original folk art creation by Baker & Co. Designs Ltd.* $265–300.

Toy, Stuffed Mouse. "Berry Mousekin." 10" beige mohair mouse, wool felt ears and tail. He has vintage ribbons and a wool strawberry. Original folk art creation by Baker & Co. Designs Ltd. New. Mint condition. **$180–210**

Wind-up Egg Music Box. Marked "Mattel, Inc., Los Angeles, Calif. Stock #513. Music arranged by Ted Duncan. Décor by Louis Song. Copyright by Mattel Inc., 1954. Pat. Nos. 2,630,655 2,504,666. Pat. in Canada 1953." Very good condition. **$18–24**

Arbor Day (Last Friday in April)

Arbor Day began in 1872 in Nebraska with Julius Sterling Morton's idea that both Nebraska's landscape and economy would improve if the vast plains were planted with trees. He began the work by planting trees on his own property, and encouraging others to do the same. The idea worked. By the following year, over a million trees had been planted. Nebraska made April 22 (Morton's birthday) a state holiday the year after that, and other states followed suit. In 1970 President Nixon declared the day a national holiday, and since that time, some countries around the world have made it an international holiday. Currently, all U.S. states have declared different times to celebrate the holiday, but the majority celebrate on the last Friday in April. At that time, homeowners are encouraged to plant a tree or to take care of the ones they currently own. Each state has also taken special responsibility for the tree designated as their state tree.

The National Arbor Day Foundation encourages people to celebrate the holiday by taking care of trees, having parades, getting people together for celebrations, or by starting a seedling in a cup. They also give each new member of the foundation ten seedling trees to plant, so Morton's heritage will continue.

Collectors will discover that the day's celebrations produce more than trees: items like posters, greeting cards, coffee and coffee cups, and gift packages are available for collection.

PRICE LIST: ARBOR DAY COLLECTIBLES

Art, Woodcut Block, Limited Edition. Titled "Twas Arbor Day in Potters Field." 1926 linocut by John Held, Jr. 10" × 17", plus margins. Impression from second printing, done in 1964 by Mrs. John Held, Jr. Limited edition of 100; numbered 20/100; signed and dated in pencil by Mrs. Held. Excellent condition. **$110–130**

Photograph, Arbor Day Rhode Island, 1908. Very large scale reproduction of an original panoramic photograph of Arbor Day Festival in Providence, Rhode Island taken in 1908. 52½" × 9", printed on very heavyweight satin paper. Excellent condition. **$30–35**

Postcard, Sixtieth Anniversary, Founding of Arbor Day. One hundredth anniversary of the birth of J. Sterling Morton. Posted on April 22, 1932, Nebraska. Excellent condition.
$12–15

Poster, Movie. Titled "Little Rascals Arbor Day." Re-release 1953. Fully restored with linen backing. 27" × 41". Excellent condition. **$70–75**

Stamp, First Day Cover. 1932 717-3 two cent Arbor Day FDC, 1st Douglas Stamp Company Cachet. Excellent condition. **$15–18**

Stamps, First Day Covers. Republic of China, Taiwan, Arbor Day Scott 2400-03, full sheet of twenty-five blocks, mint never hinged, issue of March 12, 1984, folded once, couple of minor wrinkles on two corners of the sheet, not affecting the stamps. Very good condition. **$18–20**

Confederate Memorial Day (April 26)

This holiday, instituted as a loosely celebrated honoring of dead Civil War soldiers in 1866, became more organized with formal programs to honor soldiers who had fought in that war. In 1868 the holiday was adopted officially. Although states throughout the South celebrate the holiday on different dates, I have included it in April because the 26th is the earliest date that celebrations take place. By 1916, Florida, Georgia, Alabama, and Mississippi had designated that day to be their Confederate Memorial Day, while North and South Carolina chose to celebrate on May 10, Virginia on May 30, and Kentucky, Louisiana, and Tennessee on June 3.

Most services to honor the fallen soldiers were begun by women's organizations, such as the Daughters of the Confederacy, and those women usually had family members who had been victims of that war. Mrs. Charles J. Williams, the wife of Major C.J. Williams, is credited with beginning Confederate Memorial Day when she started leaving flowers on soldiers' graves after her own husband's death. She actively pursued various newspapers, politicians, and associations, begging them to support her idea for the holiday, until her wish was granted in 1868. At first, simple floral arrangements representative of the South (like magnolia blossoms) were laid on soldiers' graves, but later, speeches, prayers, and sermons were arranged, and some states held reenactments of Civil War battles.

The holiday is not as well known or attended as the national Memorial Day, but in those states where the women's organizations are strong and the history of those battles respected, ceremonies are still held and states still maintain the right to close their offices.

Items to collect from this holiday include medals, pins, postcards, greeting cards, mugs, and flags. Collectors who look for items associated with this holiday might also search for "Civil War collectibles" or "Confederate collectibles," since some of the items might not be listed as Confederate Memorial Day collectibles.

PRICE LIST: CONFEDERATE MEMORIAL DAY COLLECTIBLES

Mug, Confederate Memorial Day Mug. Ceramic, with handle; features three different Confederate flags on the front. Mint condition. **$7–8**

Postcard, Four American and Confederate Flags. Poem over the image of the flags. Colorful lithograph. Standard postcard size (3½" × 5½"). Circa 1900-1910s. Publisher: Raphael Tuck & Sons. Excellent condition. **$30–35**

Postcard, Confederate General Joseph E. Johnston Memorial Day. Image of the general with confederate flag below his bust. Colorful lithograph. Standard postcard size. Circa 1900–1910s. Publisher: Raphael Tuck & Sons. Excellent condition.   **$35–40**

Postcard, Confederate Memorial Day Veterans' Medal. Depicts the medal below the flag. Colorful lithograph. Standard postcard size. Circa 1900–1910s. Excellent condition. **$75–80**

Postcard, Confederate/GAR Memorial Day. Images of Generals Grant and Lee and both flags. Colorful lithograph. Standard postcard size. Circa 1900–1910s. Excellent condition.
$35–40

– 5 –
MAY

May Day (May 1)

Like many modern holidays, May Day has a pagan tradition. In Britain, the Druids considered May Day their second most important holiday. It was originally the festival of Beltane, which was the last of the spring festivals, the "Return of the Sun." The Druids thought Beltane/May Day was the date that divided their year in half. Their custom was to light a new fire at that time. The holiday was also very important to the Romans, who celebrated with a five-day festival called the Floralia, in honor of Flora, the goddess of flowers. When the Romans settled Britain, they brought their traditions and customs with them, and when marrying into the tribes already settled there, the people blended the holidays of Floralia and Beltane. The result? May Day.

During the Middle Ages, every village had a maypole, a tall pole erected in the center of the area and decorated with greenery to celebrate the occasion. Some time later, the poles were permanent, but religious groups objected to the poles since they were associated with the old Druid holidays. In the 1600s, when the Puritans came into power, such celebrations were curtailed. Since Puritans were the first settlers in the Colonies, they did not bring the celebration with them. It was not until other groups began traveling to the New World that some introduced the once-popular celebration to Americans.

However, school children might be introduced to the holiday as part of the historical English tradition. They celebrate May Day by dancing and singing around a maypole festooned with colorful streamers or ribbons. Celebrants move back and forth around the pole with the streamers, and tradition states that you choose a May queen and hang May baskets on neighborhood doorknobs.

Collectors can find greeting cards, postcards, stamps, and other ephemeral collectibles for this holiday, as well as baskets and maypole-type items, such as the ribbons and flowers used to decorate the pole. Surprisingly enough, quite a few May Day collectibles are politically-oriented, since demonstrations by communist, anarchist, and socialist groups have also been held on this date.

PRICE LIST: MAY DAY COLLECTIBLES

Baskets, Longaberger May Day Collection. Five baskets: 1994, Lilac; 1995, Tulip; 1996, Sweet Pea; 1999, Petunia; 1999, Daisy. All baskets are combinations. Excellent condition.
$275–325

Book, *May Day with the Muses.* Written by Robert Bloomfield, published in 1822. Marbled cover with leather spine. Several black and white illustrations. Good condition.   **$20–25**

Crewel Kit, May Day Bouquet. Embroidery crewel kit designed by artist Michael A. Leclair. Screened on 100% linen fabric, presorted wool crewel yarn, cotton floss, metallic thread, needles, and instructions. Finished size: 18" × 14". Mint condition.   **$30–32**

Magazine cover, May 1, 1915, *Saturday Evening Post.* Cover depicts young girl dancing with flowers on May Day. Illustrated by Sarah S. Stilwell Weber. Artist initials in print, bottom right of image. Good condition.   **$20–25**

Pot Lid, May Day Dancers at the Swan Inn. Depicts the inn with a group of people standing outside watching some men doing a jig. Metal. Good condition.   **$100–125**

Print, May Day. Original Le Blond print, number 85, May Day. Scene of military gentleman dancing to a drum outside the Swan public house. Signed "Le Blond" London and "Elliot" of Boston. Circa 1885. Very good condition.   **$125–150**

Whirligig, May Day. Circa 1950s. *Erzgebirge Windmill from East Germany.* 8" tall. Children dance around the maypole decorated with pastel multicolored flowers. When candles are lit, the windmill starts to spin from the heat and children turn. Very good condition.
$60–70

Cinco de Mayo (May 5)

On May 5, 1862, four thousand Mexican soldiers of the government of Benito Juárez reclaimed their country from a French army of eight thousand (including some Mexicans loyal to France). The Battle of Puebla, near Mexico City, was important for the Mexicans because it harkened back to their battle for independence from Spain in 1821, a time of bloody struggles that crippled the Mexican economy. When the Mexican soldiers won at Puebla, they were able to depose Napoleon's relative, Archduke Maximilian of Austria, who had been put in place to rule Mexico. The holiday celebrates the freedoms that Mexico won in that lopsided battle, and it has become a holiday celebrated by Americans as well.

Although the holiday is becoming more widespread and popular in towns along the Mexican-American border, it is traditionally celebrated in areas with a large Mexican population. Parades and concerts are held to celebrate Cinco de Mayo, and festivities highlight Mexican food, music, beverage, and customs.

Items created for this holiday include clothing, posters, greeting cards, and poker chips, which have been specially made for this holiday by some of the larger casinos.

PRICE LIST: CINCO DE MAYO COLLECTIBLES

Bicycle Jersey, Cinco de Mayo. Depicts Corona bottles on front. 19" hidden zipper, elastic waist and cuffs, three back pockets for storage. Mint condition. **$50–60**

Bowls, Pottery. Cinco de Mayo vintage Mexican pottery bowls. Signed. Stackable red clay bowls with brightly colored handpainted designs in the bowl itself. Excellent condition. **$19–24**

Costume, Cinco de Mayo. Serape and sombrero costume created for the Cinco de Mayo holiday. Excellent condition. **$24–30**

Garden Flag, Fiesta. Cinco de Mayo flag. Yard art. Depicts sombrero and canastas. 28" × 44". Very good condition. **$15–20**

Pin, Cinco de Mayo. Hard Rock Café. Aztec figure playing guitar. 2005. Mint condition. **$17–20**

Poker Chips, Hard Rock Cinco De Mayo. $5/$25 chips. Two chips only. Mint, uncirculated condition. **$125–135**

Sneakers, Nike Air Force 1 LA Cinco de Mayo. Green, white, and red design. Made only for Los Angeles market. Mint condition. **$50–60**

Mother's Day (Second Sunday in May)

Mother's Day has its roots in paganism, as do many other holidays. The Greeks and Romans celebrated holidays based on goddesses or mothers of gods such as Rhea (Greece, mother of Demeter, Hades, Hera, Hestia, Poseidon, and Zeus) and Cybele (Rome, mother of the gods). When Christians started blending their holidays with the pagan holidays, they added their own special mother to the mix: Mary, Mother of Jesus. The feast to celebrate Cybele was called Hilaria and ran from March 15 to 18. During the 1600s, the fourth Sunday in Lent was named as the day to honor Mary, but the English designated it as a holiday to honor all mothers, calling it Mothering Sunday. On this holiday, all servants had the day off to spend time with their own mothers. A mothering cake was designed especially for the occasion.

Mother's Day began largely as a side thought in the United States in 1872 when Julia Ward Howe (who wrote "Battle Hymn of the Republic") suggested that the holiday should be dedicated to peace. It was not an official holiday until 1907, when Ana Jarvis wanted her mother's church in Grafton, Virginia, to celebrate the death of her mother (Anna Reese Jarvis) on its two-year anniversary. The following year, the city of Philadelphia celebrated the holiday, and Jarvis and her friends were hard at work trying to convince other American citizens to make the holiday national. By 1911 almost every state was celebrating Mother's Day, and in 1914 President Woodrow Wilson officially declared that the holiday would be celebrated nationally on the second Sunday in May. Other countries throughout the world also celebrate Mother's Day, though their dates do not coincide with the one instituted by the United States.

The celebrations for Mother's Day often start in church and end up in a restaurant. Usually a mother will get the day off, which means that her family either waits on her all day or takes her out. Flowers and candy are popular gifts, as are specially written cards, poetry, and love letters.

Collectibles for this holiday include greeting cards, postcards, limited edition plates, mugs, teacups and saucers, jewelry, figurines, and stuffed animals.

PRICE LIST: MOTHER'S DAY COLLECTIBLES

Basket, Longaberger 2004 Mother's Day Weekend Tote. Retired. Market Stripe liner, an Heirloom Floral liner (both in original bags), protector, 3" ceramic purse mirror (flower), red leather straps and product card. 16" × 6.5" × 11". Red leather weave and a woven bottom with metal feet. Mint condition. **$150–175**

Basket, Longaberger 1996 Mother's Day Vanity Full Set. Circa 1996. Measures 14.5" × 7.5" × 4.5" × 6.5". Pink on classic weave. Excellent condition. **$110–150**

Basket, Longaberger 2004 Mother's Day Weekend Tote Combo. Measures 16" × 6.5" × 11". Red on warm brown weave. Near mint condition. **$130–160**

Baskets, Lot of Seven. Longaberger Lot Hope 95-99, Mother's Day 98, Cake L+P. Collection of the first five Horizon of Hope Baskets dated from 1995 to 1999: All of these baskets come with protectors and matching Garden Splendor liners. All in excellent condition. **$250–350**

Bell, 1977 Mother's Day Musical Bell by Reuge Collectors. Marked on the bottom "Reuge." Made in Switzerland. Plays "Alouette." Mint condition. **$110–125**

Book, Mother's Day 1985 Ideals Book. Photographs, illustrations, poetry, articles, and recipes. **$8–10**

Bowl, Swarovski Crystal Mother's Day Daisy Bowl 2005. Bleikrstall crystal; 24% Pbo. Swarovski swan stamped on the bottom. Approximately 8" × 3". Mint condition. **$300–325**

Candle Holder, "I Love You, Mom." Glass plaque candle holder. Mirror base. Tealight not included. 4¼" × 3½" × 5". New. Mint condition. **$15–20**

Candle, Scented Mother's Candle. "Chamomile tea" scented candle is embedded with dried flowers and a lovely poem for Mother. Excellent condition. **$5–8**

Crystal figure. 3-D laser-etched crystal piece engraved with the words "On Mother's Day with Roses Flowers." 2" × 2" × 3". Mint in box condition. **$3–5**

Fan pull, Happy Mother's Day Girl. On pull chain/ceiling fan. Excellent condition. **$4–5**

Figurine, "Gift of Love." Mother and Children. Made by Lladro. Numbered 5596. Depicts mother and two children. Mint condition. **$290–300**

Hanging Glass "Mom" Heart. Spun-Glass heart 3¼" diameter; bevel glass base 2" × 4¾" high. Mint condition. **$15–20**

Heart, Spun Glass. Engraved "Mom." Porcelain flower atop it. 3¼" × 2" × 3½" high. Mint condition. **$18–20**

Jewelry Box, Halcyon Days Enamels, Mother's Day 1979. "Mother's Day 1979" written on the top of the box. Approximately 2" × 3". Mint condition. **$140–160**

Music Box, A Daughter's Heart by Ardleigh Elliot. Hand-painted, heart-shaped music box, decorated with handcrafted details and Swarovski crystal. Sculptural collectible music box highlighted with 22K gold and platinum accents. Mint in box. **$40–50**

Plate, Avon. 1981 Avon Mother's Day plate. Cherished Moments Last Forever. Mint in Box. **$15–20**

Plate, Avon. 1983 Avon Mother's Day plate. Love Is a Song for Mother. Mint in Box with stand. **$10–12**

Plate, Bing & Grondahl Mother's Day Plate, 1969. "Cocker Spaniel and Pups." Blue tones and great details. Approximately 6" diameter. Marked "Mors Dag 1969." Mint condition. **$135–150**

Plate, Rockwell Society Mother's Day Plate, 1976. Mother's Love. Mint in box condition. **$55–65**

Plate, Rockwell Society Mother's Day Plate, 1977. Faith. Mint in box condition. **$40–50**

Plate, Rockwell Society Mother's Day Plate, 1978. Bedtime. Mint in box condition. **$38–45**

Plate, Rockwell Society Mother's Day Plate, 1979. Reflections. Mint in box condition. **$25–30**

Plate, Rockwell Society Mother's Day Plate, 1980. Mother's Pride. Mint in box condition. **$25–30**

Plate, Rockwell Society Mother's Day Plate, 1981. After the Party. Mint in box condition. **$25–30**

Plate, Rockwell Society Mother's Day Plate, 1983. Add 2 Cups Love. Mint in box condition. **$30–35**

Plate, Rockwell Society Mother's Day Plate, 1984. Grandma's Courting Dress. Mint in box condition. **$30–35**

Plate, Rockwell Society Mother's Day Plate, 1985. Mending Time. Mint in box condition. **$25–30**

Plate, Rockwell Society Mother's Day Plate, 1986. Pantry Raid. Mint in box condition. **$25–30**

Plate, Rockwell Society Mother's Day Plate, 1987. Grandma's Surprise. Mint in box condition. **$25–30**

Plate, Schmid Disney Mother's Day Plate, 1974. Flowers for Mother. Mint in box condition. **$35–45**

Plate, Schmid Disney Mother's Day Plate, 1975. Snow White and the Seven Dwarfs. Mint in box condition. **$35–45**

Plate, Schmid Disney Mother's Day Plate, 1976. Minnie Mouse and Friends. Mint in box condition. **$25–35**

Plate, Schmid Disney Mother's Day Plate, 1977. Pluto's Pals. Mint in box condition. **$25–35**

Plate, Schmid Disney Mother's Day Plate, 1978. Flowers for Bambi. Mint in box condition. **$25–35**

Plate, Schmid Disney Mother's Day Plate, 1979. Happy Fleet (the whole Disney group dances). Mint in box condition. **$25–35**

Plate, Schmid Disney Mother's Day Plate, 1980. Minnie's Surprise. Mint in box condition. **$20–30**

Plate, Schmid Disney Mother's Day Plate, 1981. Playmates (Dalmations). Mint in box condition. **$25–35**

Plate, Schmid Peanuts Mother's Day Plate, 1972. Linus holding rose. Mint in box condition. **$25–30**

Plate, Schmid Peanuts Mother's Day Plate, 1975. A Kiss for Lucy. Snoopy kisses Lucy, hearts around edge of plate. Mint in box condition. **$25–30.**

Plate, Schmid Peanuts Mother's Day Plate, 1976. Linus and Snoopy. Mint in box condition. **$25–30.**

Plate, Schmid Raggedy Ann/Andy Mother's Day Plate, 1978. Hello, Mom. Mint in box condition. **$25–30.**

Plate, Schmid/Disney Mother's Day Plate, 1982. A Dream Come True (Mickey, Minnie, and the boys). Mint in box condition. **$30–40.**

Plates, Lot of Thirty-five Bing & Grondahl Mother's Day Plates 1969–2005. Complete set with many in their original boxes and includes the very valuable #1 1969 plate. 6" diameter plates. Mint condition. **$500–600**

Postcard, Commemorative Cachet. Mother's Day 1932. Shows the "Home of Mary, the Mother of Washington, 1775–1789, Fredericksburg, Va." The cachet has been postally cancelled with Scott #707 (i.e., a plate block single). Excellent condition. **$40–50**

Postcard, Mother's Day Founder Jarvis 1908. Grafton, Va. Four view postcard shows a photo of Miss Anna Jarvis, her mother, Andrews Methodist Episcopal Church, and the home or birthplace of Anna Jarvis (Webster. . W. Va.). Postmarked 1952. Very good condition. **$15–20**

Postcards, Lot. Eleven Mother's Day postcards. Circa 1908. One has a one cent stamp and the others have no stamps. Very good condition. **$10–15**

Rose, Crystal, Blue. Blue glass stemmed rose. Few green leaves are attached along the stem. Approximately 13" long. Mint condition. **$3–5**

Trivet, Daffodil Flowers. Mother's Day trivet by Angela Reitter for Papel Giftware. Mint condition. **$6–10**

Vase, Swarovksi Crystal. Decorated with two enamel daisies at the bottom of the vase. 8" tall. Excellent condition. **$125–135**

Memorial Day (Last Monday in May)

Originally called Decoration Day, the actual Memorial Day holiday was officially declared by General John Logan, commander of the Grand Army of the Republic, on May 5, 1868. Until that time, various communities honored their dead in their own ways, depending upon their traditions. Some visited grave sites, while others gathered to pray or talk about their dead. In the South, women began a tradition of cleaning up cemeteries that led to the Confederate Memorial Day (see Confederate Memorial Day in April). But Logan's holiday sought to be one that would commemorate all American soldiers who had died in the line of duty.

The first observance of the holiday on May 30, 1868, was celebrated by placing flowers on soldiers' gravesites in Arlington National Cemetery. New York led the way in recognizing the holiday as a statewide celebration in 1873, and most northern states had followed suit by 1890, but the federal version of Memorial Day was not officially declared until 1971, when Congress stated that the holiday would be celebrated on the last Monday in May. In 1966 President Lyndon Johnson cited Waterloo, New York, as the "birthplace of Memorial Day," although several other cities had made that claim previously.

Today, the holiday is still celebrated at Arlington National Cemetery, as well as throughout the United States. Small American flags are placed at each soldier or sailor's gravesite, and usually the president or vice president makes a speech at the Tomb of the Unknowns (formerly the Tomb of the Unknown Soldier). Parades are held, politicians speak, and Americans celebrate their heritage.

Collectibles for the occasion include numerous items decorated with flags and images of those who fought for the country, including postcards, greeting cards, posters, plaques, photographs, flags, figurines, and books.

PRICE LIST: MEMORIAL DAY COLLECTIBLES

Postcard. "They fought like heroes, long and well, and then like heroes died." Circa 1910. Colorful graphics. Depicts old soldier with one wooden leg and children at his knee. Good condition. **$5–6**

Postcard, Black and White Graphics. USS *Cachalot*, Memorial Day 1938. Good condition. **$10–12**

Cachet, Memorial Day. Groton, Conn., Submarine Base, Memorial Day, painted naval. Wentworth hand-painted cachet, cancelled on Memorial Day, Groton, Conn., May 29, 2000. Very good condition. **$15–18**

Figurines, Soldier Bears. Special order for Collector's Showcase in 2004. Factory decorated. Part of holiday bears sets, one for each of the twelve major holidays. Set includes two bears: one sitting bear and one baby bear. Dressed in black boots, camouflage, and a hat. Only 150 sets made. Bottom reads, "Exclusively for Collector's Showcase," and signed by the artist. Mint condition. **$80–100**

**Patriotic Group: Willkie, Liberty Make-Do is 14",
mohair teddy with wool pincushion and vintage
flag.** Ted, 13" mohair teddy with wool felt coat and
vintage ribbons. *Courtesy of Baker & Co. Designs.*
$400.

Menu, Memorial Day Dinner, 1956. SS *Brazil* cruise ship in the Port of Trinidad, May 30,
1956. Slick white heavy paper foldover with blue cord spine. Menu in three languages along
with list of staff. 10" × 7". Very good condition.   **$6–8**

Pin, Disney, Memorial Day. Disneyland, Memorial Day 2004. Surprise release 3-D. Rear
level is American flag in the shape of an oval background. Upper level Mickey, Donald,
Goofy, and Pluto in the uniforms of the four branches of service. Two dangles on bottom:
Memorial Day 2004, Disneyland. Mint condition.   **$20–25**

Pin, Grand Army of the Republic. 1913 Memorial Day Pin. Pin and attached ribbon feature
the famous GAR medal design. Ehrman back paper still intact. 1¼" with attached ribbon.
Very good condition.   **$18–22**

Poster, Van Halen Memorial Day. Depicts the rock group in the famous Iwo Jima "raising
the flag" pose. Originally made for the U.S. rock festival in 1983. Excellent condition.
                        $15–18

Postcard, Grand Army of the Republic. Embossed card with colorful graphics of a medal
worn by Union veterans against a flag background. Circa 1900–1910. Very good condition.
                        $12–15

Poster, Memorial Day Veteran. Fine art giclee reproduction of vintage poster depicting old
soldier saluting children to celebrate Memorial Day on May 30. 24" × 36". Excellent condition.   **$10–15**

Postcard, Memorial Day Souvenir: Capture of San Juan Hill. Colorful lithograph depicts
soldiers running up the hill with American flag. Circa 1910. Winsch Publishers. Excellent
condition.   **$10–15**

Promotional Blowup, Coors. Inflatable sun created for Coors Beer as part of Memorial Day
promotion. 30" × 30". Never sold in stores. Mint condition.   **$6–8**

– 6 –
JUNE

Flag Day (June 14)

This holiday was the brainchild of B. J. Cigrand, a teacher in Wisconsin, who wanted to celebrate "Flag Birthday" on June 14, 1885, the 108th anniversary of the official adoption of the American flag. However, it was another teacher, George Balch of New York, who convinced the New York Board of Education to observe Flag Day in 1889. Other organizations followed that lead until President Woodrow Wilson officially proclaimed the holiday in 1916. The date June 14 wasn't designated until President Harry Truman signed an Act of Congress confirming the date for the holiday in 1949. In 2002 President George W. Bush proclaimed the week of June 14 as National Flag Week.

Flag Day is celebrated by honoring the flag, and is a time when schoolchildren learn about respecting Old Glory and taking care of the flag properly. For example, flying it from only dawn to dusk, lighting it at night if it's flying, folding it properly, flying it above all other flags, and retiring it properly when it's old.

It would make sense that the collectibles available to celebrate this day are all related to the flag, so in addition to the flags themselves, there are banners, quilts, photos, and postcards.

PRICE LIST: FLAG DAY COLLECTIBLES

Art, Watercolor. "To Ramsonville" by Harry G. Ackerman (circa 1900–circa 1985). Circa 1935. Watercolor and gouache on smooth, heavy paper, 15½" × 22½", unframed. Signed with estate stamp, lower right. Excellent condition. **$30–35**

Coin, Hawaii Flag Day Dollar. So-Called Dollar, Hibler-Kappen 547, choice uncirculated condition. Struck in 1960 to commemorate the addition of the 50th star to the U.S. Flag. Obverse pictures two flags and a rendition of King Kamehameha. Reverse pictures a map

Blue Patriot. 17" tall. Mohair with a ruff of vintage flag bunting and vintage buttons. Original design. *Courtesy of Baker & Company Designs.* $395.

of the state of Hawaii. Measures 39 mm, copper-nickel, choice uncirculated. Mint condition. **$11–15**

Photograph, Flag Day Celebration at Fort Sam Houston. Panoramic taken near San Antonio, Texas, taken in 1918. 52½" × 10½." Printed on very heavyweight satin paper. Excellent condition. **$30–35**

Pin, Walt Disney World. Pluto is depicted against an American flag in the background. 2005. Mint condition. **$10–12**

Poster, Elmhurst Flag Day. Dated June 18, 1939. Reproduction of vintage poster. Printed on fine art paper. 24" × 36". Mint condition. **$10–12**

Quilt Kit, Flag Day. By Alice Wilhiot Designs. The pattern and all of the fabric for the quilt top is included. Quilt is done in red, white, blue, soft blue, and gold. Instructions included. Finished size 38" × 54". Mint condition. **$30–35**

Father's Day (Third Sunday in June)

Father's Day is celebrated in the United States on the third Sunday in June, thanks to Sonora Dodd of Spokane, Washington, who had the idea for the holiday when she was listening to a Mother's Day sermon. Her father, William Smart, a veteran of the Civil War, was the man she wanted to honor because he had raised his five children alone after his wife died while giving birth to their sixth baby. William Smart's birthday was June 5, so in 1909 Mrs. Dodd asked her church minister to devote a special church service to all fathers on her father's birthday. Because it was too late for him to prepare for that particular date, the minister performed the celebration on June 19 instead. After that time, the state of Washington celebrated Father's Day on June 19.

Roses were traditionally used to celebrate the day (red for a living father and white for a deceased), but J. H. Berringer of Washington, a minister who conducted Father's Day services starting in 1912, preferred white lilacs.

President Woodrow Wilson approved the holiday in 1916, and President Calvin Coolidge made it official in 1924. President Lyndon Johnson put the final seal of approval on the holiday by signing a presidential proclamation in 1966 stating that the third Sunday in June would be the official holiday.

The most common Father's Day gift has been the necktie, but other gifts include humorous items and sports items. Collectibles include ties, pins, plaques, mugs, gag gifts, plates, greeting cards, postcards, and figurines.

PRICE LIST: FATHER'S DAY COLLECTIBLES

Tickets, Nextel Cup Father's Day Event. Four tickets to the June 18, 2006, Michigan International Speedway event. Mint condition. **$425–450**

Basket, Longaberger. Chess Game Father's Day Basket, 2001. Includes checkerboard lid and pewter chess pieces. Excellent condition. **$325–350**

Baskets, Desk Set. Longaberger three-piece set, 1998. Includes 14" long envelope basket with organizer plastic protector, 8" long address card organizer basket with unused address cards and plastic protector, and 5" tall basket with plastic protector. Very good condition. **$65–75**

Baskets, Pocket Change Set. Longaberger "pocket change" basket, 2003. Used atop a bureau. Almost square, leather trim, wood lid. Excellent condition. **$45–55**

Figurine, Father's Day. Lladro #5584. Retired in 1989. Depicts a father in his pajamas reading to child on his knee. 9" tall. Excellent condition. **$215–230**

Cel, Superman "Father's Day" Episode. Warner Bros. from the animated classic Superman "Father's Day" episode. Piece measures 15½" × 17½" and cel itself measures 7½" × 9½". Comes with Certificate of Authenticity. Excellent condition. **$1,200–1,500**

Race Car, Dale Earnhardt. Autographed by Dale Earnhardt, Jr. Depicts his #8 Budweiser/Father's Day 2004 Monte Carlo. 1:24 scale action car. Mint condition. **$50–60**

Race Car, Terry Labonte. #5 Kellogg's Racing "Happy Father's Day" Edition action die-cast 1:24. Mint condition. **$35–40**

Plate, Delft. Depicts the Santa Maria and honors Father's Day. 7" diameter. Back: Delft Crown and made in Holland and upper side "Happy Father's Day—Santa Maria of Columbus 1492" First of a series of famous ships throughout the ages. Excellent condition. **$25–30**

Plate, "Heidelberg Castle." 1971 Bareuther Father's Day Plate. 3rd issue in the Father's Day series by Bareuther Porcelain Factory, Waldsassen, Bavaria, Germany. Artist Hans Mueller perfectly captures this thirteenth-century castle located on the Neckar River as it towers above the university city of Heidelberg. Fine porcelain. 7¾" diameter. Mint condition. **$20–25**

Pin, Artist's Proof, Mr. Incredible & Family. Walt Disney World, Father's Day 2005. Reads "Father's Day 2005" around the white border. Bottom says "Walt Disney World." Martha Widener from Disney Design Group created the artwork for this pin. Mint condition. **$25–30**

Plaque, Father's Day. Hand-cut sheet metal is skillfully shaped for 3-D effects, hand-painted and intricately detailed with rod, reel, line and sinker. Rust-resistant; 17" × 15" long. Hangs from metal chain. Custom-engraved with "Happy Father's Day." Mint condition.

$17–20

Figurine, Austin Sculpture. Signed by Dee Crowley. Dated 1989. Depicts father on all fours with child on his back. Leaflet on bottom of sculpture calls it "Father's Day." Excellent condition.

$16–20

Mug, Pillsbury Dough Boy. Marked "Father's Day Gift" and depicts the Dough Boy cooking something for the holiday. 2001. Dishwasher safe. Excellent condition.

$15–18

T-shirt, In Dad We Trust. Extra large. Mint condition.

$10–12

Poster, Father's Day Tie. French poster for the French version of Father's Day. Reproduction of a vintage poster. 20" × 30". Mint condition.

$10–12

Belt Buckle, Dad. Pewter and blue belt buckle. Measures 3⅜" × 2¼". Mint condition.

$10–15

Pin, New York Yankees Father's Day Tie. Pin in shape of tie with NY Yankees logo. Officially licensed by the baseball team. 1" long. Mint condition.

$8–10

– 7 –
JULY

Independence Day (July 4)
The Holiday

As any American schoolchild knows, the United States declared its independence from Britain on July 4, 1776. This is the most celebrated strictly American holiday on the annual calendar. The Declaration of Independence, adopted by the Second Continental Congress on July 4, stated that "all men are created equal" and became the most important governmental document in the nation's history. The original document is exhibited in the Rotunda for the Charters of Freedom of the Capitol building in Washington, D.C. It was signed by fifty-six delegates from the thirteen original colonies.

For more than a year, Americans had been fighting a Revolutionary War against the British. On June 7, 1776, Congress met with Richard Henry Lee, who strongly advocated independence. A committee, consisting of Thomas Jefferson, John Adams, Benjamin Franklin, Roger Sherman, and Robert R. Livingston, was appointed to draft a declaration of independence. By June 28, that draft, written mostly by Jefferson, was available and read to Congress for the first time, then debated and revised. But time was running out for the delegates, and they knew they had to move quickly because the British fleet would soon arrive. On July 2, the British fleet arrived in New York and Congress declared its independence. They followed up that verbal declaration with the written Declaration of Independence on July 4, then had John Dunlap print broadsides, or printed posters, of the document. There are twenty-four of Dunlap's broadsides still in existence, two of which are in the Library of Congress. As president of the Continental Congress, John Hancock ordered the copies disbursed to the New Jersey and Delaware legislatures. Although the document was printed in the newspaper in Pennsylvania on July 6, it was not delivered verbally to the American people until it was read aloud in Philadelphia on July 8, and the following day, read to the troops in New York at the request of General George Washington. Finally, an embossed copy was signed by Congress on August 2, just as a reinforcement of British troops arrived in New York. The states each received their signed, official copies in January 1777.

Signing the Declaration and building a government for what was now known as the United States didn't end the Revolutionary War. The war itself continued for some time after the signing, and didn't officially end until 1783, when the British left New York City. The document that declared the war over and acted as an agreement for peace was the Treaty of Paris, signed on September 3, 1783. At that point, the thirteen colonies were recognized as the United States.

Celebrations of July 4 are held all across the United States. The flag is flown, parades are held, politicians speak, and many other celebrations are enjoyed. Today, the holiday typically calls for fireworks, barbeques, games, and music. In the past, those events would have been a little tamer and a lot more connected to patriotism, but the general ideals are the same, even though generations have adapted different ways of relishing the moment the United States became free.

The Symbols

Certain icons are now connected with the holiday, including Uncle Sam, Columbia, the Statue of Liberty, Yankee Doodle, and the American eagle. Stories about how these icons came into being differ.

Uncle Sam

Troy, New York, claims to be the home of the original Uncle Sam: Samuel Wilson, a meat packer during the War of 1812 who was born in Arlington, Massachusetts, on September 13, 1766. They even sport a full-size statue of the man at the corner of River Street and Third Street. During the time he was a meat packer, there was a standing joke that the "U.S." stamped on the meat barrels he sent to the Army stood for "Uncle Sam." Supposedly, Wilson was known for his fairness, honesty, and reliability. Wilson died in Troy, New York, on July 31, 1854. Congress passed a resolution in 1961 recognizing Samuel Wilson as the inspiration for Uncle Sam.

Thomas Nast (1840–1902), the famous nineteenth-century political cartoonist, is responsible for creating the images we know as Uncle Sam today, yet they do not resemble Samuel Wilson, who was clean-shaven rather than bearded. Nast first drew the lanky, bearded figure dressed in red, white, and blue with a distinctive top hat in 1830. The figure personified the United States and often represented the nation's conscience in Nast's political cartoons.

But the most powerful of the Uncle Sam images may be the one created by James Montgomery Flagg (1877–1960), an illustrator who designed the poster "I Want You" depicting Uncle Sam, stern and finger pointing, asking for volunteers for the U.S. Army in 1916. World War I was just heating up, and Flagg's depiction of Uncle Sam, originally used as a cover of *Leslie's Weekly* magazine on July 6, 1916, is said to be the most famous poster created during the history of the United States.

Sam. 13" tall. Mohair with wool felt paws. Wears a wool felt jacket. Original design. *Courtesy of Baker & Co.* $345.

Sam's Hat. 12" tall. Mohair rabbits with ruffles of vintage flag bunting sit in a painted wool felt hat. Original design. *Courtesy of Baker & Co.* $495.

Band Stand Sam Candy Container. 9½" tall. Papier-mâché. ©*Lori C. Mitchell, 2004.* $350–400.

Columbia

Columbia, the female personification of the country, did not become as recognizable as Uncle Sam, and since the 1920s has been rarely seen. Like Uncle Sam, she was used in political cartoons through the early twentieth century, and her image came from the poetic term for the nation, largely derived from Christopher Columbus. The term fell out of use in the twentieth century.

The Statue of Liberty

Another female icon for the United States is the Statue of Liberty, designed by French sculptor Frédéric-Auguste Bartholdi. He was commissioned to design a statue for the centennial of America's independence from England, but the statue was not complete until 1886. Another famous Frenchman, Alexandre-Gustave Eiffel (who later designed the tower that bears his name), designed the wrought-iron skeleton of the statue. The statue was in place and dedicated to the American people on October 28, 1886. She stands over 305 feet tall from the ground to the top of her torch, weighs 27,000 tons, and holds a tablet in her right hand upon which is inscribed the Roman numerals for the date July 4, 1776. The poem "The New Colossus" (1883) engraved on her base was written by Emma Lazarus, who coined the famous lines:

> Give me your tired, your poor,
> your huddled masses yearning to breathe free,
> The wretched refuse of your teeming shore;
> Send these, the homeless, tempest-tost to me,
> I lift my lamp beside the golden door.

Since the time she arrived in New York Harbor, the statue has become an icon for the United States, and her figure is found in many different representations. She has also become a symbol for all of the immigrants who have poured past her to arrive at nearby Ellis Island, as well as for New York itself.

Yankee Doodle

"Yankee Doodle" is a tune that came to represent all that Americans were fighting for during the Revolutionary War. The original meaning of the term is unknown, but "Yankee" generally referred to New Englanders, while "doodle" meant a silly person or country bumpkin. "Macaroni" was a degrading term meant to poke fun at British soldiers, whom the colonists thought dressed like dandies. On April 19, 1775, the tune was played by British troops as they marched to relieve a regiment posted at the battle of Lexington and Concord. When the Americans fought back, they also chose to rewrite the verses of "Yankee Doodle" to turn the meaning of the song around: no longer was it derisive to Americans but to the British themselves. By 1777 the tune had become an unofficial American anthem, celebrating the pluckiness of those Revolutionary soldiers who fought back against the British. The physical image most often associated with "Yankee Doodle" is actually a painting entitled "The Spirit of '76," created by artist Archibald M. Willard in 1876. After the war was won, the song remained popular, showing up in musicals, operas, and plays, until George M. Cohan immortalized the song in his Broadway play "Little Johnny Jones." The play later became a movie entitled "Yankee Doodle Dandy," starring James Cagney as Cohan.

The American Eagle

Last, but not least, the American eagle has been an icon symbolizing the nation's strength and freedom. Congress deliberated for six years before deciding on the bald eagle as the national bird, finally making it official on June 20, 1782. The eagle has found its way onto our money, federal and state seals, and the president's flag.

Today's collectors can find a plethora of items reflecting the patriotic history of the United States, including flags, replicas of the Declaration of Independence, images of the signers of the Declaration, posters, postcards, statuettes, snow globes, plates, mugs, greeting cards, jewelry, costumes (e.g., Uncle Sam), toys, banks, games, ornaments, and songbooks.

PRICE LIST: INDEPENDENCE DAY COLLECTIBLES

Abstinence Pledge. Dated July 4, 1844. Temperance Celebration Pledge of the Pawtucket and Central Falls Washington Total Abstinence Society. Measures approx. 3¼" × 9". Very good condition. $175–200

Art, "Best Seat in the House." Hand-enhanced giclee canvas by William S. Phillips. Image is of fireworks in the sky above the Bay View Inn. Released in June 2004, only 300 produced. Signed by artist. 24" × 30". Excellent condition. $540–575

Art, "Statue of Liberty, New York, 2005." By Ng Woon Lam, nationally recognized artist. Original, signed by artist. Oil on canvas. 24" × 20" × ¾". Unframed. Mint condition.

$300–350

Bank, Uncle Sam. Mechanical bank. Iron. Circa 1886. Manufactured by The Shepard Hardware Company. All original. Excellent condition. $2,000–2,250

Bowl, Norman Rockwell. Made for Bicentennial in 1976 by Gorham. Norman Rockwell design. 8¾" wide × 5¾" tall. Mint condition. $30–40

Box, Statue of Liberty. Halcyon Days enamel box. Made in Bilston, England. Designed by Tiffany & Co. On side of box: "Statue of Liberty, 1886–1986." Mint condition. $115–125

Card, Uncle Sam's Home Defense. #104 Enlisting Home Guard, from the 1941 series by Gum, Inc. Boy Scout image on card. Very good condition. $125–150

Charm, Statue of Liberty figure. Circa 1960s. 9 kt. Gold. ¾" tall. Excellent condition.

$30–35

Coin, 100th Anniversary of Statue of Liberty. 1986, France. Platinum Statue of Liberty 20 G. In box with original papers. Mint condition. $610–700

Clock, American Eagle. Mid-nineteenth century. Wood case, brass clockface. Eagle, leaves and vine designs in high relief brass. Face, 3¾". Frame 6¾" × 8¼". 4½" deep. Good condition. $225–275

Clock, Statue of Liberty. Motion lamp/clock made by the United Clock Corporation from Brooklyn, N.Y. Bronzed cast metal replica of Statue of Liberty. The lamp motion is in the base: New York Harbor scene with ships. Excellent condition. $350–375

Doll, Barbie. "Statue of Liberty Barbie" designed for FAO Schwartz for 110th anniversary of the Statue in 1996. Mint condition. $80–100

Ants On Parade. 5" tall. Made of resin. 2003. *Courtesy of Bethany Lowe Designs, Inc.* $14.99–16.

Figurines, Ants On Parade. Set of three. 5" tall. Made of resin. Two ant figurines stand on all legs while third holds small pseudo-American flag and sits back on "haunches." Introduced 2003. Mint condition. **$14.99–16**

Firecracker Label. "Roaring Lion Firecrackers." Depicts lion against red, green, and yellow background. 1½" tall. Excellent condition. **$50–60**

Folk Art, Uncle Sam Jack. Wood, papier-mâché, and tin figure. 10" tall. Original folk art by Trout Creek Folk Art, Napa, Calif., 1997. New. Mint condition. **$55–75**

Folk Art, Miss Liberty. Papier-mâché figure. 11"" tall. Original folk art by Trout Creek Folk Art, Napa, Calif., 2004. New. Mint condition. **$155–180**

Folk Art, Americus Mouse. 7" tall. Papier-mâché. ©Lori C. Mitchell, 2004. Mint condition. **$220–240**

Folk Art, Band Stand Sam. Candy container. 9½" tall. Papier-mâché. ©Lori C. Mitchell, 2004. **$350–400**

Folk Art, Uncle Sam Flag Holder. "Outsider art," constructed from pine boards and having a good weathered paint surface. Full-figured Uncle Sam, painted in traditional red, white, and blue, and stars and stripes uniform, outstretched arm in a finger pointing gesture with drilled hole to accept a flagpole (flag not present). Possibly from a World War II era recruitment center, American, mid-twentieth century, 71" × 27". Very good condition. **$350–500**

Magnet, Americana Ant Magnet. 4" × 2½". Hand carved wood. Ant is sitting atop a red clip with white stars. Introduced 2003. Mint condition. **$6.95–8**

Music Box, Yankee Doodle. Raggedy Andy as Yankee Doodle, playing drum. Base of music box marked 1776–1976. Music box rotates while music plays. Label: Schmid Bros/Disney. Good condition. **$45–50**

Ornament, American Eagle. 1989 Gorham Sterling. Christmas ornament. 1⅞" × 4¾". Mint condition. **$275–300**

Uncle Sam Jack

Lady Liberty

Uncle Sam Jack. 10" tall. 1997. Wood, papier-mâché, and tin. *Original folk art by Trout Creek Folk Art, Napa, Calif.* $55–75.

Miss Liberty. 11" tall. 2004. Papier-mâché. *Original folk art by Trout Creek Folk Art, Napa, Calif.* $155–180.

Americus Mouse. 7" tall. Papier-mâché. ©*Lori C. Mitchell, 2004.* $220–240.

Paperweight, Statue of Liberty Standing on Globe. Paper lithographed lead figure. Very good condition. **$200–250**

Photograph, Print. Statue of Liberty by renowned photographer Margaret Bourke White. Circa 1930. 16" × 20". Black and white. Limited edition. Number 25/100. Mint condition. **$1,500–2,000**

Pinback, Yankee Doodle Trio. Circa 1912. Taunton, Mass. 1.25" celluloid pinback from the July 4th celebration. Multicolored image of the famous Yankee Doodle Trio, by Archibald Willard, formally known as "The Spirit of '76." "Yankee Doodle" and "Fourth of July Carnival, Taunton, 1912" in block letters around the perimeter. Rim curl has Bastian Bros., Rochester, N.Y. Reverse has original backpaper from Bastian Brothers. Excellent condition. **$35–45**

Postcard, Independence Day. Embossed Raphael Tuck July 4th patriotic postcard. Postally unused, no postmark, no writing on back. Very good condition. **$6–8**

Postcard, Independence Day. Depicts flags and fireworks. Colorful lithograph. Banner at the top says: Independence Day, July 4th. Mailed to Cuyahoga, Ohio, in December 1910. Good condition. **$6–8**

Postcard, Lady Liberty/Columbia. Lady Columbia shown laying a wreath at a soldier's grave. Colorful lithograph, embossed, unused, and features a small gold lettered verse at the bottom right: "Let Loving hands place lovely wreath / On valiant Soldier's grave, To honor him who lies beneath—A warrior true and brave." Excellent condition. **$15–20**

Postcard, Photo. Independence Day in Paris. Depicts a 1918 parade in Paris of military personnel flying both the American and French flags. Very good condition. **$5–6**

Poster, "Join the Quartermaster Corps." World War I–1919 poster. Artist: John W. Sheeres. 17" × 26". Lower edge: "Keep the stars shining for Uncle Sam." Shows Uncle Sam in doughboy outfit, thumbs up toward purple, starry heavens. Quartermaster motif all around. Very good condition. **$200–225**

Poster, "The Living Uncle Sam." Dated January 13, 1919, by Mole & Thomas, Chicago, Ill. Photo taken at Camp Lee, Va., Major General Omar Bundy, Comd'g. Picture measures 14" × 11" and depicts 19,000 officers and men standing, kneeling, and lying down in a pose together depicting the Uncle Sam character. Very good condition. **$450–500**

Poster, "Yankee Doodle Dandy." Original 1942 movie poster. 11" × 14". Good condition. **$275–325**

Ring, American Eagle Design. Circa 1940s. Size 11¾. Pilot's wings insignia on the top with "E Pluribus Unum." 10k on Sterling, ¾" wide tapering to ⅛" wide at the back of the band; weighs 9.4 grams. Good condition. **$110–125**

Salt and Pepper Shaker Set, Statue of Liberty. Made of Bakelite. Red and yellow shakers. Souvenirs from 1930s–1940s. Approximately 1⅝" tall. Excellent condition. **$195–215**

Tabletop Decoration, Picnic Ants See Saw. 13" × 6". Made of paper pulp. Introduced 2003. Mint condition. **$29.95–35**

Tabletop Decoration, Picnic Ants. 2003. 13" × 6".
Paper pulp. *Courtesy of Bethany Lowe Designs, Inc.*
$29.95–35.

Tieback, Battersea. Early nineteenth century Battersea curtain tieback, with an American eagle, in full color enamel. 1⅞" in diameter. Grey, pink, and blue on a white background. Very good condition.   **$500–600**

Toy, Stuffed Bear. "Red Ted." 13" red mohair teddy bear with wool felt paws. He has a squeaker in his belly and his ruffle is of vintage flag bunting. Original folk art by Baker & Co. Designs Ltd. New. Mint condition.   **$225–250**

Toy, Stuffed Bear. "Sailor Ted." 13" brown mohair teddy bear. Wool felt paws and squeaker. Wears a wool sailor shirt. Original folk art by Baker & Co. Designs Ltd. New. Mint condition.   **$260–300**

Toy, Stuffed Bear. "Sam." 13" red mohair bear with wool felt paws. Wears a wool felt jacket. His hat is vintage as is the drum he stands on and his flag. Original folk art by Baker & Co. Designs Ltd. New. Mint condition.   **$345–400**

Toy, Stuffed Bunny. "Red Patriot." 17" red free-standing mohair bunny. He wears a ruff of vintage flag bunting and vintage buttons. His pack basket is filled with vintage and new goodies. Original folk art by Baker & Co. Designs Ltd. New. Mint condition.   **$395–425**

Toy, Stuffed Bunny. "Blue Patriot." 17" blue free-standing mohair bunny. He wears a ruff of vintage flag bunting and vintage buttons. His pack basket is filled with vintage and new goodies. Original folk art by Baker & Co. Designs Ltd. New. Mint condition.   **$395–425**

Toy, Stuffed Elephant. "Willie." Gray mohair elephant. 13" wearing a wool sailor shirt. Original folk art by Baker & Co. Designs Ltd. New. Mint condition.   **$245–300**

Toy, Stuffed Teddy. "Lil Patriot." 13" light brown mohair teddy with glass eyes and wool felt paw pads. Wears a ruff of vintage flag bunting. Original folk art by Baker & Co. Designs Ltd. New. Mint condition.   **$225–250**

Toy, Stuffed Bunny. "Blue Bunnies." 12" and 15" gray mohair bunnies, ruffles of vintage flag bunting. Wool felt ear linings. Original folk art by Baker & Co. Designs Ltd. New. Mint condition.   **$215–250 and $265–300**

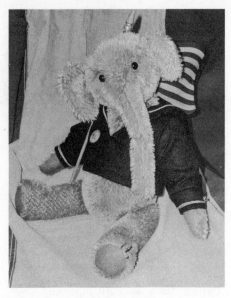

Sailor Ted. 13" tall. Mohair with a wool sailor shirt. Original design. *Courtesy Baker & Co.* $260.

Willie. 13" tall. Mohair with a wool sailor shirt. Original design. *Courtesy of Baker & Co.* $245.

Toy, Stuffed Teddy. "Liberty Make Do." Small beige mohair teddy sits atop a hand dyed wool ball, decorated with appliqué, feather stitching, and bells. Holds a tiny vintage flag. 14" overall. Original folk art by Baker & Co. Designs Ltd. New. Mint condition. **$245–300**

Toy, Stuffed Bunny. "Willkie." 17" beige mohair freestanding rabbit. Dressed in a wool felt coat and vest. He has a collar cut from a vintage one and carries an antique silk flag. Original folk art by Baker & Co. Designs Ltd. New. Mint condition. **$395–425**

Toys, Stuffed Animals. Patriotic Group Willkie (17" beige mohair freestanding rabbit), Liberty Make Do (14", mohair teddy and wool pincushion, with vintage flag) and Ted (13" with wool felt coat, vintage ribbons). Original folk art by Baker & Co. Designs Ltd. New. Mint condition. **$395, $245, and $225**

– 8 –
AUGUST

Sisters' Day (August 3, August 7, or first Sunday in August)

When a holiday isn't officially proclaimed, it's often confusing when it is actually celebrated. That's the case with Sisters' Day. Though meant for those who have some kind of familial connection, this holiday is often celebrated by people who feel they have a "sisterly" connection with another female. Friends, coworkers, people who share the same interests—all might celebrate this holiday.

Though this holiday is a fairly young one on the list of annual holidays, there are still some collectibles out there, and I'm sure there will be more as the holiday grows in popularity. Stuffed toys, embroidered items, greeting cards, and jewelry are already available to the collector.

PRICE LIST: SISTERS' DAY COLLECTIBLES

Jewelry, Pin. Limited Edition (of 750) Sisters' Day Pin. Made by Disney. 2005. Depicts Cinderella between her two stepsisters. Mint condition.   **$10–12**

Plate, Sisters. Hummel plate. 8¼" diameter. Border of plate reads: "Sisters, together tasks are lighter, days are brighter." Excellent condition.   **$16–20**

Calendar, Perpetual. Everyday Thoughts/Sisters. Excellent condition.   **$13–15**

Toy, Stuffed Animal, Beanie Baby. "Sis" born August 5, 2004. Sad-eyed dog with tag that reads: "You've helped me through good times and bad / You've cheered me up when I've been sad / A better friend I never knew / Happy Sisters' Day to you!" Excellent condition.
          $6–8

International Friendship Day (August 7)

This holiday is meant to celebrate bonds with friends of all shapes and sizes—those you've just met, those you work with, those on teams, those with family connections, and those you've known forever. Celebrations include sharing gifts, flowers, friendship bracelets, going to sleepovers, special trips, to the movies or a restaurant—anything you enjoy doing with friends.

Some of the items available for collectors include embroidered pillows, jewelry, stuffed animals, plaques, and plates. Surely as the holiday becomes more popular, many more collectibles will be created.

PRICE LIST: INTERNATIONAL FRIENDSHIP DAY COLLECTIBLES

Figurine, "You Just Can't Chuck a Good Friendship." Precious Moments® Members Only Figurine, 1988. #PM-882. Excellent condition. **$15–20**

Jewelry, Bracelet. 7" friendship charm bracelet features a large heart charm with the word "Friendship" engraved on it and a smaller heart charm with word "Forever" engraved on it. Bracelet tiles feature scrolling detail and message: "Friendship is the only cement that will ever hold the world together!" Mint condition. **$6–8**

Toy, Stuffed Animal, Steiff Bear. Friendship Bear. Exclusive edition for Germany Ltd.; 2,000 pcs. in 2003. Mint condition. **$125–150**

International Left-Handers' Day (August 13)

Left-Handers' Day was first celebrated in 1976 by members of Lefthanders' International (LI). The first holiday was on August 13, a Friday; it was scheduled on that day to poke fun at all of the many superstitions about left-handed people. The celebration is designed to bring awareness to the difficulties faced by left-handed people.

The Left Handers Association was formed in 1990 to keep fellow left-handers aware of new developments and manufactured items that could help them.

PRICE LIST: LEFT-HANDERS' DAY COLLECTIBLES

Book, *The World's Greatest Left-Handers*. Published in 1995. Excellent condition.
$15–18

Calendar, The Left-Handers 2006 Day-to-Day Boxed Calendar. Each page includes information about left-handed people. Mint condition. **$10–12**

Mug, Official Left-Handers Mug. Ceramic. Made by Recycled Paper Products. Mint condition. **$5–7**

Women's Equality Day (August 26)

When Bella Abzug, a Democratic congressional representative from New York, suggested a holiday called Women's Equality Day in 1971, Congress agreed and set aside August 26.

Designated as the time when people would recognize the struggles women went through to obtain the right to vote in 1920, the observance celebrates the passage of the Nineteenth Amendment, as well as the continued work toward equality for women.

On this holiday, the National Women's History Project urges celebrants to wear purple, gold, and white, the colors of the suffrage movement. Programs to celebrate the holiday include parades, video presentations of the original suffrage speeches, lectures by educators and politicians, and recognition of women who have made a difference in the world.

Collectibles inspired by this holiday include posters, videos, jewelry, photos, books, T-shirts, plaques, and mugs.

PRICE LIST: WOMEN'S EQUALITY DAY COLLECTIBLES

Book, *A Women's History Gazetteer to England, Scotland and Wales.* By Jane Legget, published by Pandora, London. 1988. 8 vols. Black and white photo illustrations throughout. Excellent condition.   **$4–6**

Book, *Women's Suffrage in History.* Written by Elizabeth Frost and Kathryn Cullen-Dupont. Published in 1992 by Facts on File. Mint condition.   **$10–12**

First Day Cover, President Ford Designates Women's Equality Day, 1974. Photos on left of Ford and women representatives. Posted in Washington, D.C. Mint condition.   **$7–9**

Jewelry, Dancing Woman. Sterling silver. Approximately 2" long. Mint condition. **$15–18**

Pin, Lapel. National Women's History Project lapel pin. 1¼" × ¾". 2005. Mint condition.
                                                                                                                                     $10–12

Pin, Lapel. Women's History. Round. Circa 1985. Mint condition.   **$3–5**

– 9 –
SEPTEMBER

Labor Day (First Monday in September)

Labor Day is probably the only holiday not devoted to a particular event, person, or conflict. Instead, it is a creation of the labor movement and is dedicated to all workers. Most sources say that Peter J. McGuire, the general secretary of the Brotherhood of Carpenters and Joiners, and a cofounder of the American Federation of Labor, was the first to state that a day should be set aside to honor all those who endeavored to build the nation. However, others state that a machinist, Matthew Maguire, was responsible for proposing the holiday in 1882 while he was secretary of the Central Labor Union in New York.

The Central Labor Union adopted the idea and held a demonstration and picnic on September 5, 1882. They celebrated on the same day the following year, but in 1884, the Knights of Labor designated the first Monday in September as the day all future Labor Day celebrations would be held. The first state to hold an official Labor Day celebration was Oregon in 1887. By June 28, 1894, Congress passed an act making Labor Day an official holiday throughout the United States. Labor Day is celebrated in Canada, as well as in many other industrialized nations.

Celebrations of the holiday include parades with trade and labor organizations marching to show their strength, followed by picnics or festivals for the workers. Politicians traditionally give speeches, and most workers have the day off for the holiday.

Items created for this holiday include pins, postcards, greeting cards, medals, pinbacks, stamps, and many other pieces of memorabilia dedicated to the workers of the world.

PRICE LIST: LABOR DAY COLLECTIBLES

Art, Limited Edition Print. Artist: Charles Wysocki. "Labor Day in Bungalowville." Artist signed and numbered print from a sold-out edition of 1,250 published in 1998 by AMCAL. Measures 35" × 16". Mint condition. **$300–325**

Badge, Painters Union. 1911. Labor Day Painters Union, no. 102–Cleveland, Ohio, Aide badge. 2¾" × 8½" badge with hanging tassels and fringe on the lower part. Union Bug (stamp) on the lower part of the ribbon. Very good condition. **$100–125**

Medal, Swim Race. Labor Day Swimming Medal for Lewes, Dela., from the 1956 Lewes Beach Race. Very good condition. **$10–12**

Photograph, Women Union Parade. 1909. Labor Day Parade, New York. 8" × 10". Good condition. **$10–12**

Pin, Seventh Annual Labor Day. Official souvenir badge from the Seventh Annual Labor Day Demonstration, Western Pa., Sept. 4, 1905. In the shape of Pennsylvania's traditional keystone. 2½" × 1½". Hallmarked "The Whitehead & Mead Co. Newark NJ." Very good condition. **$60–75**

Postcard, Photo. Labor Day, 1909. Woodland, Maine. Very good condition. **$15–18**

Program, Race. 1962 Du Quoin USAC Big Car Labor Day program. Very good condition. **$25–30**

Silver Bar, Sixtieth Anniversary. Labor Day silver bar. Marked 1913–1973. Very good condition. **$8–10**

Spooner, Ruby Glass. Labor Day, 1903. 3½" × 3". Good condition. **$10–12**

Stamps, International Labour Day. Sheet of stamps. 1919–1969. Near mint condition. **$8–10**

Grandparents' Day (First Sunday following Labor Day)

Marian Lucille Herndon McQuade, a housewife from West Virginia, is given credit for founding Grandparents' Day in 1970. By 1973 she had convinced the legislators in West Virginia to make it a statewide holiday, and through her efforts and the contacts her team made with governors, senators, and congressmen, she pushed the holiday through all the way to the president. In 1978 President Jimmy Carter signed a proclamation declaring that the holiday would be celebrated nationally on the first Sunday following Labor Day. McQuade became a premier proponent of senior citizens' interests and a leader in many organizations, including the Vocational Rehabilitation Foundation, the West Virginia Health Systems Agency, the Nursing Home Licensing Board, and the Bi-Centennial Centenarian Search for the West Virginia Commission on Aging.

The holiday is celebrated by families, churches, and senior organizations with special events that spotlight the contributions of grandparents. The celebrations reflect the humanitarian attitude of the holiday's founder, who has fifteen children and forty grandchildren. Because of her efforts, McQuade has received many awards and, according to the National Grandparents' Day web site, "[t]he U.S. Postal Service issued a 10th anniversary commemorative envelope bearing a likeness of Mrs. McQuade on September 2, 1989."

Hallmark Cards created a line of Grandparents' Day cards in 1978, after President Carter declared it an official holiday, and many other firms followed suit. They offered to give Mrs.

McQuade's group a small royalty to help with expenses, but she refused, saying that the holiday is not about money, but rather about the quality time intergenerational families should spend with each other.

In spite of Mrs. McQuade's insistence that the holiday is not about gifts but about family connections, there have been many items created for this holiday, including jewelry, plates, posters, postcards, greeting cards, books, and figurines.

PRICE LIST: GRANDPARENTS' DAY COLLECTIBLES

Pin, Olympic Games. 1999 Grandparents' Day for the 2002 SLC Olympic Games. Code SLO-1154. Depicts a grandmother and grandfather on a ski lift. Made by Aminco. Excellent condition.   **$5–7**

Bottle, Coca-Cola. Celebrates twentieth anniversary of Grandparents' Day. Full Coke 8 oz. bottle. Marked 1978–1998. Coke bottle number is 1998-1520. Excellent condition.   **$2–4**

Pin, Disney. Disneyland. Donald Duck's Nephews Huey, Louie, and Dewey. "Happy Grandparents' Day 2003." Limited edition (1,500). Excellent condition.   **$7–8**

Needlepoint, Charles Wysocki. The late artist Charles Wysocki created a series of original designs to commemorate specific holidays in an annual Americana Calendar. In 1994 his wife, Elizabeth, executed his design for Grandparents' Day in needlepoint. This original needlepoint is double matted and professionally framed; image measures $2\frac{7}{8}$" × $3\frac{1}{4}$"; frame $10\frac{1}{2}$" × $10\frac{1}{2}$". Signed in pen by both artists, Charles Wysocki and Elizabeth Wysocki, on the outer mat underneath the image. Excellent condition.   **$350–400**

Plate, Royal Copenhagen. 2003 Grandparents' Day plate. Depicts grandmother and granddaughter feeding chickens. Entitled "Feeding Time." $5\frac{1}{8}$" diameter. Mint condition.

$30–35

Stuffed Animal, Beanie Baby. Grams dressed in shawl and slippers. Poem reads "Grams, you're always there for me, you love me unconditionally, it brings a smile to my face when I'm in your warm embrace." Excellent condition.   **$7–10**

Plates, Two. Painted by Josep Castari "Grandparents' Day Series." Bradford Exchange Limited Edition. "The Cookie Tasting" and "The Swinger." $8\frac{1}{2}$" diameter. Bradex Number 84-K41-43 and 84-K41-44, 1982 plate number 2926F, 3rd in series. 1983 plate number C426, 4th in series. Excellent condition.   **$25–30**

Rosh Hashanah (1st and 2nd Days of the Hebrew month Tishri)

Rosh Hashanah, which means "new year" in Hebrew, is one of the most important days in the Jewish year. It is a time to celebrate the act of creation, and according to tradition, it is the time when God opens his Book of Life and decides who will live another year. It is a holy celebration marked by an expanded daily liturgy in the synagogue and a moratorium on working. The holiday begins at sunset, extends for two days, and ends at nightfall. It's a time when Jews are introspective and think about the year that has past, as well as the one they are about to begin. They ask for God's forgiveness, then pray for a good year and a good life.

A special prayer book (called a *machzor*) is used in the synagogue, and the *shofar* (a trumpet made of a ram's horn) is blown for a total of one hundred notes on each day. One of the other customs of the day is eating honey-dipped apples and bread, as well as other sweet items, which signify the wish for a good new year. Celebrants also practice *tashlikh*, or "casting off." This custom calls for Jews to walk to flowing water and empty their pockets, or throw bread crumbs, symbolically casting off their sins.

Some of the items representative of this holiday include plates, dishes, art, hanging decorations, jewelry, glassware, greeting cards, needlepoint, books, and tableware.

PRICE LIST: ROSH HASHANAH COLLECTIBLES

Art, "Rosh Hashana Meditation." By chassidic folk artist Michoel Muchnik. Limited edition giclé. 18" × 26". Excellent condition.   **$400–500**

Bezalel Cover. Machzor, Rosh Hashanah. Sinai Publishing, Tel Aviv, Israel, 1961. Large size, written in Hebrew and Yiddish, has Bezalel's cover with copper image of Jerusalem. Approximately 6¼" tall. Excellent condition.   **$40–50**

Book, *Machzor, Prague, 1846.* Jewish prayer book for second day of Rosh Hashanah. Published and printed in 1846 in Prague by M. I. Landau. This Machzor contains full page ancient engravings printed on one side of the page. 272 pages. Good condition.   **$75–90**

Challah Cover/Dekel, Israeli Silk. Handmade and hand-painted. Suitable for Rosh Hashanah and the High Holy Days. Dekel measures 16" × 20"; hand painted in Israel. Mint condition.   **$20–25**

Hanging Decoration. Rosh Hashanah Blessings. Hanging decoration. The pomegranate is decorated with Hebrew blessings for the new year. Approximately 9" long. Mint condition.   **$28–35**

Jar, Glass. Hand-painted Rosh Hashanah jar with tray. Decorated with apples. Includes glass honey spoon. 4¼" × 10". Excellent condition.   **$30–35**

Mobile, Pomegranate and Fish Mobile. For Rosh Hashanah. Silver plated pewter. 9" × 3¾". Fish's belly is a red bead and two others connect it to pewter trim. Mint condition. **$25–30**

Toys, Kids' Rosh Hashanah Set. Made by KidKraft. Hand painted wooden Rosh Hashanah set comes with everything to practice the Rosh Hashanah rituals, including a set of candlesticks, kiddush cup, apple and honey, shofar, and two round challahs. The apple slices are attached with Velcro, so children can pretend to slice the apple and dip it into the honey. Mint condition.   **$20–25**

Patriot Day (September 11)

This holiday was started by President George W. Bush on December 18, 2001, as the day when flags would be flown at half mast to remember those who perished in the attacks on

September 11, 2001. The presidential proclamation also asks that a moment of silence be observed at 8:46 A.M. to recognize the innocent victims of the terrorist attacks.

The day honors those aboard the flights that flew into the World Trade Center, the Pentagon, and the field in Somerset County, Pennsylvania, as well as the people in the World Trade Center and the Pentagon, and those who gave their lives trying to save the victims of the tragedy.

Americans display their patriotism on this day in varying ways, including flying the flag or displaying their pride on their bodies, cars, homes, or desks. Many items have been created commemorating the horrific events of that day, including jewelry, plaques, posters, T-shirts, and stuffed animals.

Price List: Patriot Day Collectibles

Art, Lithograph. "America's City of Heroes and Angels" by South Carolina artist Madeline Carol. Signed and numbered limited edition, #654 of 9/11. Shows new skyline with the Twin Towers ghosted where they once stood. In the sky, ghosted images of a peace dove and angels in the sky. 16" × 29". Title on the center bottom below the image reads "America's City of Heroes and Angels." Excellent condition.   **$40–50**

Candle Holder, Angel. Created by Heather Goldmine. White spots are light reflections and not damages. 14½" high. Two small peace doves hanging on chain in front. Inside bottom is marked "Blue Sky Corp. 2001." Front of base is hand marked "Peace," and back is signed Heather Goldmine, September 11, 2001. Excellent condition.   **$50–60**

Flag, "The Cost of Freedom." #22 of 10,000 for purchase. The limited edition flag is a copyrighted Image of the Pentagon, Trade Towers, and United Flight 93, located inside the thirteen stars and thirteen stripes, designed as a tribute to all lives lost on September 11, 2001. Mint condition.   **$375–400**

Flag, Mosaic. Made up of over 1,000 photos of 9/11. Finished picture depicts the American flag furling in the wind. Excellent condition.   **$20–25**

Gemini Jets, Model. "United We Stand" 747-400. 400 scale die-cast metal model. #1 of limited edition run of 1,000, commemorating 9/11. Excellent condition.   **$80–100**

Newspaper, *New York Times.* September 12, 2001, issue with photo of World Trade Towers in flames. Intact, never been read. Mint condition.   **$35–45**

Patch, Statue of Liberty Hero Patch. September 11, 2001. Circular patch showing the Twin Towers. Words around trim read: "Our Hearts Remember the Past, Our Eyes See the Future." Excellent condition.   **$18–22**

Pin, Disney World. Patriot Day 2004. Depicts Minnie and Mickey with their hands over their hearts. Mint condition.   **$8–10**

Print, "The Record." Fine art print. 22" × 28". Depicts firemen raising the flag in front of the downed Trade Towers. Mint condition.   **$25–30**

Quilt, handmade. September 11 Quilt. King size. Embellished with images of the World Trade Center, the American eagle, the Statue of Liberty, and the American flag. Mint condition. **$200–250**

Stuffed Animal, Eagle. Ty Valor Patriot Day Beanie Baby. Eagle has a medal hanging around his neck. Mint condition. **$8–10**

Ticket, Baseball Game. Chicago Cubs vs. Cincinnati Reds. September 11, 2001. Excellent condition. **$20–30**

– 10 –
OCTOBER

Yom Kippur (10th Day of the Hebrew month Tishri)

Yom Kippur is considered the most important Jewish holiday and is celebrated on the tenth day of *Tishri* (the seventh month of the Jewish year). Often referred to as the Sabbath of Sabbath, Yom Kippur itself means "Day of Atonement" and is the time when people of the Jewish faith atone for the sins they have committed against God throughout the past year. The sins they have committed against other humans must be dealt with separately and before Yom Kippur. In fact, they are to have righted any wrongs committed, if possible, before this holiday.

Traditionally, one does not work, eat, or drink on Yom Kippur—a complete twenty-five hour fast, starting before sunset the evening before Yom Kippur and ending after nightfall on Yom Kippur itself. In addition, the Talmud, a Jewish holy book, states that one should not anoint one's body (using deodorants, cosmetics, or perfumes), wear leather shoes, or have sexual relations. Most practitioners wear white on this holiday and some wear a *kittel*, the white robe in which the dead are buried.

Most of the day is spent in prayer at the synagogue, sometimes breaking in the middle of the day to return home briefly. At the end of the services, a long blast of the *shofar* (a trumpet made of a ram's horn) signifies the conclusion of the holiday.

A special prayer book, called the *machzor*, is used for Yom Kippur and Rosh Hashanah. A series of prayers make up the extended liturgy for Yom Kippur, including two parts for the confessional called the *Ashmanu* and *Al Chet*. *Ashmanu* is a "short list" with generalized descriptions of the transgressions of the worshipper, while the *Al Chet* is a detailed extension of what kind of sin it was and why and when it occurred. The holiday's final prayer is called *Ne'ilah* and usually lasts about an hour. People in the congregation stand during this prayer and the ark (where the Torah scrolls are kept) is open throughout. This part of the service is sometimes called "the closing of the gates" because it is the time when the worshippers try to get in one last good word for themselves before the Day of Atonement concludes. Once all the prayers are done and the holiday is over, the *shofar* is blown to signify the conclusion of the day.

PRICE LIST: YOM KIPPUR COLLECTIBLES

Art, Painting, "Yom Kippur, 1986." By the late Charles Wysocki. Original acrylic painting for an annual Americana Calendar. Double matted, professionally framed, 3½" × 3½" image size and 12" × 11½" frame size. Signed in pen by artist on the lower right side. Image features a synagogue, the Star of David, and flowers. Mint condition.   **$150–175**

Book/Artscroll, Yom Kippur. *Yom Kippur, Its Significance, Laws, and Prayer: A Presentation Anthologized from Talmudic and Traditional Sources.* By Rabbis Nosson Scherman, Hersh Goldwurm, and Avie Gold. Published by: Mesorah Publications, 1989. Soft cover; 178 pages. Excellent condition.   **$10–15**

DVD, "Story of the Yom Kippur War." October 1973. 30 minutes. Excellent condition.
          $12–15

Machzor, Yom Kippur. Made for Paris, 1852. Translation to French by Rabbi Elchanan Dorlacher. Leather binding. Very good condition.   **$20–25**

Medal, Bronze, IDF. Israel 1973. Yom Kippur war. Owl image. Very good condition.
          $10–15

Record, Israeli. Folk LP entitled "Songs of the Yom Kippur War." 1973. Features Hebrew folk and folk-pop songs about the Yom Kippur War. Very good condition.   **$6–8**

Snuff Bottle Cap, Yom Kippur. Silver set. Circa 1940. Excellent condition.   **$50–75**

Columbus Day (October 12 or first Monday in October)

Christopher Columbus, a native of Genoa, Italy, is said to have reached the New World on October 12, 1492. He had begun his journey in Spain with a fleet of three ships (the *Niña*, the *Pinta,* and the *Santa María*) and believed he would establish a new route to Japan and the East Indies. In the past, people believed he had actually reached the shores of North America, but in actuality he landed on San Salvador, a small island in the Bahamas. Although it was believed for many years that Columbus was the first explorer to reach our shores, it is more likely that others, including some Vikings, preceded him. He returned to Spain, but not before establishing a port in Santo Domingo (Hispaniola).

The Society of St. Tammany (or the Columbian Order) in New York City first celebrated Columbus's landing in 1792, three hundred years after the original event. The holiday was legally proclaimed at the opening of the Columbian Exposition in Chicago in 1892. President Benjamin Harrison was responsible for declaring the holiday a national tradition, although it was originally called Discovery Day (in the Bahamas, the holiday is still known by this title). Now, it is celebrated every year on the first Monday in October in the U.S. In New York, the holiday is traditionally celebrated with a huge parade up Fifth Avenue. Other cities and states celebrate likewise or reenact the landing or hold patriotic ceremonies. Some Latin American countries (where it is known as *Dia de la Raza* or Day of the Race), as well as cities in Italy and Spain, also celebrate Columbus's discovery, while other celebrations are distinctly anti-Columbus. Some Native American and African American groups believe that celebrating this holiday is offensive since Columbus is representative of the European invasion and massacre of indigenous peoples and, ultimately, that he greatly contributed to the enslavement of millions of people.

In recent years, the holiday has come up against some criticism, because historians have proven that Columbus was not the first explorer to reach North America. Since there are no holidays that celebrate the other explorers, some feel that Columbus Day is unfair. Others believe that, by celebrating Christopher Columbus, Native American people are being ignored. The result is that certain cities or establishments might choose to celebrate the way the town of Berkeley, California did in 1991: by canceling Columbus Day and celebrating a holiday called Indigenous Peoples Day.

Collectibles for this holiday include replicas of the ships or of Christopher Columbus, postcards, greeting cards, statues, figurines, posters, and books.

PRICE LIST: COLUMBUS DAY COLLECTIBLES

Art, Serigraph, "Christopher Columbus." Artist: Melanie Taylor Kent. Kent was the first artist to be licensed by the Walt Disney Company to portray Disney theme parks in limited edition prints. 1992. 30" × 22". Depicts the three ships sailing through the sky right past the Statue of Liberty and a sky full of fireworks. Mint condition. **$110–125**

Book, *The Life of Christopher Columbus.* Published 1891. Many illustrations and maps. Very good condition. **$100–150**

Button, Columbus Day Celebration. Victorian era. Celluloid button worded: "Columbus Day Celebration." 1¼" diameter. Reverse has a brass pin and original maker's label: "W. F. Miller, Patent Applied For, 158 Park Row, New York." Ribbon and rosette are green, white, and red (Italy's national colors). 2¹³⁄₁₆" × 4¾". Very good condition. **$48–54**

Dolls, Madame Alexander, Queen Isabella and Christopher Columbus. 8" dolls depicting the ruler of Spain who gave Columbus the wherewithal to travel across the ocean, and the explorer himself. Excellent condition. **$100–150**

Figurine, Sebastian. Christopher Columbus figure with paper Marblehead label on base. 3¾" tall. Green paper label marks the figure as a Marblehead Sebastian figure. Copyright 1951, P. W. Baston. Excellent condition. **$75–100**

Mug, Royal Doulton. Christopher Columbus character jug made by Royal Doulton. 6¼" high. Made to commemorate 500th anniversary of Columbus's discovery. Excellent condition. **$110–125**

Pin, Disney Columbus Day. Depicts Mickey as Christopher Columbus. A jumbo character pin made by Walt Disney World. Limited edition of 100. 2005. Mint condition. **$22–25**

Pinback, Christopher Columbus. Columbus's portrait flanked by both Italian and American flags. Made in New York. Martin and Naylor Co. 1¾" diameter. Excellent condition.

$12.50–15

Plate, Desimone. Depicts Christopher Columbus and the Santa Maria ship. 10" in diameter. Signed on bottom of plate. Excellent condition.

$85–100

Poster, Columbus. Depicts a tall ship ready for October 12. #6 in series of monthly inspirational posters for American school rooms. Made in 1938. Printed by T. G. Nichols & Co. of Kansas City. Excellent condition.

$10–15

Ribbon, National Public School. National Public School Celebration of Columbus Day, 1892, the 400th Anniversary of Columbus's discovery of America in 1492. Ribbon says it is an official badge, but apparently provided by Linn & Scruggs Dry Goods and Carpet Co. Very good condition.

$10–15

Teapot, Fitz & Floyd. Limited edition. #2342 of 7500. Made in 1992. Columbus holds ship in one hand and map in the other. Handle looks like rope. 8" × 10½". Mint condition.

$18–25

Halloween/All Hallows' Eve (October 31)
The Holiday

The origins of Halloween stretch back to the pagan celebration called *Samhain*, a Celtic harvest festival held to honor Saman, the lord of the dead, at the beginning of winter. People believed that the spirits of the dead roamed the earth, and it was said that Samhain was the night when the walls between the worlds of the living and the dead were thinnest. The Celts believed that all of the dead who had passed during the previous year actually united and traveled to their final resting place together on this evening.

It was a time that Druids (Celts) prayed for the dead and honored the living. Bonfires were lit, fruits and vegetables carved, and people disguised themselves with masks and costumes so that the dead would not recognize them and thus would not take them to the nether world. As celebrants hoped to appease the spirits of the dead, charms, spells, and predictions of the future were particularly important on Samhain eve.

As the Christian religion gained strength throughout the British Isles, the lines between Celtic, Druid, and pagan celebrations and Christian beliefs began to blend. Though Christians tried to change what they could about the old ways of life, they could not eradicate those beliefs that had been in place for thousands of years, so they tried to adapt the old holidays to the new, saving the dates but changing the names and meanings of the holidays themselves. Pope Boniface IV was responsible for re-creating Samhain in the seventh century. Instead of honoring spirits of the dead, the new holiday, known as All Hallows' Eve, sought to convince people to pray for the dead and honor Christian saints.

The American version of Halloween came to this country during the mid-nineteenth century with the Irish descendants of the Celts who had once celebrated Samhain. Some of the

Goblin Enjoying Ice Cream. 6" tall. 2005. Papier-mâché and wire. *Original folk art by Trout Creek Folk Art, Napa, Calif.* $145–200.

Lantern, Cob Goblin. 15½" × 5". Composition and papier-mâché. *Original design, sculpted and created by Scott Smith, owner of Rucus Studio.* $375–475.

Halloween Cat. Wooden Circa 1920. *Courtesy of Holly Knight.* $175–200.

customs they brought with them included bobbing for apples and lighting jack-o'-lanterns. Those folk customs coexisted with the agricultural traditions of the Americans with whom the Irish commingled. Thus, the harvesting of nuts and apples blended with the old pagan rituals of foretelling the future and dabbling in the occult.

Children adapted to the holiday without problem, donning masks and costumes and wandering from house to house to wish the occupants a happy Halloween in return for gifts of fruit and nuts. They were now imitating the supernatural creatures their ancestors had once feared. The trick-or-treat custom is apparently an American invention that might be related to a holiday called English Plough Day when ploughmen went begging for a gift. If they didn't receive one, they threatened to damage the area with their ploughs. If a person gave a treat, they would have good luck; if not, they would have bad luck.

The actual phrase "trick or treat" is an American phrase that dates back to the 1930s, combining the begging traditions of England with the ancient supernatural beliefs. Originally, the tricks that were played were designed to look as though otherworldly forces were behind them. Some of the tricks played during the early twentieth century included "threshold tricks" like ringing the doorbell and running away or soaping windows. Just as the farmers had to protect their crops during the ancient Samhain season, so the homeowners had to protect their homes against the trickster.

By the 1950s, children celebrating Halloween were more concerned with getting candy than with playing tricks. During the 1960s and 1970s, there were isolated instances where children themselves became victims of cruel tricks, like razor blades and pins hidden in the apples and candy that was given to trick-or-treaters. Nowadays, fewer children go door to door, with parents favoring private parties as opposed to allowing kids to roam the streets.

The Symbols

The symbols of this holiday are as rich and varied as the history behind it. We have already mentioned jack-o'-lanterns, but there are other icons just as recognizable, such as black cats, goblins, witches, costumes, bats, nuts, apples, and scarecrows.

Jack-O'-Lanterns

Jack-o'-lanterns came to the United States from England or Ireland. In the days before flashlights, people who traveled the boggy areas or marshes of the British Isles often carried lanterns lit by candles. If you were to see one of those lanterns from a distance, they would resemble a ghostly head bobbing along; thus they became called "lantern men," "will-o'-the-wisp," or "jack-o'-lantern."

Another type of light that could cause a shiver along the spines of the bravest people was the spectral light that hovered over graves that existed in marshlands. Though the light was probably a result of methane gas caused by rotting plant or animal life, it was a phenomenon that caused superstitious people to believe that the dead were waking up to walk the earth.

Combine these two types of lights, and you have a legendary folk figure called Jack-o'-lantern. The story is that Jack was a blacksmith who was so evil that he wasn't allowed in heaven, but he had outwitted the devil, so he didn't go to hell either. Instead, he was destined to wander the earth forever. To light his way, he would pick up a glowing ember with a vegetable he might be eating.

Originally, jack-o'-lanterns were turnips (Scotland) or potatoes (Ireland), but once immigrants to the United States found pumpkins, that vegetable became the one of choice for the Halloween jack-o'-lantern. Harvested at the perfect time of year, they could be displayed for more than a month, illuminated by a candle and used to symbolize the world of the dead.

Black Cats
The history of black cats begins in the Middle East, particularly Egypt, where they were worshipped as a type of divinity. The Celts believed that cats had once been evil human beings, and it was tradition during the Samhain holiday to throw cats into the fire. Cats were also believed to be helpmates to witches, since they can see at night and travel about noiselessly.

Goblins
The evil spirits said to roam the world on All Hallow's Eve were called goblins by the French, though the Celts called them leprechauns or pixies. The word goblin (or *gobelin*) comes from the Greek *kobalos*, which means rogue or knave. By the twelfth century, a cleric named Ordericus Vitalis stated that *Gobelinus* was a spirit that haunted the neighborhood of Evreux. Legend has it that these evil spirits emerged during Samhain and that they lived underground or in dark places. They wore green to blend in with the foliage around them and lived much like the faerie folk about which many Irish stories have been written. The actual history of these mythical creatures might be more linked to reality than we expect. According to some scholars, a race of small people actually might have existed during the Stone Age, and their habits could very well have been like those attributed to goblins or leprechauns, such as stealing children, holding up travelers, and threatening people. It's quite possible that these people married into the Celtic race, thus blending the lines of reality and the supernatural.

Witches
The symbol of a witch (or her hat) is linked to the actual religion practiced by people during the time of Samhain. The religion was *wicca*, which means "wise one" in the Saxon language. Witches gathered at Samhain in a sacred spot where they would initiate new witches, perform marriages, and practice fertility dances. Legend has it that they might have ridden horses or imitated that type of riding on a broomstick.

As Christianity became more powerful, the harvest festivals that the witches attended were frowned upon. Because of the knowledge these women possessed, uneducated villagers began to fear them. The witches often knew how to cure certain illnesses with natural herbs and remedies, and they could predict weather or the success of a particular harvest by using their knowledge of the moon and stars' positions in the sky. That type of power became associated with a willingness to sell one's soul. Pretty soon, members of

Witch on Owl. 22" × 8". Composition, papier-mâché, and painted fabric. Sitting on an architectural wood base. Original design. *Sculpted and created by Scott Smith, owner of Rucus Studio.* $1200–1400.

Witch Candy Container. 22" × 9". Composition, antique fabric and trims. Standing on a wood base. The witch separates under the skirt to reveal a candy container tube. *Original design, sculpted and created by Scott Smith, Rucus Studios.* $900–1000.

Folk Art Figure, "There Was an Old Witch" by Bethany Lowe Designs, Inc., 2005. 30" tall. Hand sculpted, one of a kind. *Courtesy of Bethany Lowe Designs, Inc.* $695–750.

what we now know as the wicca religion were as feared as goblins. (Gerald Gardner, a scholar of the religion and author of several books on the subject, coined the term in his 1949 book, *High Magic's Aid.*

When immigrants from Europe came to the United States, they brought these old superstitions and fears with them. Pennsylvania Dutch farm buildings sported hex signs to ward off witches, and iron and salt were placed by new babies' bedsides because they were items that witches would not touch. The image of a witch degraded to the fearful black-haired, hook-nosed version depicted in Halloween symbolism today, and black cats became their only companions.

Masks and Costumes

A great many practitioners of various religions have, at some point in time, donned a mask or costume to scare off devils or avert some type of natural crisis. Masks were worn by ancient Egyptians and sub-Saharan Africans, as well as by Aztecs, Chinese, and Native Americans. The European people are no different. Once the Samhain holiday started losing its pagan importance and Christianity began to change its meaning, Europeans did not want to be recognized if they left their houses at night during this holiday period, so they dressed up in costumes resembling the types of creatures they were most frightened of: ghosts, demons, goblins, and witches. Today, costumes are still fearful, but children are also likely to wear masks that allow them to impersonate popular figures of the day.

Bats

Bats are associated with the supernatural and with witches, and on Halloween they are used as representatives of evil. According to some sources, witches who attended a special gathering or Sabbath might rub bats' blood ointment on their bodies and include the bodies and blood of bats in their brews. Witches' cloaks also resemble the way bats' wings fold down over their bodies as they hang upside down.

Nuts and Apples

Nuts and apples are symbols of the harvest that usually occurs in early autumn, at about the same time as Halloween. In the British Isles, nuts are so strongly associated with Halloween that the holiday used to be called "Nutcrack Night." There is an old Scottish myth that if you put two nuts into a fire, believing they represented a certain couple, and the nuts burned together, the couple would be happy. If the nuts broke apart, the couple would fight and separate. It is also believed that nuts might have been "sacrificed" instead of living animals during Samhain.

Apples, a symbol of fertility, were also used to make predictions about love. Bobbing for apples was one way to find out whether a girl wanted a boy as her boyfriend: if that boy came up with an apple in his mouth, the girl wanted him; if he was unlucky and couldn't grab one, he would go loveless. In addition, peeling an apple on Halloween would allow a girl to see what her future husband's name would be. She would keep the peel in an unbroken strip, swing it three times over her head, and toss it over her left shoulder. The way the strip of peel fell would be the initial of her future husband's name.

Accordion Paper Scarecrow Decoration. Approximately 12" tall. Circa 1960s. *Courtesy of Holly Knight.* $15–20.

Scarecrows

Scarecrows symbolize harvest time, and when a scarecrow is brought out of the garden or field, it signifies the end of the summer growing season and a time to bring in the harvest to protect it from the scavengers who might eat it in the fields.

The Collectibles

Halloween collectibles number in the thousands, so collectors have a field day with this holiday. Some of the items available include art and folk art, books, candles and candle-holders, candy containers, costumes, dishes, figurines, games, greeting cards and postcards, jack-o'-lanterns, jewelry, lanterns, nodders, noisemakers, ornaments, pipes, table and party decorations, teapots, and toys. Prices for Halloween collectibles range from the inexpensive to the priceless. Because so many collectors have jumped on the Halloween bandwagon in the past decade or so, prices have risen dramatically above what was paid only ten years ago.

Art and Folk Art

Many of today's premier folk artists create items for Halloween. Some of their work echoes the items created in the past, but other artists are carving inroads with innovative new images of the holiday. Some of the artists included in this volume who create Halloween items are Bethany Lowe, C. S. Post, Jamieson Studios, Lori Ann Baker, Lori Mitchell/Ladeedah, Rucus Studio, and Trout Creek. These artists are profiled elsewhere in the book (see the Easter and Christmas sections).

Books

Books about Halloween range from children's books written about the ways to celebrate the holiday to tales of witches, goblins, and other things that go bump in the night. Collectors tend to gravitate toward brightly illustrated vintage children's books, like Robert Bright's *Georgie's Halloween* or Dennson's *Bogie Book*, a catalog of Halloween games, crafts, and fes-

Stack of Jack-O'-Lanterns. Reproduced from Vintage Originals. 4" × 4" $20; 4" × 5½" $24; 6" × 7" $28. *Courtesy of Jamieson Studios.*

Bucket O' Bunny. 12". Mohair. Original design. *Courtesy of Baker & Co.* $245.

Candy Containers, Boo Hoo Pumpkin and Sourpuss in Costume. Boo Hoo Pumpkin is 10" × 3", made of resin. $18.50–22. Sourpuss is 12" × 5", made of papier-mâché. $36.95–40. *Courtesy of Bethany Lowe Designs, Inc. 2005.*

Happy Tree Bucket. Approximately 11" tall. 2005. Papier-mâché and vellum. Happy acorn baby attached, also in papier-mâché. $110–140.

tivities. Others might want to collect books about Halloween icons, such as witches, goblins or vampires. Whatever the case, a book's condition is paramount. Watch for broken spines, foxing (discoloration or brown spots), or silverfish (a small silvery wingless insect that eats paper), which can destroy a book's value.

Candles and Candleholders

Candles and candleholders have been created for the Halloween holiday to continue the tradition of keeping a candle or lantern lit in order to either keep away spirits or to light one's way past said spirits. Most of the candles made for the holiday are figurals created in the shape of the most popular Halloween icons (witches, bats, cats, jack-o'-lanterns), and though there are many companies who have made candles for the season, the ones made by Gurley have made it into almost every collection. W & F Manufacturing of Buffalo, New York, created wax products, including Gurley candles, for many years. The height of popularity of these candles was from about 1930 to 1960, but the candles were created right up until the time the company closed in 1991.

Candy Containers

Candy containers are a very popular item during this holiday, particularly because of the trick-or-treating, but a majority of these containers are actually table decorations rather than containers a child might carry from house to house. Since more candy is sold at Halloween than at any other holiday, it makes sense that candy containers are one of the most popular collectibles. The containers hold an assortment of small candies for the holiday. Once the candies inside are eaten, children keep the containers and play with them as toys. The early containers are glass, and later versions can be pressed cardboard, plastic, or celluloid. Most candy containers are figurals, often created in the shape of Halloween icons, like witches, jack-o'-lanterns, black cats, or goblins.

The first American candy containers were produced in the late 1800s, and once their popularity was established in the early 1900s, they were manufactured for all holidays, as well as historical occasions. Molds were designed in the shape of whatever the container would be, and the glass was pressed into the mold. Once the glass container was cool, women would handpaint the decorative accents (e.g., eyes on a jack-o'-lantern or the details in a character's face). The manufacturing process continued in this manner until the Great Depression. During the Depression, there was a moratorium on producing these items, but production picked up again in 1940, when the automated assembly line made it possible to create many more types of candy containers. After this time, the metal container tops were replaced by wood, cork, or waxed cardboard. In the 1950s, glass candy containers were replaced by plastic versions.

Because of the availability of materials in one particular area of Pennsylvania, most of the manufacturers of these items were located in the towns of Jeannette and Grapeville. Some of the companies involved in producing candy containers included West Brothers Co., T. H. Stough, Westmoreland Specialty Company, Westmoreland Glass Company, Jeannette Glass Company, Victory Glass, L. E. Smith, J. H. Millstein, and J. C. Crosetti Company.

Costumes and Masks

Costumes have been worn on this holiday since it was celebrated by the ancient Celts and called Samhain. When celebrants were walking home from the bonfire, they worried about spirits, so they dressed up in costume and carved scary faces in the hollowed-out vegetables in which they held their candles so that they would scare the spirits away. The tradition continued as Christians celebrated All Hallows' Eve. Masks and costumes were often made out of bits and pieces of whatever was available, so they weren't necessarily saved. In our modern Halloween parties, adults dress up as scary figures, following the ritual created by travelers who wanted to make sure they weren't bothered by spirits. This is why witches with high cone-shaped hats, ghosts, devils, skeletons, and black cats are typically costumes created and worn by partygoers.

Before costumes and masks were produced commercially, pattern makers such as Butterick's created Halloween costume designs that home sewers could make in a variety of sizes and materials. The company, begun in 1863, offered patterns for costumes in the early 1900s. Store-bought costumes were first produced by Dennison's, the catalog company that also made paper decorating items. They offered the costumes themselves—hats, masks, wigs, teeth, beards, and makeup. Some of the costumes were made out of paper, while others used more durable material. Because they were not meant to last more than one night, costumes worn by children are not often found in excellent condition.

As the years progressed, costumes continued to resemble the most well-known Halloween icons, but today, costumes may be scary or representative of famous or infamous people. Some of the older costumes are particularly collectible since they were often discarded.

Dishes

Dishes made for the holiday are often created to hold candy and most are either in the shape of Halloween icons or decorated with the same. Many Halloween dishes are in the traditional orange and black colors. Though most of the dishes collectors find today are ceramic, there are glass, plastic, and porcelain examples as well. Most of the glass and porcelain examples tend to be vintage or antique, but in order to determine the piece's age, one should have information about the company or the design. Some of the finest porcelain companies, like Royal Doulton and Lenox, have created items for Halloween.

Figurines

Figurines of various Halloween icons have been created since the Victorian era. You can find ghosts, witches, black cats, haunted houses, and many horror characters, like Dracula, Frankenstein, werewolves, and vampires. Both vintage and contemporary examples are available. Napco, Royal Doulton, Enesco, and the George Good Corporation created figurines during the 1930s through the 1960s, and Doulton continues to produce holiday figures. Some of the more contemporary companies that produce Halloween-related figures include Department 56, Byers Choice, Boyds Bears, Snowbabies, Annalee, Charming Tails, and many others.

Games

Games have been played on Halloween since the earliest times the holiday was celebrated. In fact, bobbing for apples was played during the days when the Romans and Celts were blending the two cultures, and games of divination were played for Samhain. Those games were kept but modified a bit when the holiday became Christian. A lot of the new games were like the divination of old: fortune telling, crystal gazing, or the once-popular Oujia Board. Some of the companies that have created collectible games are R. Peck DeSnoyers, American Novelty Company, Milton Bradley, and Parker Bros.

Cards

Greeting cards and postcards made for Halloween are bright and colorful, and highly collectible. Early versions (from the turn of the century) depict the usual Halloween icons like witches, pumpkins, and frightening beings. Illustrations by certain illustrators have become as collectible as the cards themselves. For instance, John O. Winsch, a publisher of postcards from 1910 to 1915, hired several illustrators whose work has become well known. Samuel Schumacker created stunning images of women for Winsch: beautiful witches, delectable devil women, and romantic women in costumes for the Halloween holiday. Schumacker also worked for Tuck and Whitney Publishers to create series of cards and postcards for them. Another Schumacker artist, Jason Friexa, created illustrations of wide-eyed children for Halloween greeting cards and postcards. The colors are so vivid on these greeting cards and postcards because there is a high metal content in the printing process—which also makes the cards highly toxic.

Through the years, many other greeting card and postcard publishers printed Halloween cards, including Raphael Tuck, Paul Finkenrath of Berlin, Whitney Publishers, E. C. Banks, Clapsaddle, H. L. Woehler/NY, Frances Boundage, Gibson Art Company, Bernhardt Wall, and many others. There are upwards of six thousand Halloween postcards available for collectors, enough to keep anyone busy for the rest of his or her collecting career!

Jack-O'-Lanterns

Jack-o'-lanterns are one of the most popular and valued of all Halloween collectibles. Some of the earliest examples from Germany are worth thousands of dollars, while the contemporary plastic examples can be found in any discount department store. Handmade jack-o'-lanterns are increasingly difficult to find, because they are traditionally made of real pumpkins that are tossed into a compost heap after the holiday is over.

The German jack-o'-lanterns, made from the early 1900s up to the 1940s (World War II stopped the production of holiday collectibles coming from Germany), were often handcrafted and creatively designed. They were made of composition, papier-mâché, and cardboard. Though the typical "vegetable face" is common, there are other types of jack-o'-lanterns that are favorites among collectors, such as devil faces, cats, monkeys, and bears. These examples are rare, and their prices tend to be high.

American jack-o'-lanterns were made from the early 1900s, and the material used was pulp or slotted cardboard. They were not lit with candles, since that would have been extraordi-

Jack-O'-Lanterns, Germany. Composition. 4¼" tall. *Courtesy of Tom Pritchard.* $2,500–3,000 each.

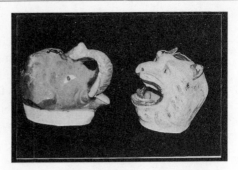

Jack-O'-Lanterns, Japanese. Elephant has inserts in eyes and mouth. Gray colored with flesh-toned trunks and white color. Top of lantern has some dents and breakage. Japanese lion lantern has original insert and great molding detail. 5½" tall. Some paint flaking. Very good condition. Rare. *Courtesy of Tom Pritchard.* $1,000–1,500.

narily dangerous. Instead, they were used as decorative accents on porches or in windows throughout the Halloween holiday season. Some of the American jack-o'-lanterns were molded into whatever shape the maker wanted.

The paper and cardboard lanterns were sold in local discount or "5 & 10¢" stores, like Woolworth's, Kresge's, and others. Sizes ranged from a couple of inches to a couple of feet, but the majority were 6–8" high. Though most examples are the typical pumpkin jack-o'-lantern, collectors are attracted to those that are not the norm, such as cat faces, devils, witches, or animals.

American pulp lanterns are reproduced by artists and companies, but if the collector remembers a few simple rules, the original will easily be recognized. For example, old versions have rounded bottoms and circular rings impressed in the bottom. New reproductions are stamped and signed by the artist. In addition, the newer versions are slightly smaller than the old ones, and the original jack-o'-lantern's nose is open while the new one is closed.

After 1950, plastic lanterns were made and often used as candy containers by trick-or-treating children. One of the companies that made hard plastic Halloween items was Rosbro. The most important thing to remember about plastic jack-o'-lanterns, as well as other plastic Halloween items, is that they have been reproduced, so the buyer should beware. Make sure the dealer you purchase your piece from is reputable and knowledgeable. Some collectors don't mind buying reproductions because the prices are more in line with their budgets, but if you are more interested in value and authenticity, you need to educate yourself about what the true originals look and feel like.

Battery-operated jack-o'-lanterns, which are a lot safer than the lighted candle or kerosene versions, appeared around 1960. Though most of the old jack-o'-lanterns that collectors will find are made of molded papier-mâché, some are made of lithographed sheet tin or flammable paper tissue, and the newer ones of plastic.

Parade lanterns created in the jack-o'-lantern image were made mostly in Europe where Halloween parades were fairly common; however, they were also used in the United States at the turn of the twentieth century. These lanterns were similar to those used at political rallies. Some are made of tin, others glass. The lantern was mounted on a pole. Because they are fairly rare, parade lanterns are pretty expensive and hard to find.

Jewelry

Halloween jewelry ranges from cheap plastic pumpkin earrings to bejeweled coffins. Though there are some vintage pieces of Halloween jewelry, it appears the majority of jewelry pieces attributed to the spooky holiday were made after 1940. Most of the pieces you'll find are made of molded plastic. As with other collectibles, the icons of the holiday are depicted on earrings, bracelets, necklaces, and rings.

Nodders

Halloween nodders (bobbers, bobbin' heads, bobbleheads) were first made in Germany during the 1930s, out of bisque. Most were fairly small (3–4" tall) and represented the typical Halloween icons. They are fairly rare (especially the nodders that are also candy containers), and are priced accordingly. In the 1950s, Japanese firms began making nodders and continued to produce the bulk of those available to collectors. The heads are made from papier-mâché. Because nodders are constantly moving, it is hard to find them in mint condition.

Noisemakers

Noisemakers have been used since the very beginning of the Halloween celebrations, when people thought that making a loud noise while out at night would scare away demons and ghosts. At first, travelers would simply bang something, but later, horns, whistles, and rattles were used. The tradition of making noise continued, and when the holiday became less connected with pagan rituals and more related to an excuse to have a party, the noisemakers were produced in decorated wood or tin. Whistles, drums, horns, tambourines, ratchets, clangers, and rattles decorated with witches, black cats, bats, skeletons, and other Halloween icons have been made by manufacturers such as Bugle Toy, Chein, Kirchhof, and T. Cohn. One of the ways a collector can determine whether the noisemaker is old is if the handle is carved wood. Later versions have plastic handles.

Because all types of noisemakers are still being produced and many of them are reproductions, the buyer should beware. Since this type of item would have been used by children and banged around on a regular basis, it will be very rare to find a noisemaker that is not showing some wear around its edges or on the handle. If it looks too new and perfect, it probably is. Remember: Halloween items were not generally put away from year to year, as Christmas decorations were, thus the perfectly preserved items are few and far between. Because of that, many companies have reproduced the most popular of the old items. If you are a collector who does not mind purchasing a less expensive reproduction, then go for it, but if you are concerned with buying only antique or vintage items, be sure to do your homework!

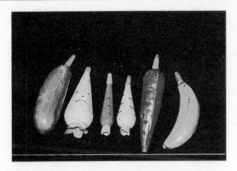

Horns, German. From 5½" to 8" long. Cardboard. *Courtesy of Tom Pritchard.* $45–85 each.

Drum whistles, German. Group of six. Paper faces and wood frames. *Courtesy of Tom Pritchard.* $85–115 each.

Noisemakers, American. *Courtesy of Tom Pritchard.* $20–40 each.

Paddles, Diecut. German. Approximately 6" long. Cardboard. *Courtesy of Tom Pritchard.* $125–300.

Ornaments

Ornaments featuring Halloween symbols were made during the end of the nineteenth and beginning of the twentieth centuries. The blown glass balls, which featured witches, skeletons, pumpkins, and the like, were created by the same companies that made Christmas decorations. These items are often part of Christmas collections, rather than Halloween. Today, one of the best known Christmas ornament makers, Christopher Radko, creates a line of Halloween ornaments, as do Krinkles, Terry's Village, Olde World Christmas, Department 56, and many others.

Party Decorations

Halloween parties were generally adult events until after World War II, and then children became the center of attention. Table and party decorations for the Halloween season were treated with less respect than those made for Christmas, so quite a few of them were disposable, made of paper or plastic. Most of the examples collectors will find date from 1900 to 1950. The Dennison Manufacturing Company in the United States is the major source for these decorations, but others were made in Japan or Germany and will be marked "Germany" or "Japan" if they were made before 1930. If they are marked "Made in Germany" or "Made in Japan," they were made from 1930 to 1941. Pieces made in Germany from 1941 to 1949 will be marked "U.S. Zone Germany."

Dennison, based in Framingham, Massachusetts, produced an abundance of decorations in the U.S. from 1909 to 1934. At one point in the early 1900s, there were ten thousand dealers of Dennison products in the United States. In addition to supplying paper goods, they also created a popular catalog called *Dennison's Bogie Book*, a party book containing suggestions for decorating the table, creating invitations, staging games, making costumes, and carving pumpkins. The books themselves, which were put out annually, have become a hot collectible. Due to the suggestions made by Dennison's, the business of Halloween decorations expanded exponentially, and soon the whole country enjoyed dangling orange and black streamers in their dining rooms, bought cardboard cutout decorations for their doors and windows, and set their tables with accordion-style figures of skeletons and black cats. Paper napkins matched paper plates and cups, paper bats and jack-o'-lanterns decorated the walls, and pumpkin centerpieces sat in the middle of the party table.

Dennison was bought out by Avery in 1990, and the new company was called Avery Dennison. They are still in the business of making paper products, but the party side of the business does not thrive to the same extent that it did during the mid-twentieth century.

Today's party supplies largely come from overseas manufacturers, with no single company maintaining a corner on the market, yet the Beistle Company, an American company, is probably the most important to Halloween collectors. The Beistle Company of Shippensburg, Pennsylvania, the major producer of party decorations during the early 1900s, is still in business today. Like many other businesses, Beistle stopped producing during World War II, concentrating instead on the war effort. After the war, however, business went back to normal. There are several signatures and marks used by this manufacturer during the time it produced collectible Halloween items, including "Copyr. H.E. Luhrs" (Luhrs became the president of the company), the printed signature (The Beistle Company), the Beistle Diamond trademark, "Bee-Line" (or the symbol of bee in flight), and Art Tissue Westminster Bells (tissue). The marks are embossed, stamped, printed, or applied with a paper label, depending upon the type of product. The Beistle Company is still in business today, and their Halloween items include diecut jointed figures, party decorations, centerpieces, and floor displays.

Teapots and Tea Sets
Teapots and tea sets have been created in the shape of Halloween icons, such as jack-o'-lanterns. German, Japanese, and American versions are available for today's collectors, and values are determined by the country of origin, as well as manufacturer, condition, and rarity. Children's tea sets with flying witch transfer decorations were available in America at the end of the nineteenth century, but most were made in Germany or England.

Toys and Gag Toys

The toys available for the Halloween collector include all of the monster toys, like Dracula, Frankenstein, the Munsters, ghosts, scary movie figures, as well as toys that contribute to the spooky, creepy, horrible aspect of the holiday. Some of the items that would normally be included in the toy category have already been described because they are collectible in their own right, like nodders, noisemakers, and games.

Rosbro, the company that made quite a few of the hard plastic candy containers and jack-o'-lanterns, made a series of Halloween pull toys (some of which were also candy containers).

Since Halloween is also a "dark comic" occasion, collectors will discover some gag toys like H. Fishlove & Co.'s Talking Skull. Other Halloween gag gifts include bugs in fake ice, remote controlled cockroaches, bats, or spiders, and rubber severed fingers or fake brains.

Jack-in-the-box toys have been created since the turn of the century, but the majority were produced during the period from the 1920s to the 1960s. One of the most desirable jack-in-the-box figures is the devil, though other Halloween icons have been made as well.

Movies that inspire toys that fall into the Halloween category include *Nightmare Before Christmas, Halloween* (all 9 versions), *Beetlejuice, Frankenstein, Dracula, The Werewolf, Friday the 13th, The Addams Family,* and many others. Character figures are popular, as are mechanical toys, games, costumes, masks, dolls, candy, lifesize props, and the standard movie collectibles: posters, ads, and the movies themselves.

PRICE LIST: HALLOWEEN COLLECTIBLES

3-D Picture. U.S. 7" tall witch stirring a cauldron candle scene in relief. Very hard to find. Very good condition. **$45–65**

Album, Napkins. U.S. Album of miscellaneous napkins, variety of designs. Many hand-tinted. 30+ napkins ranging from common to hard to find. Hard to find. Very good condition. **$60–80**

Animatronic, Shivering Mummy. Free-standing prop made of hard, durable foam with elastic and spring loaded joints allows the internal motor to make this mummy shake and shiver. 5' tall. Can be plugged into 110-volt plug. Excellent condition. **$300–350**

Blowout, Jack-O'-Lantern Face. Molded cardboard, German. Round, orange, angry face with blue eyes. Works great. Hard to find. Excellent condition. **$65–75**

Bobber, Jack-O'-Lantern. German. Jack-O'-Lantern head bobber with pickle nose. Has bow tie and bowler hat, but no arms. Pull slide bottom. Rare. Near mint condition. **$700–800**

Bobblehead, Halloween Witch. German. 6½" high. Made of paper, papier-mâché, and composition. Brim of hat and base are cardboard, and bottom marked "Made In Germany" in a circle. Wooden post and spring inside of the head. Head nods really well. Very good condition. **$800–875**

Bowl, Halloween Memories. 2004. Ceramic. *Courtesy of Bethany Lowe Designs, Inc.* $25.50–30.

Book, *Dennison's Bogie Book.* Picture of two kids peering over pumpkin with witch coming out of it. Great graphics. Marked with original price of 10 cents. Very hard to find. Excellent condition. **$135–160**

Book, *Dennison's Bogie Book.* Circa 1924. Haunted tree picture and little boy carrying pumpkin on front. Great graphics. Very hard to find. Excellent condition. **$105–130**

Book, *Dennison's Bogie Book.* Circa 1926. Black and orange cover that offers ideas on how to entertain on Halloween. Great graphics. Very hard to find. Excellent condition. **$145–165**

Book, *Dennison's Bogie Book.* Circa 1922. Price of 5 cents on cover. Full of decorating ideas, costumes, games. Very good condition. **$500–525**

Bounce House, Inflatable. Measures 10' × 8' × 9'. Includes foam entrance mat and fan marked "Classified UL Listed Commercial" then plugs into any standard outlet, cinch straps with wheels, spiral stakes, and a repair kit. Made by Gemmy Industries. Very good condition. **$275–300**

Bowl, Halloween Memories. Images of Halloween encircle perimeter of the bowl. Orange and black checkered rim. Inside of bowl is decorated with Halloween sayings. Ceramic. Introduced in 2004. Mint condition. **$25.50–30**

Bracelet, Vintage. Charm bracelet with glass beads. Thirteen pewter charms depicting the typical Halloween icons: black cat, bat, scarecrow, web and dangling spider, devil with pitchfork, skeleton, witch face, spider, owl, witch, trick or treat bag with dangling candy, skull, and cat. Bracelet is 7½", 8" including closure. Excellent condition. **$30–40**

Cabinet, The Witch's Pantry, King of Mice Studios. Original, one-of-a-kind, large solid wood cabinet, featuring an auburn-haired witch reaching for something to throw in her cauldron. Her black cat dozes on the shelf above. Fine details such as the pumpkin knobs, and the many jar labels, books, herbs, and utensils. Hand-painted in acrylics and finished with a clear acrylic varnish. Signed and dated on the bottom by the artist. Measures 31" × 10½" × 5". Mint condition. **$650–800**

Candleholder, Witch Taper, Pam Schifferl Collection. #553046 Pam Schifferl witch taper candleholder. 4½" × 11", made of resin and metal. Does not include a candle. Pam Schifferl will not be producing items with Midwest after 2005, so this is highly collectible. Mint in box. **$35–45**

Candleholder. Probably U.S. 7" metal candleholder with painted witch on a moon. Handle on wall for hanging. Hole in handle for hanging. Minor wear on paint. Circa 1930s. Excellent condition. **$175–225**

Candle, Owl and Pumpkin Scene. U.S. 7" × 1½" candle with scene of an owl and pumpkin on one side, witch and pumpkin on the other. Burnt a little bit. Hard to find. Good condition. **$25–40**

Candle, Skeleton. U.S. 9" Gurley skeleton with orange cape. Candle in relief. A little bit dirty. Hard to find. Good condition. **$60–80**

Candle, Skull. U.S. 7" tall Gurley orange skull candle. One slight indentation by the mouth. Hard to find. Very good condition. **$10–15**

Candle, Witch. U.S. 5" wax witch head candle with candle holder in rear. Unused. Very hard to find. Excellent condition. **$95–115**

Candle, Witch. U.S. 8" tall Gurley witch candle. Fairly common. Excellent condition. **$20–30**

Candles, Gurley, Group. Four candles. All 4–5" tall. Two ghosts, a pumpkin boy, and a witch. Common. Very good condition. **$60–75**

Candles, Gurley. U.S. Group of Gurley candles includes three pumpkins, a Jack-O'-Lantern wearing a tall witch's hat, a witch's face, a black cat, and an owl. Common. Very good condition. **$35–50**

Candles, Gurley. U.S. Group of Gurley candles includes two pumpkins, two pumpkin figures, a black cat, a witch, and an owl. Common. Very good condition. **$65–75**

Candy Box, Kitty. German composition kitten perched on a candy box. 2" tall. Hard to find. Very good condition. **$155–175**

Candy Container, Bee. German. 11" tall. Molded cardboard with reticulated neck. Separates in middle for candy. Chenille arms and antennae with original paper eyes. Slight crazing on feet and neck. Replaced antennae. Rare. Very good condition. **$575–625**

Candy Container, Black Cat on Jack-O'-Lantern. German. Composition. Original bottom. Great face, some paint crazing and flaking. 6" tall. Very hard to find. Very good condition. **$225–250**

Candy Container, Black Cat. Composition. 3" black cat on small candy box. Minor chips on ears. Hard to find. Good condition. **$125–150**

Candy Container, Black Cat. German. 2½" black cat on jack-o'-lantern candy container. Almost miniature. Missing plug. Scarce. Excellent condition. **$325–350**

Candy Container, Black Cat. German. Composition. 6" tall. Scarce. Excellent condition. **$55–75**

Candy Container, Black Cat. German. Nodding black cat on nervous pumpkin. Cat head on a string, crepe bow tie. 3½" tall. Scarce. Excellent condition.   **$475–500**

Candy Container, Black Cat. U.S. 7" papier-mâché black cat. American pulp kitty with large open sack for candy on back. Very hard to find. Excellent condition.   **$450–500**

Candy Container, Boy in Sailor Suit. German. 3" tall. Boy carries jack-o'-lantern balloon. Exquisite detail in painting. Minor flaking on feet of boy. Scarce. Excellent condition.   **$650–700**

Candy Container, Cat on Pumpkin. German. Papier-mâché. 4". Original pull-slide. Scarce. Very good condition.   **$350–375**

Candy Container, Chef. German. 4½" tall composition chef. Slight dirt from wear. Scarce. Very good condition.   **$475–500**

Candy Container, Devil Head. German. 3¾" composition devil head container with crepe color. One minor flake above right eye. Very hard to find. Excellent condition.   **$500–600**

Candy Container, Devil. German. 6" composition devil candy container with scuffing on nose, ears, and horn. Replaced plug. Scarce. Very good condition.   **$475–525**

Candy Container, Figure, Witch. U.S. 8" papier-mâché witch container has wear to brim of hat and face. Very hard to find. Good condition.   **$350–400**

Candy Container, Goblin. German. Composition. 3" high. Green outfit, dark hair, black shoes. Stands on blue container. Hard to find. Near mint condition.   **$60–75**

Candy Container, Goblin. German. Composition. 3" high. Green hat, yellow outfit. Stands on blue container. Hard to find. Near mint condition.   **$60–75**

Candy Container, Goblin. German. Composition. 3" high. Very large ears, black hat, yellow outfit. Stands on blue round container. Hard to find. Near mint condition.   **$205–225**

Candy Container, Goblin. German. Composition. 3" high. Orange face and green outfit, including hat. Stands on bluish round container. Rare. Near mint condition.   **$105–125**

Candy Container, Jack-O'-Lantern. U.S. 7" papier-mâché, solid-faced jack-o'-lantern candy container. Very hard to find. Near mint condition.   **$105–125**

Candy Container, Jack-O'-Lantern. Probably German. Glass container. Early 1900s. Has most of its original paint, original metal bell and screw lid. Very hard to find. Excellent condition.   **$400–450**

Candy Container, Jack-O'-Lantern. Probably German. Glass container. Early 1900s. Lemon-colored eyes. Original metal bale and screw lid. Rare. Excellent condition.   **$400–450**

Candy Container, Large Witch. Witch in dress with crescent moon and star design and wearing orange cape, holds staff with black cat bucket hanging on it and carries jack-o'-lantern. 19" × 8". Made of resin. Introduced in 2004. Mint condition.   **$110–130**

Candy Container, Lollipop Lady. German. 7½" tall. Jack-o'-lantern face lady with stiff neck and cardboard body. Great paint, slight bend on one of her arms. Scarce. Excellent condition.   **$275–300**

Candy Container, Owl. U.S. Papier-mâché owl. 10" tall. Glass eyes. Hard to find. Excellent condition. **$335–360**

Candy Container, Pirate. German. 4½" tall composition pirate candy container with saber. Scarce. Excellent condition. **$450–500**

Candy Container, Pulp Owl. U.S. Made by Unger Toy Company American. Orange owl with yellow eyes. Has the original Unger label on base. 10½" tall. Scarce. Very good condition. **$175–200**

Candy Container, Pumpkin Boy with Parade Lantern. German. 4½" tall pumpkin-headed boy. Early composition. Head lifts off for candy. Rare. Excellent condition. **$700–750**

Candy Container, Pumpkin Boy. German. 7" wood and felt-bodied spring neck, cardboard pumpkin-headed candy container. His backpack is the candy container. Small tear below mouth. Rare. Very good condition. **$500–600**

Candy Container, Pumpkin Girl. German. 7" pumpkin girl candy container with molded cardboard head, crepe bonnet, and dress. Candy tube and closure are missing. Very hard to find. Very good condition. **$125–150**

Candy Container, Pumpkin Girl. German. 6½" tall. Composition. Wears white bonnet, blue kerchief around neck, red and white blouse, purplish skirt, yellow shoes. Scarce. Excellent condition. **$350–375**

Candy Container, Pumpkin-head Man. German. 4½" tall. Composition pumpkin-head man carrying a bat and wearing a hat. Very hard to find. Very good condition. **$325–350**

Candy Container, Pumpkin Head Sandlot Sammy. German. 3½" tall. Early composition piece. Sammy wears a striped shirt and carries a ball. Head lifts off for candy. Very little wear to piece. Scarce. Excellent condition. **$550–600**

Candy Container, Pumpkin Head Witch. German. 3½" tall. Witch holds black cat. No hair on the witch's head. Little scuffing on cat and hat, bit of dirt wear. Scarce. Very good condition. **$250–275**

Candy Container, Pumpkin Head Witch. German. 6" tall. Original broom. Slight scuffing and crazing. Scarce. Excellent condition. **$525–550**

Candy Container, Pumpkin Head Witch. German. 7" tall. Head lifts off. Slight crazing in eyes. Collar needs glue where candy comes out of head. Broom has been replaced. Scarce. Very good condition. **$375–400**

Candy Container, Pumpkin Head. German. 6" composition candy container with pumpkin head. Nose paint has worn off. Scarce. Very good condition. **$400–450**

Candy Container, Pumpkin-headed Boy. German. 4" tall. Composition. Pull off head. Great face. Very hard to find. Excellent condition. **$295–325**

Candy Container, Pumpkin Man. German. 6" composition head pumpkin man. Circa 1920s. Appears to have high collar white shirt, green ascot, and yellow vest. Scarce. Excellent condition. **$525–550**

Candy Container, Pumpkin Man. German. 9" tall cardboard pumpkin man. Bobbing pumpkin head on spring. Open ball type bottom. Scarce. Very good condition. **$325–350**

Candy Container, Pumpkin Wearing Party Hat. German. 9½" high. Cardboard candy container with reticulated neck, crepe around the brim. Crepe ball and fringe on hat. Small flaking. Has original "Jordan Marsh" (Boston) price sticker (75 cents). Rare. Excellent condition. **$575–625**

Candy Container, Radish Head. German. 6½" tall. Cardboard spring neck and arms. Small old tape mark on stomach where ball separates for candy. Scarce. Very good condition. **$125–150**

Candy Container, Red Cat. German. 3" tall. Composition cat on candy box. Scarce. Excellent condition. **$185–215**

Candy Container, Standing Jack-O'-Lantern Man. German. 14" tall. Cardboard Jack-O'-Lantern head, black hat. Body slides open in the center for candy. Wood base, dressed in shredded crepe. Rare. Excellent condition. **$1,000–1,250**

Candy Container, Standing Witch. U.S. Huyler Candy Company 6" witch candy container. Composition head with exquisite detail. Felt clothing, wood base. Pulls apart at waist for candy. Some paint crazing. Scarce. Very good condition. **$775–850**

Candy Container, Veggie Boy Straddling Pumpkin. German. 3½" tall. Composition. Original pull plug, very early primitive piece. Minor paint loss, hairline on side. Scarce. Very good condition. **$425–475**

Candy Container, Witch on Rocket. U.S. Large, hard plastic, witch on rocket with pumpkin wheels. Original candy and wrapper. 8" × 5½". Scarce. Mint condition. **$500–550**

Candy Container, Witch, Composition. German. 3¾" tall. Slight crazing. Dress is red. Black hat has red stripe. Hard to find. Very good condition. **$95–115**

Candy Container, Witch. German. 4" witch on pumpkin. Pull out bottom. Hard to find. Very good condition. **$425–475**

Candy Container, Witch. German. 6" composition witch without hat. Replaced plug, some wear on face. Scarce. Good condition. **$350–400**

Candy Container, Witch. Japan. 5¼" tall cardboard witch. Slight rubs on nose and chin. Circa 1920s. Scarce. Very good condition. **$575–625**

Candy Container, Witch. Probably German. Original metal base. 4¾" tall (5½" to top of bale). Paint in good condition. Original bale and closure. Rare. Very good condition. **$550–600**

Candy Container/Lantern, Black Cat. German. 30" high combination candy container/lantern. 6" lantern molded cardboard head, reticulated neck. Head and shoulders lift off from body to reveal candy holder. Protruding glass eyes and red glass nose. Whole piece is flocked. Minor repair done inside neck on string to enable neck to move back and forth. Restoration to left foot. Rare. Very good condition. **$2,750–3,000**

Candy Container/Nodder. German. Vegetable head combination nodder and candy container. Featured on cover of *Halloween in America*. Slight hairline in head. Scarce. Very good condition. **$525–575**

Candy Container/Squeaker/Mechanical, Pumpkin-headed Clown. German. 10" tall pumpkin-headed composition and wood clown. When squeezed, tongue sticks out and he

Candy Containers, Pumpkin with Cat and Old Witch. Both 2001. Pumpkin is 5" × 8", made of papier-mâché. $19.95–23. Old Witch is 4" × 9", made of resin. $24.95–28. *Courtesy of Bethany Lowe Designs, Inc.*

squeaks. Raise him up to reveal candy box on base. Arms move up and down. Dressed in felt, crepe accessories. Rare. Excellent condition. **$600–700**

Candy Containers, Boo Hoo Pumpkin and Sourpuss in Costume. Boo Hoo is jack-o'-lantern on skinny legs standing on circular container. 10" × 3", made of resin. Sourpuss is a black cat in skeleton costume, holding skull on stick and carrying jack-o'-lantern bucket. 12" × 5", made of papier-mâché. Both figures were introduced in 2005. Mint condition. **Boo Hoo: $18.50–22. Sourpuss: $36.95–40**

Candy Containers, Pumpkin with Cat and Old Witch. Both introduced in 2001. Pumpkin is a bucket with curly wire handle. 5" × 8", made of papier-mâché. Mint condition. **$19.95–23**

Old Witch Candy Container. 4" × 9", made of resin. Mint condition. **$24.95–28**

Candy Tin, Mrs. Stevens. U.S. 10" diameter tin with witch on broom on cover. Mrs. Stevens homemade candy. Minor wear. Great graphics. Very hard to find. Very good condition. **$45–65**

Chocolate Molds, Jack-O'-Lantern. Two-part early metal mold with three pumpkin molds. Scarce. Excellent condition. **$255–275**

Costume, Chewbacca from Star Wars. Made by Rubies Costume Company, comes complete with body suit and mask completely covered with hand-layered multicolored long hair fur, for an authentic "blended" look complete with latex hands, bandolier, and pouch. An official Star Wars costume. Extra Large. New. Mint condition. **$375–400**

Costume, Beatles' Yellow Submarine. Costume made by Collegeville. The mask is the blue-faced creature from the movie. Original cellophane is 100% intact. $1.99 price sticker on the front. Near mint condition. **$550–600**

Costume, Disney Beauty and the Beast. Plush costume of the Beast from Disney Store. One piece plush jumpsuit with attached cape, hand and feet covers, and beast hood. Size 7/8. Very good condition. **$100–125**

Cutout Halloween Decorations, Cardboard. Two movable black cats. One pumpkin. One black cat face. Circa 1950s. Excellent condition. **$45–55 each**

Dancing Figures. U.S. Lot of two paper honeycombed dancing figures with crepe accordion arms and legs. One cat and one witch. Unused. Hard to find. Excellent condition. **$35–50**

Die-cut, Arched Black Cat. German. 5" tall. Black and orange. Very hard to find. Very good condition. **$55–70**

Die-cut, Bat in Crescent Moon. German. 5" in diameter. Full circle die-cut depicts bat, crescent moon and star. Orange and black. Very hard to find. Excellent condition. **$95–115**

Die-cut, Betty Boop Pumpkin Face. German. 9½" diameter. Hard to find. Excellent condition. **$105–125**

Die-cut, Black Cat Face. German. 13" tall. Slight loss of paint in the eyes. Hard to find. Very good condition. **$85–115**

Die-cut, Black Cat Face. German. 9" tall. Hard to find. Excellent condition. **$105–125**

Die-cut, Black Cat with Cane. German. 15½" tall standing cat with cane wearing hat and big orange bow tie, as well as orange shorts. Minor scuffing. Hard to find. Very good condition. **$55–75**

Die-cut, Black Face Jack-O'-Lantern. German. 13" tall, 16" wide. Minor wear on top, stem, and ruffles. Slight bend in ear. Extremely hard piece to find and largest version of this piece. Scarce. Excellent condition. **$250–300**

Die-cut, Devil. German. 19½" tall. Slight scuffing on nose and crazing. Black and orange. Holds pitchfork. Hard to find. Very good condition. **$95–105**

Die-cut, Flying Witch on Broom. German. Orange and black. 13½" with original easel stand. Hard to find. Very good condition. **$85–100**

Die-cut, Flying Witch. German. 5" tall. Black and orange. Very hard to find due to unusual size. Very good condition. **$50–65**

Die-cut, Jack-O'-Lantern. German. 13" with tissue backed nose, eyes, and mouth. Slight bend in the stem. Very hard to find. Excellent condition. **$80–100**

Die-cut, Lady with a Cat. German. 3" standup figure of jack-o'-lantern lady figure with cat. Orange and black. Hard to find. Excellent condition. **$65–85**

Die-cut, Mickey Mouse Band Members (Six). All are 7½" tall. One plays trumpet, the next plays sax, next is on accordion, then the drums, the banjo, and bass drum. Each is in excellent condition and all are very hard to find. **Values range from $65–125**

Die-cut, Owl on Branch. German. 5" tall. Black and orange. Hard to find. Very good condition. **$65–80**

Die-cut, Owl on Crescent Moon. German. 3" tall. Dated 10/12/29. Hard to find. Excellent condition. **$80–100**

Die-cut, Owl. German. Has very large eyes and outspread wings. Brown, yellow and orange. 11" × 14½". Very hard to find. Very good condition. **$115–125**

Die-cut, Sitting Cat. German. 3" tall. Standup figure. Hard to find. Excellent condition.
$65–85

Die-cut, Standing Cat. German. 3" tall. Black cat wearing big orange bow. Hard to find. Excellent condition. $55–75

Die-cut, Standing Cat. German. 3" tall. Standing cat wearing big orange bow. Very hard to find. Excellent condition. $110–130

Die-cut, Walking Witch. German. 15½" tall. Slight wear on paint, slight tear on dress, slight crazing. Black, orange and white. Holds cane and has broom over shoulder. Very good condition. $100–115

Die-cut, Waving Skeleton. German. 19" skeleton with slight rubs and creases. Very hard to find. Good condition. $85–100

Die-cut, Witch Carrying Broom. German. 3" tall. Orange and black. Hard to find. Excellent condition. $85–105

Die-cut, Witch Head. German. Glossy finish. Slight creases to hair on right side. Very hard to find. Very good condition. $75–100

Ephemera, Party Goods. U.S. Selection of party cards, tally cards, and party invitations from 1930s–1940s. Very good condition. $30–50

Fence, Cardboard. American paperboard "fence" with scarecrow, black cat, and pumpkin. Hard to find. Near mint condition. $80–100

Fence, Paper. U.S. Dennison fence scene. 3 sections: 5½" tall × 7" wide. Pumpkin-headed people decorate whole fence. Very hard to find. Very good condition. $65–85

Figure, Black Cat. German. Composition spring-necked figure. 3" tall. Great grin. Minor crazing. Very hard to find. Excellent condition. $175–200

Figure, Folk Art. "Fright Flight" by Bethany Lowe Designs, Inc. 24" × 20" × 62". Depicts witch in flying car. Pumpkin figure hangs off front bumper and dressed black cat off back bumper. Hand sculpted, one of a kind. Introduced 2005. Mint condition. $5,995–6,500

Figure, Folk Art. "Get Spooked" by Bethany Lowe Designs, Inc. 31" tall. Pumpkin head figure in patchwork quilt jacket and tall hat with jack-o'-lantern design. Wears short pants and striped stockings. Holds sign that says "get spooked" and a candy container. Introduced 2005. Hand sculpted, one of a kind. Mint condition. $695–750

Figure, Folk Art. "Halloween Queen" by Bethany Lowe Designs, Inc. 30" tall. Depicts witch in gray plaid skirt, black velvet jacket, conical hat. Carries broom in one hand and jack-o'-lantern on stick in the other hand. Introduced 2003. Hand sculpted, one of a kind. Mint condition. $595–750

Figure, Folk Art. "Large Folk Art Witch" by Bethany Lowe Designs, Inc. 41" tall. Depicts witch in crooked black hat, carrying crooked broom, dressed in tattered clothes in patchwork style. Introduced 2005. Hand sculpted, one of a kind. Mint condition. $1,795–2,000

Figure, Folk Art. "Party Pumpkin" by Bethany Lowe Designs, Inc. 24" high. Depicts pumpkin-faced figure dressed in black cap and matching clown-type jacket with large ruffled color and striped stockings. Holds cone-shaped candy container. Introduced 2005. Hand sculpted, one of a kind. Mint condition. **$695–750**

Figure, Folk Art. "There was an Old Witch" by Bethany Lowe Designs, Inc. 30" tall. Depicts witch with full gray hair, wearing black cape, red checked blouse and long white apron. Wears tall coned hat, carries stick with black cat head on end and has a conical shaped candy container over her arm. Introduced 2005. Hand sculpted, one of a kind. Mint condition. **$695–750**

Figure, Folk Art. "Top Hat Cat" by Bethany Lowe Designs, Inc. 27" tall. Black cat figure dressed in short orange pants, wearing striped stockings, tall hat with jack-o'-lantern design, and holds an orange wreath. Introduced 2005. Hand sculpted, one of a kind. Mint condition. **$695–750**

Figure, Jack-O'-Lantern Head. 5½" lantern-headed figure. Base was added to provide greater stability. Original insert. Small, repairable fracture around eye. Great paint. Scarce. Very good condition. **$1,500–1,750**

Figure, Morgan with Witch Mask. Little girl parading as witch, wearing green cape and orange witch's hat, holding mask away from face. 7" × 3½". Introduced in 2005. Mint condition. **$28.50–34**

Figure, My First Halloween, Lang & Wise. #20010804 Pumpkin Shed (retired). Part of "My First Halloween Village." Lighted, with decorative box with molded styrofoam 6" × 4½". Near mint condition. **$80–100**

Figure, Party Goater. Depicts jack-o'-lantern figure riding a goat; figure holds a black cat face on stick. 9½" × 4". Made of resin. Introduced in 2003. Mint condition. **$29.95–35**

Figure, Ride a Jack Pumpkin. Masked boy holding lantern and candy bucket sits astride large pumpkin. 9½" × 7". Introduced 2004. Mint condition. **$44.95–50**

Figure, Spencer in Skeleton Suit. 7½" × 2" tall little boy in skeleton costume, carries skeleton head on stick. Figure made of resin. Introduced in 2005. Mint condition. **$24.95–30**

Figure, Standing Jack-O'-Lantern Figure. 3" tall. Figure has pointed hat and big green bow tie. Hard to find. Excellent condition. **$70–100**

Figure, Turnip Horn. German. 6½" cardboard turnip face with big scowl. Very hard to find. Very good condition. **$145–170**

Figure, Witch Sitting on Pumpkin. U.S. 6" papier-mâché witch on pumpkin. Hard to find. Excellent condition. **$125–150**

Figures, Folk Art, Boo Tuxedo Pumpkin Man and Pumpkin Queen. Designed by Folk Artist Dee Foust for Bethany Lowe Designs. Boo Tuxedo: 18" × 5½"; made of paper pulp. Introduced in 2004. **$44.50–50.** Pumpkin Queen: 14" × 7"; made of paper pulp. Introduced in 2004. Mint condition. **$39.95–45**

Figures, Folk Art, Pumpkin Skeletons. From the Hobgoblins collection. Designed by Bethany Lowe Designs from the vintage and antique holiday collections of Bruce Elsass. Figures have pumpkin heads and skeleton bodies. Both appear to be dancing. 8½" × 7";

Morgan with Witch Mask. 2005. 7" × 3½". *Courtesy of Bethany Lowe Designs, Inc.* $28.50–34.

Party Goater. 2003. 9½" × 4". Made of resin. *Courtesy of Bethany Lowe Designs, Inc.* $29.95–35.

papier-mâché heads; paper wrapped wire frame bodies. Introduced in 2005. Mint condition. **$52–55**

Figurine, Bride of Frankenstein, Creepy Hollow Collection. #06663-8 Bride of Frankenstein (retired). The Bride of Frankenstein is an early accessory for the Creepy Hollow Collection. High quality resin, 3" high. Rare. Excellent condition. **$25–35**

Figurine, Cat Witch, Eddie Walker Collection. #16571-3 Cat Witch (retired). 11½" high, made of resin, carries a pumpkin in hand and wears an apron. Excellent condition. **$80–100**

Figurine, Composition. German. 5¾" composition devil straddling skull lantern. Scarce. Near mint condition. **$950–1,000**

Figurine, Outhouse, Creepy Hollow Collection. #10648-6 Resin Outhouse (retired). Outhouse with ghost lurking out back. Made of resin, 3" high. Excellent condition. **$18–25**

Figurines, Pam Schifferl Enchanted Hallow's Eve collection. #471326 Pam Schifferl Halloween characters: Owl, Black Cat, Witch, Pumpkin-head Man, set of four. Made of resin, stand 5" high. Excellent condition. **$45–55**

Finger Puppet, Kooky Spooky Ghost. Ghost holding umbrella. Approximately 3¼", without umbrella, ghost is yellow and umbrella has hot pink trim. Marked on the back "Hasbro, 1966, Hong Kong." Good condition. **$325–340**

Folk Art Cat, Ratchet Dance, Scott Smith Rucus Studio. Dancing cat with Halloween ratchet is an original handcrafted collectible made in the U.S. by Scott Smith of Rucus Studio. This piece is made of composition, papier-mâché, fabric, and wood. Measures 11" tall. Mint condition. **$250–350**

Folk Art, Acorn Prince. Papier-mâché and dried moss. 9" tall. Original folk art by Trout Creek Folk Art, Napa, Calif., 2001. New. Mint condition. **$110–125**

Folk Art, BeWitched. 7" tall. Papier-mâché. ©Lori C. Mitchell, 2004. Mint condition. **$210–230**

Folk Art, Black Cat Boogie. 9" tall. Papier-mâché. ©Lori C. Mitchell, 2004. Mint condition. **$225–250**

Folk Art, Candy Container, Halloween Pig Ride. Made in the traditional German style, using composition, antique fabric from a child's costume and sitting on candy container flocked pig. The pig separates at the head and body to reveal a candy container tube. Approximate size: 13" × 11". Original design, sculpted and created by Scott Smith, owner of Rucus Studio. New. Mint condition. **$475–575**

Folk Art, Candy Container, Missy Mouse's Carriage Ride. 7" × 5". Papier-mâché. ©Lori C. Mitchell, 2004. **$250–275**

Folk Art, Faerie Halloween Chair. Papier-mâché and wire. 8" to the top of chair bank. Back of chair looks like a leaf, attached to chair with spider web. Original folk art by Trout Creek Folk Art, Napa, Calif., 2005. New. Mint condition. **$85–105**

Folk Art, Figure, Witch of Cobbler Hollow. Made using composition and an antique shoe last. Approximate size: 8½" × 9". Original design, sculpted and created by Scott Smith, owner of Rucus Studio. New. Mint condition. **$190–250**

Folk Art, Fly Gal. Papier-mâché on a wood base. 8" tall. Turnip body, cabbage head, dressed in Halloween skirt, handbag, and hat. Original folk art by Trout Creek Folk Art, Napa, Calif., 2003. New. Mint condition. **$135–175**

Folk Art, Ghostie Bucket. Bucket has ghostly face, handle, and three feet. Papier-mâché. 4" tall. Original folk art by Trout Creek Folk Art, Napa, Calif., 2000. New. Mint condition. **$55–75**

Folk Art, Happy Tree Bucket. Papier-mâché and vellum bucket with jack-o'-lantern type face on it. Approximately 11" tall. Happy acorn baby attached; also in papier-mâché. 2005. Mint condition. **$110–140**

Folk Art, Jack Sprat. 6" tall. Papier-mâché. ©Lori C. Mitchell, 2004. Mint condition. **$225–250**

Folk Art, Kitty Back Jack. 8" tall. Papier-mâché. ©Lori C. Mitchell, 2004. Mint condition. **$235–255**

Folk Art, Lettie's Leap Frog. 12" tall. Papier-mâché. ©Lori C. Mitchell, 2004. Mint condition. **$375–400**

Folk Art, Midnight Moon Ride. 10" tall. Papier-mâché. ©Lori C. Mitchell, 2004. Mint condition. **$375–400**

Folk Art, Moon Pie Magic. 7¼" tall. Papier-mâché. ©Lori C. Mitchell, 2004. Mint condition. **$225–250**

Ratchet Dance Toy. 15" × 8". Papier-mâché and painted fabric. Miniature. German Reproduction. *Original design, sculpted and created by Scott Smith, owner of Rucus Studio.* $450–575.

Acorn Prince. 2001. 9" tall. Papier-mâché and dried moss. *Original folk art by Trout Creek Folk Art, Napa, Calif.* $110–125.

Black Cat Boogie. 9" tall. Papier-mâché. © *Lori C. Mitchell, 2004.* $225–250.

Candy Container, Missy Mouse's Carriage Ride. 7" × 5". Papier-mâché. © *Lori C. Mitchell, 2004.* $250–275.

Ghostie bucket

Ghostie Bucket. 2000. Papier-mâché. *Original folk art by Trout Creek Folk Art, Napa, Calif.* $55–75.

Kitty Back Jack. 8" tall. Papier-mâché. © Lori C. Mitchell, 2004. $235–255.

Folk Art, Peter, the Great Pumpkin Eater. 6" tall. Papier-mâché. ©Lori C. Mitchell, 2004. Mint condition. **$190–220**

Folk Art, Sculpture, Mystic Meow. One-of-a-kind sculpture. Made using composition and antique fabric and trims. Lighted crystal ball. Approximate size: 17" × 11". Original design, sculpted and created by Scott Smith, owner of Rucus Studio. New. Mint condition. **$800–1,000**

Folk Art, Sculpture, Soul Seeker. One-of-a-kind sculpture. Made using composition, papier-mâché, painted fabric, and sitting on an architectural wood base. Approximate size: 22" × 13". Original design, sculpted and created by Scott Smith, owner of Rucus Studio. New. Mint condition. **$725–800**

Folk Art, Sculpture, Witch on Owl. Made using composition, papier-mâché, painted fabric, and sitting on an architectural wood base. Approximate size: 22" × 8". Original design, sculpted and created by Scott Smith, owner of Rucus Studio. New. Mint condition. **$1,200–1,400**

Folk Art, Sculpture, Witch Riding Cat. Made using composition, papier-mâché. The cat is covered in antique black velvet and is mounted to a wood base. The witch is a nodder. Approximate size: 20" × 16". Original design, sculpted and created by Scott Smith, owner of Rucus Studio. New. Mint condition. **$1,500–1,750**

Folk Art, Sissy and Her Cat. 9" tall. Papier-mâché. ©Lori C. Mitchell, 2004. Mint condition. **$265–300**

Soul Seeker. 22" × 13". Composition, papier-mâché, and painted fabric. Sitting on an architectural wood base. *Original design, sculpted and created by Scott Smith, owner of Rucus Studio.* $725–800.

Folk Art, Skeleton Cat. Papier-mâché and wire figure of a cat skeleton. 5" tall. Original folk art by Trout Creek Folk Art, Napa, Calif., 2003. New. Mint condition.   **$110–130**

Folk Art, Toy, Ratchet Dance. Made using papier-mâché and painted fabric. Miniature German reproduction ratchet. Approximate size: 15" × 8". Original design, sculpted and created by Scott Smith, owner of Rucus Studio. New. Mint condition.   **$450–575**

Folk Art, Trick or Treating Goblin, Resting. Papier-mâché and wire. 7" tall. Original folk art by Trout Creek Folk Art, Napa, Calif., 2001. New. Mint condition.   **$135–160**

Folk Art, Veggie Bucket. Papier-mâché bucket in shape of pumpkin with winking eye and three smiling cherry tomato feet and green bean handle. 9" tall. Original folk art by Trout Creek Folk Art, Napa, Calif., 2001. New. Mint condition.   **$95–125**

Folk Art, Witch Lantern. Papier-mâché, wire handle, paper inserts. 9" tall. Original folk art by Trout Creek Folk Art, Napa, Calif., 2001. New. Mint condition.   **$85–115**

Game, "Children's Take a Chance Stunt Game." U.S. 8½" × 9". Great graphics. Very hard to find. Very good condition.   **$75–100**

Game, Bridge Tallies. U.S. Early paper bridge tallies (set of 5 in Halloween icons, including jack-o'-lantern, devil, several black cats). Very hard to find. Excellent condition.   **$55–75**

Game, Bridge Tallies. U.S. Early paper bridge tallies (set of 6 showing children in various Halloween outfits/poses, including one as witch on pumpkin, another with black cat, several with pumpkins). Hard to find. Excellent condition.   **$60–75**

Game, Cat and Witch. U.S. 20" × 19" paper pin-the-tail on the cat and witch game. Original box. Whitman Publishing. Game has all the tails. Part of them have been cut. Very hard to find. Very good condition.   **$75–100**

Game, Ghostly Stunt and Fortune. 4" × 6" ghostly stunt fortune game. Paper punch outs. Hard to find. Excellent condition.   **$40–60**

Game, Jack-O'-Lantern Target. Parker Brothers target game in original box with original targets, guns, stands, directions, and corks. Great graphics. Early 1900s game. Scarce. Near Mint. **$625–650**

Game, Old Witch Brewsome Stunts. 9½" × 7½" unpunched game. Very hard to find. Near mint condition. **$55–80**

Game, Owl Tell Your Fortune. U.S. Stunts and fortune game. Minor flake on tip of one ear. Owl is 9" tall. Unused. Hard to find. Near mint condition. **$115–130**

Game, Punch Out. U.S. 9½" × 7½" paper punch-out old witch brewsome stunt game. Hard to find. Excellent condition. **$35–50**

Game, Spin the Wheel. USA. 10" tin spin the wheel fun game candy tin. Miss Southern Homemade Sweets. Minor scratches. Scarce. Very good condition. **$75–100**

Game, Spin the Wheel. USA. 9½" × 7½" paper punch-out old witch stunt game. Hard to find. Excellent condition. **$35–50**

Game, Stunt Halloween Quiz. U.S. Luhrs. 9" × 8". Great stunt game. Hard to find. Excellent condition. **$40–60**

Game, Whirl-O Halloween Fortune and Stunt Game. U.S. 9" × 7". Has a spinner on the front. Fairly common. Near mint condition. **$45–65**

Garland, Halloween. Tissue paper. Orange and black. 2½" × 9". Introduced 2004. Mint condition. **$8.50–10**

Garland, Vintage Glass Bell Garland. Halloween bells in black, silver, and gold-range. 1½" blown glass bells on silver 6' garland. Introduced 2005. Mint condition. **$36.50–40**

Figures, Group: Pumpkinhead Ghost, Candy Corn, Pumpkin Bat. Introduced in 2004. Ghost is papier-mâché, 27" × 18". **$55–60**

    Candy Corn is papier-mâché, 22" × 16". **$54.95–60**

    Pumpkin Bat is papier-mâché, 13" × 34". **$54.95–60**

Halloween Barrels, Cut-out. Luminarias (before they were mass-produced). Handmade out of regular house barrels. Approximately 12" and 15" tall. Circa 1950s. Excellent condition. **$35–55 each**

Halloween Cat, Folk Art, Wooden. Arched back cat is white with black spots. Crazed all over with age. Tail has been fixed (old staple repair) and one paw is chipped. Circa 1920. Good condition. **$175–200**

Halloween Prop, Lifesize, Dracula. In cape with blood coming down his chin. Made of resin and handpainted with great detail. Approximately 6' tall. Excellent condition. **$550–650**

Halloween Prop, Lifesize, Father Zombie. Over 6' tall. Handmade original by Chris Russell at *TwistedToybox.net*. Posable at the shoulders and elbows, and breaks apart at the waist for easy storage or shipping. Mint condition. **$650–700**

Vintage Glass Bell Garland. 2005. 1½" blown glass bells on silver 6' garland. *Courtesy of Bethany Lowe Designs, Inc.* $36.50–40.

Hanging Figure, Party Skeleton. 2005. 32" × 10". Paper pulp. From the Hobgoblins collection. Designed from the vintage and antique holiday collections of Bruce Elsass. *Courtesy of Bethany Lowe Designs, Inc.* $76.50–80.

Hanging Figure, Folk Art, Party Skeleton. From the Hobgoblins collection. Designed by Bethany Lowe Designs from the vintage and antique holiday collections of Bruce Elsass. 32" × 10"; made of paper pulp. Introduced in 2005. Mint condition. **$76–80**

Hanging Figure, Witch Spider. Witch with spider face hangs from string in her center. She has orange and black stockings on her spider legs and wears an orange witch hat. 13½" × 21". Made of papier-mâché. Introduced in 2004. Mint condition. **$110–130**

Hanging, Pumpkinhead on Bat. Resin figure has pumpkin head and wears green suit. Bat is realistic. 13" × 12½". Made of resin. Introduced in 2002. Mint condition. **$49.95–55**

Hat, Felt. Unknown origin. Felt hat with bells on top, orange and black, with a cat face. Very hard to find. Excellent condition. **$65–80**

Hats, Crepe. German. 9" tall, paper rims with figures. Some tears. Hard to find. Good condition. **$5–10**

Hats, Tissue. German. Lot of four tissue hats. 7" × 11". Hard to find. Excellent condition. **$15–25**

Hats. German. Three hats, all 9" × 9", each with different die-cut figure decoration. Very hard to find. Very good condition. **$125–150**

Hats. Seven different heavy paper hats. Fairly common. Good to excellent condition. **$90–120**

Horn, Cardboard. American lithographed horn depicting red devil's face, black cat, and other Halloween icons. 6" tall. Works. Very hard to find. Excellent condition. **$60–75**

Horn, Cardboard. German. 24" cardboard horn, orange and black, stripe lithographed paper with pumpkin ball and crepe ruffle. Scarce. Good condition. **$65–85**

Horn, Mickey Mouse. U.S. 6½" tall horn/ratchet combination noisemaker. Mickey and Minnie adorn this highly sought after early American piece. Scarce. Excellent condition. **$115–140**

Horns, Cardboard. U.S. Four cardboard paper lithographed horns. Graphics are all different. Hard to find. Good to very good condition. **$115–130**

Jack-O'-Lantern, "Cauldron." 3" jack-o'-lantern on three wire legs. Scarce. Excellent condition. **$800–900**

Jack-O'-Lantern, American. "Scowler" pulp lantern with original Pulpco label and candleholder plug. Excellent color with green highlights. Very hard to find. Excellent condition. **$340–360**

Jack-O'-Lantern, American. Very unhappy/frowny face pumpkin. 6" tall. All original. Hard to find. Very good condition. **$135–150**

Jack-O'-Lantern, Boy. U.S. Papier-mâché head/boy. 7½" tall, original insert. Slight dent in corner of one eye; excellent paint with few minor chips and flakes. Hard to find. Very good condition. **$375–400**

Jack-O'-Lantern, Cardboard. Googly eyes, painted teeth in red and white. 3½" diameter. Made in Germany. Hard to find. Excellent condition. **$155–175**

Jack-O'-Lantern, Centerpiece. German. Cardboard centerpiece is 7" high. Crepe skirt around base. Black "lipstick." Scarce. Excellent condition. **$575–600**

Jack-O'-Lantern, Composition. Huge German composition jack-o'-lantern with leaves. 5" high. Great expression. Rare. Near mint condition. **$2,100–2,250**

Jack-O'-Lantern, German. Distinctive lantern marked "DRNG." 5" tall with extended molded cardboard nose. Highly painted facial features. Hand-painted, original and unique, because it has both red and black in the detailing. Rare. Very good condition. **$725–775**

Jack-O'-Lantern, German. Molded cardboard jack-o'-lantern with a lot of definition in the molding. 5" tall. Great face. Some discoloration in the rear. Very hard to find. Very good condition. **$275–300**

Jack-O'-Lantern, German. 3" tall. Red painted lips. Replaced insert. Hard to find. Very good condition. **$165–190**

Jack-O'-Lantern, German. Unusual 5" molded cardboard with original green eyes and red cellophane mouth. Scarce. Excellent condition. **$185–200**

Jack-O'-Lantern, Japan. 2½" tall. Early (1920s–1930s). Japanese. Very dark color, almost burnt red. Nice example of early piece. Original bottom and insert. Scarce. Very good condition. **$205–225**

Jack-O'-Lantern, Japan. 3½" cardboard. Circa 1930s. Scarce. Near mint condition. **$205–230**

Jack-O'-Lantern, Japan. 4" tall. Early (1920s–1930s) Japanese lantern. Replaced base. Original insert, original leaves. Scarce. Excellent condition. **$155–175**

Jack-O'-Lantern, Pumpkin. German. 4" cardboard lantern with composition feet, felt rim under mouth. Break from eye to nose and from nose to mouth. Very unusual. Scarce. Very good condition. **$350–400**

Jack-O'-Lantern, Witch. German. 7½" early molded cardboard witch jack-o'-lantern. Hair in curls by cheek, witch's cap atop head. Hat removes to reveal lantern with original candle and candle holder. Open at the base. Probably a candy container, but the plug or paper is missing. Molded hands across her belly. Missing part of eye insert. Rare. Very good condition. **$1,750–2,000**

Jack-O'-Lantern. German. 7½" glazed cardboard. Scarce. Excellent condition. **$500–550**

Jack-O'-Lantern. German. Marked "DNGM Germany." 6" glossy finish. Red lips, eyebrows around eyes. Scarce. Excellent condition. **$500–550**

Jack-O'-Lantern. U.S. Papier-mâché. 7½" tall. Original insert with the tongue sticking out (rare insert). Large size. Has some stains and scuffs. Scarce. Very good condition. **$225–250**

Jack-O'-Lantern. U.S. Papier-mâché. 5½" tall. Original inserts. Slight tear on both eyes. Pug-nosed, dimpled cheeks, original crepe on handle. Scarce. Very good condition. **$375–400**

Jack-O'-Lantern. German. 5½" "Mr. Mustache." Glazed finish, hand-painted mustache, eyebrows and goatee, red lips. Slight tear in one eye. Small hole in base, but does not distract from pumpkin. Scarce. Very good condition. **$475–525**

Jack-O'-Lantern. German. 2¾" tall cardboard jack-o'-lantern. Painted lips, original inserts, and arched eyebrows. Very hard to find. Near mint condition. **$265–295**

Jack-O'-Lantern. German. 3" tall. All original inserts. Hard to find. Excellent condition. **$215–235**

Jack-O'-Lantern. German. 5½" tall. Cardboard. Replaced base, replaced partial insert. Yellow-green stripe. Crack on lip by mouth. Very hard to find. Very good condition. **$300–325**

Jack-O'-Lantern. German. 5" tall molded cardboard with cotton batting nose and red lips. Small tape mark on back. Scarce. Excellent condition. **$550–600**

Jack-O'-Lantern. German. Huge fully molded lantern. 12" tall, early cardboard lantern was originally a store display in 1910 at New Hampshire general store. One eye replaced insert. Great detailing on face. Rare. Excellent condition. **$4,000–4,500**

Jack-O'-Lantern. Japan. 4" tall early cardboard lantern. Very hard to find. Near mint condition. **$135–150**

Jack-O'-Lantern. Japan. 5" high lantern. Original insert. Slight tear in insert in mouth and small holes. Original cellophane candy holder on handle. One small hole on base in front of jack-o'-lantern, not noticeable. Scarce. Very good condition. **$175–200**

Jack-O'-Lantern. Japan. 5" tall. Original insert. Painted eyebrows arched upward. Very hard to find. Excellent condition. **$260–300**

Jack-O'-Lantern. Probably Japanese. 3½" composition "man in the pumpkin" lantern. Asian features. Rare. Near mint condition. **$900–1,000**

Jack-O'-Lantern. Unknown origin (probably American). 13" stem atop jack-o'-lantern with muslin insert. Great molding, fabulous expression with flared nostrils, realistic eyes, teeth with several missing. Early piece. Rare. Excellent condition. **$3,000–3,500**

Jack-O'-Lantern. U.S. 8" solid-faced papier-mâché jack-o'-lantern. Minor scuffing on the eyebrows, lips, face. Very large. Very hard to find. Good condition. **$175–210**

Jack-O'-Lantern. U.S. Smiling pumpkin with original inserts. Rough pulp finish, circa 1920s. Slight damage. Scarce. Very good condition. **$190–225**

Jack-O'-Lanterns, Stacking. Reproduced from Vintage Originals. Mint condition. 4" × 4", **$20–24.** 5" × 5½", **$24–28.** 6" × 7", **$28–32.**

Jack-in-the-Box, Devil. German. Early devil jack-in-the-box. 3¼" square when closed; 5¼" when open. Paper lithographed over wood box with original cloth hinge. Composition devil head dressed in crepe. Rare. Very good condition. **$425–450**

Jack-in-the-Box, Pumpkin Head. German. 3" × 4" box with German litho paper. Pumpkin head wears top hat. Rare. Very good condition. **$425–450**

Jack-O-Lite Pumpkin. U.S. 7½" Jack-O-Lite lantern in choir boy style. Molded pumpkin, has special metal bracket on top and is open on base. Designed to be used as lampshade for bridge lamp, a ceiling fixture, or early 1940s flashlight. Original box, original insert. Box in very good condition. Scarce. Very good condition. **$325–350**

Jewelry, Halloween Charm Bracelet. Loaded with original polymer clay Halloween beads, Austrian crystal, lampwork, Czech glass, and all sterling silver findings. Wire wrapped ghosts, pumpkins, cats, witch hats, bats, candy corn, glow in the dark and more. Bracelet adjusts from 7" up to 8" with extender chain. Mint condition. **$50–60**

Jewelry, Earrings, Silver. Handmade witch cauldron earrings. Excellent condition. **$10–15**

Jewelry, Ring, Silver skull. Circa 1950. Halloween costume jewelry. Marked sterling silver. Excellent condition. **$25–35**

Jewelry, Handmade, Earrings. Spider on web, with dangling charms: pumpkin, ghost, skeleton, and crystals. Excellent condition. **$15–18**

Lantern, Arched Black Cat. U.S. Papier-mâché, full body, arched black cat lantern. Original insert, slight tear in mouth. 6" × 7". Scarce. Excellent condition. **$875–1000**

Lantern, Black Cat Head. Japan. 6" loofah sponge lantern. 9½" to top of candle holder. Felt ears. Scarce. Very good condition. **$450–475**

Lantern, Black Cat. German. 4½" cardboard lantern, replaced bottom, original insert. One ear bent. Paint in excellent condition. Scarce. Very good condition. **$350–375**

Lantern, Black Cat. German. 3¾" tall molded cardboard black cat lantern with bow tie. Original insert in base. Scarce. Near mint condition. **$725–750**

Lantern, Black Cat. German. 4" flocked with molded nose. Hard to find. Very good condition. **$675–700**

Lantern, Black Cat. German. 5½" tall, molded cardboard black cat lantern. Original insert and base. Scarce. Near mint condition. **$675–725**

Lantern, Black Cat. German. Great detail. 5" tall. White painting around mouth. Original insert. Very hard to find. Near mint condition. **$875–950**

Lantern, Black Cat. German. Primitive style 5" black, molded cardboard and wood cat lantern. One wood ear replaced with cardboard. Hand-painted face with lots of detail. Minor flaws. Scarce. Good condition. **$325–350**

Lantern, Black Cat. U.S. Black cat peering over fence. Molded. 7½" tall. Original price tag from G. Whacker (20 cents) on bottom. Fairly common. Near mint condition. **$250–275**

Lantern, Black Man Face. German. 4" composition black lantern. 4" × 5". Black hair, brown skin. One hairline above right eye. Original inserts, original bottom. No tears. Rare. Excellent condition. **$3,300–3,500**

Lantern, Cardboard Cathode. Jack-o'-lantern type, but has "ears" where handle inserts. German. Glazed finish. 4" molded cardboard cathode lantern. All original. Very hard to find. Excellent condition. **$225–250**

Lantern, Cardboard. German. Four-sided lantern. 11" tall. Cardboard framed, lighter paper. Original bottom. Never been used. Very hard to find. Near mint condition. **$60–75**

Lantern, Cat Face. German. 4¼" tall composition cat head with white moustache. Minor crazing of paint and minor tear on right eye. Rare. Very good condition. **$2,600–2,725**

Lantern, Cat Head. U.S. Black papier-mâché cat head lantern. 5½" tall, original insert. Minor tear in mouth insert. Excellent paint. Hard to find. Excellent condition. **$225–250**

Lantern, Cat Head. U.S. Orange cat head papier-mâché lantern. Original insert with no tears, minor flakes. 6½" tall. Slight scuffing on one ear. Hard to find. Excellent condition. **$275–300**

Lantern, Cat. German. 6" cardboard cat lantern type with ears. Original insert and bottom. Very large painted red lips and nose. Scarce. Excellent condition. **$600–650**

Lantern, Devil Head. German. 5" tall "veggie" (squash) devil lantern. Composition head with green leafy ears. Charming grin. All original. Minor tear in mouth insert. Hairlines front and back. Rare. Good condition. **$2,600–2,800**

Lantern, Devil. U.S. 6½" papier-mâché. Orange fades to green. Slight tear in eye insert. Minor wear to horns. Scarce. Excellent condition. **$400–475**

Lantern, Elephant. Japan. Early elephant lantern. Inserts in eyes and mouth. Great detail to lantern. Gray colored with flesh toned trunk and white collar. A little bit of staining on bottom of collar. Top of lantern toward back has some denting and breakage. Rare. Good condition. **$1,250–1,400**

Lantern, German. 3" tall, on a stick with bells. Replaced insert. Overall length 12". Some scuffing. Scarce. Very good condition. **$200–250**

Lantern, Ghost. German. White ghost lantern with original red inserts. 5" tall. Scarce. Excellent condition. **$600–700**

Lantern, Ghost. German. 4¼" tall. Minor flaking. Original insert. Replaced base. Scarce. Very good condition. **$650–675**

Lantern, Gore. Japan. 4" early gore lantern with leaves. Original insert and lift-out metal candleholder. Rare. Excellent condition. **$1,200–1,300**

Lantern, Lion. Japan. Early and rare lion lantern. Original insert. Great molding detail. 5½" tall. Little bit of paint flaking. One ear has broken off cleanly and could be re-attached quite easily. Rare. Very good condition. **$1,000–1,200**

Lantern, Monkey Face. German. 3¾" tall composition monkey head lantern, exquisite detailing. Original insert. Cracked on both sides on seam but can be repaired. Slight flaking on lips. Rare. Good condition. **$2,800–3,000**

Lantern, Monster Cat. U.S. 8" tall cat jack-o'-lantern face with body. Papier-mâché. Slight tear in insert. Scarce. Excellent condition. **$900–1100**

Lantern, Orange Cat. U.S. Orange cat peering over fence. Molded. 7½" tall. All original. Fairly common. Near mint condition. **$225–250**

Lantern, Owl. Japan. 4½" tall cardboard lantern. Rare. Excellent condition. **$575–625**

Lantern, Paperboard and Tissue. Decorated with jack-o'-lanterns on top of each piece; typical Halloween scenes on each panel. 8" tall. Reproduced from Vintage Originals. Courtesy of Jamieson Studios. New. Mint condition. **$6–10**

Lantern, Parade. Early 1900s parade lantern by Toledo Sign Company 1905 (U.S.). Original stick and metal. Near mint paint. Original insert. 27" long from bottom of stick to top. Lantern is 7" tall. Has original candle holder and candle inside. Scarce. Near mint condition. **$2,550–3,000**

Lantern, Parade. U.S. 10" metal parade lantern. 1906 Toledo Sign Company. Complete with candle holder, screw-type mount, and stem top. Missing insert and paint loss are consequence of this lantern being used once. Scarce. Good condition. **$750–850**

Lantern, Pumpkin. U.S. Pig-nosed lantern. Rough pulp look. 5½" tall. Circa 1920s. Some slight damage. Scarce. Very good condition. **$400–450**

Lantern, Red Devil. U.S. Papier-mâché with exquisite, detailed molding. Original insert reinforced. Very hard to find. Very good condition. **$365–400**

Lantern, Skull. German. 5½" tall. Molded cardboard, replaced insert. Original bottom. Small amount of wear. Very hard to find. Excellent condition. **$350–375**

Lantern, Skull. U.S. 7" cardboard, slotted skeleton lantern. Some tears in inserts. Very hard to find. Very good condition. **$80–110**

Lantern, Witch Head. German. 8" tall. Early composition piece. Pull slide plug in base for candle. Minor wear to nose, eyebrows, and chin. Rare. Excellent condition. **$4,000–4,250**

Lantern, Witch Head. German. Extremely unusual 3½" tall witch head composition lantern. Salesman's sample with catalog sticker. Rare orange hat, which is slightly bent. Original insert. Slight scuffing on face. Rare. Excellent condition. **$2,950–3,200**

Lanterns, Pumpkins. U.S. Two cardboard jack-o'-lanterns. One is 4½" tall and the other is 6" tall. Excellent condition. **$130–150**

Masks, Six. U.S. Set of six Halloween paper party masks, 7–8" tall. Many came as part of promotional advertisements. Set includes skull, devil, ghoul, screaming cat, witch, black cat. Hard to find. Excellent condition. **$50–75**

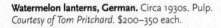

Watermelon lanterns, German. Circa 1930s. Pulp. *Courtesy of Tom Pritchard.* $200–350 each.

Lanterns, German. Circa 1930s. Cardboard and papier-mâché. Familiar Halloween icons, including skull, black cat, devil, and jack-o'-lantern. *Courtesy of Tom Pritchard.* $175–275 each.

Drum, Miniature. German reproduction drum. Approximate size: 15" × 8". Original design, sculpted and created by Scott Smith, owner of Rucus Studio. New. Mint condition. **$425–475**

Lantern, Miniature. German reproduction lantern, sitting on an architectural wood base. Approximate size: 15½" × 5". Original design, sculpted and created by Scott Smith, owner of Rucus Studio. New. Mint condition. **$375–475**

Molds, Chocolate, Jack-O'-Lanterns. Assortment of jack-o'-lantern molds. German. Circa 1930s–1960s. Sizes range from 2" to 4" tall. Excellent condition. **Values range from $100–300**

Molds, Chocolate, Witches. Assorted witch chocolate molds. German. Circa 1930s–1940s. Largest mold is 6" tall. Excellent condition. **Values range from $200–800**

Mug, Halloween Memories. Mug is decorated with Halloween figures, including boy looking at pumpkin, girl dressed in witch outfit looking at cat she's holding, and girl dressed in orange clown costume. 4" tall. Ceramic. Introduced 2003. Mint condition. **$9.50–12**

Musical Instrument, Tambourine. German. Jack-o'-lantern faced tambourine. 7" paper lithographed center with wood frame. Very hard to find. Excellent condition. **$155–200**

Nodder, Jack-O'-Lantern. German. 5½" tall. Happy nodder. Great paint. Minor crazing. Scarce. Excellent condition. **$400–450**

Nodder, Pig. German. 5" composition board is slightly dirty and paint is flaking. Scarce. Very good condition. **$150–175**

Nodder, Pumpkin Head. German. Head has surprised look. Great mechanical action. Wood base. Slight hairline in back. Scarce. Very good condition. **$300–325**

Nodder, Pumpkin. German. Green hat atop jack-o'-lantern head. Very hard to find. Very good condition. **$275–300**

1 Belsnickle Santa. Circa 1890–1900. Approximately 5" tall. Brown papier-mâché with gold glitter. Very rare. *Courtesy of Gary Heidinger.* $1,300–1,500.

2 Belsnickle Santa. Circa 1920. Approximately 7½" tall. Papier-mâché with feather tree in his arms. Very rare. *Courtesy of Gary Heidinger.* $1,200–1,400.

3 German Santa. Circa 1920. Approximately 8" tall. Papier-mâché with red mohair coat on a wooden base. Rare. *Courtesy of Gary Heidinger.* $800–900.

4 Siegnitz boat ornament circa 1900. 3¼" × 2½". Wire and cotton with fabric flowers, sprigs of evergreen, foil-covered pine cones, and a wax baby sitting inside. *Courtesy of Gary Heidinger.* $650–750.

5 Siegnitz spinning wheel ornament. Circa 1900. Approximately 4¼" × 1¼". Wire, chenille, and cotton with Dresden wheels. *Courtesy of Gary Heidinger.* $600–650.

6 Rabbit ornament with basket on back. Dresden. Circa 1890. 3¼" tall. Fabric flowers in basket and green dried sprigs (very fine). Silk ribbon on basket to rabbit's chest. Very rare. *Courtesy of Gary Heidinger.* $1,200–1,500.

7

8

9

7 Candy container, elephant head with silk bag. Circa 1890. 4" long. Dresden. Very rare. *Courtesy of Gary Heidinger.* $1,500–1,800.

8 Siegnitz coach ornament. Approximately 5" × 2¾". With Dresden wheels, angels, a wax baby, a horse with attached mane and tail, and two pinecones on the front. Very unusual. *Courtesy of Gary Heidinger.* $1,500–1.700.

9 Zeppelin ornament. Circa 1910–1920. 5" long. Dresden. *Courtesy of Gary Heidinger.* $1,000–1,200.

10

11

10 Siegnitz plane ornament. Circa
1890–1900. 4½" long. Wire and
crepe paper, and cardboard
covered with foil. Wax baby with
angel hair/spun glass. Dresden
wheels. *Courtesy of Gary
Heidinger.* $700–900.

11 Dresden horse and rider
ornament. Circa 1900–1910.
Approximately 2⅛" tall. *Courtesy
of Gary Heidinger.* $650–800.

12 Santa on antique steamroller.
1999. 25" × 24". Hand sculpted,
one of a kind. *By (and courtesy
of) Bethany Lowe Designs, Inc.*
$2,495–2,600.

13 Bottle brush trees with small
houses. All introduced in 2004.
12" tree in white house, $21–25.
9" tree in blue house, $15.50–20.
7" tree in pink house, $11.50–15.
*Courtesy of Bethany Lowe
Designs, Inc.*

12

13

3

14

14 Bead sticks and Noel letters. Antique bead sticks, lengths of 7" and smaller, $4–11. Ceramic letters with holders in tops, 1¼" × 4" × 3", $44–50. *Courtesy of CSPost.com.*

15 Candy castle ornament. Rare and retired ornament was originally made in 1998. 7" tall, and stands on its own. Made by Christopher Radko, for Starlight members only. Limited edition, Style Number 98–SP–36. *Courtesy of Seller Dropoff.com.* $70–100.

16 Sugar holiday ornament. 6" tall. Made by Christopher Radko. A portrait of one of Elizabeth Taylor's dogs and created for her AIDS Foundation. *Courtesy of Seller Dropoff.com.* $38–48

17 Candy container, bunny with baskets on back. Circa 1940s. Three different colors available: blue is 6", yellow is 7½", and pink is 9". *Courtesy of Cocoa Village Antique Mall.* $50–100 each.

18 Chicks in basket. Cotton. Circa 1940s. Marked "Made in Japan". *Courtesy of Cocoa Village Antique Mall.* $40–50/set.

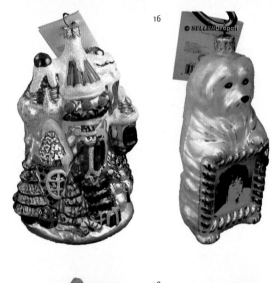

15

16

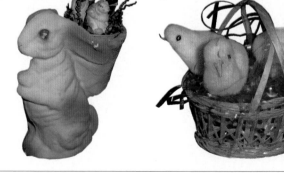

17

18

19

20

21

22

23

24

19 Devil's head ornament. Approximately 3" high. Victorian. *Courtesy of Cocoa Village Antique Mall.* $175–200.

20 Santa, reticulated hanging figure. Circa 1950s. Approximately 30" tall. Paper decorated with sparkles. *Courtesy of Holly Knight.* $140–160.

21 Bunny make–do in pink. Approximately 18" tall. Small mohair bunny atop a hand dyed wool "make–do" pincushion with feather stitching and beading adorning the ball. Bunny holds a wool flower. *Courtesy of Baker & Co.* $245.

22 Uncle Bigelow. 7½" tall. Papier-mâché. © *Lori C. Mitchell, 2003.* $225–250.

23 Ornamental elf folk-art sculpture. 21" × 13". Papier-mâché and vintage glass ornaments and original package, mounted on a wooden base. Sculpted and created by Scott Smith, owner of Rucus Studio. Mint condition. *Courtesy of Scott Smith.* $800–900.

24 Scherenschnitte art. Standing art deco–style deer with flowers. 11" × 14", including mat. *Photo and Copyright © Sharyn Sowell. All rights reserved.* $60–75.

25 St. Basil cathedral music box. About 10". Handmade and painted in Moscow. *Photo Courtesy of The Russian Shop.* $100–120.

26 Santa Claus playing golf. About 12½". Wood carving, painted and signed. From the village of Bogorodsk, Russia. *Photo Courtesy of The Russian Shop.* $400–425

27 Snowmen chocolate molds. All are European, circa 1920s–1960s. From 3" to 7" tall. *Courtesy of Trout Creek Folk Art.* Values range from $100–600.

28

29

30

28 Snowboy goes off to the sauna. 2000. 7" tall. Papier-mâché. *Original folk art by Trout Creek Folk Art, Napa, Calif.* $65–85.

29 Clown cat toy. Approximate size: 15" × 8". Papier-mâché and painted fabric. Miniature German reproduction drum made by Scott Smith. Original design, sculpted and created by Scott Smith, owner of Rucus Studio. $425–475.

30 Band Stand Sam candy container. 9½" tall. Papier-mâché. ©Lori C. Mitchell, 2004. $350–400.

31

32

33

31 Roosevelt Rabbit. 15". Golden
kid mohair with wool felt
coat and vest. *Courtesy of
Baker & Co.* $280.

32 Nodders, German. Circa 1930s.
Composition. *Courtesy of Tom
Pritchard.* $175–375 each.

33 Owl candy containers,
American. Circa 1940s. Pulp.
Courtesy of Tom Pritchard.
$200–375 each.

Chocolate Molds, Jack-O'-Lanterns. German, circa 1930s–1960s. Sizes range from 2" to 4" tall. $100–300.

Mug, Halloween Memories. 2003. 4" tall. Ceramic. $9.50–12.

Tin Noisemakers. 5" rattles. Reproduced from Vintage Originals. *Courtesy of Jamieson Studios.* $16–20.

Nodder, Pumpkin Head. German. Wears yellow suit with white color, red buttons, green gloves and hat. 5" tall. Excellent mechanics. Scarce. Near mint condition.　　**$550–600**

Nodder, Screaming Pumpkin Girl. 6½" tall composition jack-o'-lantern headed nodder. Jack-o'-lantern girl has her mouth wide open. Minor flaking on back of head. Rare. Near mint condition.　　**$1,000–1,250**

Nodder, Witch. German. 8½" tall. Cardboard. From bottom of her stand to top of her hat 11½". Stand made exclusively for her. All original with original broom. Very great detail on face. Minor chips. Full bodied nodder, rocker type with whole dowel going up, so her whole body dances. Scarce. Excellent condition.　　**$900–1,000**

Noisemaker Rattles, Tin. Reproduced from Vintage Originals. Both are 5" long. Courtesy of Jamieson Studios. New. Mint condition.　　**$16–20 each**

151

Nut Cups, Halloween. Set of five. Designed by Gail and Glenn Giaimo of Dresden Star Heirloom Ornaments. Reproduction of original ornaments made from vintage glass, antique tinsels and trims, paper "scrap" images. 1½" × 1½". Introduced 2005. Mint condition.
$56.95–60

Nut Cups, Jack-O'-Lanterns. Japan. Lot of four papier-mâché nut cups. 2½" tall. Two closed mouth design; one with open mouth. Minor flake on one cheek. Hard to find. Excellent condition.
$130–150

Ornament, S'more "Witch on Broom Ornament." #548769. 3¼" high, made of resin. Excellent condition.
$10–15

Ornaments, Halloween Cornucopias. Set of four. Designed by Gail and Glenn Giaimo of Dresden Star Heirloom Ornaments. Reproduction of original ornaments made from vintage glass, antique tinsels and trims, paper "scrap" images. 10½" × 4½". Introduced in 2005. Mint condition.
$88–95

Paper Cones. Set of two Halloween paper cones, decorated with jack-o'-lanterns. 6" × 3", made of pressed paper. Mint condition.
$14.95–18

Party Favors, Cardboard Hats. U.S. Two cardboard hats and horns. One is 14" high with two different designs on either side. Other is 19" high with design on one side of a boy holding a pumpkin with crepe fringe. Small one is in very good condition. Other is in good condition with some bending and creasing. Both wood tip horns work. Very hard to find. Good condition.
$25–35

Pipe Horn, Black Man. German. Black face with gray top hat, big red lips. 4½" tall, 6" long. Very minor paint flaking, slight crease in hat. Scarce. Excellent condition.
$275–300

Pipe Horn. German. 5½" paper lithographed pumpkin design. Wonderful graphics. Very hard to find. Excellent condition.
$105–130

Pipe Horns (Two). Japan. Cardboard pipe horns. One is ghost and the other is dark green veggie. White "ghost" horn has painted face; the other has no face. Wood tips. Very hard to find. Excellent condition.
$35–50

Pipe Horn, Devil. German. 8" long cardboard pipe horn with wood tip. Works. Scarce. Very good condition.
$135–155

Pipe Horn, Pumpkin. Japan. 5½" cardboard pumpkin-faced pipe horn with great face. Scarce. Very good condition.
$135–155

Pipe Horn, Watermelon. German. Cardboard watermelon pipe horn with great face. 8" long, slight crease by wood tip. Works. Scarce. Very good condition.
$175–200

Place Cards, Set of Six. Halloween party place cards by Ellen Clapsaddle, Wolff Publishing Company. All show little children in "party mode." Circa 1920s. "Halloween Greetings." 3½" × 5¼". Scarce. Near mint condition.
$50–75

Plate, Children's (Two). Girl in witch costume raising black cat or boy looking at jack-o'-lantern. Ceramic. 9" diameter. Both introduced in 2004. Mint condition.
$26.50–30

Plate, Pumpkin Party Girl. Ceramic. Depicts girl in pumpkin colored "clown" costume, surrounded by Jack-O'-Lanterns with a black cat at her feet. 14" diameter. Introduced 2003. Mint condition.
$32.50–35

Print, Bess Cleveland. U.S. 6" × 8½". Artist designed several sets of scarce Halloween postcards, and the print has similar proportions. May have been a design she created for a postcard around 1910. Hand-tinted Halloween artwork. Scarce. Excellent condition.   **$35–50**

Puzzle, Jigsaw. Wood. Unusual and early jigsaw puzzle of standing jack-o'-lantern holding crow on arm. Words in upper right read "Don't dare try to frighten me!" Similar to postcards of 1907–1912 era. Appears to be Whitney Publishing design. 5" × 3½" × 1". Rare. Excellent condition.   **$175–200**

Puzzle, Jigsaw. Wood. Features witch and cauldron with words "Happy Halloween" in upper right hand corner. Signed by artist "A. Pona". Appears to be circa 1907–1912 and made by Whitney Publishing. 5" × 3½" × 1". Scarce. Excellent condition.   **$175–200**

Scarecrow Decoration. Accordion, paper. Approximately 12" tall. Circa 1960s. Excellent condition.   **$15–20**

Sparkler, Black Cat. U.S. 8" early tin Roscoe black cat sparkler. Very hard to find. Good condition.   **$800–1,000**

Squeaker, Pumpkin Figure. German. Mushroom-capped pumpkin squeaker. Red shoes marked "Germany." Circa 1920s. Rice paper has dissolved and squeaker is no longer functional. Scarce. Very good condition.   **$115–135**

Squeaker, Witch. German. Composition headed witch squeaker on wood shoes. 4½" tall. Dressed in orange. Squeaker is not working properly. Circa 1920s. Scarce. Very good condition.   **$200–250**

Sucker Holder. U.S. 4½" tall hard plastic jack-o'-lantern faced sucker holder. Fairly common. Excellent condition.   **$10–15**

Tablepiece, Pumpkin House with Witch. Black pumpkin, white fence, witch going to the door. 11" × 11", made of paper pulp. Introduced 2003. Mint condition.   **$64.50–70**

Tabletop Centerpiece, Folk Art, Cat in Jack's Hat. Designed by Folk Artist Dee Foust for Bethany Lowe Designs. 9½" × 5¾"; made of paper pulp. Introduced in 2005. Mint condition.   **$32–35.**

Tabletop Display, Box of Bones with Hat. Skeleton in coffin that reads "here lies party skellington beloved fright producer–R.I.P." Made of paper pulp. Introduced 2004. Mint condition.   **$110–130**

Tambourine, Chein. Pumpkin face tambourine with all cymbals. Circa 1920s. 6¾" diameter. Made in the U.S. Very hard to find. Very good condition.   **$380–400**

Tissue Garland. Orange and black variegated. 25'. Reproduced from Vintage Originals. Courtesy of Jamieson Studios. New. Mint condition.   **$10–15**

Toy, Black Horse. U.S. Black horse on orange wheels. 5" tall. Fairly common. Very good condition.   **$105–125**

Toy, Cat Pushing Pumpkin on Wheels. U.S. 6½" × 6". Hard plastic. Rare variation with wheels and platform. Tab in front of platform broken off but cat and pumpkin in excellent condition. Very hard to find.   **$125–150**

Tabletop Centerpiece, Cat in Jack's Hat. 2005. 9½" × 5¾". Paper pulp. Designed by Folk Artist Dee Foust for Bethany Lowe Designs. *Courtesy of Bethany Lowe Designs, Inc.* $31.95–35.

Toy, Cat Pushing Pumpkin. U.S. 4½" × 6½" hard plastic cat pushing pumpkin on wheels. Minor wear on paint. Hard to find. Very good condition.   **$125–150**

Toy, Clown. U.S. Plastic orange clown on wheels. Fairly common. Very good condition.
$175–200

Toy, Cowbell Noisemaker. U.S. 6" tin lithographed cowbell with wood handle. Orange with lithographed scenes. Scarce. Excellent condition.   **$175–200**

Toy, Drum Whistle. German swinging drum with whistle has black cat on front. 4" diameter. Red background, black cap. Paper face, wood frame, slight tear in back. Carved handle incorporates whistle. Scarce. Good condition.   **$85–100**

Toy, Drum. German. 9" paper lithographed horn with 3½" drum. Two-faced with pumpkin on one face and cat on the other. Very hard to find. Good condition.   **$85–100**

Toy, Ghoul. German. Ghoul-headed toy, composition head, cloth body, wood legs and feet. Holds cardboard jack-o'-lantern in his arms. Remnants of soap string suggest this piece may have been a marionette in the 1920s. Scarce. Very good condition.   **$1,000–1,250**

Toy, Gun. U.S. 3½" × 6½" hard plastic trick or treat gun. Very hard to find. Very good condition.   **$105–130**

Toy, Horn. German. 8½" red carrot cardboard horn. Minor flakes and crazing. Very hard to find. Excellent condition.   **$85–100**

Toy, Horn. German. 5¼" cardboard, jack-o'-lantern-faced horn. String on mouth to modulate sound. Slight wear on face. Very hard to find. Very good condition.   **$155–180**

Toy, Horn. German. 5½" cardboard parsnip horn with painted face. Hard to find. Excellent condition.   **$85–115**

Toy, Horn. German. 7½" cardboard pickle horn. Minor creasing. Hard to find. Very good condition.   **$75–100**

Toy, Horn. German. 7" cardboard banana horn. Hard to find. Very good condition.
$85–115

Toy, Horn. German. 9½" paper lithographed horn. Face of a jack-o'-lantern on front (4¾" across). The horn goes through the center and is made of cardboard with a wood tip. Slight tear on face cover. Very hard to find. Very good condition.
$300–350

Toy, Horn. German. Cardboard horn topped with pumpkin and lithographed cover of horn is covered with pumpkins. Black shredded crepe collar. 16" long. One slight bend near ball. Very hard to find. Excellent condition.
$300–350

Toy, Horn/Blowout. German. 6½" pumpkin faced horn/blowout with messy crepe hair. Works great. Minor cracking of face paint. Very hard to find. Very good condition. **$55–75**

Toy, Kazoo. U.S. Kirchoff 4" metal kazoo. Tin litho noisemaker. Scarce. Excellent condition.
$120–150

Toy, Kitty. German ratchet toy. Kitty has black face, big smile, yellow eyes, red ruffle around neck. Very unusual. Scarce. Excellent condition.
$115–125

Toy, Metal Pan Slapper. U.S. Jack-O'-Lantern slapper. 8½" long. Two-sided. Very hard to find. Very good condition.
$105–125

Toy, Noisemaker Slapper. Unknown origin. 6½" cardboard noisemaker slapper with cellophane nose, eyes, and mouth. Minor wear to edges. Very hard to find. Excellent condition.
$50–75

Toy, Noisemaker. German. 2½" cardboard ball blowout noisemaker. Minor wear on the face. Very hard to find. Excellent condition.
$105–125

Toy, Noisemaker. 6¾" can paper lithographed noisemaker. Can itself is 3" × 3¼". Pumpkin face and other designs. Minor tears in paper. Hard to find. Very good condition. **$45–65**

Toy, Noisemaker. German. 24" long paper lithographed cat noisemaker. Face on drum is 5½" in diameter. Crepe add-ons. Very hard to find. Very good condition.
$300–350

Toy, Noisemaker. German. 6½" two-sided die-cut owl slapper noisemaker. One owl die-cut has repaired tear. Very hard to find. Good condition.
$75–100

Toy, Noisemaker. German. 7¾" high noisemaker in black cat image. Paper and wood. Some creasing on paper. Very hard to find. Very good condition.
$85–100

Toy, Noisemaker. German. 7¾" lithographed black cat noisemaker. Some creasing on paper. Crepe paper wrapped around the handle missing in a couple of spots. Very hard to find. Very good condition.
$95–125

Toy, Noisemaker. U.S. 19" long. Early American paper lithographed over paperboard noisemaker. Very unique whistle. Orange with black figures. Scarce. Excellent condition.
$55–75

Toy, Pan Slapper. U.S. Chein pan slapper with children holding a pumpkin. Great lithograph. 8" long. Very hard to find. Very good condition.
$95–115

Toy, Pan Slapper. German. Wooden pan slapper noisemaker. 6" tall. Black face. 2¼" wide, crepe covering the wood paddle for the noisemaker. Orange crepe bow tie. Double sided wood clapper, both original lead bongers. Scarce. Excellent condition.   **$275–325**

Toy, Pan Slapper. U.S. Pan slapper noisemaker with a horn handle. Lithographed paper pumpkin for a face. Early piece. Very hard to find. Very good condition.   **$135–155**

Toy, Pan Slapper. U.S. U.S. Metal Toy Company pan slapper. Scene of witch flying over a house. Hard to find. Very good condition.   **$70–90**

Toy, Peep Show. German. 3" high. Squeeze wood squeaker in back to make little molded cardboard pumpkin face go up and down. Red, white and blue stage. Minor bend on right hand side. Scarce. Very good condition.   **$305–350**

Toy, Pumpkin Man. German. Mushroom-capped pumpkin man dressed in felt (black and orange), swinging on a stick toy. Early ratchet toy. 10" × 4". Scarce. Excellent condition.   **$350–400**

Toy, Ratchet. German metal ratchet with great litho Halloween icon figures in black on orange background. 5" long. Wood handle. Scarce. Excellent condition.   **$65–75**

Toy, Ratchet, Black Cat. German. Grinning composition kitty nestled atop wooden ratchet. Moveable tail (may have been replaced). Early piece. Overall size 7½" × 5". Scarce. Excellent condition.   **$275–300**

Toy, Ratchet, Cat and Pumpkin. German. Very large cardboard and wooden ratchet. Classic black cat and jack-o'-lantern adorn twin-bladed dual noisemaker with whistle carved in handle. Normal amount of creases and bends. Scarce. Very good condition.   **$215–230**

Toy, Ratchet, Cat. German. 7½" tall. Composition and wood. Crepe collar, missing a wood blade. Very hard to find. Excellent condition.   **$135–150**

Toy, Ratchet, Devil. German. 8½" × 5" wood ratchet of full-bodied devil. Composition head, crepe collar, cloth skirt. Some crazing on back of head. Scarce. Very good condition.   **$475–525**

Toy, Ratchet, German Skull. Lithographed skull on paper/wood ratchet. Some creasing on the paper lithograph. 6½" across. Scarce. Good condition.   **$145–165**

Toy, Ratchet, Jack-O'-Lantern Man. German. 9" × 6½" man. Cardboard lithographed pumpkin face with crepe collar, wood body. Part of the flag that he is holding is missing. Rare. Excellent condition.   **$225–250**

Toy, Ratchet, Jack-O'-Lantern. German. Two-faced, molded cardboard, jack-o'-lantern headed wood ratchet with crepe collar. Very hard to find. Excellent condition.   **$300–350**

Toy, Ratchet, Pumpkin Head. German. 4½" × 5½" wood ratchet. Two cardboard jack-o'-lantern faces, one on each side of the blade. Faces measure 1¾" each. Unusual. Scarce. Very good condition.   **$125–150**

Toy, Ratchet, Pumpkin Head. German. 7¼" × 4¼" cardboard lithographed wood ratchet. Crepe top hat on pumpkin's head. Marked "Germany" across bottom of pumpkin face. Very hard to find. Excellent condition.   **$75–100**

Toy, Ratchet, Pumpkin Man. German. 9½" × 4" pumpkin man with composition head and felt attire. Scarce. Excellent condition. **$130–150**

Toy, Ratchet, Safety Cracker. U.S. 7" wood toy ratchet. Minor wear to lithographed paper. Hard to find. Good condition. **$50–75**

Toy, Ratchet, Sitting Black Cat. German. 9" paper lithographed black cat ratchet. Cat is 6" tall. Minor paper loss on lower right; minor flaking on right ear. Scarce. Very good condition. **$105–130**

Toy, Ratchet, Skull. German. Unique composition skull on wooden ratchet. Two bladed. Ratchet itself is 7" × 5". Minor wear to skull. Scarce. Excellent condition. **$115–130**

Toy, Ratchet, Veggie Guy. German. 9" veggie guy ratchet with minor wear on tip of hat. Crepe "clothing" has minor wear. Scarce. Excellent condition. **$250–300**

Toy, Ratchet, Witch. German. 10½" cardboard lithographed witch. Paper litho is 6½" tall. Two-sided. Scarce. Excellent condition. **$215–240**

Toy, Ratchet, Witch. German. 9" × 4" ratchet. Witch has wood body, composition head, crepe clothes. Scarce. Very good condition. **$285–315**

Toy, Ratchet, Witch. German. Composition headed witch ratchet. Orange crepe collar, detailed face with bright red lips. Missing one blade. Hard to find. Very good condition. **$125–150**

Toy, Ratchet, Witch. German. Composition witch with black cat perched on wooden German ratchet. 5" × 6", two-bladed. Minor wear. Rare. Very good condition. **$125–135**

Toy, Ratchet. U.S. Chein circular 4" party scene with children bobbing for apples. Minor scrape on front; minor rust on back. Very hard to find. Very good condition. **$30–50**

Toy, Ratchet. German. 7½" × 6" veggie man ratchet. Cardboard lithograph. Very hard to find. Very good condition. **$160–200**

Toy, Ratchet. German. Pumpkin face ratchet. 6" × 6". One of four blades is missing. Slight paper loss on face. Scarce. Very good condition. **$115–130**

Toy, Ratchet. German. Two-bladed ratchet slapper. Paper lithograph with figures, one bonger, two half blades. Scarce. Good condition. **$65–80**

Toy, Ratchet. German. Witch riding black cat. Composition. Three bladed ratchet. 11" × 5". One blade missing tip. Scarce. Very good condition. **$100–125**

Toy, Ratchet. U.S. 3½" metal ratchet. Patented Feb. 22, 1916. Great lithograph of witch flying on broom. Very hard to find. Very good condition. **$75–100**

Toy, Ratchet. U.S. Chein party scene ratchet. Great litho. Very hard to find. Excellent condition. **$95–115**

Toy, Rattle, Tea Cone. U.S. Horn/rattle combination with face painted on front. 12" long. Great early piece. Very hard to find. Very good condition. **$95–110**

Toy, Rattle. German. 9" paper lithographed pumpkin-faced rattle with horn in handle. Small dent on paper litho face. Very hard to find. Very good condition. **$85–100**

Toy, Rattle. German. 9" jack-o'-lantern faced paper lithographed rattle with bells. Small tear below mouth on right. Very hard to find. Very good condition. **$95–125**

Toy, Rattle. German. 3½" cardboard, round rattle with pumpkin faces on either side. Slight wear. Original string attached. Hangs. Great face. Very hard to find. Excellent condition. **$65–80**

Toy, Roly Poly, Cat. German. 8" tall. Red hat with slight bend on brim of hat and one ear. Excellent paint. Spring tail and crepe bow tie. Scarce. Excellent condition. **$300–350**

Toy, Sammy the Strolling Skeleton. Japan. Mechanical windup. Original box. Early 1950s. 5½" tall. Hard to find. Near mint condition. **$300–350**

Toy, Scissor. German. 5¾" (opens to 11") scissor toy with a composition veggie head and crepe collar. Scarce. Excellent condition. **$275–300**

Toy, Slapper. Chein mini pan slapper. Made in U.S. Original wooden bongers. Scared kitty face on pan. Metal. Very hard to find. Excellent condition. **$200–250**

Toy, Squeaker, Jack-O'-Lantern Face. German. 2¼" cardboard squeaker candy container. Squeaker works. Hard to find. Very good condition. **$105–125**

Toy, Squeaker. German. 3¾" fuzzy jack-o'-lantern-faced squeaker. Similar to an old powder puff. Fabric pillow with paper eyes and mouth attached. Scarce. Very good condition. **$70–100**

Toy, Squeaker. German. 4½" two-sided squeaker. Pumpkin on one side, witch on other. Paper lithograph. Squeaker does not work. Scarce. Very good condition. **$75–100**

Toy, Stuffed Bear. "Hallooo." 13" black mohair teddy with rust wool felt paws, hat, and ruffle. Wears orange and black party hat and ruffled collar. Glass eyes and a squeaker in his belly. Pumpkin candy container is handmade by "Stamm House." Original creation by Baker & Co. Designs Ltd. New. Mint condition. **$235–275**

Toy, Stuffed Bunny. "Bucket O Bunny." 12" mohair bunny with ruffled orange and black collar sitting in a painted tin bucket with Halloween finery. Ear linings, hat, and ruffle are wool felt. Original creation by Baker & Co. Designs Ltd. New. Mint condition. **$245–300**

Toy, Stuffed Bunny. "Jack O Make-Do." Mohair bunny with orange ruffled collar sitting on a hand dyed wool "make-do" pincushion that resembles jack-o'-lantern. 14" overall. Original creation by Baker & Co. Designs Ltd. New. Mint condition. **$245–300**

Toy, Stuffed Mouse on a Pumpkin. Black mohair mouse with orange and black party hat and ruffled collar, sitting on a mohair pumpkin. Wool felt ears, tail, hat, and ruffle. 15" overall. Original creation by Baker & Co. Designs Ltd. New. Mint condition. **$265–300**

Toy, Stuffed Mouse. "Harvest Mouse." Brown mohair mouse sitting atop a mohair pumpkin. Wool felt ears and tail. Wool leaves and vintage ribbons. 15" overall. Original creation by Baker & Co. Designs Ltd. New. Mint condition. **$255–300**

Toy, Stuffed Mouse. "Ole Shoe." 10" mohair mouse tucked into a vintage black leather shoe. Ears, tail, hat, and ruffle are wool felt. 12" overall. Original creation by Baker & Co. Designs Ltd. New. Mint condition. **$255–300**

Hallooo. 13" black mohair teddy with glass eyes and rust wool felt paws, hat, and ruffle. Pumpkin candy container is handmade by "Stamm House". Original design. *Courtesy of Baker & Co.* $235–275.

Harvest Mouse. Brown mohair mouse sitting atop a mohair pumpkin. Wool felt ears and tail. Wool leaves and vintage ribbons. 15" tall. Original design. *Courtesy of Baker & Co.* $255–300.

Toy, Stuffed Rabbit. "Rusty Rabbit." 12" rust mohair rabbit with black party hat and ruffle with orange polka dots. Wool felt ear linings, ruffle, and hat. Original creation by Baker & Co. Designs Ltd. New. Mint condition. **$225–275**

Toy, Stuffed Squirrel. "Aww Nuts!" 11" mohair squirrel with hand-dyed wool acorn. Original creation by Baker & Co. Designs Ltd. New. Mint condition. **$185–225**

Toy, Tambourine. U.S. Chein tambourine with two cats on fence. 6¾" diameter. Some minor denting on face. Original cymbals. Hard to find. Good condition. **$135–155**

Toy, Tambourine. U.S. 6" metal tambourine with kids dancing around a pumpkin. Fairly common. Near mint condition. **$40–50**

Toy, Whistle. U.S. Kirchoff sliding whistle. 8½" long. Extends to 14½". Great lithograph. Scarce. Very good condition. **$210–230**

Toy, Windup, Cat. Mechanical celluloid cat. 3½". Cat is holding cane. Cat wobbles when you wind it up. Key included. Rare. Near mint condition. **$625–675**

Toy, Witch in Rocket. U.S. 8" × 6". Hard plastic witch on pumpkin wheels. Original candy in cellophane wrap. Scarce. Near mint condition. **$600–650**

Toy, Witch. German. 8½" tall. Composition mechanical walking witch. Cloth clothes, felt shirt. Slight smudging. Rare. Excellent condition. **$1,800–2,000**

Toy, Wooden Noisemaker. U.S. T. Cohn black cat wooden noisemaker. Bongers are on the backside to create noise, and bars on back double as cat's eyes. Cardboard ears with a little creasing. Scarce. Very good condition. **$155–175**

Toys, Cat Figures. German. Four small cat figures. Two are 2" tall, mohair bodies. Two are small red composition candle holders, 1½" tall. Hard to find. Excellent condition. **$300–400**

Toys, Clickers. U.S. Set of five 4½" metal clickers. Fairly common. Excellent condition. **$105–125**

Toys, Noisemaker Slappers. Unknown origin. Two early and unique wood noisemakers. 8" slappers with lithographed designs. Very hard to find. Very good condition. **$15–25**

Toys, Noisemakers. U.S. Two slapper noisemakers. One is 8¼" cardboard skeleton slapper. Other is 7" molded cardboard skeleton rattle with wood handle. Hard to find. Very good condition. **$80–100**

Toys, Noisemakers. Unknown origin. One 3½" primitive tin whistle, orange and black. One cardboard 3" horn, missing a tip. Very hard to find. Good condition. **$15–30**

Toys, Noisemakers. U.S. Three American tin lithographed noisemakers. Fairly common. Excellent condition. **$60–75**

Toys, Squeakers, Black Cats. Two Japanese black cat squeakers. 3½" full body composition cat with bell. 3¾" composition head with clothes. Both work. Very hard to find. Excellent condition. **$150–175**

Treat Boxes, Vintage Cat and Witch. Both boxes are made of paper pulp and are 9½" × 4½". Cat is a black cat with orange bow tie. Witch has orange hair. Both sit on circular bases/containers decorated with stylized black Halloween figures. Introduced in 2005. Mint condition. **$24.95–30**

Votives, Party Cat and Parade Cat. Party Cat, 16" × 8", made of tin. Parade Cat with marble eyes, 15" × 7", made of tin. Both introduced in 2003. Mint condition. **Party Cat: $32.50–35; Parade Cat: $19.95–24**

Votives, Witch Tree and Pumpkin Tree. Pair of votives made of tin. Witch tree is 12" × 6". Pumpkin tree is 9½" × 6". Both introduced in 2001. Mint condition. **$16–18 each**

Wall Dressings, Mr. Pumpkin and Party Skeleton. Mr. Pumpkin is 12" × 15" with Hat. Pellon strips hang down 57"; outstretched arm length is 71". Party Skeleton's head is 10¾" × 15"; pellon strips hang down 54"; outstretched arm length is 70". Both were introduced in 2005. Mint condition. **Each hanging is $119–130**

Wall Hanging, Cat in the Moon. Three-dimensional papier-mâché. 16½" × 3". Black cat peers up into crescent moon face. Introduced in 2001. Mint condition. **$57.50–60**

Winking Cat. Standup honeycomb base. Reproduction of 1949 version. Produced by Beistle Company. 13" tall, 7" diameter. **$12–15**

Witch, Papier-mâché. British. 8¼" tall. Very large hat. Black and light orange. Hard to find. Very good condition. **$375–400**

– 11 –
NOVEMBER

All Saints' Day (November 1)

A Christian feast, this holiday honors all Christian saints. Catholics, Lutherans, and Anglicans celebrate the festival, often known as Hallowmas or All Hallows. Catholics celebrate it on November 1, while Orthodox churches celebrate it the first Sunday after Pentecost. The first Christian to celebrate this feast on a particular day was St. Chrysostom of Constantinople, who died in 407, but All Saints' Day was not recognized by the Church until Bishop Boniface IV stated the Pantheon would be used for Christian purposes in May 609. The holiday was switched to November 1 by the Bishop of Rome, Gregory III, when a chapel in St. Peter's Basilica was dedicated to All Saints. Catholics do not work and are required to attend mass on All Saints' Day.

During the time of Charlemagne, the festival was celebrated by the Western church and was made a day of obligation in the Frankish empire. After the Reformation, the holiday was kept on the Church of England's calendar.

Collectibles for this holiday are similar to those for Halloween, even the costumes and masks. However, the holiday appears more widely celebrated in England than anywhere else.

PRICE LIST: ALL SAINTS' DAY COLLECTIBLES

Art, Engraving. Double page. Titled, "All-Saints Day in New Orleans: Decorating the Tombs in One of the City Cemeteries." Drawn by John Durkin. Published in "Harper's Weekly," Nov. 7, 1885. Dimensions of the engraved area: 14¼" × 20". Excellent condition.
$55–65

Book. *All Saints' Day* by Charles Kingsley. Published 1890. Macmillan & Co., London. Fourth Edition. Red binding. Very good condition. **$15–20**

Graphic Novel, X-Man. "X-Man All Saints Day" Marvel graphic, 1997. Graphic is complete. Near mint condition. $4–5

Postcard, All Saints, Hereford. Depicts the Chained Library. Postally unused. Good condition. $2–3

Poster, All Saint's Day. Art by W. Bouguereau. Reproduction of original painting depicting two women dressed in black holding funereal wreaths, sitting in front of a gravestone. Fine art giclée reproduction on heavyweight paper. 13" × 19". Mint condition. $15–20

Stamp, "Happy All Saints' Day." 3" long. Mint condition. $3–4

All Souls' Day (November 2)

This holiday was set by the Roman Catholic Church to commemorate the dead. It is believed that the dead who didn't commit any venial sins and who have not seen the true vision of God will be helped by those on Earth who pray for them and attend mass. Odilo, the abbot of Cluny, first established this feast in the early part of the second century.

The story was that a pilgrim found the point on Earth where the living were separated from the dead by a space called purgatory. According to legend, he overheard the demons complaining that the prayers of Abbot Odilo and his followers for those who had died had helped the spirits trapped in purgatory to make it into heaven. After the pilgrim told the abbot of his discovery, the abbot named November 2 as the day intercessionary prayers would be given for those souls in purgatory. Soon, some dioceses in France adopted the holiday, and it spread throughout the West.

On this holiday, it is common for celebrants to decorate the graves of the dead. Some of the traditions followed by certain cultures have a pagan influence. Pagans believed that the dead would return on this holiday for a meal with the living. For example, Tyroleans left cakes on the table for the dead and kept the room comfortably warm for the spirits. Brittons visited graveyards and dropped holy water or milk on the hollows at the top of the tombstone, and supper was left on the table for the souls before the family went to bed. Others left candles in the windows to guide the souls home and set an extra place at the table for them. Mexicans made offerings (*ofrendas*) to those dead souls, often accompanied by marigolds (*zempasuchitl*), the traditional flower for the dead. Incense is often used on the altar (with the offerings) and mementos, as well as photos of the dead, also decorate the *ofrenda*.

Collectibles for this holiday are limited, and they usually are closely related to the ones produced for the Day of the Dead.

PRICE LIST: ALL SOULS' DAY COLLECTIBLES

Book, *All Souls Day.* By Cees Nooteboom. Published by Harcourt, 2001. Excellent condition. $25–28

Book, *All Souls' Day.* By Bill Morris. First edition. 1997. Excellent condition. $8–10

DVD, "Herbert Von Karajan: All Souls' Day Concert, 1984." Excellent condition. $10–14

Engraving. Published in *Illustrated London News.* 9¼" × 12". Title: "Praying For Luck And Honoring The Dead—Drawn by G. D'Amato. All Souls' Day in Naples—Worshipers at The Altar Of Skulls." Very good condition.   **$175–225**

Day of the Dead (November 1 and 2)

El Dia de Los Muertes (the Day of the Dead) is celebrated in early November. Mexican people gather in their local cemeteries to honor their departed ancestors and to celebrate the continuity of life. Though customs practiced during this holiday vary from region to region because of its complex history, in many Mexican homes *ofrendas* (temporary altars) are constructed to hold flowers, bread, fruit, candy, cigarettes, and sometimes even tequila as offerings for the dead. The Day of the Dead celebrations, which honor the ancestors of people of Mexican heritage, are becoming more popular in the United States, particularly in the Southwestern states.

The history of the festival dates back to Mesoamerican traditions, particularly the Aztec feast during the month of *Miccailhuitontli*, which means "Little Festival of the Dead." The holiday was presided over by the Lady of the Dead and was meant to honor ancestors and children.

Celebrants welcome the dead into their homes and also visit graves, sprucing them up and decorating them with flowers, then setting out a sumptuous picnic near the gravesite and telling stories about the dead. It is their hope that the dead will take part in the celebrations, as well as the living.

Special foods are made for the holiday, such as "Day of the Dead bread." This is traditionally a round loaf, but in some communities the bread is made a little differently, sometimes inserting a small plastic or ivory skeleton inside the dough as the bread bakes, or shaping the bread dough into the shape of a body or burial wrap.

During this festival, handmade tin and papier-mâché skeletons called *calacas,* dressed in Mexican garb (such as ponchos and sombreros), dance in the streets, symbolizing a positive image of the afterlife. Often these skeletons are recreated as figurines, which celebrants use to decorate their homes or altars.

Some Native American tribes (Zuni, Acoma, and Laguna) celebrate a holiday very similar to the Day of the Dead called *ahoppa awan tewa* ("the dead their day") at the end of October. The saint's crier announces the holiday four days ahead of time from the top of a roof, calls for wood to be brought in, and a portion of whatever is cooked on the holiday is carried by the males of the household to the place where the deads' possessions are traditionally buried. The night the holiday is announced, the boys of the tribe pay household visits, making the sign of the cross at doorways, and saying prayers. The inhabitants of each house give presents of bread and meat to the boys.

The holiday resembles Halloween in that the dead are recognized, but it is different in that the holiday is an accepted part of the Catholic religion in Mexico. Mexicans celebrate by offering prayers. They also set up candles, as well as a ball of food with a bit of everything the family is about to serve, on the graves of their loved ones. The food is left on the grave for the dead, a custom which has been common to many people throughout time.

Day of the Dead collectibles imitate the celebrations of the holiday and all it represents. For instance, many of the figures created for this day are in the image of the skeletons that parade in the streets and graveyards during *El Dia de Los Muertos*. Typical collectibles for the holiday include figurines, altars, altar cards, greeting cards, masks, skulls (painted and beaded), dolls, and artwork.

PRICE LIST: DAY OF THE DEAD COLLECTIBLES

Art, Painting. "Celebracion" by Anthony Saldivar. Acrylic on gallery wrapped canvas. 2001. 16 pieces, each is 12" × 12" × 1½" deep over 48" × 48". Mint condition.   **$1,500–2,000**

Art, Yarn Painting. Created by Excelente Castro. Measures 24" × 24". Excelente learned his trade from his father, Eliseo Castro, and his grandfather, the late Daniel Castro, a well respected shaman or *Mara'akame,* who is widely recognized as one of the foremost pioneers of the yarn art in the 1960s. Scene in this work is typical of Day of the Dead activities. Excellent condition.   **$425–450**

Candy Holder, Skeleton. Department 56 Day of the Dead Skeleton. Stands 5' tall. Rests on metal stand. Excellent condition.   **$100–125**

Card, Altar. Pop-up altar card inspired by Mexican Day of the Dead scenes. Mexican. Depicts *ofrendas* and their traditional offerings. Excellent condition.   **$5–6**

Card, Los Mariachis. Pop-up altar card. Depicts group of mariachi players with skulls for heads. Excellent condition.   **$5–6**

Figurine, Bride and Groom. 3½" × 2". La Fuente Imports. Mint condition.   **$11–13**

Figurine, Day of the Dead. Frida Kahlo. Wears long dress with cape and carries her beloved monkey on her shoulder. Calla lilies embellish front of dress. 19" tall. Head is movable and removable. All handmade and handpainted. Mint condition.   **$160–175**

Figurine, Frida Kahlo with Monkey. 5" × 1¾". La Fuente Imports. Mint condition. **$15–17**

Figurine, Mariachi Player. 4½" × 1½". La Fuente Imports. Mint condition.   **$9–12**

Folk Art, Chest. Day of the Dead decoupaged chest, covered with images from Frida Kahlo's paintings, including those from "Roots," "The Wounded Deer," and "Self-Portrait Between the Mexican Border and the U.S.," as well as a couple of skulls and a skeleton image. Mint condition.   **$75–100**

Jewelry, Bracelet. Charm bracelet with skulls, marigolds, and other flowers. Skulls are acrylic, flowers are porcelain, papier-mâché, and plastic. Orange glass beads and freshwater pearls accent the charms. Circa 1940s. 7¾" long, foldover clasp. Mint condition.   **$150–165**

Mask, Dia de Los Muertos. By Zarco Guerrero. White skull with decorations and a necklace of beads. Made of fiberglass. Excellent condition.   **$500–550**

Plate, Day of the Dead. By artist Javier Ramos Lucano. Depicts young woman with long hair playing guitar. Measures 18" diameter. Signed on back of plate. Mint condition.

$100–115

Skull, Beaded. By Guadalupe Carillo Marquez. Large skull coated in wax and set with hundreds of tiny beads in various designs and images sacred to the Huichol Indians and their cosmology. Peyote buds, snakes, deer, scorpions, spirits, and coyotes evident. Almost 9" in length and 6½" in height and width. Excellent condition.

$165–180

T-shirt, "La Fiesta." White T-Shirt. Medium. Mint condition.

$16–18

T-shirt, "Los Burros." Black T-Shirt. Mint condition.

$16–18

Guy Fawkes Day/Bonfire Night (November 5)

In England in 1605, King James I was not tolerant of the English Catholics. Thirteen men, led by Robert Catesby, obtained 36 barrels of gunpowder and stored them in the basement under the House of Lords, intending to blow up the building. But during the planning, some of the men realized that innocent people might be injured during the explosion, and they started having second thoughts. One of them sent an anonymous letter to Lord Monteagle on November 5 explaining the whole thing.

Guy Fawkes, one of the conspirators, was in the basement of the building when authorities caught him. He was captured, tortured, and finally executed. Because he was in prison alone for two days, Fawkes's name became synonymous with the Gunpowder Plot, as well as the one connected with the holiday.

All the conspirators confessed to their wrongdoings and conveniently implicated a couple of innocent Jesuits in the plot, which gave the government excuses to mistreat even more people who believed in Catholicism.

Every year on November 5, Bonfire Night is celebrated with the burning of an effigy of Guy Fawkes and setting off fireworks. The English government instituted the holiday, which was illegal not to observe, in celebration of the fact that the plot to blow up the House of Parliament was foiled. Depending upon the community, the festivities are either extensive or rather small. Lewes, in the Southeast of England, is famous for its Guy Fawkes festivities, and thousands of people travel there each year for the holiday. Bonfire Night is not only celebrated in Britain. It was celebrated in New England (and called "Pope Day") until the eighteenth century, and it is still celebrated in New Zealand and Newfoundland.

Guy Fawkes collectibles include mugs, T-shirts, postcards, greeting cards, posters, and beer steins, because drinking is a major part of this holiday.

PRICE LIST: GUY FAWKES DAY COLLECTIBLES

Beer Stein. Bears Guy Fawkes image and "Remember, Remember . . ." poem. Ceramic with gold trim. Mint condition.

$18–20

Miniature Figure, Guy Fawkes by C. J. Nokes. Royal Doulton. 4" high. 1988–1991. Excellent condition. **$15–20**

Mug. "Remember, remember, the fifth of November." White mug with Bonfire Night slogan in red above a black and white depiction of gunpowder barrels. Mint condition. **$15–17**

Poster, Guy Fawkes Gunpowder Plot. Reproduction poster on fine parchment paper. 16½" × 11½" paper. Details about Fawkes's and conspirators' execution. Excellent condition. **$5–7**

Print, Guy Fawkes Bonfire on Ice Floe. Circa 1876. Published in *The Graphic*, illustrated newspaper. 5" × 12". Very good condition. **$10–12**

Tote Bag. Gunpowder slogan in red across white bag. Mint condition. **$17–20**

Veterans' Day (November 11)

Once known as Armistice Day, Veterans' Day is set aside as a holiday to celebrate the anniversary of the signing of the Armistice, the agreement between the Allies and Germans in 1918 that ended World War I. Both sides lay down their arms after the agreement was signed at 5 A.M., and the celebration of peace began in earnest with people in all the affected nations throwing parties, closing down businesses for the day, and organizing parades.

President Woodrow Wilson issued the Armistice Day proclamation that November, but in 1927, it was President Calvin Coolidge who called for American people to display the flag on November 11—and it was President Franklin Delano Roosevelt who, in 1938, made the holiday a legal one in the District of Columbia. On that day, solemn observances—often held by the American Legion or other groups of American veterans—commemorate the veterans of World War I, as well as the other wars in which Americans have fought. Presidents recognize the occasion with a visit to the Tomb of the Unknowns (formerly the Tomb of the Unknown Soldier) at Arlington National Cemetery, laying a wreath there and holding a short ceremony. The Tomb was inaugurated in 1921 to be the final resting place for a soldier of World War I, one of the many who had not been identified after the major battles in Europe during that war.

In 1954 an act of Congress changed the name of the holiday from Armistice Day to Veterans' Day, so that all veterans could be honored. President Eisenhower encouraged all American citizens to join him in recognizing those service people who fought, not only in World War I, but also in World War II and the Korean War.

Americans celebrate Veterans' Day with ceremonies at Arlington National Cemetery, as well as at other military cemeteries throughout the country. Cities hold parades marked by marching military bands and groups of soldiers from all branches of the service. Most schools and public buildings are closed on this holiday.

Collectibles for this holiday include posters, photographs, T-shirts, flags, postcards, wreaths, and military ribbons and pins.

PRICE LIST: VETERANS' DAY COLLECTIBLES

Badge and Ribbon, Veterans' Day. Gettysburg, New York. Monument dedication badge and ribbon. Belonged to veteran who attended New York Day at Gettysburg Battlefield, July 1, 2, and 3, 1893. Good condition. **$75–100**

Belt Buckle, Siskiyou Commemorative 1989 American Veteran D Day. #682 of a limited edition of 2,500. Made of heavy metal. Measures 3¼" × 2½". Front of the buckle has a detailed scene of the D-Day Invasion including men, ships, and plane. Front reads "American Veteran D-Day June 6, 1944, Commemorative 1989." Back reads "D-Day began on June 6 1944 with General Eisenhower telling his forces: You are about to embark upon a great crusade. The D-Day Invasion included almost 3 million men, 5,000 large ships, 4,000 smaller landing craft and more than 11,000 aircraft." Excellent condition. **$10–15**

Helmet, Presentation. Chrome. Based on an M-1 rear seam. Awarded after World War II and presented "by the members of Co. B in memory of Philip L. Russ, 1st Sgt., Co. B., 2nd Bn., 115th Inf. Maryland Army National Guard. 29 Years Continuous Service." Excellent condition. **$125–135**

Lithograph, "Daddy's Girl." Personally signed by artist Danny Day. Depicts mother and daughter sitting in front of VietNam Wall. Limited edition of 2,500. Approximately 21" × 28". Signed and numbered. Excellent condition. **$25–35**

Pin, Hard Rock Veterans Day. 2004 pin. Features a blonde girl saluting in blue navy uniform with U.S. flag and "Veterans' Day 2004." The red stripes on the flag sparkle. Pincraft pin in a Limited Edition 300. 2" × 1¼ ". Mint condition. **$15.95–18**

Pin, Walt Disney World, Veterans' Day, 2005, Mickey Mouse. Limited edition of only 3,500. Disney Design Group Artist Mark Seppala created the artwork. Pin released on 11/8/05. Mint condition. **$16.95–18**

Veterans Day Silver Bar. This one-ounce silver bar of .999 fine silver was produced to commemorate Veterans' Day 1973 by the Madison Mint. Patriotic image depicts Iwo Jima Memorial. Excellent condition for its age. **$10–15.**

Thanksgiving (Fourth Thursday in November)
The Holiday

The ultimate harvest holiday, Thanksgiving was first celebrated in 1621 by the Puritans who had just come to America. The holiday commemorated their first harvest in their new home. The Puritans had endured a long and eventful cross-ocean trip, overcome the problems of settling in a strange, new land, and beat incredible odds to stay alive despite inhospitable conditions, language issues with the Natives, and illnesses no one had expected. Their first year was devastating. But the Pilgrims were determined to make this New World their home, and once they harvested the foods they'd learned to plant from their new neighbors, they felt the need to celebrate their good fortune.

The Pilgrims were at peace with their Native American neighbors, and Governor William Bradford thought that was good enough reason to proclaim a day to be filled with thanks and good spirits. The Pilgrims and the Natives shared a meal that included turkey, ducks, geese, venison, lobsters, clams, fish, root vegetables, Indian corn, wheat flour, barley (for making beer), raspberries, blueberries, gooseberries, nuts, onions, leeks, cabbage, eggs, and spices. Some of the foods we now include in a traditional Thanksgiving meal that would not have been available to the Pilgrims are corn on the cob (the corn Indians grew was only good for making cornmeal, not for eating off the cob), potatoes, sweet potatoes, cranberry sauce (no sugar), and ham (no pigs).

Though Native Americans celebrated that first harvest with the Puritans, the holiday was not an official one for many years. George Washington was the first president to suggest that the holiday be celebrated by Americans in 1789, but his date for Thanksgiving was November 26. Americans kept celebrating the holiday throughout the early years of the country, even though some states celebrated on different dates. The holiday wasn't recognized nationwide until Mrs. Sarah Josepha Hale started lobbying presidents in 1827 and pushed for federal recognition of the holiday. As editor of a ladies' magazine and of *Godey's Lady's Book*, she had extensive influence with the women of the country, who got behind her plea to make the holiday a national one. Nevertheless, she was not successful, and the holiday was not officially recognized until 1863, when President Lincoln proclaimed that the day should be celebrated across the nation. In 1939 President Roosevelt designated the holiday to occur on the fourth Thursday in November, as it is today. Currently, there is a move toward an International Day of Thanksgiving, spearheaded in 2000 by Kofi Annan, secretary general of the United Nations. It calls for a holiday to promote peace and understanding among all people of the world.

It must be noted that, for today's Native Americans, Thanksgiving is not celebrated as a holiday but rather as a National Day of Mourning. The first time this commemoration was held was in 1970, when a group of Native Americans gathered to hear a speech given by Wampanoag leader Frank James at the top of Coles Hill, overlooking Plymouth Rock in Massachusetts. His angry speech highlighted the fact that while most Americans celebrate that first Thanksgiving, the Native Americans who fed those early settlers were later robbed of their lands and heritage. He spoke of the fact that early settlers often took Native Americans into bondage, and that the culture and language of his people are almost extinct as a result of the theft of their lands and the disenfranchisement of Native Americans. His speech reminds us that there is another side to this holiday and shows that there are many different voices in this country. What can be seen as a joyous celebration to one group of people can be cause for great mourning by another.

On Thanksgiving morning in modern times, many Americans begin the celebration by watching the annual Macy's Thanksgiving Day Parade (New Yorkers attend the parade in droves, and a huge number arrive the night before to see the big balloons inflated). The parade started in the 1920s when employees of Macy's, who were largely immigrants, wanted to celebrate their newfound nation with a celebration that echoed the ones they enjoyed in their old countries. They banded together and marched from 145th Street to 34th Street in various costumes and with floats, bands, and borrowed animals from the Central Park Zoo. The parade was a huge hit, and it became an annual tradition. In 1927 gigantic float-

Pilgrims and Pilgrim Boy with Turkey. 2004. All made of resin. Man is 10" × 5", woman is 9½" × 4". Set is $48.95–52. Pilgrim boy with turkey is 4½" × 5". $16.95–18. *Courtesy of Bethany Lowe Designs, Inc.*

Pilgrim Boy with Turkey Cart. 8½" × 12". Made of resin. *Courtesy of Bethany Lowe Designs, Inc.* $58.50–65.

ing balloons were added to the parade. During World War II, the parade went on hiatus in order to conserve the valuable commodities it took to create the balloons. In the 1950s, the whole nation began to enjoy the parade when it became televised. The parade has become such a strong tradition that other cities have begun holding Thanksgiving parades as well.

After the parade is over, the annual football games begin. During the early years of the twentieth century, the principal game was between the Detroit Lions and the Green Bay Packers, but now almost every major team, as well as college and high school teams, hold competitive games on the fourth Thursday in November. Traditionally, rival teams play each other on Thanksgiving, rather than varying teams, as they do throughout the rest of the playing season.

One of the most uniquely American additions to this holiday—which is heralded as the beginning of the Christmas season—is the day after Thanksgiving, or "Black Friday," (also called Blitz Day). This is the day that Americans start the frenzied holiday shopping season. Retailers believe that Black Friday is the turning point in their retail year. While much of the retail year may be financially uncertain, retailers know that from Black Friday through the end of the year, they should be making plenty of money.

The Symbols

Cornucopia

The cornucopia, one of the main symbols of Thanksgiving, comes from a Greek legend. Zeus was reportedly raised by a beautiful maiden who supplied his food and drink through a goat's horn that miraculously filled with goat's milk and food every night. Because of this legend, the cornucopia became associated with an endless supply of food and drink. To this day, the cornucopia, or horn of plenty, is associated with Thanksgiving and is pictured filled with squashes, pumpkins, gourds, and corn on the cob.

Dinner

The festivities on this holiday center around the traditional Thanksgiving dinner, though it is different than the one originally shared by the Native Americans and the Puritans, as noted above. In the early days of celebrating the holiday, people decorated their tables with foods of the harvest season. That laden table—overflowing with a golden-roasted turkey, cornucopia filled with gourds, resplendent cranberry sauce, luscious pies, and freshly harvested vegetables—has become one of the symbols most strongly associated with the holiday. Traditionally, friends, families, and extended families share dinner together, gathered around the largest table they can find.

Other Symbols

Other symbols include the Pilgrims and Native Americans themselves, the turkey (though it was not the only meat available on that first Thanksgiving table), and the pumpkin. All of these Thanksgiving symbols have been immortalized on everything from dinnerware to ornaments for a Christmas tree.

The Collectibles

Collectibles created for this holiday often echo the symbols of the day: turkeys as candy containers, pilgrims as salt and pepper shakers, cornucopias as centerpieces for the table, and autumn leaves for decorative accents. The good news for collectors is that though Thanksgiving has been around for hundreds of years, collectibles for this holiday are still relatively inexpensive and easy to find. I suspect that Thanksgiving items will be the next hot item, following the tremendous success of Halloween collectibles. That said, let's talk about what's available.

Serving Pieces and Table Decorations

Most households have at least one serving piece for the dinner table designed specifically for Thanksgiving. The most common piece found in an American home is the turkey platter, but whole dinner settings are often brought out on this holiday. Some of the companies that make Thanksgiving-themed serving pieces and dinner services include Wedgwood, Homer Laughlin, Johnson Brothers, Fitz & Floyd, Wood & Sons, Spode, Royal Staffordshire and many others.

Candy containers have been used on Thanksgiving since the late nineteenth century. Most are made in the shape of a turkey, often full-figure. The heads usually come off these metal-bodied candy containers, and the turkeys often have glass eyes. Glass containers with designs of turkeys, as well as other fowls, are also available.

The holiday calls for a plentitude of sweets to follow those huge dinners, so naturally chocolate candy molds made of pewter and tin are collected by fans of Thanksgiving. Full-figure turkeys, as well as pumpkins, cornucopias, and wheat sheaves are some of the Thanksgiving symbols that have been made into chocolate. German pewter molds are the most desirable.

Sweets are also set out on the table as favors. Set at each place setting, nut cups are made of papier-mâché, plaster, or cardboard/paper. Many of these collectible favors were produced

Turkey Candy Container. 6½" tall. Papier-mâché. Reproduced from vintage original. *Courtesy of Jamieson Studios.* $30.

in Germany from 1910 through 1940. Dennison created paper nut cups after that time and became the company that produced the majority of the paper decorations for this holiday.

Other paper decorations created for Thanksgiving include tablecloths, napkins, paper plates and cups, and centerpieces. Many of these examples are lithographed in bright autumn colors. As already stated, Dennison was the manufacturer of note for home decorations; however, collectors will also discover a wealth of other decorative items on the market, including some woven-reed nut cups and other decorations made in Japan. Some of these were filled with plastic replicas of fruits and vegetables. Crepe paper is another material widely used for decorations, and the orange and brown examples made in the 1950s were often filled with candy corn. Table decorations, specifically the lithographed and accordion-style turkeys and cornucopias, were used for several years, but they were not made to last, and are hard to find in perfect condition.

Candle figures molded in the shape of turkeys, cornucopias, pumpkins, candy corn, Pilgrims, and Native Americans have decorated Thanksgiving tables for at least a century. Candle companies like Gurley and Knorr Beeswax have created figurative candles that are now finding their way into collections.

Today's Thanksgiving table is often decorated with porcelain or china cornucopias, pumpkins, turkeys, or Pilgrim figures. The companies who produce dinner sets also create delicate figurines of John and Priscilla Alden, one of the first Pilgrim couples to marry in the new world, or an Indian chief and maiden. Lenox makes glass and china cornucopias, pumpkins, and turkeys. Hummel and Precious Moments both produce figurines of Puritans and turkeys. Lefton also has made Thanksgiving-based figurines.

Paper Ephemera

Paper ephemera for Thanksgiving includes postcards, greeting cards, magazines, books, posters, and photos. Dennison and other magazines offered readers suggestions for Thanksgiving menus, decorations, party favors, and ideas for celebrating the holiday. All of the ephemeral items for Thanksgiving have been produced since the beginning of the federal observance of the day. The postcards, created by companies like Raphael Tuck, Gibson, John Winsch, and Nash, depict the typical Thanksgiving symbols like turkeys, cornucopias, corn, and pumpkins—often accompanied by figures of Uncle Sam, Native Americans and Puritans.

Toys and Dolls

Toys created for Thanksgiving include stuffed animals, hard plastic pull toys, and puppets. Plush turkeys, Native American dolls, and teddy bears impersonating Native Americans are commonly made by companies such as Steiff, Danbury, Barbie, and Annalee. Banks created in the shape of a turkey or the other Thanksgiving icons are also available in iron, tin, and ceramic.

There are many more collectibles created for the Thanksgiving holiday, most of which are reasonably priced. This is one holiday that still hasn't hit its peak, so there's plenty of room for the amateur collector.

PRICE LIST: THANKSGIVING COLLECTIBLES

Art Cel, Snoopy and Peanuts. From the original *Peanuts Thanksgiving Special*. Snoopy is fighting with a chair. Professionally framed. Mint condition. **$1,500–2,000**

Bank, Turkey, Cast Iron. 1905 A. C. Williams cast iron turkey bank. 3½" high. Excellent condition. **$275–300**

Bowls and Cups, Fitz & Floyd. Made in Taiwan. Three cups with handles made of pilgrim figures. Dated 1990. 3¾" × 3¼" around rim. Three carrot serving dishes. Dated 1991. 5¼" × 2¼". Very good condition. **$150–175**

Candleholders, Fitz & Floyd. Huntington pheasant candleholders. Marked on bottom: "Fitz & Floyd Classics Huntington." Mint condition. **$78–85**

Candles, Pilgrim Boy and Girl. VintageThanksgiving candles in hunter green and white. 5½" tall. Excellent condition. **$9–12**

Candy Container, Turkey on a Log. Composite candy container. Marked Japan. Circa 1920s. Turkey on spring legs stands on log. Approximately 2¾" tall. Very good condition. **$75–90**

Candy Container, Turkey. German. Made in U.S. Zone. Circa 1945–1949. 7½" × 5½". Very good condition. **$150–175**

Candy Container, Turkey. German. Papier-mâché body; lead feet. Circa 1920s. Measures 6¾" from bottom of feet to top of his head, with a length of approximately 7", and a 3¾" width across the belly. Turkey's head comes off, and candy was stored inside. Stamped "Germany" inside the neck. Very good condition. **$625–650**

Candy Containers, Set of Four. Germany. Circa 1890s. Two made by Schaller and two of unknown origin. Largest: 8" tall. Made of a composite. Medium: approximately 6" tall. Two small ones: approximately 4" tall. All have lead feet. Very good condition. **$600–650 (for set)**

Candy Containers, Turkeys. Papier-mâché. Reproduced from Vintage Originals. Courtesy of Jamieson Studios. New. Mint condition. The large one is 6½" × 4¼"; **$30–35.** The small one is 5½" × 3¼"; **$22–25**

Card, Thanksgiving, Angels with Bluebirds. Postmarked 1909. Two cupids with blue wings sitting on grass among red hearts. Green and gold frame. Very good condition.

$40–50

Centerpiece, Turkey. Paper. Patent number dates it to 1926. 8½" × 7". Crepe paper has faded with age. Good condition. **$60–70**

Character Doll, Pilgrim. Simpich Thanksgiving man. Handmade character doll. 14" tall. Very good condition. **$155–175**

Chocolate Mold, Turkey. Antique and used for seasonal turkey treats, wax decorations or soaps. Very good condition. **$75–100**

Cookbook, Holiday. Features turkey on cover. Published by Culinary Arts Institute. Soft cover. 1973. Very good condition. **$14–20**

Cupcake Picks, Thanksgiving Icons. Seven small turkeys and one large turkey. Very good condition. **$3–5**

Decoration Set, Beistle. Set includes two 36' brown and orange tissue paper garland, three large tom turkey wall decorations, measuring 26¼" tall each, two male Pilgrims 23¾" tall, two lady Pilgrims 24½" tall, and two Indian figures 24¾" tall each. Wall decorations marked "USA." One large Honeycomb ball 16" in diameter and two small balls 14" in diameter. No mark. One large pumpkin 17" across and two small pumpkins 12" across. Stems marked "Made in USA." One large honeycomb turkey measuring 20" × 16" and two small turkeys measuring 13½" × 8½". Marked "Beistle, Made in USA." Near mint condition.

$75–90

Dinnerware Set, Churchill Thanksgiving Set. Forty-four pieces. Service for eight. No covered sugar or creamer. Mint condition. **$175–225**

Dish, Casserole. Copeland Spode's Reynold's pattern. Depicts autumn fruits and flowers, typical of Thanksgiving. 11⅝" × 7⅜". Excellent condition. **$300–325**

Doll, "The Turkey May Crow." Apple Whimseys Teddy Bear Turkey Doll by Lita Gates. Original tag, signed by Lita Gates 1/100, 8/5/99. Bear with turkey atop head. Array of red, orange, brown, and black feathers and fruit basket adds a distinctive touch of character and personality. Holds turkey baster and fruit and vegetable basket. Measures 26" tall. Apple Whimseys Company was composed of seven designing artists, all women, in business for almost twenty-five years. Mint condition. **$385–400**

Figures, Pilgrim Boy with Turkey Cart. 8½" × 12". Made of resin. Boy sits astride pumpkin with wheels and has a harness on the turkey. Mint condition. **$58.50–65 (pair)**

Figures, Thanksgiving Pilgrims and Pilgrim Boy with Turkey. Male and female Pilgrims (woman holds child in her arms, while man has pumpkin under one arm). 10" × 5", 9½" × 4". Made of resin. Introduced 2004. Mint condition. **$48.95–52**

Pilgrim Boy with Turkey. 4½" × 5". Made or resin. Introduced 2004. Mint condition.

$16.95–18

Figurine, Female Pilgrim. Fitz & Floyd Harvest Heritage figurine. Dressed in Puritan clothing, carries a basket with autumn flowers and vegetables. 18" tall. Mint condition.
$140–160

Figurine, Precious Moments®. "Squashed with Love." Depicts Native American girl with pumpkins. Mint condition.
$52–60

Figurine, Royal Doulton. "Thanksgiving." Gentleman in overalls feeding his turkey. Dated 1972–1976. Marked on base. Excellent condition.
$150–175

Figurine, Thanksgiving Angel. Made by Lefton, circa 1946–1953. 4½" × 3" × 2¼". Lefton paper label on bottom. Excellent condition, no chips or cracks.
$12–15

Figurine, Thanksgiving at Grandmother's House. Department 56 Original Snow Village®. Made of high quality resin and ceramic. Village building comes with a couple figurine, a child-with-dog figurine, an autumn tree, and a hay bale with assorted pumpkins. Lights up with batteries. Mint condition.
$75–85

Figurine, Thanksgiving Turkey, Porcelain. Made in Japan, marked on bottom. 2⅛" high. Excellent condition.
$10–12

Figurines, Native American Couple. Made of resin. Made by Pacific Rim Collectible. Approximately 18" tall. Looks like carved wood. Mint condition.
$75–90

Figurines, Thanksgiving Couple. Meant to be centerpieces. 17" tall. Contemporary. Excellent condition.
$85–100

Homemade Card, Thanksgiving, Pilgrim Boy and Girl. Made of felt. Pilgrim Boy and Girl. Circa 1950s. Very good condition.
$15–20

Magazine, *Pioneer* edition, 1953, Fall issue. Issue titled *Pioneer*, with articles on Wilderness, American Pioneer Spirit, Great West, Fall Harvest. Excellent condition.
$15–20

Menu, Thanksgiving, Chicago vs. Michigan Football Game, 1905. Embossed design of a football with the Chicago and Michigan University pennants and the score of 2 to 0. Inside page: small engraving of the Congress Hotel, noting R. H. Southgate as President. Menu designed and printed by Bicker. Measures 7" × 6" with blue, burgundy, and yellow ribbons on spine. Good condition.
$500–550

Ornament, "Holiday Inn," Radko. Shows turkey on one side, holiday decoration on back. Can be used for Thanksgiving. Excellent condition.
$36–46

Plate, Dinner. King Tom ironstone plate. Transferware design. Turkey in the middle of the design. Very good condition.
$40–45

Plates, Dinner (Twelve). Transferware. Turkey design. 10¼" diameter. Brown design, turkey in center and repeated in border. Marked Nikko Stone China, Japan. Excellent condition.
$450–500

Platter and Salt and Pepper Shakers, Turkey. Fitz & Floyd. Pastel colors. Platter measures 18" × 12½". Very good condition.
$28–32

Platter, Turkey, Ironstone. Transferware design in mostly black and white with splashes of color. 18¾" × 14½". Very good condition.
$63–75

Postcard, "May Thanksgiving Offer You the Fruit of Content". Circa 1910s. *Courtesy of Cocoa Village Antique Mall.* $12–15.

Platter, Turkey. Johnson Bros. Woodland Wile Turkeys design. Made in England. Patent No. 474.050. 20¼" × 15½" × 1½" deep. Excellent condition.   **$115–125**

Platter, Turkey. Johnson Bros. turkey platter. Circa 1880s. Windsor Ware. 20" × 15½". Brown floral pattern in background and trim. Turkeys (two) are brown, red, and green. Excellent condition.   **$200–225**

Platter, Turkey. Vintage gold trim platter with a turkey and barnyard scene. 15" × 13". Excellent condition.   **$55–75**

Postcard, "A Joyful Thanksgiving." Vintage card in excellent condition, marked in pencil on back "Fredrick from Lucille." Unsigned Brundage, Series 252D. Very good condition.
                    $12–15

Postcard, "Wishing You a Happy Thanksgiving," signed Clapsaddle. Printed in Germany. Published and copyrighted by International Art Publishing Co. in 1907. Very good condition.   **$9–12**

Postcard, Beaded Thanksgiving. 1910. Appliqué Nash postcard. Depicts two children on each side of a Thanksgiving menu. Color linen card. Very good condition.   **$3–5**

Postcard, Chef Bringing in Turkey Dinner. German. Light grey with gold leaves background. Little chef is holding open kitchen door with her foot. Antique. Very good condition.   **$55–75**

Postcard, Harvest Scene. Pictures Pilgrim bringing home turkey. Series 256A. Unused, some soiling and corner wear. Good condition. Circa 1907–1915. Very good condition.   **$10–15**

Postcard, May Thanksgiving Offer You the Fruit of Content. Grapes with inset of oval picture of cows. Circa 1910s. Very good condition.   **$12–15**

Postcard, Pilgrim Lady with Pie. Vintage, circa 1912, Series 642. Embossed picture of Pilgrim lady with pie and man with muzzle-loader and turkey. Very good condition.   **$12–15**

Postcard, "Thanksgiving Greetings". Circa 1910s.
Courtesy of Cocoa Village Antique Mall. $12–18.

Postcard, Thanksgiving, Pilgrim with Musket and Wishbone. Embossed. Printed by H.S.V. Lithographing Co., New York, as part of Series 800. Very good condition. **$13–16**

Postcard, Thanksgiving Greeting. Turkey in bright colors, framed by gold border. No stamp, but postal stamp and date on back (Oct 29 1912). Germany Series No. 7043. Very good condition. **$10–15**

Postcard, Thanksgiving Greetings, Girl with Turkeys and Pumpkins. Little girl in blue feeding big turkey. Never posted. Circa 1907–15. Excellent condition. **$10–15**

Postcard, Thanksgiving Greetings, Pilgrim Lady with Pie. Frances Brundage card. Copyright 1910, Series #130. Embossed. Excellent condition. **$13–18**

Postcard, Thanksgiving Greetings. Young girl driving two turkeys and cart. Circa 1910s. Excellent condition. **$12–18**

Postcard, Thanksgiving Greetings. Vintage. Fall colors showing Pilgrim couple, red apples, gold background, gold trim. Very good condition. **$10–12**

Postcard, Thanksgiving House Scene. 1911. Bas Relief Ellen H. Clapsaddle postcard. Series No. 2445. Dated Nov. 28, 1911. Published by International Art Publishing Company. Good condition. **$4–6**

Postcard, Turkey Carrying American Flag. Embossed. Beige, bark-like textured background. German. Never used. Near mint condition. **$45–55**

Postcard, Turkey on Stage with Cottage in Background. Dated 1911, postmark Friendship, NY. One cent stamp. Very good condition. **$10–15**

Postcard, Turkey. Shows harvest of fruit and flags. Excellent condition. German. Circa 1915. Near mint condition. **$85–95**

Postcard, Victorian Thanksgiving Turkey with Pilgrim Boy. Colorful gold background and pumpkin, corn, haystacks, turkey, boy in Sunday best, two-piece outfit. Unmailed M132. Very good condition. **$10–15**

Postcards, Lot of Four Vintage Cards. Some damage, but wonderful colors, turkeys, pumpkins, fall scenes. Very good condition. **$24–30**

Pottery, Turkey. Acoma pottery turkey by artist Terrance M. Chino, Sr. 6½" tall. Signed by artist. White, orange and brown stylized turkey. Mint condition. **$165–185**

Prop, PETA Turkey Puppet Prop. Lifelike turkey puppet. Movable parts. Lifelike feathers, beak, feet, etc. Used in commercials. Excellent condition. **$400–450**

Sugar, Creamer, Butter, Turkey Accessories. China kitchen items. All pieces are approximately 3" tall, made in the shape of a turkey. Excellent condition. **$25–35 for set**

Table Set, Children's. Pottery Barn. 29-piece table set for Thanksgiving. Set of four turkey placemats; four turkey "gobble gobble" napkins; four leaf coasters; four turkey place card holders; one Thanksgiving table runner; one Thanksgiving melamine dish set: service for four (four plates, four bowls, and four tumblers). Mint condition. **$155–175**

Tablecloth, Fall Colors and Pattern. 74" × 54". Durable cotton fabric. Red, yellow, and green on white background with white edges. Excellent condition. **$45–55**

Tablecloth, Turkey and Pumpkin. Thanksgiving tablecloth in vibrant colors. Features a Thanksgiving turkey surrounded by pumpkins. Border is harvest produce. Circa 1940s. 60" × 82". Excellent condition. **$75–100**

Tureen, Turkey. Fitz & Floyd, Autumn Bounty Collection. Majolica pottery. Turkey has rich colors: red head, gold beak, brown body feathers, long tan wing feather, brown-tipped orange tail feather, golden harvest corn and ripe purple grapes. 13¾" tall. Excellent condition. **$250–275**

VIP Passes (Four), Macy's Thanksgiving Parade, 2005. Passes will enable holders to view the Parade from the 77th and Central Park West Grandstands. Mint condition. **$2,850–3,000**

Yard Decoration, Mickey and Minnie. The Disney characters are dressed as pilgrims. Happy Thanksgiving Pumpkin between them. Made from ½" plywood. Mickey is 26" × 12". Pumpkin is 21" × 24" and Minnie is 26" × 13". Excellent condition. **$300–350**

– 12 –
DECEMBER

Saint Nicholas Day (December 6)

This holiday occurs early in the Advent season and celebrates "the real Santa Claus," who is patterned after Saint Nicholas, a bishop in fourth century Turkey. He passed away on December 6, 310, and that day is still the time Dutch children await the visit of Sinterklaas (the Dutch version of Saint Nicholas). When the Dutch began to emigrate to the United States in the seventeenth century, they brought their traditions with them and Sinterklaas became Santa Claus.

Saint Nicholas is depicted as wearing his bishop's hat and long evangelical robes. He often holds a staff or cross in his hand and is sometimes shown on a donkey, or putting gifts into children's shoes, as was customary.

People believe Saint Nicholas was extraordinarily kind and capable of performing miracles. Some of the things he is credited with doing include saving sailors, protecting young prostitutes from continuing their lives of crime, and bringing three young murdered boys back to life. He is considered the patron saint of sailors, unmarried girls, and children.

Christians today celebrate this holiday throughout Northern Europe, and one of the traditions is to leave gifts in children's shoes, like sweets and nuts. Tradition warns that children who have not behaved through the year will receive lumps of coal. German families put a shoe outside their bedroom doors before they go to sleep, expecting it to be filled with candy canes or other treats the next morning. This tradition is the precursor of the American habit of filling stockings on Christmas Eve.

Some parents impersonate Saint Nicholas or his nemesis, Krampus (also called Black Peter), and try to coerce their children into talking about their behavior throughout the year. In some families, it is customary to bake Saint Nicholas cookies, a type of sugar cookie made in the shape of the bishop. The Krampus figure began in Austria, and to this day,

Candy Container, Krampus on Wooden Shoe. Approximate size: 6" × 6". Composition with antique trims. The silk bag is the candy container. *Original design, sculpted and created by Scott Smith, owner of Rucus Studio.* $135–150.

there are two schools of thought about the figure. The secular version depicts Krampus as a scary creature who horrifies children on December 5 (the night before Saint Nicholas rewards them with gifts for being good). The magical or mystical version depicts Krampus as a figure that scares away evil spirits.

Americans moved this holiday closer to what is believed to be the traditional birthday of Jesus Christ in order to make the holiday more appropriate for the baby Jesus and his symbolic love for children.

Collectibles for this holiday are often confused with the ones produced for Christmas, so I will list a few of the images of Saint Nicholas and include the rest of them in the Christmas collectibles list.

PRICE LIST: SAINT NICHOLAS DAY COLLECTIBLES

Chocolate Mold, Saint Nicholas. Approximately 6" tall. Two-part mold. Depicts Saint Nicholas in bishop's robes. Circa 1860s. Excellent condition.   **$30–45**

Figurine, Sinterklaas. Depicts Saint Nicholas in red robes with bishop's hat. He holds a gift box. Peeking out from behind him is Black Peter. 12" tall. Wood. Manufactured by Beachcomber, Inc. Mint condition.   **$50–60**

Icon, Bronze, Russian. Approximately 2½" × 2". Eighteenth-century Russian Orthodox bronze icon depicts Saint Nicholas Chudotvorec holding open book. On his left and right are depictions of Jesus and the Virgin Mary. Decorated with original enamels. Very good condition.   **$50–75**

Icon, Russian. Circa 1750. Depicts Saint Nicholas, the Miracle Worker. Scraper-planed board with an ark, gesso ground, tempera, drying oil. Hagiographic icon. Saint Nicholas image in the middle with scenes from his life all around the border. Cleaned professionally. Very good condition.   **$450–500**

Postcard, Sinter Klaas. Circa early 1900s. Embossed postcard with image of Saint Nicholas/ Sinter Klaas. From Netherlands. Postally used in 1909. Good condition. $20–25

Hanukkah (25th day of the Hebrew month Kislev)
The Holiday
Hanukkah (which means "rededication" in Hebrew) is celebrated for eight days and eight nights, starting on the 25th day of Kislev on the Hebrew calendar. This holiday commemorates the Jews rededicating their temple to the worship of their own God in 165 B.C.E. Three years prior to that, the Syrian-Greeks had taken over the temple and dedicated it to the worship of Zeus. It took three years of fighting and the loss of many lives, including that of the Jewish High Priest, Mattathias, who had been instrumental in leading his fellow Jews into a rebellion against the Greek soldiers.

When Mattathias died, his son Judah took over the fight. Judah and his army were called the *Maccabees*, which means "hammers" in Hebrew, because they hammered away at the huge Assyrian army, finally winning the battle. The holy temple had been damaged and quite a few of the relics were missing or destroyed, including the golden menorah (a seven-branch candelabra that is the symbol of Israel). Talmudic legend states that Judah and his people cleaned and repaired the temple, and when they were finished, they decided to have a celebration, but after searching everywhere, they could only find a small amount of oil for the lamps. They used it, and amazingly that small bit of oil lasted for eight days.

Because of this miracle, Jews now celebrate the holiday by lighting a special menorah with nine branches that is made specifically for Hanukkah, called a *chanukia*. One candle is lit for each of the eight nights of the holiday. Originally, the Shammaite tradition was to light all eight candles the first night, then remove one per night for the following seven nights. However, the Hillelites began the tradition of lighting one candle the first night and adding another each of the seven remaining evenings. The candles are lit from left to right, though the candles themselves are placed in the menorah from right to left. The *shumash* (servant) candle, which is the highest one in the menorah, is used to light the rest of the candles. It is customary for families to light as many candlestands or oil lamps as they have doorways to their home. Perhaps this is why the holiday is often called the Festival of Lights.

Another tradition followed during Hanukkah is to play with a spinning top called a dreidel. Families give these to their children, and there are many collectible versions of these tops, some made of wood, some of metal, others of pottery; all are painted with a Hebrew letter inscribed on each side. The letters (*nun, gimmel, hay,* and *shin*) stand for the phrase *Ness Gadol Hayah Shem* which means "A Great Miracle Happened There." (In Israel the dreidels have a *pay* instead of a *shin*, standing for the phrase "*Nes Gadol Haya Po*" which means "A great miracle happened *here*.") These letters are also used in the game of dreidel to tell the players what to do on their turn.

There are special foods made on this holiday that are usually cooked in oil, including *latkes*, a type of potato pancake, and *sufganiyot*, which are similar to jelly doughnuts. Gold-wrapped chocolate coins called *gelt* are part of the celebration, and children receive these, in addition to real silver or gold coins.

The Collectibles

Collectible items for this holiday include menorahs and dreidels, as well as decorations for the holiday, dinnerware, artwork, toys, jewelry, postcards, greeting cards, and spiritual items.

Menorahs

Menorahs are made of a variety of materials, including metals, pottery, wood, and glass. Some hold candles, while others are made to light with oil. Decorative accents range from the traditional Lions of Judah, to flowers, Star of David, scrolls, and other symbolic elements.

Dreidels

Dreidels are made of wood, pottery, pewter, sterling silver, or glass. All dreidels are four-sided and inscribed with the Hebrew letters *nun*, *gimmel*, *hay*, and *shin* (except those made in Israel, as noted on the previous page).

Decorations and Dishes

Decorations for the holiday include linen tablecloths, placemats, and napkins, as well as paper versions made by the same companies, like Dennison's, that create paper decorations for many other holidays. Most of the decorations are created in the colors of the Israeli flag, which are blue and white.

Hanukkah dinnerware is made by the major companies like Lenox, Nambe, Waterford, Limoges, and many others. It is common for the dishes and serving pieces to be embellished with Judaic symbols and Hebrew letters, and blue and white are often the colors used.

Art and Jewelry

Artwork for Hanukkah often depicts the spiritual aspects and includes symbols of the holiday, like the menorah and dreidel, as decorative accents. A common theme is family togetherness during this season.

An example of the jewelry created for Hanukkah would be charm bracelets with the symbols of the holiday depicted on the charms. Gold Hanukkah menorahs can be hung on gold chains to make necklaces. The Star of David is often used as a charm or pendant as well. Blue and white stones decorate many pieces of jewelry created for the holiday.

Toys and Books

Hanukkah toys include teddy bears, finger puppets, candlemaking kits, books about the holiday and its history, and child-sized menorahs.

Cards and Postcards

Postcards and greeting cards for this holiday have been made by most of the major greeting card publishers, such as Hallmark, American Greetings, and Disney. Vintage postcards and greeting cards are hard to find because sending out greetings for this holiday isn't as common as for some other holidays.

PRICE LIST: HANUKKAH COLLECTIBLES

Doll, Chanukah Holiday Doll, Madame Alexander. Retired. 8" tall. The first Hanukkah doll Madame Alexander had made, dressed in blue and gold, wearing Star of David necklace. Excellent condition. **$120–130**

Figurine, Hanukkah Lights. Made by Lladro. #6027 retired in 1999. Depicts a young boy on his knees, with a dog by his side, looking at a Hanukkah candle. Mint condition. **$500–550**

Lamp, Hanukkah. Galicia. Cast bronze. Circa end of nineteenth century. 10" × 7". Handmade with lions on front. Good condition. **$90–100**

Lamp, Hanukkah. Libya. Cast bronze. Circa beginning of the twentieth century. 8" × 6½". Decorated with vase of flowers in middle of arch. Good condition. **$75–90**

Menorah, L'Chaim, Lenox. Made of Lenox ivory fine china, accented with gold. Decorated with a floral pattern and the Hebrew word for peace: *shalom*. Excellent condition. **$160–175**

Menorah, Sterling Silver. Approximately 12" tall. Made in U.S. Stamped "Sterling" on the bottom. Excellent condition. **$450–500**

Ornament, Hanukkah Dreidel Polonaise Ornament by Kurt Adler. Poland. Approximately 5" tall. Blue and gold glass. Mint condition. **$25–30**

Serigraph, "Homage to Chanukah." Artist: Yaakov Agam. This piece was specially commissioned for a Jewish organization in Canada, with only 99 regular editions printed, as well as ten artist's proofs. 28" × 28". Numbered and signed. Excellent condition. **$500–550**

Sign, LED, Happy Chanukah. 24" × 12". Blue motion lights. Mint condition. **$50–60**

Teddy Bears, "Chanukah Gelt Pooh" and "Dreidl Pooh." 5" plush bears made by Gund and discontinued. Original ear tags. Mint condition. **$40–50 (pair)**

Tidbit Tray, Star of David. Metallic silver accents. Approximately 6" wide. Mint condition. **$15–20**

Saint Lucia Day (December 13)

One of the traditional holidays in Sweden is Saint Lucia Day, or *Luciadagen*. Marking the beginning of the Christmas holiday season, this day is devoted to celebrating the life of Saint Lucia, a young Roman woman who is said to have been extraordinarily kind, and who gave up her life after being tortured and having her eyes gouged out. Even after losing her eyes, she could miraculously see, and thus became known as the patron saint of blindness. On December 13 (one of the shortest days of the year), one young girl from every village is chosen to represent Saint Lucia and is paraded through the town wearing a red ribbon around her waist and a ring of candles on her head. The holiday is also called the Festival of Light, because Saint Lucia overcame the darkness with her own type of light.

According to some stories, Lucia also endured an extremely painful death, which her followers believe was a miracle. A man loved her, but Lucia did not feel the same, and the man wasn't happy about his love not being reciprocated. When Lucia's mother requested that she marry the man, Lucia refused, and the man said he would burn her to death. Lucia was extremely religious, and prayed to God that she would withstand the fire. She survived, and when the man saw that she was not dying, he took a sword and stabbed her in the throat. Still she survived, and continued to speak for several hours before finally succumbing to death.

Another version of her story states that the man who loved her (whom she didn't love in return) admired her eyes, so she gave him her eyes and grew another pair. Her new eyes were even prettier than the originals, so he asked for those as well, and when she refused, he drove a knife into her heart.

Others say that Lucia took food to the Christians trapped in tunnels when the Romans were sending Christians into battle with lions. Another story chronicles her life as a Christian woman who was tortured and killed by the Roman emperor Diocletian in the first century. When tales of her life were brought to Sweden, she became known as the Lucia Bride, and it was said that she would go out in the early morning wearing white and a crown of candles to bring food and drink to the poor. It is the last story that is reenacted every year on December 13. The Swedish girls chosen to represent the Saint, as well as her siblings, wear white and carry lit candles. They bring their parents coffee and saffron buns early in the morning.

On Saint Lucia Day, families bake spicy gingerbread biscuits and *Lussekatter* (saffron buns), and fish and ham. Children in Sweden get out of school early. The holiday is also celebrated in towns in the United States that have been settled by Scandinavian immigrants.

Saint Lucia is also honored in her hometown of Sicily, where people gather with torches and build bonfires to celebrate her birth.

Collectibles made to represent Saint Lucia include figurines, ornaments, dolls, stamps, and coins. The items produced for this holiday are in the shape of Saint Lucia as she is portrayed in the Swedish celebration of her day: a young blonde girl dressed in white with a red sash around her waist and a candelabra on her head.

PRICE LIST: SAINT LUCIA COLLECTIBLES

Doll, Saint Lucia. American Girl Doll. 18" tall. Wears Saint Lucia gown, red and white striped stockings, and hair in braided buns. Includes Kirsten's Christmas Story pamphlet, Saint Lucia tray, wooden candle, heart shaped candleholder, sprig of holly, and checkered cloth. Good condition.   **$75–100**

Doll, Saint Lucia. Porcelain doll with LED lighted crown. 18" tall. Long blond curls. Holds coffeepot on tray in her hand. Mint condition.   **$30–40**

Prayer Card, Saint Lucia. Circa 1950. Includes a medal marked "S. John Vianney pray for us" and the other side says "S. Philomena pray for us." Card made in Italy. Very good condition.   **$3–5**

Recipe Collection, Saint Lucia Day. Recipes include traditional foods served on Saint Lucia Day, such as *Lussekatter*, *Glog*, *Köttbullar*, and *Pepparkokar*. Mint condition.   **$5–7**

Stamps, Saint Lucia. Christmas 1979 stamp sheet. Depicts various paintings of Saint Lucia from Italy. Very good condition. $5–7

Tree Topper, Saint Lucia. Ceramic tree topper. 12" tall. Depicts Saint Lucia in prayer with candles atop her head. Cone underneath her dress. Very good condition. $14–15

Las Posadas (December 16–24)

Las Posadas is celebrated by people of Mexican descent. The holiday allows celebrants to re-live the mystery of the journey Mary and Joseph took to Bethlehem. The trip is reenacted during this series of evening events. *Las Posadas* actually means "shelters" in Spanish, which defines the manger in which the Christ child was born.

Neighborhood parties are held every night during Las Posadas. Children are dressed to im-itate the Holy Family, with processions following them, playing music, singing litanies, and carrying candles. A child dressed as an angel leads the procession to a house where half of the group begs for food and shelter from the other half. The doors to the house are then opened, and the procession enters to enjoy food and treats. Once the festivities begin, the most popular event is swinging at a piñata, an earthenware figure filled with gaily wrapped candies and other treats. The piñata was traditionally shaped like a star to symbolize the one that led the three wise men to the manger to discover the baby Jesus, but contemporary piñatas come in many different shapes, including donkeys, like the one upon which Mary rode to Bethlehem.

The last night of Las Posadas, Christmas Eve, is the most important because the evening's festivities are followed by midnight mass at church. When I visited Puerto Vallarta several years ago during the Christmas holidays, we took part in the Christmas Eve Las Posada, as well as midnight mass at Our Lady of Guadalupe Church. The streets were full of cele-brants that evening and the skies lit up with fireworks after the evening service was over.

Las Posadas collectibles include books, songbooks, nativity decorations, and of course, piñatas. Most of the items are Mexican-made, though the holiday has gained in popularity in the United States and some collectibles are now being made here or mass-produced in Hong Kong and Taiwan. Vintage piñatas are desirable and rare because piñatas are made to be cracked open on the night of festivities.

PRICE LIST: LAS POSADAS COLLECTIBLES

Book, *Las Posadas: A Bilingual Celebration for Christmas.* For Parishes and Groups. By Kathryn J. Hermes, FSP, and Marlyn Monge. Includes an explanation of the holiday, words and music to the songs, and information for children. Mint condition. $2–3

Book, *The Christmas Piñata.* By Jack Kent. Parents' Magazine Press, New York; 1975 copyright. Hardcover; 7½" × 10¼". Excellent condition. $25–30

Book, *The Night of Las Posadas.* By Tomie dePaola. Scholastic Press. Soft cover. Mint con-dition. $8–10

Pin, Disney. Retired 2002 "Las Posadas" pin depicting the Three Caballeros, characters from the Disney movie. 1¼" wide. Cloisonné. Mint condition. **$8–10**

Piñata, Bull. Jose Cuervo bull. Circa 1970s. Cuervo sign on side. Shades of pink, orange and yellow crepe paper covering the bull and its horns. Stuffed with newspaper. Trap door for candy in belly of bull. Very good condition. **$40–50**

Piñata, Donkey. Crepe paper 23" tall donkey. Ready to fill with candy and toys. Mint condition. **$15–18**

Christmas Eve & Christmas Day (December 24 and 25)
The Holiday
The most popular holiday of the year is also one of the last to be celebrated. Christmas, the day Christians celebrate the birth of Jesus Christ, is a religious occasion, but through the years, it has also become a day connected with peace and joy. People all over the world get together with loved ones or with strangers who become friends and rejoice in Christ's birth by giving either their time, their love, or their gifts. Stories of Christ's birth in a manger in Bethlehem are told in churches and living rooms, and a feeling of tranquillity and harmony prevails.

The Symbols
Though traditions for celebrating this holiday differ, depending on region or family customs, there are many recognizable icons and symbols associated with this holiday. Some are religious (the manger with nativity scene) while others have grown as a result of cultural and spiritual traditions (Santa Claus). The two figures who represent the holiday are very different from each other, yet both have a religious base.

Baby Jesus
Jesus as the Holy Child is usually depicted in a cradle, lying on a mattress of hay, with Mary and Joseph, his mother and father, beside him. The Bible states that an angel came to shepherds in the field, saying "And this shall be a sign unto you; Ye shall find the babe wrapped in swaddling clothes, lying in a manger" (Luke 2:12). The Infant Jesus is depicted on ornaments, figurines, candles, and many other places.

Santa Claus
The persona now known as Santa Claus is the figure most children instantly think of when Christmas is mentioned. Most people have no idea where this legendary figure comes from, and it is a common misconception that Santa Claus is mythical and has no basis in reality. The truth is that the icon that has morphed into a white-bearded man wearing a suit of red velvet with white fur trim was actually a holy figure himself. Saint Nicholas, a bishop in fourth century Turkey, was known for his kindness and compassion, especially toward women, children, and sailors (see Saint Nicholas Day for more information).

Through the centuries, this religious figure became the center of attention and children would look forward to his visits on December 6, but by the time of the Protestant Reforma-

Nativity Ornament, Siegnitz. Circa 1890–1900. Approx. 2¾" × 2¾". Wire and scrap. Figures made of lithograph scraps. *Courtesy of Barbara Brunner and Gary Heidiger.* $350–450.

Dresden Angel Ornament. Circa 1880–1890. Approx. 4½" tall. Gold. *Courtesy of Barbara Brunner and Gary Heidiger.* $1,000–1,200.

Angel Ornament. 4" long. Wax with Spun Glass. Germany. Victorian. *Courtesy of Cocoa Village Antique Mall.* $175–200.

Wood Nativity Set. About 6". Carved, painted and signed. From the village of Bogorodsk, Russia. *Photo Courtesy of The Russian Shop.* $200–225.

tion in the sixteenth century, people no longer thought it wise to celebrate the birthday of a saint. Saint Nicholas, in his bishop's robes and high hat, usually holding a staff, transformed into a figure dubbed "Father Christmas," and the two holidays (Saint Nicholas Day and Christmas) blended together in many cultures.

Early illustrations of this figure depict him as a tall, thin gentleman wearing floor-length robes with a wreath of holly or mistletoe on his head. Sometimes the robes are trimmed in fur, sometimes he carries a staff, sometimes he holds a bag of toys for the children, sometimes he carries a yule log or a small fir tree, and in some cultures he carries a handful of switches (one of the legends tells that he comes to the household to determine whether children have acted properly throughout the year, and if they haven't, he gives them switches or coal). Every culture has a slightly different image of Saint Nicholas, including his clothes and his physical appearance.

Grandfather Frost Matryoshka Dolls. About 3½". Painted birch wood. Bielarus label. *Photo Courtesy of The Russian Shop.* $25–40.

Winter Bell Dolls. About 4". Painted and signed. From Rostov on the Don, Russia. *Photo Courtesy of The Russian Shop.* $50–60.

Old World Santa. 20" tall. *Courtesy of Jean Littlejean Santas.* $795.

Old World Father Christmas. 1996. 5'7" tall. Hand sculpted, one of a kind. *Courtesy of Bethany Lowe Designs, Inc.* $5,995–6,250.

He is also known by many different names. Saint Nicholas is still the name used in Northern Europe, while Sinter Klaas is what he's called by the Dutch, and Kris Kringle (a variation of the name the Germans use for the Christ Child) is what he was called by the Germans who settled in Pennsylvania in America's early days. There have even been negative connotations attached to the figure, represented by the story that Saint Nicholas was accompanied by another person called Krampus or Black Peter, who was responsible for meting out punishment to the children who hadn't been good. In the 1800s, these sinister figures were one of the most popular Christmas items and known as Belsnickles.

It would be neglectful if I didn't mention some of the artists who have brought Santa Claus alive, particularly the ones who have created the images and stories of the distinctly American version of Santa. The story most American children associate with this holiday is the one told in 1822 by author Clement C. Moore (1779–1863), who reportedly wrote *A Visit from St. Nicholas* as a gift to his own children for Christmas. The story of the night before Christmas and the cherry-nosed gentleman who came down through the chimney to deliver toys for the children has represented the December 25 fantasy ever since. It was first published anonymously on December 23, 1823, in a Troy, New York newspaper as a poem, but later it was published as *'Twas the Night Before Christmas* in an anthology of Moore's work, and the first illustrated version was published in 1849. That illustration depicts Santa wearing a fur hat, jacket, and knee britches.

In 1999, descendants of another poet, Henry Livingston, Jr., began debating the claim that Moore wrote the poem, and through careful research, scholars have discovered that their claim might be correct, since the newspaper has retained copies of a letter Moore wrote asking if anyone knew the author of the poem before he included it in his own anthology and claimed it as his own. However, until someone prints the poem with Livingston listed as the author, the Hunt Library at Carnegie Mellon University (which houses most of the illustrations of the famous holiday poem) claims they will continue to give Moore credit.

Since that time, many well-known illustrators have taken up their pens and brushes to create their version of this popular figure, such as Thomas Nast, Grandma Moses, Jessie Wilcox Smith, and Arthur Rackham. Each year, around the beginning of October, various publishers produce their newest illustrated version of the classic tale, with award-winning illustrators attempting to make their St. Nick more attractive or distinctive than the last one. Some of the contemporary versions feature illustrations by Jan Brett, Mary Engelbreit, Christian Birmingham, Tasha Tudor, and many others.

One of the most famous Santa Claus images produced in the United States was created for an advertising campaign for Coca-Cola® by Haddon Sunblom, a Michigan-born artist who eventually used his own image to create the "jolly ol' soul." Sunblom read *'Twas the Night Before Christmas* to get inspiration for the image his company wanted to use in their holiday advertising campaign, and he created a robust figure in a red and white velvet, fur-trimmed suit. It was a warmer and more human image than the previous examples of Santa Claus created by illustrators like Thomas Nast. Earlier depictions of Santa were more elf-like or holy, often with a tan coat and long robes, most closely associated with the Saint Nicholas figure revered in Europe. But Sunblom's Santa was totally American, and from 1931 to

Books. Selection of children's Christmas books. *Courtesy of Karen Pinkney.* $10–18 each.

Chenille Star Ornaments. Approximately 6". Reproduced from vintage originals. *Courtesy of Jamieson Studios.* $6.

1966, he graced Coke ads and became ingrained as the American public's idea of the Santa Claus image.

Stars

There are a few other symbols that have also come to represent Christmas. Perhaps the earliest is the star. In the book of Matthew, the Bible states that the wise men had followed a star to find the baby in the manger. From that holy occasion came the star used to decorate Christmas trees and homes for the holiday. The star most people place at the top of their Christmas tree symbolizes the star the wise men followed.

The Christmas Tree

The Christmas tree is often depicted as a pagan symbol of this purely Christian holiday, and it is true that it started out as a Druid tradition to signal the beginning of spring. In fact, even the prophet Jeremiah wrote about the vain customs of men cutting down a tree and decorating it. Romans used the pine tree to symbolize Attis, the son of Cybele. The Cybele cult chose a pine tree every March 22, decorated it, and mourned over it as if it were the person himself.

Perhaps the first connection of the pine tree with Christmas itself was in the eighth century, when the German missionary Saint Boniface gathered the Christians around him and cut down an oak that pagans had used in sacrifices and considered sacred. When the tree fell, it split and revealed a healthy pine growing in its center. The Christians took the pine tree as a symbol of their faith, at the suggestion of Boniface, who noted that its top pointed heavenward.

When the Puritans came to power in England, they demanded their followers not continue some of the old traditions, such as burning the yule log, using mistletoe, singing Christmas carols, decorating the Christmas tree, or anything else that were deemed "heathen traditions." The Pilgrims in America banned the same traditions; in fact, Governor William

Bradford ordered all "pagan mockery" stamped out. Christmas trees were not decorated in America in those early years.

The decorated Christmas tree as we know it started in the sixteenth century in Germany and was not popular elsewhere until the nineteenth century. During those years, the tree was a small one, placed on tables and decorated simply with candies, fruit, and cookies that the guests of the household would eat. These trees were called "sugar trees," and when the treats that hung on them were replaced with paper, they were facsimiles of the original fruits and candies. It is assumed that this is the tradition that Pennsylvania Germans brought with them to the United States in the mid-eighteenth century. A children's book published in Philadelphia in 1845 entitled *Kris Kringle's Christmas Tree* depicted Santa carrying a pine tree.

There are many legends surrounding the Christmas tree. One states that the fir tree was the original tree of life and had once grown with fruits, leaves, and flowers, but when Eve ate from it, it lost the ability to produce these things. Another story is that the Holy Family hid inside a pine tree when being chased by Herod's soldiers and that the Christ Child blessed the tree. Austrians and some other Christians believe that all the trees of the earth blossomed the night Christ was born, and for that reason, they bring branches of hawthorn, cherry, and pear trees inside, then put them in water so that they will bloom in time for Christmas. Legend also has it that all Christmas trees bow down on the eve of the Christ Child's birth in deference to him.

Holly

The Druids believed holly to be sacred, and Christians believed that holly miraculously grew its leaves to hide the Holy Family from Herod one evening. It is also said that holly is one of the trees that Christ's cross was made from. Christ's crown of thorns is thought to have been made from a wreath of holly. Early saints and Christians hold a branch of holly in pictorial depictions because it is said to represent their reflection upon Christ's passion. Holly is thought to have the power to keep away evil. Its connection with Christmas also includes a belief that English virgins hung it by their beds to protect themselves from goblins. Because of these superstitions, early Christians were forbidden to use the plant because of all the pagan superstitions associated with it. Once holly became more strongly associated with Christmas, it became an accepted part of the season and symbolic of the holiday.

Ivy

Ivy symbolizes the everlasting love and devotion Christians feel for Jesus. Ivy clings, thrives in the shade, and is green year round. It also stands for eternal life and resurrection, and before it was associated with Christmas, it was associated with resurrection in both Egyptian and Roman history.

Mistletoe

There are many legends surrounding the symbolism of mistletoe. One is from Scandinavia, where mistletoe is associated with Frigga, the goddess of love. The other legends come from pagan and Druid tales that extoll the strength of mistletoe. Romans noted that Druids cut away mistletoe from trees but knew of its strength, so they spread white cloth on the ground

Feather Tree. Circa 1970s. 8" tall. Decorated with wooden clip-on birds. *Courtesy of Holly Knight.* $40–50.

Feather Tree. Circa 1930s. Approximately 4' tall. Victorian. Decorated with ornaments, mostly glass. *Courtesy of Cocoa Village Antique Mall.* $600–700.

Feather Tree. Decorated with Shiny Brite ornaments, with box at base. *Courtesy of C.S. Post.* $45–75.

in order to keep it from losing its sacred powers. They used it in sacrificial acts and hung it over doorways so that the household would be protected from evil.

The legend most closely associated with Christ is that his cross was made from mistletoe wood and that from his death forward, the plant was destined to exist as a parasite.

The actual practice of kissing under the mistletoe comes from Norse traditions, which were brought to England by early invaders. Norsemen would lay down their arms and declare a truce if they met enemies in a forest (thus, the tradition of kissing under the mistletoe, a plant commonly found in the forest). In England, the minister of York hung a branch of mistletoe in the cathedral and declared that it represented a universal pardon.

Wreaths

Wreaths are symbolic of Christmas because they are circular, having no beginning and no end, just like Christ's love. The Advent wreath, used in Catholic celebrations of the Christmas holiday, is made of an evergreen, including three purple candles and one pink candle. Each Sunday during the month of Advent, one candle is lit, the purple ones first, then the pink, each representing a week during the Advent period. Some people place a large white candle in the center, which is lit on Christmas Day.

Candy Canes

Candy canes are shaped like either an upside down J (for Jesus) or a shepherd's staff. The white and red colors signify the purity of Jesus and the red blood he lost at his death. It is said that the first person to make candy canes was a German choirmaster who fashioned sugar sticks into the shape of a shepherd's staff. He passed them out to children during the Christmas service, and soon the candy became a popular holiday custom, decorated with roses. It wasn't until the 1900s that the canes became red and white striped and peppermint flavored. A candy maker in Indiana started the story that the cane symbolized the story of the birth of Jesus. Traditionally, the three red stripes on the cane are said to represent soldiers' stripes by which Christians are healed, and the wide red stripe represents Christ's blood on Calvary. The three small white stripes represent the Trinity, while the larger one represents Christ's passion. Sometimes there is a green stripe on the cane, which represents giving, as Jesus was God's gift to humankind.

Candles

Candles were used long before Christmas was celebrated. Pagans worshipped a sun god called Balder. People believed that fires would bring back the sun god, so fires and candles were lit. During the early days of Christiandom, candles or lanterns were used on Bible stands to signify eternal hope, faith, spirituality, and devotion to a singular passion. They were used in marriage and fertility rites because of their phallic shape. Candles also symbolize Christ's purity and salvation, and the flame represents His divine nature, while the candle represents His body.

Bells

The use of bells to signal a call to worship began in 431 A.D. with Bishop Paulinus of Nola. Pagans used bells to cast spells, communicate with the dead, and summon demons, but

Ornament Wreath. A mix of antique and modern ornaments. *Courtesy of CSPost.com.* $25–45.

Christians used bells to frighten away storms and evil spirits. The bells remind Christians to come to church and to keep the Sabbath day holy. They can ring for a marriage or a funeral, for a warning or for a celebration, but the bells on Christmas Day ring to remind everyone of the joyous hour of Christ's birth.

Red and Green

The colors red and green are symbols of the blood Christ shed for mankind and the color of spring and new growth. During the Christmas season, these colors indicate both the love and suffering Christ endured during his life, as well as the hope for Christians in both this world and the next.

Stockings

The stockings that celebrants hang on Christmas Eve may have their origins in a story about Saint Nicholas. Legend has it that he delivered some coins to three sisters who had no money to spend on their weddings. They had put their stockings by the fireplace to dry that evening and the coins landed on the stockings, starting the tradition of putting stockings out for St. Nick or Santa Claus to fill on Christmas Eve.

The Collectibles

Unlike many other holidays, decorative items and collectibles made for Christmas were designed to stand the test of time. Cultural influences impact the type of items each family preserves, and sentiment also determines what each person collects. Items that collectors treasure include Advent calendars, advertisements, banks, beads, bells, books, candelabras and candles, candy containers, cards (greeting cards and postcards), chocolate molds, cookie cutters, cookie jars, dinnerware, dolls, feather trees, figures and figurines, folk art, garlands, jewelry, lamps and lights, mangers and nativity sets (including figures), nodders, nutcrackers, ornaments, plates, salt and pepper shakers, Santas (of all shapes, sizes, ages, and types), snow babies, snow globes, stamps, stockings, tablecloths and towels, toys, trees, tree toppers, tree stands, wreaths, and a thousand other items too numerous to name or count. Suffice it to say there's something for everyone, and I will attempt to offer a bit of information about each of these collectibles below.

Advent Calendars

A German man named Gerhard Lang printed the first Advent calendar in 1908. The Advent calendar is meant to mark the twenty-four days until Christmas either by marking a line through the dates, opening little doors on each day to reveal small gifts or candies, or lighting a candle for each evening of the Advent season.

Calendars were not produced during World War II because of the shortage of paper, but in 1946 Richard Sellmer Verlag began producing a series of Advent calendars that are still sold today. The 1946 version of a house with windows and doors that opened was produced in German, English, and Swedish. (Check the bibliography for a link to an online museum of Verlag's Advent calendars.)

Advent calendars can be made of wood, cardboard, or paper. They stand up to display their openings or hang on a wall. Though the traditional Advent calendars depicted houses, churches, or stores, there are many more modern ones in the shape of Santa or another figure. The doors or windows open to display pictures, or might have a piece of chocolate or a small toy hidden behind them.

Today most greeting card companies produce Advent calendars, and companies such as Disney and Mattel have their own versions.

Advertisements

Every company with a product to sell tries its hardest to get that product to the public during the Christmas buying season. Collectors tend to choose advertisements for certain products or from certain stores. All of the major department stores have had full page ads for Christmas since the mid-1800s. The advertising companies realized that they could boost sales for retail businesses tremendously by promoting products during the season when most people were inclined to be buying presents anyway. As a result, ads, brochures, signs, trading cards, postcards, and letters selling Christmas items, as well as regular items being pushed during the season, are readily available and are often fairly inexpensive.

When retailers began selling ornaments and decorative accents for Christmas trees in the mid-1800s, they knew they would need ways to lure buyers into their stores. Macy's Department Store of New York discovered that the benign and jolly figure of Santa Claus was a great draw. They billed themselves as the "official Santa headquarters" in 1862 and began promoting themselves as the store where Santa had left his supply of Christmas gifts. Other stores followed Macy's lead, and before the turn of the century, Christmas became a retail holiday with Macy's, Marshall Field's, Sears, and other prominent department stores filling the newspapers with ads for the goods they were selling that holiday season.

Certain iconic figures have been created strictly for the Christmas season and are recognizable to most Americans, like the Coca-Cola® Santa. Brand recognition is important for products, especially during the holiday season when most companies make the bulk of their annual retail dollars. Other retail icons simply don Christmas outfits during the season (such as red caps, decorative wreaths, or lights).

When collecting advertising, the most important thing for the collector to remember is to watch for condition. Buy the best item you can afford, especially since advertising is meant to be "for the moment" and you might not be able to find that particular item again. Also remember that paper, cardboard, and tin items damage easily and are meant to be temporary, so keeping ads, trade cards, postcards, and other paper items from year to year requires special care, like keeping the items in dark, dry, and cool storage areas. Store the items flat rather than folding or rolling. Pack especially fragile or valuable items in acid-free alkaline folders, polyester film folders, or alkaline mats, which neutralize acidity.

Banks
Though most collectors prize the iron mechanical banks that were popular at the turn of the nineteenth century, some simply want banks manufactured in the shape of Christmas icons, like Santa Claus. The early iron banks made in the shape of Santa Claus often depict him in clothing typical of the European-style Saint Nicholas figure, rather than the jolly, fat figure dressed in red and white who became popular in the United States.

The mechanical bank was meant to take a coin, and uses some type of mechanical action to drop it into the slot. This type of bank was extremely popular during the Victorian age, and the original versions were made from 1880 to 1920. After that time, banks took a back seat to other toys, but the ones that were still produced were either cast iron, tin, or ceramic, until the widespread use of plastic in the 1950s made it possible to manufacture banks more cheaply. Now most banks are made of plastic.

The Stevens Company made a cast iron bank in 1889 depicting Santa Claus putting money into a slot in the chimney. A Santa Phone Bank was also made in the early 1950s and 1960s in Japan, though the manufacturer is unknown. A number of novelty plastic Santa banks were made in the 1950s by Harret-Gilmar Inc. of New York City.

Beads
Beads became popular during the Victorian era, and were used to decorate the Christmas tree, as well as to hang on mantles and across doorways. The early decorative beads were made of glass and were usually manufactured in Eastern Europe. Store-bought ornaments, beads, and household decorations started becoming popular in 1870. Christmas beads are still used for decorative purposes, but most modern ones are either ceramic or plastic.

Bells
During pagan celebrations, bells were rung to frighten away evil spirits. Bells are also used in many cultures to "ring out" the old year and to "ring in" the new. As Christian and pagan elements were combined, bells became part of just about every Christmas celebration, whether in a church service or as part of a community festivity. Bells are rung for fires and to call people to church; they are used to warn people of hurricanes or to summon townspeople together for meetings. Some bells are used to "tag" animals (like cow bells), while

Garland and Sled. Brightly colored glass beads of various sizes stretch over 8½'. $16.50–20. Ceramic sled measures 2½" × 5" × 2½". $30–35. *Courtesy of CSPost.com*

others are musical. There are so many different types of collectible bells that collectors have formed an association to share information about their finds called the American Bell Association.

Holiday bells are typically thought to announce the birth of Jesus Christ, and they have become an integral part of the Christmas season. Many seasonal songs have been composed to highlight the sound of bells (like "Jingle Bells" and "Silver Bells"). When Santa figures ring the bells, they are often asking for donations for the poor; typically, Salvation Army volunteers also use a bell when asking for donations during the holidays. But the type of bells most collectors choose to collect are decorated specifically for the season.

Bells have been made of wood, iron, glass, porcelain, silver, pewter, and any other material that will produce a ringing sound. They were first cast in the United States in the 1700s, but they had been made throughout the rest of the world for many hundreds of years before that time. The Meissen Porcelain Factory of Germany was the first to cast porcelain bells in the late eighteenth century. Paul Börner, an engineer and artisan, is credited with the creation of four porcelain bells in 1929, a feat most consider his masterpiece. Some of them are cast, like the pewter bells created by sculptor Michael Ricker, while others are pressed glass or hand-painted bone china.

Some of the companies currently making collectible bells for the holidays include Hutschenreuther, Lefton, Avon, Precious Moments, Mikasa, Lladro, Hummel, Swarovski, Disney, and many others. The bells these companies make are decorative, and often hand-painted or figural.

Books

Though one of the best-loved tales of the Christmas season is a book that has been rewritten and illustrated almost every year, *'Twas the Night Before Christmas*, there are numerous other books that are considered collectible and are quite sought after by those who love to read about the holiday.

Christmas books fall into many categories, so I'll cover only a few. Perhaps the most popular category of Christmas books is illustrated versions, and often the books that are illustrated can also be classified as children's books. The illustrations, age, and condition of the book are what determine its value. The more common the book, the lower its value. If a book was printed for only a short period of time, and the quality of the paper, as well as richness of illustrations, is high, then chances are your book will be worth more. Certain illustrators are also more collectible than others, such as Frances Brundage (1854–1937), Kate Greenaway (1846–1901), Jessie Willcox Smith (1863–1935), Trina Schart Hyman (1939–), Tasha Tudor (1915–), Richard Doyle (1824–1883), and many others.

Some collectors prefer to collect nonfiction books about Christmas, such as compendia of information about the holiday itself, Christmas icons, festivities throughout the world, and collectibles or antiques. This type of book is less valuable than the illustrated children's books, but like any other book, the value of nonfiction tomes about the holiday depends upon age, edition, and condition.

Still others like to collect works of fiction set during this holiday. Publishers will specifically ask authors to create holiday-related stories to feed the public's desire for novels of this type. For instance, well-known authors such as Charles Dickens, Fannie Flagg, Anne Perry, Oscar Hijuelos, Mary Higgins Clark, John Grisham, and many others have all contributed to Christmas-themed literature.

In addition, cookbooks and books on decorating for the season abound. Cookbooks filled specifically with Christmas recipes became popular in the early 1800s, when Christmas desserts and suggestions for decorating the home were found in ladies' magazines and books, and annual versions of holiday cookbooks became even more popular during the Victorian era. Fannie Farmer's first cookbook, published in 1896 by the Boston Cooking School, became the one most holiday chefs turned to for recipes during the season when hostesses opened their homes to friends, neighbors, and family members.

Condition is paramount when collecting anything, but is perhaps even more important for books. The book's spine must be intact and sturdy. Pages must not be dog-eared, torn, or foxed. If the book originally had a dustcover, it must be intact. First edition copies are valued more highly than any other edition. Signed copies (by either the author or illustrator or both) are highly collectible and valuable.

Candelabras and Candles

The symbol of light is closely tied to the birth of Jesus, and candles have been used to decorate Christmas trees since the very beginning of the tradition. Candles were held to the branches of the tree by a small clip attached to the candleholder. Glass candle lanterns, hung from the branches with a wire, were also used. They were made of colored glass and are quite a find for the Christmas collector.

German homes have displayed a single candle in the window to celebrate the holiday since the sixteenth century. According to legend, this candle was meant to light the way for the arrival of Kris Kringle. Today, you often see homes with a single candle in the window, a reminder of this long-ago tradition.

Figural candles have been manufactured for Christmas by companies like Gurley (you can find more information about Gurley earlier in this volume). During the 1950s, most homes had a set of Gurley candles that they had bought in a discount department store. The candles, typically choir figures, angels, nativity figures, Santas, and reindeer, are becoming more and more valuable to collectors today.

Candy Containers

Candy containers have been created in the shape of Santas and other Christmas icons since the late 1800s. Many of the earliest examples were made by Germans and typically have lithographed faces. Cardboard and paper Christmas trees were also used as candy containers, as were stockings, candy canes, snowmen, sleds, and reindeer. Typically, the head of the figure lifted off and the candy was placed inside. They were made to be given to children on Christmas day and were not meant to last longer than that holiday, so early examples are difficult to find.

Victorian-era candy containers were often made in a cornucopia shape and were meant to be hung on the tree. These chromolithographed paper candy containers might have been made by the woman of the house who had followed directions in a ladies' magazine for making the container.

Twentieth-century versions of candy containers made of wood or plastic are more readily available for collectors. Japanese examples are often poorly painted and have strange looking faces. The toys that Japanese Santas hold are often in net sacks.

Cards (Greeting Cards and Postcards)

People tend to use the holidays as an excuse to get in touch with family members and friends via a carefully chosen greeting card or postcard. The colorful holiday greeting cards became a cottage industry in themselves, one which collectors by the thousands have enjoyed examining over the centuries. The first Christmas greeting card, a three-part depiction of a family toasting one another, was created by Henry Cole of London in 1843. Though cards and postcards have been sent since the mid-1800s, the heyday of holiday postcards, the time when premier illustrators created beautiful cards in vivid colors, was from 1890 to 1930. Obviously, greeting cards and postcards were still sent after that time, but the majority of the postcards are now photographs rather than illustrations, and the quality has significantly diminished. Collectors, attracted by the images of a bygone era, tend to prefer the cards created in those earlier years.

As mentioned earlier in this book, certain publishers and illustrators are more popular and valuable than others. Collectors are often urged by professionals in the field of deltiology (postcard collecting) to narrow their collections by publisher, illustrator, date, subject matter, or type of card in order to make collecting simpler.

Christmas cards and postcards give collectors an indication of the trends of the day and the ways in which Santa and other Christmas icons were depicted. Cards produced in Europe usually showed Saint Nicholas or Santa in a long robe (not a red outfit) carrying a staff. Dolls and toys are often held by the Santa figure (offering additional information for collectors about the types of items produced during that period of time and in that area). Cards

Postcard, Santa and Child on Donkey. Circa 1920s. *Courtesy of Cocoa Village Antique Mall.* $10–15.

Postcard, "A Merry Christmas". Postmarked 1929. *Courtesy of Cocoa Village Antique Mall.* $6–10.

Postcard, "Merry Kris Kringle". Postmarked 1920. *Courtesy of Cocoa Village Antique Mall.* $6–10.

are wonderful historical references because they depict people and customs of the era. Looking at a postcard or greeting card can also show you the fashions of the day, as well as the way homes were decorated for the holidays. The illustrations are often indicators of when the card was printed.

Here is a very brief history of the postcard. The first postcard was produced in Austria in 1869. Most European and Scandinavian countries produced official postcards by 1874. During the 1890s, chromolithography (four-color reproductions) became popular (previously, cards were printed in only one color). In 1898–1900, stick-on stamps were used on postcards. In 1901 an act of Congress allowed private citizens to print photograph postcards, and in 1907 the back of a postcard was divided in half. By 1930, linen postcards were popular.

Preserving your collection of holiday postcards and greeting cards is extremely important because maintaining the condition is paramount to keeping the card's value. Professionals suggest that you keep your collection in a dry, cool, dark place, and that cards are separated from each other by acid-free paper, glassine, or Mylar. Stacking cards on their edge is preferable to lying them on top of each other, since embossing and mechanisms can become damaged by stacking.

Chocolate Molds

Originally made in Germany during the late 1800s and early 1900s, molds of all sizes were used to create solid and hollow chocolate figures of Santa, Saint Nicholas, angels, and other Christmas figures. The sizes range from a couple of inches to a couple of feet, with most being approximately 8" tall. Some of the figures are on sleds or other vehicles, while others carry Christmas trees or toys. Most molds are made of tin, though some cast iron and nickel versions have been made.

Molds fall into two categories: full figure and flat. The full figure molds come in two or more parts that have to be pinned together. The flat molds only decorate the chocolate on one side.

The chocolate-molded candies created during the latter part of the nineteenth century and the beginning of the twentieth were often accompanied by paper decorative accents. For example, a chocolate Santa might be accompanied by a paper basket full of tiny toys, or he might have a wooden staff through a hole in his chocolate hand. Figures created during that time period were realistic, but the ones created during the 1920s, the Art Deco era, were simplified fantasy figures. After the 1950s, it became common for cartoon figures to be created in chocolate, and the molds were plastic instead of tin or iron.

The companies that made these molds sold them in department stores, at candy shops, and through catalogs. Some of the well-known manufacturers of chocolate molds include Micelli (still in business today), Eppelsheimer, Anton Rieche, Jaburg Brothers of New York, and Vormen.

Today, antique molds are often used to produce figures in materials other than chocolate, and some of the folk artists included in this book employ this technique.

Chocolate Mold, St. Nicholas. Victorian. Approximately 12" tall. Good condition. *Courtesy of Trout Creek Folk Art.* $225–275.

Santa Chocolate Molds. Circa 1930s. From 3" to 11" tall. German, most made by Anton Reiche. *Courtesy of Trout Creek Folk Art.* $200–800.

Cookie Cutters and Cookie Jars

Carved wooden molds, iron and tin molds, and pottery molds have been used to create gingerbread and other types of cookies since the late nineteenth century. In addition, cookie cutters made of tin, plastic, and pottery have been used to create cookies that were often hand painted with vegetable colors or decorated with die-cut pictures. Often, these sugar cookies were strung with ribbon and hung on the Christmas trees, then eaten on Christmas Day.

Cookie cutters used by hand often have a handle as part of the tin or iron shape so that the cookie maker could exert some pressure on the dough and be certain that the iconic shape was recognizable after the cookie was baked. Cookie cutters in the shape of typical Christmas icons, such as Santa, the Christmas tree, stars, bells, candy canes, sleighs, and reindeer are commonly available for collectors at fairly reasonable prices. The older carved wooden molds are harder to find and tend to be pricier.

Naturally, where there are cookies, there are cookie jars. The history of this fairly new collectible began in the 1920s, but jars became more popular during the 1940s and hit their height in the 1950s. Some of the makers of collectible jars include Hull, Shawnee, McCoy, Red Wing, Metlox, Regal China, American Bisque, and California Originals. Today's Christmas cookie jar collectors also know that certain artists produce original cookie jars in limited editions.

Christmas Plate, Nikko. Approximately 8" diameter. *Courtesy of Jeffrey Ostroff/Seller Dropoff.com.* $20–28.

Christmas Platter, Nikko. Approximately 18" long. *Courtesy of Jeffrey Ostroff/Seller Dropoff.com.* $45–65.

Dinnerware

When the Victorians started seeing Christmas as a time to decorate their homes and throw incredible parties, proper dinnerware became extremely important. Every manufacturer of dinnerware began producing special sets decorated with holiday motifs to serve the Christmas dinner in as festive a manner as possible.

Most holiday sets are sold in sixteen-piece sets that include four place settings. Serving pieces are considered extra, though most families would purchase a large platter and at least three serving bowls. Especially important to the Victorians was a coffee set, including the pot, and during the winter months, a chocolate set (a tall pot meant for hot chocolate and requisite cups) was often a necessity.

Some of the many companies who created holiday dinnerware sets from the mid-1800s to contemporary times include Wedgwood, Lenox, Spode, Noritake, Fitz & Floyd, Villeroy & Boch, and Dansk. It is important for collectors to try to purchase complete sets, though there are services available to replace missing pieces when cousin Jack drops your porcelain tea cup on the floor.

Dolls

The most popular toy given for Christmas through the years has been the doll. In all of the early depictions of Santa shown with a basketful or bagful of toys, there is almost always a doll hanging out of the side. It is no surprise that annual lists of hot Christmas toys always include several dolls. In fact, certain companies produce holiday dolls every year.

The dolls given during the mid-1800s and early 1900s were largely porcelain-faced beauties dressed in their finest for the holidays, but they weren't necessarily "Christmas dolls." During the mid-1900s, companies began producing dolls designed strictly for the season.

One of the most important pieces of advice for doll collectors is to have a collecting focus and a set budget; otherwise, everything that comes on the market is fair game—and where dolls are concerned, that's a pretty big market! That said, here are some of the doll makers who have produced Christmas or holiday dolls: Madame Alexander, Barbie by Mattel, Chattie Cathy by Mattel, American Girl by Pleasant Company, Ginny Dolls, Annalee Dolls, Ashton Drake, Lee Middleton, and many, many others.

Figures and Figurines

In the early twentieth century, figures of Santa and other Christmas icons were made in papier-mâché, pressed cardboard, and plaster of Paris. Most of these early figures were produced in Germany and are not the round-bellied figures recognizable as today's Americanized Santa. Used as table and mantel decorations, the figures ranged from a couple of inches to a couple of feet in height and often held feather trees or candles, or were accompanied by a sleigh or reindeer.

The figures became so popular that German manufacturers began creating molded designs that appeared almost sculptured. These early depictions of Saint Nicholas or Sinter Klaas show him with his hands tucked inside his full sleeves. Their bottoms were flat so they could set on a table or mantel. Some had a wire through their head so the figure could be hung on a tree.

Dollmakers jumped on the bandwagon by 1910–1915 and created porcelain heads for the Father Christmas and Santa Claus figures. Cotton beards were attached to the porcelain faces, and the figures were often dressed in chenille robes. Santa's expression was usually one of blissful happiness.

After World War I, manufacturers in Japan started creating reproductions of the figures previously made in Germany; however, the ceramic faces they created were rougher and sandier than their porcelain counterparts. Japanese manufacturers became the largest producer of these figures, mainly because they could offer their wares at a lower price than companies in Germany or the United States.

Figures changed when the Santa created by *'Twas the Night Before Christmas* became recognized as the American version. During World War II and the subsequent years, Santa grew rounder and jollier, so later figures are almost instantly recognizable. Instead of plaster or porcelain figures, figures made of composition, celluloid, and plastic became common.

Most of the early German figures are unmarked or are simply marked "Germany," and the figures made in Japan are stamped with the country mark, unless created during the period when Japan was occupied by Allied forces (1945–1952). Today's figures and figurines are made by a number of companies including Enesco Corporation (Precious Moments, Heartwood Creek, Cherished Teddies, Disney), M. J. Hummel, Department 56, Lenox, and many others.

Folk Art

Though we don't often think about it this way, the earliest Christmas decorations were largely created by artists with little or no formal training, so, retrospectively, those items can be classified as folk art. However, most of the items created many years ago were not signed by their makers.

Japanese Santa's face. Circa 1940. *Courtesy of Jean Littlejohn.* $125–175.

Santa Doll. Circa 1950s. Approximately 20" tall. Plush figure with velvet and fur, with a celluloid and plastic face. *Courtesy of Holly Knight.* $45–75.

Today's folk artists contribute an incredible array of items for the Christmas collector. Some of the artists who were kind enough to participate in this volume on holiday collectibles are following their dream by spending long hours at their craft. We encourage you to explore the artists' web sites or to visit the retail shops that sell their goods.

To briefly introduce the artists included in this volume, let me tell you a little about each of them (contact information is located in the index).

Trout Creek Folk Art is Ginny Betourne, an artist who works in "possible truthful factoids." Her sculptures are wacky and wonderful, and she creates figures for most of the holidays. The works she has for sale are often determined by season and availability. Everything she creates is one of a kind.

Baker Company Designs, owned and operated by Lori Ann Baker-Corelis, creates handcrafted and heirloom quality bears, rabbits, and other characters. A soft sculpture artist, Lori has been making her lovable creatures for sixteen years.

Bethany Lowe Designs, owned and operated by Bethany Lowe and her "crew," is a group of folk artists who create one-of-a-kind and limited edition handcrafted holiday collectibles. Their web site and retail outlets throughout the United States showcase the artists and their wares.

Rucus Studio is owned and operated by Scott Smith, a self-taught artist with a special love for Halloween and Christmas. He uses composition and papier-mâché to create limited

Mr. Frost. 2004. 9" tall. *Original folk art by Trout Creek Folk Art, Napa, Calif.* $160–180.

Santa Gets A Ride! 8" tall. 2002. Papier-mâché, crepe, and goosefeather branch. *Original folk art by Trout Creek Folk Art, Napa, Calif.* $95–125.

Angelica. 32" long. Mohair head and hands, linen body and legs, wearing a vintage dress and shoes, holding antique Christmas accessories. Has a tinsel wreath and wooden wings. *Courtesy of Baker & Co.* $595.

Children Building Snowman. 9½" × 13". Made of resin. Introduced 2001. *By (and courtesy of) Bethany Lowe Designs, Inc.* $69.95–75.

editions of figures such as candy containers, Santa figurines, and other original holiday pieces.

Ladeedah Folk Art, owned and operated by Lori C. Mitchell, creates holiday items that are original, one-of-a-kind, licensed designs. She produced her first line of papier-mâché figures in 1999 and her first licensed reproductions with ESC Trading Company in 2003.

Jamieson Studios, owned by John Jamieson, specializes in vintage-inspired holiday recreations. Most of the pieces available for sale are created with the original molds from the 1930s and 40s. Jamieson's items are available in many museum shops.

Sharyn Sowell is a "scissor artist" who works with paper and colors in the same way German *Scherenschnitte* artists have for centuries. She creates her designs for greeting cards, framed art, garden gates, needlework kits, and more.

Jean Littlejohn creates approximately one hundred Santa dolls per year and sells them from a little shop in North Carolina. Her designs are inspired by old-time European Santa figures, and one of them resides in the governor's mansion in Raleigh.

Garlands

Early Christmas garlands were largely homemade and edible, made of things such as berries and popcorn, but the Victorians started being more inventive with their decorations and demanded more festive items for the Christmas holiday. Later garlands were made of Czechoslovakian beads or pottery beads.

Garlands are meant to be draped around the tree, swagged or circled, depending upon the decorator. Some Victorians used fabric, ribbon, or paper for garlands, which have not withstood the test of time as well as glass or pottery beads. Often the garland included decorative accents, like stars or birds, attached to the cording or tinsel.

Child holding Santa Mask. 2002. 7" × 4". Made of resin. *Courtesy of Bethany Lowe Designs, Inc.* $21.95–25.

Santa's Toy Chest. Approximate size: 18" × 13". Made in the traditional German style, using composition, antique fabric and trims, and a curly goat beard. *Original design, sculpted and created by Scott Smith, owner of Rucus Studio.* $975–1100.

I Believe. . . . 9¾" × 9". Papier-mâché. © *Lori C. Mitchell,* 2004. $600–800.

Tree Trimming Angel. 7½" Tall. Papier-mâché. ©*Lori C. Mitchell,* 2004. $225–250.

Santa Boots. 5" × 6", 7" × 8", and 11" × 12". Reproduced from vintage originals. *Courtesy of Jamieson Studios.* $22, 28 and 45.

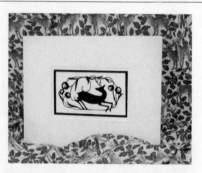

Scherenschnitte Art, Deco Deer with Flowers. 11" × 14", including mat. *Photo and Copyright © Sharyn Sowell. All rights reserved.* $45–55.

Scherenschnitte Art, Santa's Parade. 11" × 14", including mat. *Photo and Copyright © Sharyn Sowell. All rights reserved.* $165–180.

Jewelry

Decorative jewelry for the holidays has been produced for several centuries, but the bulk of what you will find on the market today was manufactured after the early 1900s. As with all types of jewelry, the buyer should rely on a reputable dealer who can identify the type of stone used or the age of the jewelry.

Much of the Christmas jewelry produced after the 1950s is considered costume jewelry and is often in the shape of seasonal icons like Christmas trees, Santas, stars, and reindeer.

Lamps, Lights, and Bulbs

In the seventeenth century, the Countess of Orleans of Germany decided to decorate her tree with candles symbolizing the birth of Christ. Though dangerous, this type of decoration persisted—some decorators even poured wax directly on the tree limbs and lit them.

Santa with Antique Dolls. 27" tall. Mounted on a black velvet covered base. *Courtesy of Jean Littlejohn Santas.* $1,495.

During the 1700s, some Americans decorated their trees with a glass container designed to float wicks with a small amount of oil. The container, designed by Baron Stiegel, could be lit and hung on the tree. The glass tumblers were colored glass, blown or molded into shape. Later, molded versions were more affordable and available to the general public.

By the eighteenth century, rings of wood set with candles were hung on the tree and lit. They were extremely dangerous, so candlemakers soon made candleholders that had metal disks attached to catch wax dripping from the candle itself. The look of a lit Christmas tree was so effective that Charles Kirchof (a German immigrant also known for inventing the yo-yo) invented a pendulum-weighted candleholder. The holder had a wax pan on top and was hung on the tree with a long, bent wire. As a weight, a clay ball hung from the bottom. This style of holder made sure that the candle remained upright on the tree.

Clip-on candleholders became popular in the 1870s, and were commonly purchased in sets of twelve. Figural clip-ons decorated with stars, birds, butterflies, angels, flowers, fruits, and children's faces were made in many different colors.

Other types of candle or lamp lighting were used, but since most of them were quite flammable, there are few examples for collectors to add to their current collections.

By the early 1920s, electric lighting had pretty much replaced actual candles as tree decorations. Electricity had become available to most Americans and was fairly inexpensive. But the lure of candles was still attractive enough that the bulbs were made to imitate the flame from a wax candle. Early light bulbs were pear shaped, like the flame of a candle, and figural ornaments became the most popular of the Christmas light bulbs produced from the 1920s through World War II. As with ornaments, the popular shapes for figural light bulbs were flowers, birds, stars, Santas, and fruits, but they were soon joined by more "contemporary" figurals like comic strip, fairy tale, and nursery rhyme characters. And after World War II, people turned back to the original image: the candle.

Candolier, Nine-light Bubble-Brite™. Shiny Brite's authentically reproduced 1940s animated candle lights exclusive to Christopher Radko. *Courtesy of CSPost.com* $40–50.

Bubble lights became a craze when Carl Otis, an employee of Montgomery Ward, invented the phenomenon. The lights resembled a lit candle, but were made of plastic with a circular base. Inside, a liquid was heated and it bubbled toward the "flame" giving the illusion of an actual candle. The lights were marketed by Noma in 1946, and the technique that powered the "bubble" was directly related to how the chemical inside the tube boiled when heated with the electrical current.

By the 1950s, a new fad had developed: the circular color wheel. Made of cellophane color panels, the wheel was placed under a tree (often an aluminum or completely white feather tree) and a floodlight placed behind. The wheel would turn and different colors bathed the tree in light.

After the color wheel, Christmas lights morphed once again into sets of twinkle lights, tiny sparkly lights that provided an effect similar to a sky full of stars. Over time, these lights have changed from all blue to various colors to all white.

To be collectible, lamp lighting, clip-ons, or electric lights must be in good condition. But the caveat is that most bulbs are either burnt out or worn by the time collectors add them to their collections. The paint on figural bulbs is often faded or nonexistent. Filaments inside early bulbs, particularly carbon, burn out easily. If collectors want to use old lighting in their contemporary decorating schemes, they would be wise to test them before putting them on the tree—and don't mix the different types of bulbs together or they'll burn out the string.

Mangers and Nativity Sets

One of the first nativity displays was set up by St. Francis of Assisi in Italy in 1223. He recreated the original manger scene with the help of some local landowners, borrowing some sheep, an ox, a donkey, and some people from the local village. From that time on, people have continued to recreate that image. By the 1700s, carvers in Germany were fashioning Mary, Joseph, the Wise Men, shepherds, animals, the manger, and baby Jesus out of native wood. Later manger displays would be fashioned from coral, marble, shell, mother-of-pearl, alabaster, pottery, and many other materials.

Nativity scenes came to the United States with Moravian peasants, who had migrated from Germany to Pennsylvania and other parts of the Eastern United States. They began producing *putz* scenes: elaborate reenactments of the manger scene. These large wood figures were set against landscapes both natural and manmade.

Crèche scenes have been portrayed by artists for hundreds of years. They range from the extremely valuable one-of-a-kind works of art created by internationally known artists to cheap imitations of the scene that are mass-produced by manufacturers who sell them for less than the price of a box of cereal. The possibilities for a collector in this field are endless.

Nodders and Bobbleheads

The earliest nodders and bobbleheads came from Germany. One was actually mentioned in the short story "The Overcoat," written by Nikolai Gogol in 1842. The dolls stand approximately 6–8" tall and have extra large heads set on smaller bodies. They are called nodders or bobbleheads because their heads are attached to their bodies with a light spring, which causes them to "bobble" around on their necks. One of the first bobbleheads was sold in the United States in the 1920s, but the bobblehead craze didn't hit the country until the 1960s. Early bobbleheads were made of papier-mâché, but the more recent versions are plastic or plaster. Bobbleheads have been made of almost every holiday figure, but the most common is the Santa Claus bobblehead, which was popular during the 1950s and 1960s. Most of the holiday nodders were made in Japan.

Nutcrackers

As with so many other Christmas legends, the Nutcracker story comes from Germany. The Erzgebirge region of Germany became the center of this woodcarving industry after its metal mining industry died out in the 1700s. Because the area had an abundance of wood, its enterprising inhabitants began carving all kinds of wooden collectibles, the nutcracker becoming the most popular. The term *nussknacker* (nutcracker) became part of the Grimm Brothers dictionary in 1830.

The legend of how the nutcracker was invented states that a farmer wanted to open his nuts easily, so he solicited the help of anyone who might have a good idea. A soldier suggested shooting it, while a carpenter thought sawing the nut might work, but the best idea came from a puppet maker, who carved a puppet with strong jaws powerful enough to crack the hard walnut.

The Sonnenberg and Erzgebirge regions made figural nutcrackers in the shape of kings and soldiers. Through the years, these figures have evolved in many ways. Now, they can be figures from movies, politicians, writers, and everyday people. My sister has a collection of nutcrackers that she displays every Christmas, including a chef, a golfer, many different types of soldiers, kings, and Santas, and she adds more to the collection every year.

There are many nutcracker makers, but several are well known. Wilhelm Fuchtner is known as the "father of the nutcracker." He became the first commercial producer of nutcrackers in 1872, using a lathe to make many of the same design. One of the companies that creates highly collectible nutcrackers is Steinbach, a German company. Christian Steinbach is considered one of the premier nutcracker makers. Today, his daughter Karla continues the tradition. Steinbach nutcrackers are signed, stamped, and dated. Another company known for fine nutcrackers is Christian Ulbricht, who took over his father's business in 1968 and has expanded the business to include two locations in Germany (one in Lauingen and one in Seiffen) run by his daughter and son.

Ornaments

The first ornaments to be placed on an evergreen tree in celebration of the Christmas holiday were edible: fruits, candies, cookies. Then decorators started making their own ornaments out of paper, popcorn, cranberries, and nuts. Those pieces ended up in chromolithographed paper cornucopia candy containers that adorned trees in the late nineteenth century.

In addition to fruit, candy, nuts, and handmade ornaments, tinsel was used to adorn the tree. Real silver tinsel was invented in 1610 in Germany. Machines stretched the metal into thin silver strips that were draped across the limbs of the Christmas tree, reflecting the light thrown by candles. Decorators used this type of tinsel right up to the twentieth century, when it was replaced by a lighter silvery-paper version.

Glass ornaments were first made in the small German town of Lauscha during the 1600s by glassblowers who had established a glassmaking center there. These glassblowers also learned how to make the same type of beads Czechoslovakian beadmakers produced to decorate the Christmas tree, as well as hollow glass balls called *kugels* that were hung from windows to protect homes from evil spirits. In addition to these glass balls, other shapes were made out of glass, like fruits and nuts, and used to decorate the trees.

Store-bought ornaments began to replace homemade ones during the Victorian era. Between 1870 and 1890, the majority of the ornaments were wax or cotton and crafted into the shape of angels or children. These ornaments typically came from Dresden, Germany.

Toy merchants in Sonnenberg, Germany, took over the making and selling of glass ornaments in the mid-1870s, and began exporting them to the United States. The first ornaments were simply decorated balls, but then they began making ornaments in the shape of fruits, vegetables, animals, and Christmas icons. One of the sillier shapes was the pickle ornament. German families hid the pickle ornament deep in the tree among the other ornaments, challenging the children to find it. Whoever found the ornament first got a special extra gift and could be the first one to begin unwrapping the Christmas presents.

For a while, German ornament makers had the market cornered, but then F. W. Woolworth, the department store giant, came along. Soon that company was selling $25 million a year in ornaments—most of which cost less than $1 per box . The ornaments were round balls decorated with Christmas scenes or greetings, birds, fruits and vegetables, nuts, vari-

Christmas Ornament, Kugel, Mercury Glass Grapes. Circa 1900s. Approximately 3" long. *Courtesy of Holly Knight.* $75–90.

Acorn Christmas Ornament. Circa 1940s. Marked "West Germany." *Courtesy of Holly Knight.* $15.

ous animals, figural Santas, Santa faces, snowmen, angels, clowns, nursery rhyme figures, Native Americans, and other human figures. The ornaments were often decorated with glass beads, spun glass tails or wings, and painted accents. There were millions of ornaments sold in a short thirty to forty year period, so every imaginable type was made, and the American public built their collection of ornaments to be used every year on the family Christmas tree.

During the latter half of the nineteenth century, glass ornaments wrapped in thin wire became popular. Very delicate, these ornaments were usually silvered and often embellished with chromolithographs depicting Santa, elves, angels, or other Christmas icons. To utilize the wire wrapping technique in a unique way, some of these ornaments were created in the shape of hot air balloons, zeppelins, and flying angels hanging from a star, as well as birdcages, umbrellas, and musical instruments. Because these ornaments are quite fragile, they are also quite rare, and usually expensive for collectors.

World War I interrupted the sale of glass ornaments, as well as the production of just about every other decorative accent. After World War I, German glass ornaments dominated until World War II again interrupted production.

The Shiny Brite company, an American-based ornament producer owned by Max Eckhardt, began selling their wares in 1937. In 1939, when England stopped all exports coming from Germany, Eckhardt made a deal with the Corning Glass Company to take over production of the ornaments. Shiny Brite became popular in department stores, filling in the

Siegnitz Baby Buggy Ornament. Circa 1890. Approximately 3" × 2¼". Wire, cotton, and wax with Dresden wheels, silk ribbon, and a wax baby inside. *Courtesy of Barbara Brunner and Gary Heidiger.* $700–800.

Auto with Baby Ornament. Circa 1890. Approximately 3" × 2½". Wire automobile with gold foil, Dresden wheels, a wax baby, and glass beads. *Courtesy of Barbara Brunner and Gary Heidiger.* $700–800.

Locomotive Ornament. Circa 1890. 3½" × 3". Wire with cotton, Dresden wheels, a lead figure, and a tin pipe spewing smoke (cotton). *Courtesy of Barbara Brunner and Gary Heidiger.* $1,000–1,300.

Heavenly Sleigh Ornament. Circa 1890–1900. Approximately 4" × 2". Dresden. Made of cardboard. *Courtesy of Barbara Brunner and Gary Heidiger.* $1,200–1,500.

blanks left by German manufacturers, and now their ornaments are experiencing a surge of interest in the collecting world, and some are starting to be reproduced.

Though glass ornaments are the most popular, there are many other kinds of ornaments available for collectors. Spun glass and scrap ornaments are made of lithographed faces or figures adorned with spun glass wings (for angels) and skirts (on Santas). The same technique was used for scrap and tinsel ornaments: the subject of the ornament was a chromo or cellophane figure, decorated or adorned with tinsel. These were popular in the early 1900s.

Cotton ornaments, popular during the early 1900s and later recreated by Japanese manufacturers, had cotton wool bodies and bisque, porcelain, scrap, or plaster faces. Cotton Santas and snowmen were the most popular figures, but angels and cotton animals were also

Dresden Eagle Ornament. 7" wide. Made of pressed paper. Turn of the century/Victorian. *Courtesy of Cocoa Village Antique Mall.* $300–400.

Stork Glass Ornament. 6" × 4". Victorian. *Courtesy of Cocoa Village Antique Mall.* $100–125.

widely made, as well as vegetables and fruits. Because they were less likely to break, these ornaments lasted longer. They hit their peak of popularity in the 1920s.

Several types of paper ornaments are popular with collectors: Dresden, scrap, papier-mâché, and pressed cardboard. Dresden ornaments are incredibly detailed and often resemble metal or glass, but they are actually made of die-cut and embossed cardboard. They were made during the latter 1800s through early 1900s (some sources say 1880s to the beginning of World War I). Often, Dresden ornaments are covered with gold or silver foil. The type and variety of decorations made in this style is immense—everything from realistic human figures to animals, forms of transportation, clocks, purses, and numerous other items. The ornaments were created by factory workers, and the finishing touches were put on by cottage industry workers, who often embellished the pieces with painstaking detail.

Between the world wars, Japan exported millions of ornaments to the United States. Most were reproductions of the original German versions, but the Japanese ones were more cheaply made and often had less attractive faces. The Japanese were responsible for 93 percent of the ornaments shipped into the United States, until war was declared against them after the December 7, 1941, attack on Pearl Harbor.

During World War II, magazines encouraged homemakers to handcraft their own decorations, harkening back to the olden days of stringing popcorn and cranberries. The new ornaments that were produced (and there weren't many) were missing the metal caps on top that usually held the hook to hang the ornament on the tree, because metal was in short supply. Paper and cardboard tops were used instead, and that allows today's collectors to easily date wartime ornaments.

During the 1950s, families decorated for Christmas more than ever. Big department stores in major cities spent the bulk of their advertising money on decorating their store windows for Christmas with moving displays and lavish holiday scenes. Plastic decorations were popular, though glass ornaments had once again become available from Germany. Plastic items were easy to use, light, unbreakable, and fun. Styrofoam balls that could be decorated with sequins, beads, and materials also became quite popular.

The 1960s was the era for dumping the old-fashioned ways of decorating for the holidays, and magazines touted the idea of "theme trees." During this decade, families bought their ornaments and lights in sets, often focusing on one color scheme. Lawn ornaments and large-scale displays became popular, encouraging families to compete against each other for scale and flashiness.

By the 1970s, ornaments returned to the basics. People wanted to decorate in the way that families had several decades before. Though lighting was still popular, Americans were energy conscious, and small and miniature lights came into vogue. Ornaments were designed to reflect a starlike quality. Magi-Glo ornaments, a type of ball that glowed in the dark, were produced to conserve electricity. The "country" look was popular, so magazines suggested decorating trees with traditional strung popcorn, cranberries, gingham bows, cookie and bread dough ornaments, corn husk figures, and anything homemade.

Limited edition ornaments became popular once the first Hallmark ornaments were produced in 1973. Their first collection consisted of six collectible ornaments and twelve yarn figures. These ornaments were available on a limited basis for a short period and were dated. Since that time, the company has created over three thousand ornaments in their Keepsakes Ornaments collection and more than one hundred groups of specifically themed ornaments. The company paved the way for others to also introduce limited edition ornaments.

During the 1980s, it became popular to sell ornaments one by one instead of in boxed sets. Manufacturers realized that most families had a full set of ornaments already, but they might be interested in a particular type of ornament or in the "newest and latest." Theme decorating sparked a revival in Victorian ornaments and an inclination to decorate the tree in whatever style the homeowner had decorated the home itself. "Trim-a-Home" or "Trim-a-Tree" departments in major department stores offered consumers the option to purchase everything in one place, and Christmas displays were set up prior to Halloween to encourage deeper-pocket spending.

In 1984 a family accident sparked the beginnings of what would become one of the most popular lines of glass ornaments: Christopher Radko. When the family had decorated the tree and put it into its new aluminum stand, an accident occurred that sent the tree crashing to the floor, breaking almost all of the family's treasured European glass ornaments. Christopher was determined to replace the family's beloved collection, so he sought out glassmakers and found one in Poland. Together, they worked with antique ornament molds to recreate a dozen of Radko's favorites. But, before putting them on his own tree, he sold them to admiring friends in New York City. Before he knew it, Radko was in the Christmas ornament business. Today, the company has retired hundreds of ornaments

Holiday Break Ornament. Made by Christopher Radko. *Courtesy of Jeffrey Ostroff/Seller Dropoff.com* $44–54.

Chub-A-Dub Santa Ornament. Made by Christopher Radko. 5½" tall. *Courtesy of Jeffrey Ostroff/Seller Dropoff.com* $40–50.

Flounder Ornament. 1997. 6½" × 3" × 4". Made by Christopher Radko, #97–DIS–84. *Courtesy of Jeffrey Ostroff/Seller Dropoff.com.* $25.

Winter Minuet Ornament. Made by Christopher Radko. Approximately 4" high. *Courtesy of Jeffrey Ostroff/Seller Dropoff.com* $40–50.

Regal Saint Nick Ornament. 5 ½" tall. Made by Christopher Radko. *Courtesy of Jeffrey Ostroff/Seller Dropoff.com* $45–55.

each year, which instantly become collectibles actively sought by his fans. Each Radko design is handblown by glassmakers in Poland, the Czech Republic, Italy, and Germany, then decorated by a cottage industry of artists—a process that takes at least seven days. These one-of-a-kind heirlooms are marked Radko, and are sent to specialty stores all over the world.

Because of the popularity of limited edition ornaments, as well as traditional ones, many collectors groups sprung up from the 1980s to 2000. A few of note include the Coca-Cola Christmas Collectors Society, the Christopher Radko Starlight Family of Collectors, Enesco Treasury of Ornaments Collectors' Club, Old World Christmas Collectors' Club, Walt Disney Collectors Society, Swarovski Collectors Society, and the Golden Glow of Christmas Past. All have web sites.

Through the years, companies have created Christmas decorations and ornaments as advertisements for their products. For example, Coca-Cola® created their version of Santa Claus in 1931 and have used it on everything from store signs to ads to ornaments ever since. McDonald's has produced Christmas versions of their characters ever since they first started producing Happy Meals in 1979. Hallmark unveils a new set of ornaments and Christmas decorations every year. And Disney has produced items for the Christmas season since 1937, when *Snow White and the Seven Dwarfs* was released at Christmastime and became the highest grossing film in history. Since that time, all of the Disney characters have appeared as ornaments or other types of Christmas collectibles.

Plates

Collectible plates were first produced by the major porcelain factories in Europe during the early 1700s. One of the premier factories was Meissen, a company that used the intricate Chinese pottery-making process. Wedgwood, Royal Copenhagen, and Spode followed shortly thereafter, and the goods these companies produced started a trend of collecting plates that monarchs, royalty, and average citizens have avidly followed ever since.

In the late 1800s, collecting souvenir plates enjoyed tremendous popularity and became an inexpensive hobby. Bing and Grondahl created the first limited edition collectible plate in 1895, a design called "Behind the Frozen Window." Rosenthal and Royal Copenhagen started producing popular Christmas plates in 1910, and soon after, the plates started becoming available in the United States.

Until the mid-1960s, when Lalique produced a glass collectible plate with an embossed design, the market for collectible plates revolved around the blue and white designs, because those are the colors Rosenthal and Royal Copenhagen used for their collectible plates. During the 1970s and 1980s, major artists like Norman Rockwell started producing painted holiday designs, and companies like the Bradford Exchange began manufacturing limited edition plates using these designs. Today's collectible plates are varied, and may be in limited editions by leading artists like Thomas Kinkade, or in mass-produced plates made by companies like Avon.

Salt and Pepper Shakers

There are many different types of salt and pepper shakers, but holiday collectors tend to focus on those made in particular figures or shapes.

Matched salt and pepper shakers were first sold in the early nineteenth century, but figural examples, such as the ones Christmas collectors are interested in, weren't popular until after World War I. Some of the shakers are identical to each other, while others are male and female versions, like Santa and Mrs. Claus. Some shakers are held in one piece (called container salt and peppers), some are nodders (with one piece that rocks back and forth), others are nesters (one sits inside the other), and still others are huggers (Santa and Mrs. Claus hugging each other and fitting into each other as a joined pair).

Companies that have manufactured shakers through the years include Avon (the company started as the California Perfume Company in 1886; in 1939, as Avon Products, they began producing cosmetic bottles that could be later used as shakers), Holt-Howard (started selling salt and peppers in 1949, and often marked them with both the year and HH for the company name), Lefton (started selling shakers in 1940 and marked them with the company name), and McCoy (this pottery company began doing business in 1899 and has undergone several changes to its name, so the marks on their shakers can help you determine their age). Other types of collectible salt and pepper shakers include those made in Japan, particularly those marked "Occupied Japan," and shakers that are considered African American in style.

Santa Clauses

The Santa Claus image has changed many times throughout the years, so the age of your Santa can often be determined by the style of the clothing and Santa's physical shape. As we already discussed, early Santas depict the figure known as Saint Nicholas and often show the icon wearing bishop's robes. Once the figure became Americanized, he gained a little weight and started wearing a red outfit, but it wasn't until the early twentieth century that he became the jolly ol' Santa wearing a red outfit trimmed with white fur. (For more information, see the sections on Saint Nicholas Day, as well as information on *'Twas the Night Before Christmas* and the Coca-Cola® Santa.)

Downhill Towards Christmas. 2003. 25" tall. Hand sculpted, one of a kind. *By (and courtesy of) Bethany Lowe Designs, Inc.* $650–700.

Children's Friend. 2003. 28" × 14". Hand sculpted, one of a kind. *By (and courtesy of) Bethany Lowe Designs, Inc.* $2,495–2,700.

Candy Containers, Santas with Pointed Hats. Circa 1930–1950s. Marked made in Germany. Large one is a bobber, 15" tall. $125–150. Smaller one is 9" tall. *Courtesy of Cocoa Village Antique Mall.* $65–75.

Grouping of Chalk Santas. Ages range from circa 1920s to early 1950s. Sizes from 2½" to 8". Most unusual and valuable is Santa on chicken. *Courtesy of Cocoa Village Antique Mall. Values from* $20–225.

Of all the icons and symbols produced for this holiday, Santa is the most popular. You can find Santa figurines, life-sized figures, wooden figures, dolls, games, and toys; as well as Santas made of lights, featured on ornaments, wreaths, paintings, posters, collectible plates, candles, coffee cups, salt and pepper shakers, beer steins, candleholders, wine bags, cookie jars, pillows, Advent calendars, postcards and greeting cards . . . need I go on?

Santa has been created in every material you can imagine. Carved wooden figures were made for the earliest Christmas celebrations. Silver spoons in the shape of Saint Nicholas were first made in the early 1800s. Santa Claus ornaments started in the mid-1800s and are so prolific that I wouldn't even dare guess how many have been created. Santa figurines have been made by every company that has manufactured Christmas items; some even have a series of Santas from every country (e.g., International Santas by Lawrence Stern, which was discontinued in 2003; Thomas Kinkade's Old World Santas; Duncan Royale's series produced in 1983; and many others).

Snow Babies

The original snow baby was actually a real person, the first white child to be born in Greenland. Marie Ahnighito, the daughter born to Admiral Robert Peary and his wife, Josephine, in 1893 was the inspiration for the figurines that came to be known as "the snow baby" after Josephine wrote a book by that name in 1901.

Snow Babies depict small children in stiff poses, dressed in Eskimo-type clothing. They are made of bisque and covered with a white chipped porcelain. They were made from 1901 through 1930 by companies like Bahr & Proschild, Hertwig, C. F. Kling, and Kley & Hahn. In Marshall Fields's 1914 catalog, the figurines sold for 90 cents a dozen. Nowadays, the price for Snow Babies is constantly rising and reflects their enduring popularity. There are other Snow Babies made during the early 1900s that are not small children. Some of them are Santas, snowmen, or animals, but they are still classified by collectors as belonging in this category.

The original versions made in Germany had realistic faces, and some of them were flecked with blue snow. There were copies made in Japan and reproductions have been made by other companies, which tend to look less realistic than the originals. The white "snow" that covers the reproductions is often flecked with black. Collectors say that you can often determine which are the fakes by examining the figure to see whether the white snow is whiter than the rest of the figure.

New versions of Snow Babies have been produced from old molds, according to author Mary Morrison, a self-proclaimed expert on Snow Babies. Her book on the subject, *Mary Morrison's Big Book of Snow Babies*, helps collectors decide the differences between the old and new versions. Snow Babies are currently being manufactured by the German Doll Company and Department 56.

Snow Globes

Snow globes (which are sometimes called snowballs, snow domes, waterglobes, or waterballs) reportedly came from France in the early 1800s (see New Years and Independence

Day sections for more information), and became popular in the United States in the 1920s. European companies have been creating snow globes since the early part of the century, but actual reports state that five companies were manufacturing them by 1879. A model of the Eiffel Tower was put into a snow globe in 1889 to celebrate the one-hundredth anniversary of the French Revolution, and it became a popular souvenir. Reportedly, the first Austrian snow globe was created by Erwin Perzy I.

At first, the globes were so artistic and new that the makers created them for monarchs and other people with enough money to ask for customized designs. The Victorians loved the uniqueness of this collectible, and the Atlas Crystal Works supplied people with a number of different versions of the globes.

Originally, the globes were leaded glass, placed over a figure or tableau, and filled with water, as well as chips of bone or porcelain that created the "snow." Later globes were constructed with thinner glass, lighter bases, and "snow" particles of gold or detergent flakes. By the 1950s, snow globes were made of plastic and filled with a water and glycerin mix, and the snow was also plastic. Some of the contemporary globes are battery-powered, which means you don't have to turn the globe upside down to have the snow fall.

Stamps and Seals

The first Christmas stamp was produced in Canada in 1898. Americans had to wait until 1964 before getting a Christmas stamp of their own. Though Christmas stamps are internationally produced now, most countries did not produce a specifically Christmas-themed stamp for quite a while after the first one was released in Canada.

Seals, which are not legal for sending a letter through the mail, began in Denmark in 1904 when a Danish postal clerk designed a Christmas seal to raise money for tuberculosis. Over four million were sold. Seeing his success, Emily Bissell, a Red Cross worker from the United States, followed suit in 1908 when she wanted to raise money for a tuberculosis sanitorium. Emily's idea was quite successful, and soon the Red Cross sponsored the printing of the seal, which sold by the hundreds of thousands throughout the holiday season. Emily's Christmas Seals continue to sell well and help raise money for victims of tuberculosis.

Stockings

The images of Christmas stockings "hung by the chimney with care" is a common one in most homes that celebrate the holiday, but that wasn't always the case. Filling stockings with small gifts, candy, and fruit is a tradition begun in Holland and brought to America by the Dutch. Earliest versions of this habit had children leaving their shoes by the hearth and filling them with straw for the reindeer that supposedly brought Sinter Klaas to their homes. In addition, a snack was left for Sinter Klaas, usually by the fireplace. The straw would disappear and would be replaced with small treats. Later, the shoes were also replaced with stockings. (For more information about this tradition, see the section on Saint Nicholas.)

After 'Twas the Night Before Christmas was published, children hung their own wool or cotton stockings on the mantel, hoping they would find them on Christmas morning stuffed with special goodies. By the turn of the twentieth century, commercially printed versions of Christmas stockings had begun to show up on department store shelves. Winter scenes and Christmas were popular themes. During the 1940s and 1950s, manufacturers began selling stockings that were already stuffed. These were often made of netting and decorated with lithographed paper scenes that acted as fasteners or closures.

Nowadays, most Christmas stockings are not the ones we wear on our feet but a more fanciful, often personalized version. They are kept from year to year, as are other decorations, and are a treasured keepsake. Though most stockings are made of fabric, there are vast differences in their style and value. Some are simple, red and white and furry, while others are lavishly decorated and made of satin and velvet.

The stocking itself has become an icon for the holiday, so items made in this shape abound. There are stocking-shaped cookie jars, vases, figurines, ornaments, jewelry pieces, articles of clothing, and more.

Tablecloths and Towels
Holiday linens make the house festive for the season. Their bright colors and designs make them popular with collectors—not only holiday collectors, but those who treasure fabrics as well.

One of the icons not yet mentioned that we often see on Christmas linens is the poinsettia. This deep red flower is a native of South America and is not really considered a flower but a grouping of brightly colored leaves. The plant was named after the first American ambassador to Mexico, Joel Roberts Poinsett, who discovered the plant and sent home samples of it to his home in Greenville, South Carolina, as well as to his gardening friends throughout the U.S. A legend states that a little boy who once wanted to bring a gift to the church picked a bunch of weeds from the side of the road. When he arrived in the church, the weeds turned brilliant colors and churchgoers believed they had witnessed a Christmas miracle.

Christmas tablecloths became prevalent during the Victorian age after the Queen insisted that a white damask tablecloth be placed on the table before the Christmas tree was erected atop it. That tradition extended to the festivities surrounding Christmas dinner, and pretty soon the tablecloth became decorated in the same styles with which other Victorian decorations were embellished.

Early tablecloths were solid colors (such as mauve or Turkey Red—a synthetic dye color invented in 1863 by William Perkins). Printed designs weren't added until the early 1900s, during the Art Nouveau period, when geometric shapes and animal symbols were used decoratively. By World War I, the dark colors of the Victorian age had disappeared, and decorations on tablecloths now included human shapes, flowers, butterflies, and many other cheerful designs. The tablecloths and other linens most available to collectors are those created from the 1950s to the present, but older versions are available, though pricey. Condition is paramount, as with any other collectible, and if the linens are used, they must be cared for gently.

Toys and Games

The wealth of items make this category one of the most popular. Christmas toys and games are not only collected by people interested in items for this holiday but are also avidly sought out by collectors of antique and vintage toys. This category is huge and my space is limited, so this is only an overview. For more detailed information, see one of the many books on the market that are specifically written about toys and games.

Besides the popular children's books that are always available for the Christmas holiday, blocks, puzzles, dolls, tin tops, spinners, lead figures, plastic figures, stuffed animals, wind-up toys, and many other toys have been made in the shape of Christmas icons like Santa, reindeer, and elves.

Lithographed paper toys, such as blocks and puzzles, became popular during the Victorian era when children could expect to find these items under their Christmas tree. Blocks depicting Santa, elves, children receiving gifts, and Christmas toys were brightly colored and incredibly popular, as were puzzles depicting Santa and his elves. Though these items were made of paper, their bases were often wood or pressed cardboard, making them sturdier than their contemporary counterparts. The American and European manufacturers who made these items included McLoughlin Bros., Milton Bradley, Bliss, W. & S. B. Ives, Raphael Tuck, and E. P. Dutton. Quite a few of the toys were marked and dated, making it easy for collectors to determine their age.

Santa Claus dolls and wind-up and mechanical figures grew in popularity after World War I, though wind-up figures have been around since the 1880s when European toymakers began producing tin lithographed figures that, through a simple mechanism, were able to move. Soon, American toy companies started selling their own inexpensive versions. Julius Chein began in 1903, Strauss in 1914, and Louis Marx manufactured them in the 1920s and 1930s. After these companies left their marks on the toy industry, others followed, with the height of the Christmas windups' popularity occurring in the 1940s and 1950s. Windups are still being made today, but the earlier ones are more valuable to collectors.

Trees, Feather Trees, Tree Toppers, and Tree Stands

More than a thousand years ago, pagans celebrated the arrival of spring by decorating trees, and the Druid priests used evergreen trees during their winter solstice rituals. The first time a tree was brought into a church was during the Middle Ages when Saint Boniface destroyed an oak tree that some pagans were worshipping, only to find a fir tree growing inside it. He saw in the triangular tree a symbol of the holy trinity, and decorated it with candles to simulate the stars in the heavens. The area where he lived, Thuringia, became well known for creating Christmas decorations. Saint Boniface's life was long, dedicated to the Roman Catholic church, and filled with important events, yet most only remember him for this one rather insignificant event in the history of Christendom.

The Christmas tree was used in various different ways before it became a popular household decoration for the season. In fact, during the twelfth century, churches typically hung the tree upside down from the church rafters in Eastern Europe, believing it to be a symbol of Christianity. The triangular shape of the pine tree was said to represent the Holy Trinity.

Feather Tree. Circa 1930. Decorated with bird ornaments. Approximately 4' tall. Birds are made of a variety of materials which range from Victorian times
to the 1950s. *Courtesy of Cocoa Village Antique Mall.*
$600–700 (undecorated).

Some say the tree was first decorated in the 1500s in Latvia, while others tell stories of Martin Luther decorating a fir tree with candles.

Germans and Dutch brought the tradition of decorating trees for Christmas with them
when they arrived in America. Both tabletop and full-size trees were decorated with candies and cookies, often in the shape of holiday symbols, as well as farm animals and human
figures.

Though trees had been decorated for centuries, they weren't considered popular home decorations for the holidays until Queen Victoria and Prince Albert of England publicized
their decorated evergreen tree in a family photo printed in *The Illustrated London News* in
1848. After that time, decorative store-bought ornaments became incredibly popular (see
the section on Ornaments for more information).

Artificial trees were developed in Germany and brought to the United States before World
War I. The earliest examples, made from dyed turkey or goose feathers, were wire
"branches" that wrapped around a trunk. Red composition berries decorated the ends of the
branches. The trees came in various sizes, some small enough to be held by papier-mâché
figures of Santa Claus, others large enough to sit by themselves on a table. The largest sizes
that stood on the floor were less common.

When World War I broke out, the United States began producing feather trees to make up
for the lack of imported trees from Germany. They were clearly marked on the base as
being from the United States. From the end of World War I to the beginning of World War
II, Germany once again became the prime supplier of artificial trees, often in colors other
than green. World War II interrupted the sale of feather trees once again, and after the war,
the shape and composition of feather trees changed—the branches were farther apart and
feathers were sparser.

Cellophane trees, briefly popular during the 1930s, were produced by the Standard Cellophane and Novelty Company. Few are available for today's collectors.

Silver Tinsel Trees. Available in 3', 4' and 6' sizes. *Courtesy of CSPost.com.* $25, $45, and $125, respectively.

In the 1950s and 1960s, a different type of artificial tree became popular: the aluminum tree. The silver trees often came with electric color wheels that reflected on the shimmery branches. These trees fit well in ranch homes with picture windows. Setting the tree in a picture window and turning on the color wheel created a spectacular sight for passersby.

Reproductions of feather trees are currently being made, and today's artificial trees resemble real fir trees so closely that it is often difficult to tell they are fake without touching them. Many sizes, shapes, and colors are made.

Wreaths

Wreaths have been made since long before Jesus was born. Romans and Greeks used the wreath to symbolize victory and celebration, sometimes even heroism. Winners of sporting events wore a circlet or wreath around their heads as their "reward." After the celebration was over, recipients of early wreaths might have hung the wreath on their wall to remind them of their victory and elongate the celebration. Instead of being disposable, the wreath now became part of the household decorations and served as a reminder of the original reason for receiving the wreath. Ancient Germans wound evergreen boughs into a circle around a fire in the dead of winter, hoping for spring to come.

The circle and the evergreen are both symbolically associated with ever-lasting life, so it is not surprising that the two ended up as icons for the Christmas holiday. The wreath is often decorated with red ribbons, signifying the blood of Christ.

Christians adopted the tradition by creating the Advent wreath, a table wreath of evergreen decorated with pink and purple candles. The Advent wreath is typically a Catholic tradition and signifies Christ's birth. Each candle is put in separately, the culmination of the ceremony taking place on Christmas Eve. A short prayer accompanies the lighting of each candle.

Today, wreaths are also made from a number of materials other than evergreen, but the symbol remains the same.

PRICE LIST: CHRISTMAS COLLECTIBLES (PRE-1960)

Advertisement, Hallmark Cards. Ad is from a 1958 magazine and depicts two boys at Christmas, one holding card for Santa. Ad is in black and white. Mint condition. **$12–15**

Bank, Santa. Iron bank circa 1925. 4¼" long and 4" tall. Tin door opens to get coins out. Bottom plate reads The Miller Bank Service 1925. Excellent condition. **$425–500**

Bead Sticks and Noel Letters. Antique bead sticks available in green, silver and gold, to accent Christmas bouquets and holiday accessories. Lengths of 7" and smaller. Excellent condition. **$4–11.** NOEL letters made of ceramic with holders in top to display Christmas accents. 1¼" × 4" × 3". Courtesy of CSPost.com. Excellent condition. **$44–50**

Bell, Santa, Japan. 5" clay face Santa with a cotton beard has a papier-mâché and mica bell body. Circa 1940s. Very good condition. **$65–75**

Beverage Set, Santa Claus Decoration. Six Santa Claus face cups and Santa mug-type pitcher. Circa 1950s. Very good condition. **$50–100**

Book, *Christmas Morning*. Part of Father Tuck's Kris Kringle Series. Printed by Raphael Tuck and Sons. Circa 1900. Great full page color lithographed prints. Very good condition. **$75–95**

Book, *Jolly St. Nick Stories*. Children's Christmas book, published by McLaughlin Bros., New York and copyrighted circa 1900. Full cover lithograph print on the cover of Santa in his workshop. Filled with a variety of stories and full black and white etchings on every other page accompanying each story. Inscription on the inside and dated Dec. 25, 1906. Good condition. **$30–45**

Book, Pop-up. Santa Claus pop-up book, circa 1930s. Very good condition, some bending of corners. **$65–80**

Book, *The Night Before Christmas*. Published by the W. B. Conkey Co. in 1903. Beautifully illustrated with black and white etchings on every page. Full color illustration of Santa in red and white robe, clothes on his back, climbing into chimney. Good condition. **$55–75**

Book, *The Santa Claus Book*. Written by E. Willis Jones and published by Walker Publishing Company, copyrighted 1976. First edition. Pictorial biography of Santa Claus and contains a variety of full color prints, black and white illustrations and poems. Illustrators such as Thomas Nast, Norman Rockwell and others are included in this book. Very good condition. **$30–40**

Bookmark, Father Christmas. Silk bookmark. Victorian era. Excellent condition. **$15–25**

Bulbs, Matchless Wonder Star Christmas Tree Light Bulbs. Vintage glass stars in original box. Double row of points of the stars are faceted crystal. Works. Ten 2" stars in the box. Most have the original hanging wires. The socket is about ⅜". Very good condition. **$500–575**

Calendar, Advent. "Christmas Angel's House." Made in Germany. Paper. Very good condition. **$15–20**

Calendar, Advent. German. From the 1930s. Looks like windows in a building which open on every day throughout the holiday season. Excellent condition. **$20–25**

Candelabra, Swedish. Wooden candle holder in shape of tree. Holds a candle on each branch. Approximately 12" tall. Circa 1950s. Some wear. Good condition.   **$55–80**

Candles, Angels. Set of three. Made by Gurley. Circa 1940–1950. Never been used. Near mint condition.   **$25–35/set**

Candles, Carolers. Set of four. Made by Gurley. Circa 1940–1950. Never been used. Approximately 3" tall. Excellent condition.   **$30–40/set**

Candles, Dwarfs. Set of two. Made by Gurley. Circa 1940s. Never been used. Approximately 3" tall. Near mint condition.   **$20–30/pair**

Candles, Gurley. Collection of vintage Gurley candles for Christmas, including angels, choir members, Santas, etc. Approximately twenty in all. Excellent condition.   **$50–60**

Candolier, Eight Light. Wooden base with cardboard tubes for eight lights in this candle-like candolier. Excellent condition.   **$40–50**

Candy Box, Japan, Santa. 7" tall Santa, clay face, cotton suit, composition boots, and cotton beard. Holding string of brass bells. Doll in sack on his back. Good condition.   **$85–100**

Candy Container, Paper Drum with Bells. German. Paper box in the shape of a drum that opens up. Three bells on the sides like a tambourine. Lithograph of a young man walking along playing a string guitar. 1¾" in diameter. Back of the box marked Germany. String on the top of this box to hang ornament on tree. Rare. Very good condition.   **$275–325**

Candy Container, Belsnickle Santa. German. White. 8¾" tall. Original closure on bottom stamped "Made in Germany." Very good condition.   **$430–475**

Candy Container, Belsnickle. German. Father Christmas stands with tree in one hand, bag over his shoulder, feet on green mound. 4¼" high. Circa 1910–1920. Excellent condition.   **$750–900**

Candy Container, Dish. Porcelain Christmas candy container decorated with elves. German. Good condition.   **$10–15**

Candy Container, Horse. German candy holder in shape of a horse. Approximately 6" tall. Circa 1890. Very good condition.   **$200–250**

Candy Container, Santa Bank. Santa Claus, figural ornament container. Hard plastic. Circa 1940s. Very good condition.   **$20–30**

Candy Container, Santa Boot. Papier-mâché boot for use as nutcup or candy container. Excellent condition.   **$10–15**

Candy Container, Santa Claus. Celluloid, mesh Santa container. Approximately 7" tall. Circa 1930s. Excellent condition.   **$90–120**

Candy Container, Santa Claus. Large figural in green cloak. Head is composition. Circa 1920. 23" tall. Excellent condition.   **$600–750**

Candy Container, Santa Claus. Papier-mâché candy container. German. Circa 1890s. Approximately 8" tall. Very good condition.   **$600–675**

Candy Container, Santa House, German. 4½" molded cardboard pink house, removable white roof and Santa in the front. Stamped, "Made in Germany" on the bottom. Circa 1940s. Excellent condition. **$75–100**

Candy Container, Santa in House. 2½" cotton batten Santa, clay face, sitting on the stoop. Bottom pulls out for candy. Circa 1940s. Good condition. **$48–58**

Candy Container, Santa in Sleigh, Japan. 7" long mica cardboard platform, papier-mâché reindeer, sleigh candy container, and 3" Santa with clay face, holds bag of glass ornaments at his feet. Circa 1930s. Excellent condition. **$55–75**

Candy Container, Santa on Bell. German 3" composition Santa, rabbit fur beard and felt robe sitting on molded cardboard bell. Pull out plug on bottom stamped "Germany." Circa early 1900s. Excellent condition. **$200–225**

Candy Container, Santa. Glass and fabric Santa in old style. Circa 1920s. He holds both arms out and container is his toy bag on his back. 10" tall. Freestanding. Excellent condition. **$100–150**

Candy Container, Santa. German. 7½" tall. Circa 1920–1930. Wears red felt coat, carries small tree, stands on wooden base. Great condition. **$700–800**

Candy Container, Vasculumn. German. Circa 1890. Paper vasculumn with thread hanger. 2½" × 1¾". Good condition. **$110–130**

Candy Containers, Santas and Sleighs. One is cotton with chalk face. German. **$200–250** One with white sleigh is made in Japan (paper with chalk face). Approximately 5½" long. Excellent condition. **$150–175**

Candy Containers, Santas with Pointed Hats. Large is a bobber (made in Western Germany) and 15" tall. **$125–150.** Shorter version is 9" tall. Marked "Made in Germany." Circa 1930–1950s. Very good condition. **$65–75**

Card, Money Holder. Santa Claus Christmas card money holder. Circa 1930s. **$5–10**

Cards, Santa Claus. Christmas Cards in display frame. Circa 1890. All eight cards are postmarked. Red suede inserts behind each card. Framed collection measures 32" × 18". Near mint condition. **$275–325**

Churches, Paper with Sparkles. Some have feather trees in front. Range from approximately 4" tall to 10" tall. Circa 1940s. Very good condition. **$15–40**

Cloth, Souvenir. Early Black Americana advertising. Christmas Happy New Year Souvenir fringed cloth from the Novelty Show, Madison Square Garden, N.Y. Measures 6¾" × 6". Original envelope in lower left-hand corner with "A Happy New Year" printed on flap and original blank card still intact inside. Very good condition. **$175–250**

Tree, Aluminum. Complete with all branches (60 of them that are placed on the pole, not counting the very top section branches), stand, and pole. Instructions included. Mint condition. **$200–250**

Cookie Cutter, Square. Tin with handle. Circa mid-1900s. Approximately 2½" square. Excellent condition. **$15–20**

Cookie Cutters, Set of Six. Cookie cutters are metal and include a Christmas tree, bell, reindeer, bell with handle, and snowflake. Circa early 1900s. Very good condition.

$10–15/each

Die-cut, Manger Scene. Victorian. Title "Gloria in Excelsis Deo" on manger. 13" × 11". Shadow-box design. Very good condition.

$20–30

Die-cut, Santa with Toys. German. Circa 1890. 12" × 6¾". Santa dressed in white, blue gloves, blue cornucopia, holding bag of toys and Christmas tree. Very good condition.

$210–250

Die-cuts, Christmas. Three die-cuts made in Germany during 1940s. One is Santa in biplane, one is snowman beside tree, third is Santa with sleigh. Good condition. $30–45

Dishes, Paper. West Germany paper Christmas dishes/plates. 6" diameter. Excellent condition.

$6–9/set

Doll, Santa Claus. Antique doll. Seems homemade. Approximately 8" tall. Good condition.

$25–35

Doll, Santa Claus. Elf doll made by Rennoc. Sitting doll, full beard, fat face, and wooden hammer. 12" tall. Very good condition.

$20–30

Doll, Santa Claus. Sitting Santa doll wearing white boots and beige lamb's wool fur trim on his outfit. Long elf's type hat. Circa 1940s. Approximately 12" tall. Very good condition.

$30–50

Doll, Santa. Composition face Santa. 3" tall. Very good condition. $10–15

Doorknob Hangers, Japan. Three 10" long and 5" wide felt hangers with two brass bells on the bottom. Mint in the package. $18–20 - set of three

Electric Candle. Off white with faux drips down side. Original paper tag by "Underwriter Laboratories, Inc., Listed, UL, Decorative Outfit, Issue No. B-9248, 8-84, For Indoor Use Only." 9" × 4¾" wide. Very good condition. $5–7

Electric Candles, Plastic. Off-white with fake wax dripping down side. Original paper tag marked "Underwriter Laboratories, Inc., Listed, UL, Decorative Outfit, Issue No. B-9248, 8-84, For Indoor Use Only." 9" tall. Circa 1950s. Very good condition. $5–8

Feather Hedge, Four Sections. Each piece is 10" long and 3½" high. Circa 1930s. Very good condition. $75–85 per section

Feather Tree, Decorated with Bird Ornaments. Approximately 4' tall. Birds are made of a variety of materials and date from Victorian to 1950s. Tree circa 1930. Very good condition.

$600–700 (undecorated)

Feather Tree. Decorated with ornaments, mostly glass, figurals, faces, mostly of Victorian vintage. Tree is feather, two-colored base. Circa 1930s. Approximately 4' tall. Tree only. Very good condition. $600–700

Feather Tree, Decorated. Possibly German. 32½" tall (including base). Fully decorated with antique ornaments and vintage lights. Eight lights on the strand in red, green and blue. Twenty-five ornaments. Wood red base has green and gold design, but no German marking. Red holly berries on some of the branches. Good condition. $200–250

Feather Tree, Faux Feathers, White. 36" tall. Good condition. **$60–75**

Feather Tree, German. Circa 1930s. Glass ornaments, real feather, star tree topper. 16" tall. Good condition. **$150–200**

Figure, Reindeer. German. 7" tall. Glass eyes. Harness. Mohair fur. Circa 1920–1930s. Good condition. **$350–375**

Figure, Santa Claus. Belsnickle papier-mâché face. Approximately 12" tall. Very good condition. **$30–45**

Figure, Santa Claus. Celluloid Santa made by Irwin. Typical round-bellied Santa. Excellent condition. **$15–25**

Figure, Santa Riding Mohair Reindeer. German. Circa 1920s. Composition with red jacket and rabbit fur beard. Stick leg type reindeer covered in mohair, glass eyes and metal antlers. 5" × 4¼". Germany sticker on Santa's foot. Very good condition. **$110–150**

Figure, Santa, Ceramic. 4½" tall. Wears a red Santa suit, green mittens and is playing a flute. White ceramic moustache and white fur beard. Sack of toys at his feet. Bottom is marked Japan. Very good condition. **$20–30**

Figure, Santa. Papier-mâché. Holds doll in one arm, teddy bear in the other. European made. 19" tall, 6" square base. Pointed red felt Santa hat, red coat trimmed in fur. Circa 1920s. Very good condition. **$250–300**

Figure, Sleigh, Santa Pulled by Huskies. Unusual German Santa set from the 1920s. 8" × 6". Santa is sitting down and measures 4" tall. Huskies have glass eyes and measure a large 4½" × 5". Together they measure about 14" long. Very good condition. **$450–500**

Figure, Snow Baby on Red Sled. German. 1½" tall. Wears stovepipe pants and has heavy black brows. Paint rubs on the corners of the red sled. Excellent condition. **$85–100**

Figure, Snow Baby, Polar Bear on Scooter. German. 1½" long. Red scooter, red painted smile. Excellent condition. **$175–200**

Figure, Snow Baby, The Whistler. German. Made by Heubach. Boy with hands in pockets. 6" tall. Excellent condition. **$800–1000**

Figure, Snow Baby. German. Boy pushing large ball. 1½" tall. Good condition. **$185–200**

Figure, Snow Baby, Heubach. German. Boy in bearskin. Has "rising sun" Heubach mark. 3½" tall. Near mint condition. **$1500–1800**

Figure, Snow Babies. German. Pair of children skiing down sides of vases. Both wear yellow mittens. 4¼" tall. Very rare. Excellent condition. **$2,200–2,500/pair**

Figures, Jointed Wood. Two German Erzgebirge jointed Santa figurines. Approximately 3" tall. Excellent condition. **$200–250**

Figurine, Porcelain. Made in Japan. December Angel. Good condition. **$10–15**

Figurine, Pottery. Christmas Elf. Very good condition. **$10–15**

Figurine, Santa Claus. German bisque figurine of Santa Claus. Very good condition. **$50–75**

Figurine, Santa Skier. Metal figure of Santa on skis. Colorful and bright. Approximately 6" tall. No markings. Very good condition.   **$30–40**

Figurine, Santa. 1912 France porcelain figurine ornament in shape of Santa. Very good condition.   **$5–7**

Figurine, Santa. Chalkware. Handpainted, marked 1946. Very good condition.   **$15–20**

Figurine, Santa. Chalkware. Handpainted. Base marked "1946." Good condition.   **$10–15**

Figurine, Santa. Early Santa figurine with green basket backpack. Approximately 3" tall. Very good condition.   **$10–15**

Figurine, Santa. Papier-mâché figurine of Santa with toy bag at his side. Circa 1930. Approximately 8" tall. Excellent condition.   **$15–20**

Figurine, Santa. Chalkware, handpainted, marked on base "1946." Good condition.

$10–15

Figurines, Mr. and Mrs. Santa Claus. Antique Mr. and Mrs. Claus. 4" × 6½" × 5". Brightly painted ceramic duo display beautiful blooms in their sack of goodies. Excellent condition. Courtesy of CSPost.com   **$64–70**

Flag, Santa Claus. Satin, embossed trumpet flag. Circa 1907. Excellent condition with bright colors.   **$15–25**

Flask, Timepiece. U.S. Porcelain. 3¾" tall. Circa 1910–1920. Merry Christmas/New Year's gift presented by West Kimmswick Bar in Missouri. Paper label has a Santa with a sack of toys stepping into a chimney. Reverse is the face of the timepiece showing time of a quarter of twelve. Good condition.   **$120–140**

Folk Art, Carved Santa. Santa stands approximately 15" tall. Old World style clothing. Holds sack on back and is stooped with its heaviness. Wood used appears to be a soft wood, like pine. Colors are soft blues and beiges. Carving is rough and unschooled. Excellent condition.   **$500–750**

Garland and Sled. Brightly colored glass beads of various sizes stretch over 8½'. Excellent condition. **$16.50–20. Napco sled holds holiday knick-knacks, candy or a holiday bouquet.** Ceramic sled measures 2½" × 5" × 2½". Excellent condition. Courtesy of CSPost.com   **$30–35**

Garland, Japan. 6½' long old glass fancy beads with 2½" foil packages. Very good condition.   **$18–24**

Icicles, Metal. Lot of 7½" twisted metal icicles, circa 1930s. Very good condition. **$15–25**

Jesus, Nativity Piece. Made of wax. Approximately 2" long. In wooden crib on bed of cotton. Circa 1880s. Very good condition.   **$175–250**

Jewelry, Lapel Studs. Santa Claus and Holly. Circa 1920s. Very good condition.   **$30–40**

Label, Sunkist Lemon. Santa Claus lemon crate label. Circa 1927. Excellent condition.

$18–25

Lamp, Motion Lamp Depicting Santa with Reindeer. Circa 1930s–1940s. All original. Outside lens has a couple cracks. Original cloth cord. 10" × 6". Very good condition. **$130–160**

Lamp, Santa Claus. Made by U.S. Glass Company of Ohio (later became Tiffin Glass Factory). Circa 1920s. Approximately 10" tall. Shows Santa coming out of chimney. Excellent condition. **$1,000–1,350**

Lamps, Santa Claus. Christmas lamps, set of two, old cotton wiring. Very good condition. **$7–10**

Light Set. Box very graphic, inside and out. Insert is beautiful, colors are bright and vibrant and very graphic. Marked "#82." Lights work. Excellent condition. **$110–150**

Light Set. Indoor/Outdoor fluorescent lights by Miller Co., circa 1945. Excellent condition. **$60–75**

Lighted Figure, Santa. Bakelite figure of Santa. Lights from inside. Circa 1940s. Very good condition. **$30–50**

Lights with Wooden Box. Box is illustrated. General Electric lights, 16 in set. Circa 1905. Rare. Very good condition. **$600–700**

Lights, Bubble Light. Parts and lights (43), circa 1940s. Very good condition. **$50–60**

Lights, Bulbs. Figural bird light bulbs. Set of nine. Excellent condition. **$45–55**

Lights, C-7. Westinghouse/GE replacement box of lights. Original box. Excellent condition. **$40–50**

Lights, Candles. Everlite Electric window Christmas candles. Set of three. Very good condition. **$5–7**

Lights, Candlesticks. Paper candlestick lights with old cloth wiring. Very good condition. **$15–20 each**

Lights, Candolier. Art Deco USALite. Five pink candolier lights in original box. Excellent condition. **$32–42**

Lights, Houses. Circa 1920s. Sixteen in the set. Cloth covered wiring and bulbholders. Complete and working. Very good condition. **$225–250**

Lights, Kingston. Large cone lights in original box. Excellent condition. **$5–10**

Lights, Noma Bubble Lites. Set with box and two bird bulbs. Very good condition. **$40–50**

Lights, Noma Star Base Bubble Lite. One bulb. Used as replacement. Works. Very good condition. **$15–20**

Lights, Noma Lites. Mazda safety plug Christmas lights. Complete set. Very good condition. **$6–10**

Lights, Paramount. Flameswirl lights, fifteen in set. Excellent condition. **$10–15**

Lights, Paramount. Set of fifteen Flameswirl lights. Excellent condition. **$15–25**

Lights, Popeye Christmas Tree Lights. U.S. King Features Syndicated, 1920. Eight Popeye plastic covers (2 blue, 2 red, 2 white, and 1 gold). The other five cartoon characters are: 1 green, 1 red, 2 blue, and 1 gold. 1¼" tall by 1⅝" in diameter. Popeye's covers are marked

"K.F.S." and the cartoon characters have "GE" in a circle. All fifteen lights work. Very good condition.　　　　　　　　　　　　　　　　　　　　　　　　　　　　　**$100–175**

Lights, Royal. Seven fluorescent lamp coral light set. Very good condition.　　**$65–75**

Lights, Royal. Seven fluorescent lamp coral/orchid light set. Cloth wiring. Very good condition.　　　　　　　　　　　　　　　　　　　　　　　　　　　　　　**$75–100**

Lights, Set. General Electric lights in box. Ten light set. Appears to have never been used. Mint condition.　　　　　　　　　　　　　　　　　　　　　　　　　　　　　**$35–45**

Lights, Spade. Box of twenty Spade Blinker transformer lights. Mint in box.　　**$30–50**

Lights, Yule-Glo Biscuit Bubble Lights. Purple color. In box. Very good condition.
　　　　　　　　　　　　　　　　　　　　　　　　　　　　　　　　　　　$50–60

Manger for Nativity. Domed glass frame, shadow box 3-D manger for nativity scene. Good condition.　　　　　　　　　　　　　　　　　　　　　　　　　　　　　**$15–25**

Garland, Merry Christmas Cutout and Bead Garland. Original design cutout from the mid-1900s. 12" × 13". White with silver glitter. Excellent condition. Courtesy of CSPost.com　　　　　　　　　　　　　　　　　　　　　　　　　　　　　**$25–30**

Garland, Antique. Red garland measures 9' to adorn Christmas tree, mantel, staircases, wreaths, or bouquets. Chipped with age. Very good condition. Courtesy of CSPost.com
　　　　　　　　　　　　　　　　　　　　　　　　　　　　　　　　　　　$4–8

Mold, Chocolate, Santa. 10½" × 4½". Circa 1930s. Marked 5936 and 15. Exterior shows nice patina; tin plating inside is scratched. Very good condition.　　　　　**$350–400**

Molds, Chocolate, Santas. Group of molds ranging up to 11" tall. German, most made by Anton Reiche. Circa 1930s. Very good condition.　　**Values range $200–800**

Molds, Chocolate, Snowmen. Group of molds all in shape of snowmen. All are European, circa 1920s–1960s. Tallest is 7" tall. Very good condition.　**Values range $100–600**

Nativity Animal, Camel. Vintage papier-mâché camel for nativity, made by Putz Co. Very good condition.　　　　　　　　　　　　　　　　　　　　　　　　　　　　**$25–35**

Nativity Animals. Lot of fine Dresden animals. Approximately 2¼" to 3¼" tall; considerable wear. Circa 1920s. Very good condition.　　　　　　　　　　　　**$10–15**

Nativity Manger. Italian manger with figures. Manger is approximately 10" tall, wooden. Figures are pottery and not finely detailed. Good condition.　　　　　　**$15–25**

Nativity Set. Eleven piece set on wood base. Figures are made of resin. Good condition.
　　　　　　　　　　　　　　　　　　　　　　　　　　　　　　　　　　$10–12

Nativity Sheep. German. Lambs' wool bodies, wooden legs, handpainted faces and feet. Circa 1920s. Very good condition.　　　　　　　　　　　　　　　　**$35–45 each**

Nodder, Santa, German. Key-wind clockwork store display. Circa 1900. When key wound, head nods backward and forward. Made of a thick cardboard with hand-painted features and glass eyes. 22½" high on a wooden base. Torso overlaid with old German newspapers.

Forearms and hands are composition joined to wire. Clothes, moustache, and beard not original. When head nods, it makes a ticking sound like a clock. Wood base. Very good condition. **$2,650–3,000**

Nutcracker, Figural, Soldier. Made in Germany by Fuchtner, circa 1950. Red jacket, yellow pants, white hair and beard. Feet molded of wood. Mint condition. **$100–125**

Nutcracker, Figural, Soldier. Made in Germany, circa 1920, by Fuchtner. Blue jacket, orange pants, handpainted face with brown moustache, blue eyes. Feet molded of clay. Very good condition. **$1000–1200**

Ornament, Acorn. Silver with white frosting. Marked "West Germany." Circa 1940s. Very good condition. **$15–18**

Ornament, American Football Player. U.S. Circa 1930s. 6" × 3". Red helmet, shirt, shoes and yellow pants and chin guard. Very good condition. **$110–125**

Ornament, American Jewels. U.S. Blown clear glass with coating applied to exterior surface. 2" × 2". Excellent condition. **$8–10**

Ornament, Anchor, Victorian. Tinsel and scrap ornament. Approximately 3" long. Very good condition. **$18–25**

Ornament, Angel. Made of spun glass and paper. 5" tall, 5" wing span. Angel's face is paper, blonde hair. Circa late 1800s to early 1900s. Some wear and discoloration. Good condition. **$10–15**

Ornament, Baby on Bell. Cotton batten baby, plaster face and paper hands, holding cotton mushroom and tree spree. Plastic sugar bell with a glass ball dinger. Circa late 1800s. Very good condition. **$25–35**

Ornament, Ball with Angel and Tinsel on Top. Ball is glass, angel is plastic. Circa 1950s. Very good condition. **$15–18**

Ornament, Ballerina. Italy. Circa 1955. Glass tube creates ballerina. Tutu original to the ornament. 5½" × 2½". Very good condition. **$110–120**

Ornament, Balloon with Basket. Bright blues and reds with gold trim. Approximately 5" tall. Excellent condition. **$85–100**

Ornament, Banana. 3½" glass banana ornament. Circa late 1800s. Very good condition. **$10–12**

Ornament, Barn. German glass ornament in shape of barn. Approximately 3" high. Rare. Very good condition. **$90–105**

Ornament, Basket. Japan. Blue and pink basket made of glass. 1⅓" diameter. Very good condition. **$4–7**

Ornament, Beaded Star. Czech glass beaded Soviet scarlet star ornament. Circa 1940s. Excellent condition. **$15–25**

Ornament, Bear. Antique German Dresden, cardboard. Circa early 1900s. Approximately 6" tall. Very good condition. **$600–675**

Ornament, Bell. 4½" with glass dinger. Excellent condition. $20–25

Ornament, Bell. Glass, USSR, handpainted Christmas bell ornament. Brass-colored and in excellent condition. $10–15

Ornament, Bird. Clip-on blown glass ornament of yellow bird. 5" long. Very good condition. $16–20

Ornament, Bird. German Dresden bird ornament. Approximately 3" long. Light colors. Very good condition. $8–12

Ornament, Blue Ball with Tassel. Circa 1920s. Very good condition. $30–40

Ornament, Blue Bell. U.S. Turquoise blue bell, paper cap. Unsilvered. Excellent condition. $8–10

Ornament, Blue Cone. Blown glass silver and blue cone ornament. Excellent condition. $10–15

Ornament, Blue Urn. Circa early 1900s. Excellent condition. $25–29

Ornament, Boy in Snowsuit and Mittens. Russia. 3" × 1¼". Circa 1960. Wears red mittens and scarf. Has clip on bottom of ornament. Very good condition. $12–15

Ornament, Boy with Goose. Clip-on. Glass. All one piece. 2½". German. Victorian. Very good condition. $75–85

Ornament, Butterfly. Large spun cotton winged butterfly on clip. Quite fragile. Very good condition. $36–50

Ornament, Cello. Victorian wire-wrapped cello, made of glass. Approximately 3" long. Very good condition. $100–115

Ornament, Chenille. Angel with wings ornament. Bendable. Circa 1930s. Excellent condition. $10–15

Ornament, Cherub Face, Glass. Glass eyes. German. 3" tall. Victorian. Very good condition. $85–125

Ornament, Chick, Dog, and Snowman. All glass. Russian. Circa 1940s. Very good condition. $25–35 each

Ornament, Chicken. Antique Christmas Dresden cardboard chicken. Good condition. $10–15

Ornament, Chicken. Clip-on glass ornament from USSR. Very good condition. $10–15

Ornament, Chimney Sweep. Circa 1890. 4¾" cotton batting figure with beard and painted face. Ladder made of tin. Very good condition. $175–200

Ornament, Clown. Antique Dresden cardboard ornament of clown. Colorful and jolly. Clown holds sides of his balloon pants. Approximately 5" tall. Very good condition. $15–20

Ornament, Clown. Vintage plastic Christmas clown ornament wearing hat. Very good condition. $6–10

Ornament, Clown. German. Circa 1890–1900. 5½" tall. Spun cotton. Clown has large buttons on his suit and a red hat. Missing part of collar. Good condition. $215–250

Ornament, Coffee Pot. Green/yellow, 4", applied papier-mâché material flower on front. Good condition. $15–20

Ornament, Coffee Pot. 2¾" red glass ornament with silver and glitter flower highlights. Circa late 1800s. Excellent condition. $25–30

Ornament, Cotillion Medals (Six). German. Circa 1890. Stamped and punched cardboard. Glitter, cork, tissue paper, silk, tinsel, iron, oblate and silk bows. 2¾" × 4". Very good condition. $300–350

Ornament, Cotton Baby on Bell. Plaster face and paper hands, holding a tree. Circa early 1900s. Very good condition. $25–30

Ornament, Cow. Europe. 3" × 4¼". Blown glass, handpainted with real tail. Restored, very good condition. $125–150

Ornament, Crocodile. Antique Christmas cardboard ornament. Crocodile is bright green and curved with open mouth. Very good condition. $15–20

Ornament, Dahlia Flower. Russia. 3" × 3". Nice mold detailing. Red and gold face, green and gold back, including sepals and stem. Very good condition. $25–30

Ornament, Devil's Head. Yellow, glass. Approximately 3" high. Victorian. Very good condition. $175–200

Ornament, Dinner Bell. 4½" with glass dinger. Excellent condition. $25–30

Ornament, Dog. Pressed cotton. Standing on his hind legs. Wearing a crepe blue, red, and gold paper jacket. 4½" tall. Excellent condition. $400–475

Ornament, Dresden, Eagle. Made of pressed paper. 7" wide. Turn of the century/Victorian. Very good condition. $300–400

Ornament, Dutch Girl. 6" × 3". Wooden shoes and pointed hat. Circa 1960. Great details. Very good condition. $80–100

Ornament, Egg. German. Circa 1900. Sebnitz ornament. 2¾" × 2". Nativity scene in foil-covered egg. Very good condition. $200–230

Ornament, Elf. Elf on tree stump. Glass. Green and gold. Approximately 3" long. Very good condition. $90–110

Ornament, Ellipsis. U.S. Pink, rose and gold bands around the ornament. 3¾" × 2". Excellent condition. $9–12

Ornament, Eskimo Child. Russia. 3¾" × 1¾". Dressed in traditional clothing. Handpainted, lovely face. Unsilvered. Very good condition. $20–25

Ornament, Fairy Godmother. Italy. 5½" × 2½". Classical fairy tale character. Glass with crystalline. Original hair. Very good condition. $100–125

Ornament, Father Christmas. European. Father Christmas is bringing a tree in for the holiday. 2½" × 1¼". Very good condition. $14–20

Ornament, Figural, Cottage. Circa 1940s. Very good condition.   **$15–20**

Ornament, Fish. Silver, spun glass. Hook is made right into the glass. Approximately 6" long. German. Victorian. Very good condition.   **$45–65**

Ornament, Fish. Vintage Dresden ornament. Glass. Approximately 2" long. Very good condition.   **$20–25**

Ornament, Floral Bouquet. Russia. 2¼" × 1¾". Front half is clear, transparent glass. Back half is silvered, with gold and rose lacquer painted on the interior surface of the back. Design looks like three flowers atop a cluster of leaves. Very good condition.   **$45–65**

Ornament, Flower Basket. German. 4½". Victorian basket with handle. Wire-wrapped basket with some red paper flowers and tinsel. Painted in soft pastel colors. Very good condition.   **$140–175**

Ornament, Flower Bowl. German. 7" tall. Wire-wrapped Victorian flower bowl. Top covered with wire, tinsel, and two paper flowers. Piece is painted. Good condition.   **$160–200**

Ornament, Girl on Swing. German. Circa 1890. 4½" tall (from feet to top of swing). Cotton girl sits on swing with rose in her hand. Dresden star on dress. Face made of scraps. Very good condition.   **$350–400**

Ornament, Girl with Red Bow. Europe. 4" × 2". Girl with long red hair, green cap, large red bow under chin. Handpainted face. Excellent condition.   **$65–75**

Ornament, Girl, Victorian. Tinsel and scrap ornament with girl's picture in the middle. Approximately 2" in diameter. Very good condition.   **$25–30**

Ornament, Girl. Country girl holding basket bowl. Circa 1920s. Mint condition.   **$10–20**

Ornament, Glass Urn. 3" green West German green urn. Near mint condition.   **$25–30**

Ornament, Glass Water Pump. 5" West German art glass water pump with delicate glass spout and turn crank. Excellent condition.   **$35–45**

Ornament, Glass, Basket. Small and adorable. Approximately 2" high. Gold, pink and silver. Circa 1920s. Very good condition.   **$30–40**

Ornament, Glass. Handblown "toy top" shaped ornament. Approximately 3" long. Excellent condition.   **$15–25**

Ornament, Glass. Songbird. Made in Germany. Looks like blue jay. Approximately 5" long. Very good condition.   **$35–45**

Ornament, Goat. 3½" × 3¾". Circa 1900. Pressed cotton. Missing a horn. Very good condition.   **$110–125**

Ornament, Gold Basket. Small glass basket. 2" × 1½". Circa 1940s. Very good condition.   **$75–85**

Ornament, Gold Peacock, Dresden. German. Circa 1900. 4". Good condition.   **$415–450**

Ornament, Grapes with Leaves. Europe. Circa 1890–1900. Wire-wrapped with tinsel. Leaves made of waxed fabric and covered with mica. Very good condition.   **$70–90**

Ornament, Grapes. West Germany. Glass. Orange-gold lacquer with glitter applied to surface. 3" × 2¼". Good condition. **$5–10**

Ornament, Green Coffee Pot. 2¾" coffee pot with perfect handle and spout. Excellent condition. **$25–30**

Ornament, Green Glass Urn. 3" with pink and white flowers. Excellent condition. **$25–30**

Ornament, Green Trumpet. 4" green horn with pink and white flowers. Circa early 1900s. Very good condition. **$15–20**

Ornament, Green Urn. 4". Circa early 1900s. Excellent condition. **$15–20**

Ornament, Head of Wheat. USSR. 5¼" × 1¾". Gold ornament, complex mold. Wheat is the symbol of the Ukraine, as well as one of the major symbols in the Bible. Circa 1940s. Excellent condition. **$50–60**

Ornament, Hockey Player. Silver glass ornament, approximately 5" long. Very good condition. **$10–12**

Ornament, Horse with Jockey, Dresden. 2⅛" × 2¼". Very good condition. **$275–325**

Ornament, Horse, Dresden. Silver prancing horse. 1¾" × 2". Originally might have been pulling a cart. Very good condition. **$235–275**

Ornament, House. 2½" with red roof and orange windows. Circa early 1900s. Excellent condition. **$15–20**

Ornament, Japanese Lady. German. Circa 1890–1900. 5½" tall. Cotton lady with painted paper mask face. Wool hair with two Dresden hair pins to keep it in place. Paper kimono with Dresden trim. Good condition. **$360–400**

Ornament, Kangaroo, Dresden. German. Circa 1890. 3-D cardboard. 2½" × 3½". Rare. Very good condition. **$875–1000**

Ornament, King and Golden Cock. Glass ornament in the character from the Christmas tale by Alexsander Pushkin. Bright colors. Excellent condition. **$25–35**

Ornament, Kugel, Mercury Glass Grapes. Approximately 3" long. Circa 1900s. Very good condition. **$75–90**

Ornament, Lamp. 2¾" lamp with a green shade and orange base. Circa early 1900s. Excellent condition. **$25–30**

Ornament, Mandolin. European. Glass. 2½" × 1½". Very good condition. **$12–15**

Ornament, Merry Christmas Santa. Paper, aluminum foil, and pipe cleaners. Marked "Made in Japan." Circa 1950s. Very good condition. **$65–75**

Ornament, Monkey, Glass. Marked "Radio" across top. German. 4½" tall. Victorian. Very good condition. **$100–130**

Ornament, Monkey. German. Circa 1920s. 3¼". Blown glass. Pearly gold with red hair around chin, red mouth, white and black eyes. Seated with his hands folded in front of him. Good condition. **$350–400**

Ornament, Moose. Circa 1890. Dresden Ornament. 3-D stamped, colored cardboard. 3⅓" × 3¾". Good condition. $550–600

Ornament, Mouse, Enesco. Mouse is stirring cup of alphabet soup with letters spelling out "Joy," "Love," and "Merry Christmas." Marked 1991, M. Gilmore Designs, Inc., Licensee Enesco Corp. Measures 2½" × 2¼". Very good condition. $16–20

Ornament, Mushroom Santa. Russia. Glass. 2¾" × 1½". Details are molded into glass. Face details nicely painted. Hat is "top" of mushroom. Very good condition. $35–45

Ornament, Ostrich. 4" × 3". Pressed cotton and feathers. Black stripes on orange legs. Excellent restored condition. $90–120

Ornament, Parrot. Silver glass parrot ornament with some color left on it. German. Approximately 3" long. Good condition. $10–15

Ornament, Peacocks (Two). Clip-on, glass with spun glass tails. 2½" tall, 3" long. German. Circa 1930s. Good condition. $40–50

Ornament, Pig with Flute. Russia. One of the pigs from the fable "The Three Little Pigs." 3¾" × 2". Unsilvered. Excellent condition. $75–100

Ornament, Pineapple. Russia. Glass ornament nubbed in gold, shortened green leaves. 4¼" × 2¾". Excellent condition. $25–30

Ornament, Pink and White Striped. Frosted white stripe. Circa 1920s. Very good condition. $25–35

Ornament, Pink Swan Boat. 9" long from nose to end of the spun glass tail. Wire wrapped with an angel scrap. Circa late 1900s. Excellent condition. $45–55

Ornament, Pink Urn. 4" pink urn with pink and red frosted flowers. Excellent condition. $25–30

Ornament, Pink Vase. German. Circa 1900. 5½". Wire-wrapped pink vase with tinsel and flower scrap in center. Excellent condition. $100–115

Ornament, Plush. Santa and feather tree on cardboard (matchbox?) sleigh. Approximately 3" long and 3" high. Circa 1940s. Good condition. $45–75

Ornament, Puss 'N Boots. Russia. 4" × 1¾". Circa 1950s. Blown glass. Puss dressed in musketeer outfit, pink boots, cape and cap; wears sword on left side. Very good condition. $45–55

Ornament, Rabbit with Ball. Vintage Christmas cardboard ornament of rabbit holding ball. Very good condition. $15–20

Ornament, Rabbit with Trumpet. Christmas cardboard ornament of rabbit blowing trumpet. Pinks and blues. Good condition. $15–20

Ornament, Rabbit. Circa 1960s. 5½" × 2½". Standing rabbit dressed in blue, green, and gold. Excellent condition. $80–100

Ornament, Radio Monkey. German. Blown glass Christmas tree ornament. Radio marked on his hat. 4½" tall. Good condition. $110–150

Ornament, Raggedy Andy. 6½" × 2½". Glass. Typical Raggedy Andy clothing. Excellent condition. **$80–100**

Ornament, Ram. Europe. 3" × 3½". Textured coat, glass horns. Missing leg. Fair condition. **$95–115**

Ornament, Red Angels Band. Red and white ornament depicting three angels playing harp, horn, and singing. Circa 1950s. Good condition. **$5–8**

Ornament, Red Ribbed Ball. U.S. 2½" × 2". Circa 1940s. Unsilvered. Excellent condition. **$8–12**

Ornament, Red Riding Hood. Silver glass with red paint. Circa 1920s. Approximately 5" tall. Very good condition. **$20–25**

Ornament, Sailboat. Russia. Circa 1950s. Glass sailboat with pink hull and 3-D sail. Very good condition. **$10–15**

Ornament, Santa Atop Wishing Well. 4" overall, 2" cotton Santa with clay face. Mica cardboard well. Excellent condition. **$45–55**

Ornament, Santa Claus. Spun cotton large Russian Santa Claus ornament. Extra wide muff of fur around neck and trim of jacket. 10" long. Very good condition. **$75–100**

Ornament, Santa Claus. Antique cotton wool figure of Santa with long beard and pointed cap. Approximately 4" tall. Very good condition. **$60–75**

Ornament, Santa Elf. Russia. 4" × 2". White beard, magenta, coral, and gold clothing. Minor loss of silver. Good condition. **$25–35**

Ornament, Santa Figurine. Papier-mâché. Old World type Santa with cotton beard and carrying small basket. 4¼" × 1½" wide. Marked 1950, 166/2000, Cindy Buy. Very good condition. **$10–12**

Ornament, Santa in Teardrop. Gold Santa figure in woodland scene. Circa 1940s. Good condition. **$20–25**

Ornament, Santa on Swing. Europe. Circa 1900–1910. 5¼". Cotton and crepe paper Santa on swing made of gold painted cardboard and wire. Both sides decorated by small feather tree branches. Very good condition. **$275–300**

Ornament, Santa on Wagon Train. Japan. 5" Santa on a flocked covered cardboard wagon ornament. Fair condition. **$14–20**

Ornament, Santa. Chenille, yellow. Approximately 3" high. Circa 1940s. Very good condition. **$30–45**

Ornament, Santa. Composition face, felt, pipe cleaners. Marked "Made in Japan" on back. Circa 1950s. Good condition. **$65–75**

Ornament, Santa. Japan. 5" flat Santa ornament, clay face, cotton beard, felt suit, cotton legs, and chenille arms. Circa 1930s. Excellent condition. **$40–50**

Ornament, Santa. Occupied Japan. 4½" clay face, paper suit, and cotton beard Santa, paper label on back "Occupied Japan." Excellent condition. **$42–50**

Ornament, Santa. German. Yellow. Made of glass. 4½" tall. Victorian. Very good condition. **$100–150**

Ornament, Santa. American. Gold glass Santa. Possibly Corning Glass. Circa 1930s. 3¼" × 1¼". Very good condition. **$40–50**

Ornament, Santa. Czechoslovakian. Purple glass Santa. Circa 1960. 3" tall. Excellent condition. **$7–12**

Ornament, Santa. German. Figural glass ornament for top of Christmas tree. German. Circa 1930s. Approximately 8" tall. Excellent condition. **$10–15**

Ornament, Santa. German. Composition face, felt suit, wooden boots. Circa 1900s. Good condition. **$125–145**

Ornament, Santa. German. Composition face, felt suit. Broken boot. Circa 1900s. Good condition. **$85–95**

Ornament, Santa. Japan. Glass Santa wearing traditional red outfit. 2" × 1¼". Circa 1930s. Good condition. **$5–8**

Ornament, Santa. 3½" Santa in orange suit holding gold tree. Mica beard and coat trim. Excellent condition. **$25–30**

Ornament, Santa. German. Circa 1890–1900. 5" tall. Made of cotton with scrap face. Holds a tree in right hand. Rare. Very good condition. **$300–350**

Ornament, Santa. Japan. 2¾" × ½". Both hands on belly, boots, gold bag over right shoulder, and blue eyes. Circa 1950s. Very good condition. **$15–20**

Ornament, Santa. Japan. Circa 1920–1930. Chenille. 5¾". Composition face, cotton beard. Holds small green chenille tree. Excellent condition. **$30–35**

Ornament, Santa. Limited edition Santa ornament, papier-mâché. Handpainted Old World type Santa with cotton beard and carrying a small basket. Measures 4¼" × 1½" × 1". Marked on base "1950." Marked on base "166/2000, Cindy Buy." Very good condition. **$8–10**

Ornament, Santa. West Germany. Glass. Traditional Santa with blue eyes. 3" × 2". Circa 1940s. Good condition. **$10–12**

Ornament, Schoolboy. German. Circa 1890–1900. 5" tall. Cotton schoolboy holding snowball and carrying backpack. Very good condition. **$375–400**

Ornament, Shepherd. German. 4" tall. Circa 1920. Pine cone shepherd wearing a lamb fur around his shoulders and a pole in one hand. Wears shepherd hat and big snowshoes and holds a *schalmai*, a traditional instrument. Body is a pine cone and the upper part of the body and his arms and legs are from cotton. Composition face. Red mittens. Very good condition. **$150–200**

Ornament, Shiny Brite. Church and village in winter scene. Circa 1950s. Good condition. **$15–20**

Ornament, Shooting Star. German. Circa 1890. 6" total length. Dresden paper star, wire-wrapped and silvered. Some paint loss. Good condition. **$110–130**

Ornament, Silver Bell. Circa 1950s. Good condition. **$6–8**

Ornament, Silver Cornucopia with Angel. German. Circa 1890–1900. 5" long. Silver paper, orange crepe paper inside, scraps, and tinsel. Good condition.   **$120–130**

Ornament, Silver Rose. Handblown glass made in Russia. Good condition.   **$10–15**

Ornament, Skater. 6½" × 2¼". Circa 1955. Made of glass. Beautiful details. Excellent condition.   **$100–125**

Ornament, Skier Girl. German. Circa 1900. 4½" tall. Cotton skier on wooden skies with pole in one hand and tree sprigs in other. Handpainted face and green ribbon around waist and shoulder. Very good condition.   **$390–425**

Ornament, Snow Princess. 7½" × 2½". Hat looks like unicorn, turquoise eyes, snowflakes on dress. Some loss of silver on the ornament. Good condition.   **$90–110**

Ornament, Snow Skier and Pine Tree. Made of glass. Tear shaped ornament with blue back panel, gold front panel, handpainted skier in red, pine tree in background in green. Circa 1940s. Very good condition.   **$30–50**

Ornament, Spun Cotton, Mushroom. Hook on end to be hung on tree. Approximately 3" long. Very good condition.   **$7–10**

Ornament, Spun Cotton, Russian. Spun cotton "snow-woman". Approximately 3" tall. Good condition.   **$25–35**

Ornament, Star. German. Circa 1890. Sebitz ornament. 4" diameter. Foil covered cardboard disc surrounded with wire. Each tip has a white glass candle with a red flame on tip. A beautiful scrap with a lovely dwarf carrying a tree is attached to the disc. Good condition.   **$275–325**

Ornament, Stork, Cotton. 4" tall. Circa 1890. Good condition.   **$150–200**

Ornament, Stork, Glass. Victorian. 6" × 4". Very good condition.   **$100–125**

Ornament, Stork. German Dresden 3-D cardboard ornament. Light pink, white, and black. 3" tall. Very good condition.   **$375–400**

Ornament, Strawberry. Circa 1920s. Approximately 2" tall. Good condition.   **$30–40**

Ornament, Strawberry. Glass. Silver strawberry was made in Russia, circa 1920s. Excellent condition.   **$10–15**

Ornament, Swan in Tinsel Wreath. 6" × 5". Free-blown glass swan hanging within tinsel wreath. Red swan, white accents on wings. Spun glass tail. Good condition.   **$15–18**

Ornament, Swan. Dresden ornament, very delicate swan. Approximately 3" long. Circa 1920s. Very good condition.   **$16–25**

Ornament, Teapot. Silver glass teapot. Approximately 6" long. Very good condition.   **$25–30**

Ornament, Teardrop. Red and silver, covered with crinkled wire. Circa 1930s. Very good condition.   **$35–50**

Ornament, Tree. German. 2¼" × 1¼". Circa 1930s. Green tree with white snow on branches. Excellent condition.   **$15–20**

Ornament, Turtle. Russia. Circa 1930s. Glass. Realistic mold. 1½" × 3". Clips on to the tree branch. Good condition. **$15–18**

Ornament, Umbrella. German. Circa 1890. Sebnitz ornament. 4" × 2¾". Umbrella accented with blue silk ribbon. Very good condition. **$310–360**

Ornament, Victorian. Tinsel and scrap ornament depicting four seasons shaped like four leaf clover. Good condition. **$15–20**

Ornament, Wax Angel with Spun Glass. Germany. Victorian. 4" long. Very good condition. **$175–200**

Ornament, White Dove. Russia. Circa 1930s. Pink beak and talons. Good condition (some paint missing). **$15–20**

Ornament, Windmill. German. Circa 1890. Sebnitz ornament. 3". Paper, golden foil, wire and cotton. Rare. Excellent condition. **$465–500**

Ornament, Yellow Bird on Tree Branch. 2½" with an incised start on the back. Circa mid-1800s. Excellent condition. **$38–50**

Ornament, Yellow Gold Urn. 3½" with perfect handles. Very good condition. **$16–20**

Ornament, Zeppelin. Antique German zeppelin glass ornament. Excellent condition. Rare. **$150–200**

Ornament/Candy Container, Paper. German. Circa 1890. Purse-like lithographed paper ornament. 3" × 3". Very good condition. **$60–70**

Ornaments and Topper. Set of ten glass ornaments and topper. Balls and acorns with some decoration. Circa 1960s. Very good condition. **$25–50**

Ornaments, Aluminum Icicles. Painted red, green, and blue. Approximately twenty icicles. Circa 1940s. Very good condition. **$8–10**

Ornaments, Balls, Twelve. Clear with tinsel inside. Circa 1940s. Very good condition. **$20–25**

Ornaments, Balls. Glass, handpainted and glittered, two-tone balls. Set of seven. Very good condition. **$8–12**

Ornaments, Bear and Carousel. Glass ornaments, 2–4" long. Very good condition. **$10–15**

Ornaments, Birds. Silver glass ornaments. Circa 1920s. Very good condition. **$10–15**

Ornaments, Box, Shiny Brite. Different colored glass ball ornaments in original box. Circa 1950s. Original price on box 59 cents. Excellent condition. **$15–20**

Ornaments, Candlesticks and Pyramids. Three ornaments with Santa Claus. German. Circa 1890. Tin plated and colored. 2½" × 2¾". Pyramids and candlesticks are hung onto the tree around a candle. As the candle warms the air, the pyramid moves and creates kaleidoscope of color. Excellent condition. **$475–550**

Ornaments, Fruits. Handblown glass lemon and pear. Excellent condition. **$10–15**

Ornaments, Glass Beads. Twelve sets of beads for feather trees. Very good condition. **$30–50**

Ornaments, Glass. Box of nine European glass ornaments (teardrops). Excellent condition. $10–15

Ornaments, Glass. Four handmade glass ornaments from mid-1940s. Good condition. $5–10

Ornaments, Glass. Lot of three ornaments. One silver Santa and two silver bulbs. Excellent condition. $10–15

Ornaments, Glass. World War II vintage glass ornaments with paper hangers (3). Very good condition. $25–35

Ornaments, Glass. Box of six European glass ornaments (balls with stripes, bells, plain). Very good condition. $9–15

Ornaments, Glass. Two German rose baskets. Early. Very good condition. $20–30

Ornaments, Handpainted and Glittered. Indents, balls and teardrops. Set of eight. Very good condition. $8–12

Ornaments, Handpainted. Blown glass Polish indents. Bright colors and nice designs. Set of twelve. Excellent condition, in box. $100–125

Ornaments, Horns and Bell. Blue and green French horns. Bell is 2¾" to glass dinger. Good condition. $10–12

Ornaments, Houses. Three glass houses/cottages. Sizes vary from 1–4" wide. Very good condition. $12–16

Ornaments, Lot of Fifty. Glass ornaments from 1950s. Very good condition. $40–60

Ornaments, Lot. 1940s glass Christmas tree ornaments and topper. Good condition. $40–50

Ornaments, Neon Brite. Twirler, glittered, star ornaments. Excellent condition. $60–75

Ornaments, Owls (Two). Silver glass owl ornaments. Circa 1920s. 3" long. Excellent condition. $15–25

Ornaments, Pine Cones. Two orange and silver 3½" pine cones. Good condition. $10–16

Ornaments, Pink. Lot of two bells with their dingers, fancy shape with turned rope, 30" fancy beaded garland, and a spiral shaped ornament. All in fine condition. $25–30

Ornaments, Porcelain. Dresden Russian ornaments. Group of five, including three birds and two Christmas trees. Very good condition. $15–25

Ornaments, Russian. Fourteen glass Russian ornaments. Assortment of balls, cones, birds. Very good condition. $20–40

Ornaments, Santa Heads. Glass, handpainted, glitter beard. Set of nine. Excellent condition. $45–55

Ornaments, Set of Ten. Silver glass ornaments from the 1940s. Some cones, teardrops, acorns. Very good condition. $15–25

Ornaments, Shiny Brite. Box of stenciled ornaments. Very good condition. $10–15

Ornaments, Shiny Brite. Eight striped and plain Shiny Brite ornament balls. Very good condition. **$11–18**

Ornaments, Shiny Brite. Four Santa ornaments with chenille accents. Very good condition. **$30–40**

Ornaments, Shiny Brite. Uncle Sam box of scenes and frosts. Excellent condition. **$10–15**

Ornaments, Silver Ice Cones. Glass, approximately 3" long. Excellent condition. **$225–235**

Ornaments, Singing Angels. 2½" cotton head angels with chenille hangers. Very good condition. **Set of three, $10–12**

Ornaments, Small Aluminum Balls on Pipe Cleaners. Circa 1940s. Very good condition. **Four for $8–10**

Ornaments, Trees. Two glass Christmas trees. Circa 1920s. Approximately 2" long. Excellent condition. **$40–50**

Ornaments, Wooden. Tiny angels on strings. Each is a different color and plays a musical instrument. Approximately 1" tall. Circa 1950s. Very good condition. **$40–50**

Plate, Santa's Head. Royal Bayreuth. German. 5" × 5". Circa 1905. Triangle plate. Depicts Santa's head, wears red cap with fur trim and holly. Royal Bayreuth mark on bottom. Excellent condition. **$2,300–2,500**

Postcard, A Merry Christmas. Embossed Santa. Postmarked 1929. Good condition. **$6–10**

Postcard, Angel. Holding music for Stile Nacht (Silent Night). Sent from Copenhagen to U.S. Good condition. **$10–18**

Postcard, Christmas Greetings and All Good Wishes. Postmarked 1913. Good condition. **$6–10**

Postcard, Merry Kris Kringle. Postmarked 1920. Good condition. **$6–10**

Postcard, Santa and Child on Donkey. Photograph. Name on back is Rudolph Wilhelm Schlesinger. 1920s. Good condition. **$10–15**

Postcard, To Wish You a Merry Christmas. Postmarked 1921. Good condition. **$6–8**

Print, Die-cut. Santa die-cut in beautiful colors. Circa 1880s. Very good condition. **$50–60**

Reindeer, Plastic. Hard white plastic reindeer. Circa 1940s. Set of ten. Very good condition. **$25–35**

Roly Poly, Santa Claus. Schoenhut. 9". Composition. Very good condition. **$900–1,000**

Santa Doll, Plush Figure, Velvet and Fur. Celluloid/plastic face. Approximately 20" tall. Circa 1950s. Good condition. **$45–75**

Santa Face, Moving. Celluloid battery-operated Santa Face. Circa 1940s. Santa figures, all made of papier-mâché. Black hat, 10½" tall, **$75–100.** Short red with pack (candy container), 4½", **$25–35.** Tall red, 10", circa 1940s–1950s, **$55–70**

Santa in Airplane, Cardboard. German. Circa 1920. Heavily embossed. 11½" long. Very good condition. **$115–125**

Santas and sleighs. All circa 1940s. 13" long, 8" long, and 6¼" long. All celluloid. Middle one has reindeer with metal on the back and is a windup. *Courtesy of Cocoa Village Antique Mall.* $60–90.

Celluloid Santa, Sleigh, and Deer. Made by Irwin. *Courtesy of Jean Littlejohn.* $125–150.

Santa in Sleigh with Deer. Japan. Cotton, 4" Santa, clay face, cotton batten coat over cardboard body, and black cotton legs stands in 4½" long mica sleigh with a brush tree and a celluloid reindeer. Circa 1930s. Very good condition. **$45–55**

Santa in Sleigh. German. 6" German Santa with papier-mâché face, rabbit fur beard, felt coat, composition boots, and holding a feather tree spree. Sits in a 7" long wood sleigh filled with cotton, brush tree, composition laying white deer, fruit, and bell. Bottom stamped "Germany" inside circle. Circa early 1900s. Very good condition. **$225–250**

Santa with Bag of Tops. Japan. 6½" Santa, clay face, cotton beard, papier-mâché boots, and flannel suit stands on mica covered base, holds sack with brush tree inside and plastic toys sewn on outside. Marked "Japan." Excellent condition. **$35–45**

Santa with Feather Tree. German. Burlap suit, papier-mâché face. All original. Circa 1900s. **$135–150**

Santa, Belsnickle. German. Red, white and blue. Open red coat with blue lining. Cloth trim. 10" high. Replaced feather tree and flag. Unmarked. Excellent condition (restored base). **$400–450**

Santa, Die-cut, Standing. Made of paper. Approximately 15" tall. Circa 1930s. Very good condition. **$65–85**

Santa, German. Large 15" Santa, head and shoulder style with a stuffed body. Porcelain head/shoulder, arms, and boots. Arms attached to body with buttons. Wool beard, metal buckle belt, and a bell on top of his hat. Missing his feather tree. Shoulder incised "G" in a circle and "ETC." Circa early 1900s. Excellent condition. **$275–300**

Santa in Chimney. Japan. Clay face, hands, and boots. Blue cotton pants, red coat, and a sack on his back. Chimney surrounded by cotton head dolls and snowmen. Good condition. **$75–100**

Santa, Japan. Sitting under lamp post. 7" Santa, clay face/hands/boots and a red flannel suit. Mica/cardboard lamp post lights. Hedge beside him, decorated with glass balls. Good condition. **$100–115**

Santa Standing Next to Chimney. Japan. 5½" tall, celluloid face, cotton suit, blue cotton pants, and black composition boots. Chimney piled high with cotton head toys, snowman, and presents. Brush tree behind him. 7" × 5". Very good condition. **$90–115**

Santa, Standing. Japan. Holding tree in one hand, cotton snowman in other, wood staff at his side. 7" tall. Clay face and hands, composition boots, cotton beard, and paper suit. Circa 1920s. Excellent condition. **$75–100**

Santa, Reticulated Hanging Figure, Paper. Decorated with sparkles. Approximately 30" tall. Circa 1950s. Very good condition. **$140–160**

Santas (Two), Celluloid. Approximately 4" tall. Both made in U.S. by Irwin. Circa 1940s. Very good condition. **$35–65**

Santas, Grouping of Chalk Versions. Various sizes, approximately twenty different versions, ranging from 2½" to 8". Ages range from circa 1920s–early 1950s. Most unusual and most valuable is Santa on a chicken. Very good condition. **Values range $20–225.**

Sign, Store Display. 15" × 17½" × 7½" Lighted, ornate frame, lion's paw feet. Painting under glass of skier waving to children on sleds, mountain in the background and a sign in front of her: "WALK-OVER SHOES Everywhere." The shoe ad (sign) illuminated when on. Fancy wooden frame has designs everywhere, four lion paws, scrollwork on the sides, a tin back. The bottom right side is marked "PERFECTIONS 78 FIFTH AVE, N.Y." Original cloth cord. Excellent condition. **$525–600**

Snowmen, Grouping. Six ranging from 3" to 10" tall. Largest is papier-mâché. Smallest is paper. Small cotton one from Japan. Tiny bobber with black hat and broom. Santa on skis with red scarf is balsa wood. Small three-legged version made of light wood. Very good condition. **$8–50 each**

Spoon, Santa. Sterling silver Christmas spoon. Marked sterling but no other hallmark. Circa 1920s. Excellent condition. **$20–30**

Squeezer, Santa Claus. German. Circa 1900. 6½" tall. Papier-mâché face, wooden arms and legs, Dresden trims, rabbit fur beard, little tree held in hands. Great condition. **$600–700**

Stamps, Christmas. Lot of stamps from Albion, Michigan, and one 1945 Christmas stamp. Good condition. **$5–7**

Stove Burner Cover, Victorian Angel. Colorful, as well as useful. Good condition. **$3–6**

Tin Box. "Christmas Card List." Decorated with Santas. Approximately 3" × 5" × 2". Good condition. **$6–10**

Tin Pail, Victorian Christmas. Primitive look. Five-color lithograph. 3⅜" height, 3³⁄₁₆" diameter; bail handle and lid intact. Stamp reads, "Pat. May—1887." Illustration has German look and feel; nice graphics of a pig / pigs (holding holly chain in mouth), corn, and berries. Front reads, "MERRY CHRISTMAS—C. M. PHERNAMBUCQ," and in tiny print, "AMERICAN CAN CO." Good condition. **$130–145**

Tin, Santa. Embossed Santa with holly berries around hood, toys around margin of tin cover. Decorations also include branches, pine cones, bells and tassels. Circa 1900. 10" × 7" × 2⅔". Very good condition. **$190–225**

Tin, Yellow Coated Santa. German. Circa 1910. 9¼" × 5" × 4¼". Lithographed tin with a heavily embossed lid. Depicts Santa with a long yellow coat that has thick fur rims. Wears red shoes and short red pants. Long beard that reaches just to his belt. In one hand he has a stick and in the other hand he holds a lantern. Carries a huge, huge back basket filled with many toys. Three of the other sides of the tin show snow scenes with dwarfs. "Gevalia" printed on two sides. Very good condition. **$200–300**

Towel, Kitchen. Linen decorated with Christmas bells. Circa 1940s. Very good condition. **$2–4**

Toy, Happi-Time Santa. 1949 cardboard Santa toy from Sears Roebuck. Good condition. **$20–25**

Toy, Pulling Sheep. Tip the sheep over for a "baaa." German. Approximately 6" long. On wooden base and rollers. Cotton sheep wool. Circa 1920s. Very good condition. **$350–375**

Toy, Putz, Country Scene with Gnomes. German. From Erzgebirge (Ore Mountains). Circa 1930. Miniature wooden houses with gnomes boxed in graphic tin can. Consists of 3 wooden houses, 3 gnomes made of composition, 3 fir trees, wooden fence w/gate. Can is 10" × 2½" × 4". Very good condition. **$200–250**

Toy, Roly Poly, Father Christmas. German. ¾" tall. Celluloid. Father Christmas wears dark blue robe, red hat, and carries a pack over his shoulder. Finely detailed. Stands up perfectly straight, and when you push him over he pops right back up. Excellent condition. **$275–325**

Toy, Santa on Train. Celluloid Santa riding a train. Approximately 8" long. Very good condition. **$100–125**

Toy, Tree with Lights. Battery-operated Christmas tree with blinking lights. Circa late 1940s–early 1950s. In original box. Excellent condition. **$40–50**

Tree Stand, Grimm's Fairy Tale Characters. German. Decorated stand is 12" diameter and 5½" tall. Characters include Cinderella, Snow White, and Little Red Riding Hood, all surrounded by angels. German names written above each. Original paint. Very good condition. **$190–225**

Tree Stand. Metal tree stand decorated with lights. Excellent condition. **$38–42**

Tree Topper, Angel. Plastic with silky blonde hair. Approximately 8" tall. Excellent condition. **$45-55**

Tree Topper, Star. Bradford ten-light tree topper star. Very good condition. **$7–10**

Tree, Aluminum. U.S. Circa 1950s. Aluminum tree, musical rotating stand, color wheel, and ornaments/decoration. Peco Christmas Pine Aluminum Tree (Model number 37) in original sleeves and original box. Tree stands 7' tall and assembles with a two-piece center pole and 160 pom-pom branches. Some usage wear. Good condition. **$350–500**

Tree, Bottle Brush. Japanese feather tree from 1930s. Approximately 12" tall with base. Very good condition. **$18–25**

Tree, Bubble Light Xmas Tree. 18". Rare purple lights. Circa 1940s cellophane tree, metal base, working lights. Probably Noma. Excellent condition. **$350–400**

Trees, Bottle Brush. Six small bottle brush Christmas trees. All are frosted with snow. Sizes range from 2"–10". Very good condition. **$60–80**

Treetop, Angel. German. Circa 1890. Ringing angel with three candlesticks with colored glass balls at chains. 14¾" × 7¾". Good condition. **$600–800**

Turtledoves. Three antique German turtledove Christmas display pieces. Cotton and feathers. Approximately 5" long each. Very good condition. **$15–25**

Urn, Cast Iron. Displays holiday floral arrangement, collection of brightly colored ornaments and other favorite Christmas knickknacks. 5" × 7" × 8". Excellent condition. Courtesy of CSPost.com **$64–70**

Vase, Victorian. German. 7½". Holiday vase with wire-wrapped ball on top. Very good condition. **$150–200**

Wreaths, Bottle Brush (Three). Two red and one green. Bows attached. One red wreath looks to have two balls missing, but is in good shape overall. 3" across. Good condition. **$10–15**

PRICE LIST: CHRISTMAS COLLECTIBLES CONTEMPORARY (1960–PRESENT)

Book, Christmas Carols. Small paper book of carols printed by John Hancock Mutual Life Insurance Company and given to customers as gift. Copyright date 1971. 4" × 6". Good condition. **$6–8**

Boots, Santa. Reproduced from a vintage original. Courtesy of Jamieson Studios. New. Mint condition. Small boot, 4" tall, **$10–15.** Large boot/holly, 8" tall. Mint condition. **$20–25**

Bucket, Saint Nicholas Head. 7" × 3½". Made of resin. Santa head with candle head wreath. American flag in top. Introduced in 2003. Mint condition. **$24.50–30**

Candle Holder, Santa. Porcelain, tealight votive holder. Scene on the holder shows Santa in a sleigh with two reindeer. Circa 1970s. Very good condition. **$5–8**

Candolier, Nine-light Bubble-Brite™. Shiny Brite's authentically reproduced 1940s animated candle lights exclusive to Christopher Radko. The candoliers come in a rainbow of colors. Streamlined lamp base is faithfully reproduced from a hard-to-find original. Courtesy of CSPost.com Mint condition. **$40–50**

Candy Container, Santa. 15½" × 6". Made of resin. Santa wears old red outfit, carries bottle brush tree and rocking horse. Toys hang off his belt and are in his bag. Introduced in 2003. Mint condition. **$66–75**

Candy Containers, Fat Santa. Two-piece European candy container. 8" tall. Reproduced from a vintage original. Courtesy of Jamieson Studios. New. Mint condition. **$25–30**

Candy Containers, Paper. Three triangular paper candy containers decorated with Santa and other Christmas icons. 6¼" × 5". Reproduced from a vintage original. Courtesy of Jamieson Studios. New. Mint condition. **$5–8 each**

Candy Dish, Santa Bear. Porcelain bear dressed in red Santa suit. Sitting in bag of toys ringing a bell. Gift bag is green and trimmed in yellow. Made by "Santa's Workbench." 6½" × 8½" × 6". Excellent condition. **$8–10**

Candy Dish, Snowman, Porcelain. Made in China. 7½" × 5½" × 6" tall. Made in 2000. Mint condition. **$8–12**

Candy Dish, Snowman. Made by Hallmark. Snowman wears cracked pot on head, green plaid scarf and apple buttons. Circa 1960s. Excellent condition. **$8–12**

Christmas Tree, Illuminated. Created by Thomas Kinkade. Limited edition by Bradford Editions. "Village Christmas" illuminated tree features scenes, houses, even the artist himself, all illuminated and approximately 15" tall. Battery operated. Contemporary. Mint condition. **$135–155**

Christmas Village, Berta Hummel. Village consists of four buildings and three Berta Hummel Figurines. Limited Edition, 2005. Buildings light up. Approximately 7½" tall (buildings). Mint condition. **each $75–100**

Cookie Dish, Snowman. Made by Fitz & Floyd. Marked "Fitz and Floyd Essentials, Made in China." 8¼" × 9½". Mint condition. **$12–16**

Dishes, Finsbury of England Christmas Saucers. One depicts Santa in front of Christmas tree holding gifts. Other is Christmas tree with gifts underneath. Both trimmed in gold and both marked "Finsbury, fine bone China, Made in England." Each measures 5" in diameter. Near mint condition. **$8–12**

Feather Tree, Decorated. Wooden clip on birds decorate this 8" tall feather tree. Circa 1970s. Excellent condition. **$40–50**

Figural House, Altstadter Bierstube. Made by Department 56. Beer Hall with window boxes around second story, beer stein hanging off sign. Approximately 4" tall. Mint in box. **$65–75**

Figural, House, Bauernhof Drescher. Set of two, exclusively from Department 56. Rustic cottages evoke the charming old farms of Bavaria. Mint in box. **$95–115**

Figural, House, Alpen Akademie der Musik. Exclusively from Department 56. School with detailed structure, including snow on roof and frescoe paintings. Approximately 5" tall. Mint in box. **$65–75**

Figural, House, Burgermeister Haus. Department 56. Large manor-like house for Burgermeister. Includes cupolas and galleries. Mint condition. **$65–75**

Figure, Child Holding Santa Mask. 7" × 4" figure made of resin. Child wears red hooded cape with ivory shift underneath. Introduced 2002. Mint condition. **$22–25**

Figure, Department 56. Snow Babies, A Gingerbread Christmas. Trio of Snow Babies are building a gingerbread house with the help of their penguin friends. The gingerbread house illuminates with the included standard switch. Mint condition. **$65–75**

Figure, Department 56. Snow Babies. Bedtime Prayers. Two Snow Babies saying their nighttime prayers. Porcelain. Mint condition. **$30–35**

Figure, Department 56. Snow Babies. Blind Faith. Snow Baby with foot poised to take a step off a log. Mint condition. **$17–20**

Figure, Department 56. Snow Babies. Bedtime Buddies. Snow Baby is ready for bed, with his favorite blanket and stuffed animal to help him drift off to sleep. Mint condition. **$20–25**

Figure, Department 56. Snow Baby, All In The Family. Snow Baby watching a penguin family play follow the leader. Porcelain. Mint condition. **$25–35**

Figure, Department 56. A Couple of Flakes. Porcelain. Mint condition. **$28–35**

Figure, Grossman/Rockwell NRX3. Caroler. 2¾" tall. 1978. Mint condition. **$25–30**

Figure, Heavenly Sisters. 9" × 6". Made of resin. Two angels. Larger one has her arm around the smaller one's shoulders. Introduced in 2004. Mint condition. **$45–50**

Figure, Santa in Moon. 16" papier-mâché figure of Santa in gold and white, holding doll under arm and star in hand, resting on a crescent moon. Introduced in 2001. Mint condition. **$67–75**

Figure, Santa Pulling Sled on Pull Toy. 12½" × 13½" resin figure of Santa holding tree over shoulder, basket of toys on back, pulling small green sled with tree and toys. Introduced 2002. Mint condition. **$90–100**

Figure, Santa, Christmas Eve Journey. Replica of Bethany Lowe's one-of-a-kind Santa. 15½" × 14". Made of paper pulp. Introduced 2002. Mint condition. **$85–95**

Figure, Santa, North Pole Express. Santa in blue work outfit sitting on black locomotive with Christmas tree on back. He holds a lamp in one hand and cuddles a teddy under his arm. 24" × 17½" × 12". Made of paper pulp. Introduced 2003. Mint condition. **$94–100**

Figure, Your Own Castle. Department 56. Depicts Snow Baby building ice castle with friendly penguin. Porcelain bisque. Approximately 4" tall. Mint in box condition. **$40–50**

Figures, Children Building Snowman. Set of three figures: two children and one snowman. By Bethany Lowe Designs, Inc. 9½" × 13". Made of resin. Introduced 2001. Mint condition. **$70–75**

Figures, Father Christmas in Sponge Car and Large Vintage German Santa. Father Christmas is made of resin, 8" × 9", and wears old red Christmas outfit. Introduced 2005. **$100–110.** Large German Santa is also resin, 19" × 7½", and introduced 2005. Mint condition. **$135–145**

Figures, Snowbunny Girl and Snowbunny Boy. Snowbunny Girl, 16½" × 10½". Bunny figure has felt body, fur trim, paper pulp face. Introduced 2005. **$52.95–58.** Snowbunny Boy, 20" × 10". Bunny figure with body made of felt, fur trim, and paper pulp face. Introduced in 2005. Mint condition. **$52.95–58**

Figures, Snowman and Snowgirl. Tannenbaum Snowman, 19" × 10½". Felt body, tulle and tinsel trim. Holds a basket of snowballs. His "hat" is a bottle brush tree. Introduced in 2005. **$42.50–46. Sugar Plum Snowgirl,** 16½" × 9". Felt body, tulle and tinsel trim. Introduced 2005. Mint condition. **$42.50–46**

Figures, Teena Flanner. Each figure is an exclusive papier-mâché work of art made from a very old mold, slowly dried, hand painted and signed by artist. Figures include Santas of different sizes, snowmen and snowwomen of different sizes, and angels of different sizes. Each piece unique and dusted with the artist's signature snow glitter. New. Mint condition. Courtesy of CSPost.com **$95–110**

Figures, Victorian Children. Set of two 7" × 2½" resin figures. Boy carries small tree and set of ice skates. Girl carries snowman head bucket. Made of resin. Introduced 2003. Mint condition. **$37–45**

Figurine, Precious Moments®, Baby Boy's First Christmas. Dated 1993. Figurine is of baby in pajamas, wrapped with ribbon. Ribbon marked "Baby's First Christmas, 1993." 3" tall. Marked on bottom of his feet "1993, PMi, Lic Enesco, 530859." Mint in box. **$30–40**

Figurine, Precious Moments®, Surrounded With Joy. Retired in 1989. The figurine depicts little boy in pale blue shirt and grey pants with Christmas wreath around neck. 4¼" tall. Marked "Surrounded with Joy, 1983 Jonathon & David, "Licensee Enesco, E-0506." Signed by Jonathon & David. Fish symbol imprinted on bottom of figure. Mint in box. **$100–120**

Figurines, Pixies. Two plastic pixies, one green, one red. Approximately 1¾" tall. Marked "Pixie, SSCO, NY, No. 2480, Made in Hong Kong." In unopened package. Excellent condition. **$5–7**

Figurines, Six Angel Musicians. Harpist, violinist, cellist, mandolin player, trumpeter, singer. Marked "Similegno, 47-2044, Hong Kong." Each is approximately 1¾" tall. Excellent condition. **$3–6**

Figurines, Ten Wooden Soldier Musicians. All are playing different instruments and appear to be hand-painted. Each is approximately 1¾" × 1". Original box is missing lid and undated. Excellent condition. **$3–6**

Folk Art, Candy Container, Johnathan Mouse's Christmas. 7½" tall. Papier-mâché ©Lori C. Mitchell, 2003. Mint condition. **$220–240**

Folk Art, 'Tis the Season Angel. 7" tall. Papier-mâché. ©Lori C. Mitchell, 2004. Mint condition. **$220–250**

Folk Art, Candy Container, Blue Santa Carrying the Christ Child. Made in the traditional German style, using composition, antique fabric/trims, curly goat beard, feather tree and standing on a mica covered wood base. The Santa separates under the robe at the boots to reveal a candy container tube. Approximate size: 20" × 10". Original design, sculpted and created by Scott Smith, owner of Rucus Studio. New. Mint condition. **$750–850**

Folk Art, Candy Container, Brownie in a Snowball. Made using composition and papier-mâché, antique fabric/trims, and feather tree. He separates at the waist to reveal a candy container tube. Approximate size: 11" × 6". Original design, sculpted and created by Scott Smith, owner of Rucus Studio. New. Mint condition. **$325–400**

Folk Art, Candy Container, Krampus on Wooden Shoe. Made using composition and antique trims. The silk bag is the candy container. Approximate size: 6" × 6". Original design, sculpted and created by Scott Smith, owner of Rucus Studio. New. Mint condition.

$135–150

Folk Art, Candy Container, Red Angel. Made in the traditional German style, using composition, antique trims, and standing on a mica covered wood base. She separates at the boots to reveal a candy container tube. Approximate size: 12" × 7". Original design, sculpted and created by Scott Smith, owner of Rucus Studio. New. Mint condition.

$325–400

Folk Art, Candy Container, Santa. Made in the traditional German style, using composition, antique fabric/trims, curly goat beard, and standing on a mica covered wood base. The Santa separates under the robe at the boots to reveal a candy container tube. Approximate size: 20" × 10". Original design, sculpted and created by Scott Smith, owner of Rucus Studio. New. Mint condition.

$750–850

Folk Art, Candy Container, Snow Friend. Made using composition and vintage trims. Separates under the robe at the boots to reveal a candy container tube. Approximate size: 14" × 6". Original design, sculpted and created by Scott Smith, owner of Rucus Studio. New. Mint condition.

$325–400

Folk Art, Evergreen Angel. 8" tall. Papier-mâché. ©Lori C. Mitchell, 2004. Mint condition.

$230–250

Folk Art, Horsing Around Santa. 6½" tall. Papier-mâché. ©Lori C. Mitchell, 2004. Mint condition.

$215-230

Folk Art, Jolly Good Fun. 7½" tall. Papier-mâché. ©Lori C. Mitchell, 2004. Mint condition.

$240–260

Folk Art, Mr. Frost. Figure in blue waistcoat and yellow outfit, holds "Frosty Winter" sign. Base looks like snow and is marked "chilly chilly." 9" tall. Original folk art by Trout Creek Folk Art, Napa, Calif., 2004. New. Mint condition.

$160–180

Folk Art, Mr. Kringle. 8½" tall. Papier-mâché. ©Lori C. Mitchell, 2004. Mint condition.

$230–250

Folk Art, Mule Tide Santa. 6¼" tall. Papier-mâché. ©Lori C. Mitchell, 2003. Mint condition.

$250–275

Folk Art, Old Father Christmas. Spun cotton beard. 9¼" tall to lantern post. Papier-mâché. ©Lori C. Mitchell, 2003. Mint condition.

$375–400

Folk Art, Santa Gets A Ride! Santa is riding upon (unhappy) snowman's back. Papier-mâché, crepe, goosefeather branch (held by Santa). 8" tall. Original folk art by Trout Creek Folk Art, Napa, Calif., 2002. New. Mint condition.

$95–125

Folk Art, Santa Jack. Santa figure made of wood, twigs, papier-mâché. No hat. Holding bells. 10" tall. Original folk art by Trout Creek Folk Art, Napa, Calif., 1996. New. Mint condition.

$45–65

Folk Art, Sculpture, Ornamental Elf. Made using papier-mâché and vintage glass ornaments and original package. Mounted to a wooden base. Approximate size: 21" × 13". Original design, sculpted and created by Scott Smith, owner of Rucus Studio. New. Mint condition. **$800–900**

Folk Art, Snowboy Goes off to the Sauna. Snowman figure with striped towel over his arm. Papier-mâché. 7" tall. Original folk art by Trout Creek Folk Art, Napa, Calif., 2000. New. Mint condition. **$65–85**

Folk Art, Snowman Bucket. Snowman face with pine branches on handle. Made of papier-mâché, goosefeathers, and felted wool. 5" tall. Original folk art by Trout Creek Folk Art, Napa, Calif., 1995. New. Mint condition. **$26–40**

Folk Art, Snowman. Chalkware snowman made from an old Obermann chocolate mold. 4" tall. Original folk art by Trout Creek Folk Art, Napa, Calif., 2001. New. Mint condition. **$45–65**

Folk Art, The Puppeteer. 9½" tall. Papier-mâché. ©Lori C. Mitchell, 2004. Mint condition. **$320–350**

Folk Art, Tree of Life Santa. 11" tall. Papier-mâché. ©Lori C. Mitchell, 2004. Mint condition. **$330–350**

Folk Art, Tree Trimming Angel. 7½" tall. Papier-mâché ©Lori C. Mitchell, 2004. Mint condition. **$225–250**

Folk Art, I Believe . . . *One of a kind.* 9¾" × 9". Papier-mâché. ©Lori C. Mitchell, 2004. Mint condition. **$600–800**

Garland. Cotton batting garland with red foil. 9' long. Courtesy of Jamieson Studios. New. Mint condition. **$15–20**

Glasses, Twelve Days of Christmas. Drinking glasses. Circa 1980s. Excellent condition. **$4.25–6 each**

Group of Bottle Brush Trees, Fat Santa Jollies, and Santa Bell Cloche. Ivory Bottle Brush Trees (set of 3). Lg. 12" × 5", med. 10" × 3½", and small 7" × 3". Introduced in 2005. Mint condition. **$27.95–35. Two Fat Santa Jollies.** 3" × 2" glass body. Introduced in 2005. Mint condition. **$14.95–16. Santa Bell Cloche.** 3" × 2" glass cloche. Introduced 2005. Mint condition. **$32.50–35**

House, Department 56, Dickens' Village Series, "Dickens' Village Church." Issued in 1985 and retired in 1989. Lighted from the back with a small nightlight-type bulb and cord on/off switch. 9¾" × 8¾". Bottom marked "Dickens' Village Church." Excellent condition. **$15–20**

House, Department 56, Heritage Village Collection, Dickens' Village Series, "Cobles Police Station." Issued in 1989 and retired in 1991. Lighted from the back with a small nightlight-type bulb and cord on/off switch. 6¾" × 6". Bottom marked "Dickens' Village Series, Cobles Police Station, Department 56, 1989." #5583-2. Mint condition in its original packing and box. **$115–125**

Jewelry, Earrings. Holiday star pierced earrings. Antiqued silver tone metal in a brushed linear finish. Circa 1960s. 2" × ¾". Front of stars are bronze color plated. All four stars twinkle in multicolor rhinestone pastes. A faux pearl dangles between the two free swinging stars. Fine condition with no missing stones. Excellent condition.   **$15–20**

Jewelry, Earrings. 1960s vintage plastic Santa clacker pin with earrings. Excellent condition.   **$18–25**

Jewelry, Pin, Christmas Tree. Sterling silver. 2½" × 1¼". Excellent condition.   **$30–40**

Nativity Set, Eleven-piece. Made of resin-type material. Mahogany-stained wood base. Mary, Joseph, baby Jesus, angel, three kings, shepherd, donkey, bull, and lamb. Each piece is 3–4" tall. Excellent condition.   **$12–18**

Nutcracker, America the Beautiful. Made by Steinbach, 2002. Uncle Sam figure with top hat. Mint condition.   **$275–300**

Nutcracker, Champion of Freedom. Made by Steinbach, 2002. Figure carries American flag. Mint condition.   **$275–300**

Nutcracker, Chubby Uncle Sam. Made by Steinbach. Holds American flag that's bigger than he is. Excellent condition.   **$120-150**

Nutcracker, Cycle Santa. Made by Ulbricht. Mint condition.   **$250–275**

Ornament Sets, Shiny Brite. Christopher Radko has reproduced Shiny-Brite glass ornaments from the 1940s–1960s in all their fantastic colors, creative designs, and unique shapes. Every ornament is entirely hand-painted and packaged in an authentic box. Courtesy of CSPost.com Mint condition.   **Boxes of one dozen vary from $29.95–54.95.**

Ornament, "Cherub with Baby," Dreamsickles. Measures approximately 2¼" × 1½". Marked on bottom "DX286, Cherub with Baby, 1994 Cast Art Industries, Inc., Made in China." Original plastic casing and box. Excellent condition.   **$40–60**

Ornament, 101 Dalmatians, Pongo & Perdita. McDonald's Mini-Snowglobe Ornament. 3" × 4". Features the happy canine couple from Disney's 101 Dalmatians riding in a sleigh with the pups in the back. Small snowdome that was a premium sold in 1999 in McDonald's restaurants. Mint in box.   **$6–10**

Ornament, Angel with Bird. 5" × 2½". Made of resin. Angel in light blue gown, holding dove in her hands. Introduced in 2001. Mint condition.   **$9.95–13**

Ornament, Angel with Gold Wings. 3" high (wings are not made of glass). Mint in box.   **$12–15**

Ornament, Bell with Clapper. Made of iron with marble bell. 3¼" diameter. Contemporary. Excellent condition.   **$12–15**

Ornament, Berta Hummel Annual Ornament. Hark the Herald. 1983. First edition. Mint in box condition.   **$25–30**

Ornament, Berta Hummel Glass Ball. 1983. Angelic Message. Mint in box.   **$9–11**

Ornament, Berta Hummel Glass Ball. 1980. Parade into Toyland. Mint in box.   **$9–11**

Ornament, Berta Hummel Glass Ball. 1981. A Time to Remember. Mint in box. **$9–11**

Ornament, Berta Hummel Glass Ball. 1990. Angel's Light. Mint in box. **$9–11**

Ornament, Berta Hummel Glass Ball. Mint in box. **$10–12**

Ornament, Berta Hummel Glass Ball. Christmas Child. 1975. Mint condition. **$9–12**

Ornament, Berta Hummel Glass Ball. Guardian Angel. 1974. First ornament, 1974. Mint condition. **$15–20**

Ornament, California Raisin. California Raisin is wearing red stocking cap trimmed in white. Marked on bottom of shoe "California Raisins, 1988, China." 3⅛" tall. Excellent condition. **$15–20**

Ornament, Candy Castle. Made by Christopher Radko. Made for Starlight members only. Limited Edition. Style Number 98-SP-36. Rare and retired ornament originally made in 1998. 7" tall, and stands on its own. Mint in box. **$70–100**

Ornament, Cherished Teddies. Teddy sitting with a box of ornaments and paintbrushes in a bucket. The box is marked "Cherished Ornaments." Marked "1996, P. Hillman, Lic. Enesco Corporation." 1¼" tall; 2" wide. Excellent condition. **$7–10**

Ornament, Child with Santa Mask. 5½" × 2½". Made of resin. Child in red hooded cape holds Santa Mask. Introduced 2002. Mint condition. **$10.50–14**

Ornament, Child with Stocking. 5½" × 2½". Made of resin. Child in white dress trimmed with red, carries red stocking in her hands. Introduced 2002. Mint condition. **$10.50–14**

Ornament, Child with Teddy. 5½" × 2½". Made of resin. Child wearing white dress and holding teddy on string from her hand. Mint condition. **$10.50–14**

Ornament, Chinese Barbie, "Dolls of the World" Collection, Hallmark Keepsake. 4½" tall, made in 1997. Excellent condition in original box. **$18–25**

Ornament, Chub-A-Dub Santa. Made by Christopher Radko. 5½" tall. Part of the Glorious Christmas line. Mint in box. **$40–50**

Ornament, Concave Ball with Decoupage Angel. 7" high. Mint condition. **$14–20**

Ornament, Disney Princesses. Three Beautiful Princesses by Disney. 4¼" tall. "Once upon a time, there were three brave and beautiful princesses, Snow White in 1937, Cinderella in 1950 and Sleeping Beauty in 1959." Ornament pictures those beautiful princesses in front of a fairy tale castle. Mint in box condition. **$20–25**

Ornament, Disney, Beauty & The Beast, Belle Figural. 4" tall. Ceramic ornament of Belle's head. Made by Schmidt. Wonderful details, deep, rich colors and an overall nice quality of workmanship. Excellent condition. **$15–20**

Ornament, Disney, Mickey Mouse Through the Years. Circa 2000. Ornament shows Mickey Mouse in several different scenes around the ornament. New. Mint in box. Box shows some wear. Good condition. **$9.50–12**

Ornament, Disney, Mickey Mouse. The Sorcerer's Apprentice Christmas Ornament, Walt Disney's Fantasia. "Abracadabra, An apprentice's first attempt to cast spells unexpectedly turns into a wild, wet adventure that has charmed audiences for over 60 years. Fantasia is Mickey Mouse's feature role. This movie is accompanied by the music of French composer Paul Dukas." A battery-operated light illuminates Mickey Mouse. Mint in box condition.

$17–20

Ornament, Disney, Pluto. Pluto is sneaking a treat. Hallmark ornament trademarked by Disney. 4" tall. "Playful Pluto seeks to sneak a tasty Christmas sample. No need to swipe the whole big tray, one cookie should be ample. Pluto thinks his fun hijinks are cleverly delicious, that is, until Mickey catches him and makes him wash the dishes." Mint in box condition.

$20–25

Ornament, Disney, Princess Ariel. Hallmark Keepsake Ornament 2004. 3" tall. This depicts "Ariel holding treasured pears on a cozy oyster chair. She is dreaming of seaside strolls with the man of her dreams, Prince Eric. The youngest of King Triton's seven daughters, this impetuous undersea princess has captivated the hearts of countless moviegoers in The Little Mermaid, released in 1989." Mint in box condition.

$15–20

Ornament, Disney/MGM Studios. 1989 Annual Christmas Ornament. Each year Disney offers a different ornament for each of their theme parks. Pictured on the front are Mickey and Minnie Mouse "filming" with Donald and Daisy as the film crew. Pluto and Goofy, along with two very funny "reindeer" complete the scene. Glass ornament with shrink wrap overlay in its original box. Mint in box.

$12.50–15

Ornament, Dolphin Duo. Poland. Made by Christopher Radko. Approximately 3" tall. Depicts two dolphins. Mint in box.

$20–30

Ornament, Ferrandiz Glass Ball. 1986. Away in the Manger. Mint condition.

$7–10

Ornament, Ferrandiz Glass Ball. 1978. Heavenly Peace. First edition. Mint condition.

$7–10

Ornament, Ferrandiz Glass Ball. 1979. Christmas Lights. Mint condition.

$7–10

Ornament, Ferrandiz Glass Ball. 1980. Babes at Christmas. Mint condition.

$7–10

Ornament, Ferrandiz Glass Ball. 1981. Mother and Child. Mint condition.

$7–10

Ornament, Ferrandiz Glass Ball. 1982. Song of Slumber. Mint condition.

$7–10

Ornament, Ferrandiz Glass Ball. 1983. Beautiful Bounty. Mint condition.

$7–10

Ornament, Ferrandiz Glass Ball. 1985. Hearts Desire. Mint condition.

$7–10

Ornament, First Christmas Together, Hallmark. Heart shaped photo holder, opens like a locket. Dated 2004.

$25–30

Ornament, Flounder. Made by Christopher Radko. #97-DIS-84. Retired ornament from 1997. 6½" tall × 3" wide × 4" deep. Rare. Mint in box.

$25–40

Ornament, Garfield. Made by Enesco. Garfield is in a Christmas shopping bag marked 'Tis Better to Get. Marked "Garfield, 1978, 1981 United Feature Syndicate, Inc., Licensee Enesco Imports Corp." 2¾" × 1¾". Excellent condition.

$8–10

Ornament, Hallmark, Night Before Christmas. Marked QX214-7. Original box. Dated 1979. Excellent condition.

$25–35

Ornament, Hallmark, Evergreen Santa. Victorian Santa holding tree and star. Sculpted and signed by Joyce Lyle. 3¼" tall. Dated 1996. Numbered QX5714. Box marked "1996, Hallmark Cards, Inc., K.C., MO 64141, Made in China." Excellent condition. **$40–50**

Ornament, Hallmark, Keepsakes Cinderella. Part of "Enchanted Memories Collection." Inspired by Disney fairy tale. Dated 1997. 4½" tall. Original packing and box. Marked QXD4045, on box "Mfd. For Hallmark Cards, Inc., K.C., MO 64141, Made in Thailand." Excellent condition. **$30–40**

Ornament, Hanging Flower with Silver Wire. 4½" high. Gold and pink. Excellent condition. **$10–15**

Ornament, Harry Potter and the Sorcerer's Stone. Made as part of promotion for the Harry Potter series in 2000. Ornament shows Harry flying on broom. Excellent condition. **$10–15**

Ornament, Holiday Break. Made by Christopher Radko. Depicts Santa half asleep in chair with glasses pushed up on his forehead. Mint condition. **$44–54**

Ornament, Jingle Pals, Hallmark. Singing Snowman and Dancing Dog. Dated 2004. Mint condition. **$30–35**

Ornament, Kristi Yamaguchi, Hallmark Keepsake. Made in 2000. 5½" tall. Mint condition. **$20–25**

Ornament, Madonna and Child. 4" high. Mint condition. **$9–15**

Ornament, Mickey Mouse. Wooden. 6" tall. Good condition. **$7–10**

Ornament, Midnight Magic. Three-piece set includes a glass ornament stand that holds Santa and his Reindeer flying above a lovely Christmas cottage. 11" tall. Mint condition. **$45–55**

Ornament, Muhammad Ali, Hallmark Keepsake. 5" tall, made in 1999. Mint condition. **$20–25**

Ornament, Nordic Rider. Santa on beautiful sleigh. 6½" wide. Mint condition. **$44–54**

Ornament, Pink and Silver Wire Bauble with Baby. 5½" high. Mint condition. **$14–20**

Ornament, Pretty Present Perch. Made by Christopher Radko. 4½" tall. Mint condition. **$47–57**

Ornament, Regal Saint Nick. Made by Christopher Radko. 5½" tall. Mint condition. **$45–55**

Ornament, Santa Cornucopias, Set of Three. Designed by Gail and Glenn Giaimo of Dresden Star Heirloom Ornaments. Reproduction of original ornaments made from vintage glass, antique tinsels and trims, paper "scrap" images. 8" × 4". Introduced in 2005. Mint condition. **$81.95–88**

Ornament, Santa Ornament. Limited edition ornament in papier-mâché. Handpainted "Old World" type Santa. Cotton beard, carrying small basket. 4¼" × 1½" × 1". Marked on base 1950, 166/2000, Cindy Buy. Good condition. **$8–12**

Ornament, Santa Riding Bird. Designed by Gail and Glenn Giaimo of Dresden Star Heirloom Ornaments. Reproduction of original ornaments made from vintage glass, antique tinsels and trims, paper "scrap" images. 4" × 5½". Introduced in 2005. Mint condition.

$34.50–40

Ornament, Santa. Limited edition Santa ornament, papier-mâché. Handpainted Old World type Santa with cotton beard and carrying a small basket. Measures 4¼" tall; 1½" wide; and 1" deep. Two small holes on the back of the base which look like they were done during the making of the piece. The bottom of the base has separated, but is not torn. It is marked on the base "1950." On the back of the base it is marked "166/2000, Cindy Buy." Very good condition.

$8–10

Ornament, Santaland Spectacular. Made by Christopher Radko. 6" tall. Mint condition.

$44–54

Ornament, Small Gold Angel. 2" high. Mint condition.

$5–8

Ornament, Spencer on Sled. 4" × 2". Made of resin. Boy in red, wearing stocking cap, on sled. Introduced 2002. Mint condition.

$11.50–15

Ornament, Spode Christmas Tree. Oval and trimmed with gold, hanging thread is gold. Original box. Marked "Spode, Happy Holidays." 2" × 2¾". Excellent condition. $16–20

Ornament, Spode. Oval ornament trimmed in gold. Depicts decorated Christmas tree and gifts. Original box. Marked Spode–Happy Holidays. 2" × 2¾" Mint condition. $16–20

Ornament, St. Ceclia's Angel. Musical ornament made in 1997 by Enesco, #293423. Wears green dress and plays Silent Night on the harp. Musical ornament. Excellent condition.

$20–25

Ornament, Star Trek, Hallmark. "City on the Edge of Forever." Dated 2004. Depicts Dr. McCoy and Captain jumping through circular hoop. Excellent condition. $35–40

Ornament, Star. Chenille. 5". Reproduced from a vintage original. Courtesy of Jamieson Studios. New. Mint condition.

$7–9

Ornament, Sugar Holiday. Made by Christopher Radko. A portrait of one of Elizabeth Taylor's dogs and created for her AIDS Foundation. 6" tall. Mint condition. $38–48

Ornament, The Baker, Reader's Digest. Porcelain ornament of small bakery with yellow roof and bay window, sign above door "The Baker." 2½" × 2½" × 2". Light can be inserted in the back. Marked "Reader's Digest, Copyright 1991, Made in China." Mint condition.

$5–7

Ornament, The Grocer, Reader's Digest. Porcelain ornament of small grocery store. Purple thatched roof, bay window in front, chimney on side, and sign above door "The Grocer." 2¾" × 2¾" × 2". Opening in back where mini-light can be inserted. Marked "Reader's Digest, Copyright, 1991, Made in China." Excellent condition. $4–6

Ornament, The Queens Inn. Porcelain inn with grey roof and dormer windows, as well as sign above door reading "The Queens Inn." Measures 2¾" × 2¾" × 2". Marked "Reader's Digest, Copyright, 1991, Made in China." Excellent condition. $4–6

Ornament, Tropical Splendor. Made by Christopher Radko. Depicts purple hibiscus. 5" high. Mint condition.   **$40–50**

Ornament, Winter Minuet. Made by Christopher Radko. Approximately 4" high. Mint condition.   **$40–50**

Ornaments, Box, Red Glass Balls. Set of twelve in original box. Marked Japan. Some wear on ornaments. Good condition.   **$15–18**

Ornaments, Box. Star-Brite ornaments, circa 1960. Plain colors. Very good condition.
                                                                                                                  $10–15

Ornaments, Christmas Trees. Plastic unopened ornaments. Red candles on each limb and trees are painted to look like snow. Undated, but marked Merri-Craft, No. 1492, Nesbit Industries, Inc., Chicago, Illinois. 1½" × 1". Good condition.   **$2–4**

Ornaments, Coca Cola Santa. Set of three 1986 Coke Santa ornaments in original box. Created by Haddon Sundblom, the artist who created what is now known as the American Santa. Mint condition.   **$45–65**

Ornaments, Delicate Angels, Set of Two. Designed by Gail and Glenn Giaimo of Dresden Star Heirloom Ornaments. Reproduction of original ornaments made from vintage glass, antique tinsels and trims, paper "scrap" images. 5½" × 2" each. Introduced in 2005. Mint condition.   **$38.95–42**

Ornaments, Miniature Christmas Tree Angels. Italian. Handpainted wood from ANRI. Angioletti. Mint condition.   **$12–15**

Plate, A Christmas Tale. Marked Bing and Grondahl, 1978. Henry Thelander is artist. Excellent condition.   **$18–22**

Plate, Christmas Cobalt Plate. Made by Lindner of Kueps, Bavaria. Dated 1976. Shows mouse family around Christmas tree. Excellent condition.   **$12–20**

Plate, Christmas Welcome. Marked Bing and Grondahl, 1976. Henry Thelander is artist. Excellent condition.   **$18–22**

Plate, Copenhagen Christmas. Marked Bing and Grondahl, 1977. Henry Thelander is artist. Excellent condition.   **$18–22**

Plate, Schmid Disney Christmas Plate. 1978. Night Before Christmas. Mint condition.
                                                                                                                  $25–30

Plate, Schmid Disney Christmas Plate. 1974. Decorating the Tree. Mint condition. **$35–40**

Plate, Schmid Disney Christmas Plate. 1976. Building a Snowman. Depicts Donald and his nephews. Mint condition.   **$25–30**

Plate, Schmid Disney Christmas Plate. Down the Chimney. Mickey as Santa with a bagful of toys ready to go down the chimney. Mint condition.   **$25–30**

Plate, Schmid/Disney Final Christmas Plate. 1991. Shows Mickey and Minnie riding a hobby horse. Mint condition.   **$30–40**

Plate, Schmid Disney Christmas Plate. 1974. Caroling. Depicts Mickey, Goofy and Donald caroling. Mint condition. **$25–30**

Pull Toy, Santa. By Bethany Lowe Designs, Inc. 7½" × 19", made of resin. Depicts Santa in white robes on small wheeled transport. Intoduced 2001. Mint condition. **$71.95–75**

Salt and Pepper Set, Snowmen. Ceramic. Snowmen dressed in black top hats, scarves around their necks and pipes in their mouths. Marked China. 2" diameter, 3½" tall. Very good condition. **$8–12**

Salt and Pepper Shaker Set, Snowmen. Snowmen are dressed in black top hats with hatbands decorated with holly and berries. Marked "China." 2" diameter, 3½" tall. Good condition. **$8–10**

Santa, Figure, Folk Art. "Americana Santa" by Bethany Lowe Designs, Inc. 35" × 24" × 28". Depicts Santa on sled banging on American drum and holding American flag. Dressed in traditional Santa clothing. Hand sculpted, one of a kind. Introduced 2004. Mint condition. **$2,850–3,000**

Santa, Figure, Folk Art. "Christmas Travelers" by Bethany Lowe Designs, Inc. 26" × 24" × 56". Santa pulling wagon full of toys, flag, and Christmas tree. Hand sculpted, one of a kind. Introduced 2003. Mint condition. **$3,495–3,600**

Santa, Figure, Folk Art. "Dog Sled Run" by Bethany Lowe Designs, Inc. 26" × 13" × 40". Depicts Santa on sled with several teddies. Hand sculpted, one of a kind. Introduced 2004. Mint condition. **$1,195–1,300**

Santa, Figure, Folk Art. "Downhill Towards Christmas" by Bethany Lowe Designs, Inc. 25" tall. Depicts Santa on skis in ski sweater and hat. Hand sculpted, one of a kind. Introduced 2003. Mint condition. **$650–700**

Santa, Figure, Folk Art. "Klondike" by Bethany Lowe Designs, Inc. 44" × 32". Hand sculpted, one of a kind. Depicts Santa as dog sled driver. He wears furs and snowshoes. Sled is full of toys. Introduced 1997. Mint condition. **$1,695–1,800**

Santa, Figure, Folk Art. "Old World Father Christmas" by Bethany Lowe Designs, Inc. 5'7" tall. Depicts Santa in fur trimmed robe, holding staff, globe, doll, and lantern. Wears a wreath on head. Hand sculpted, one of a kind. Introduced 1996. Mint condition. **$5,995–6,250**

Santa, Figure, Folk Art. "Santa on Antique Trike" by Bethany Lowe Designs, Inc. 30" × 18" × 24". Hand sculpted, one of a kind. Introduced 2003. Mint condition. **$2,495–2,600**

Santa, Figure, Folk Art. "Sky Rider" by Bethany Lowe Designs, Inc. 36" × 20" × 24". Depicts Santa in blue plane with Merry Christmas sign flying from back. Hand sculpted, one of a kind. Introduced 1995. Mint condition. **$245–285**

Santa, Figure, Folk Art. "Tinker Claus" by Bethany Lowe Designs, Inc. 21" × 14". Santa in work apron with tools, working on toys. Hand sculpted, one of a kind. Introduced 2004. Mint condition. **$695–750**

Santa, Figure, Folk Art. "Trapper Claus" by Bethany Lowe Designs, Inc. 24" × 12". Depicts Santa in full furs wearing snowshoes and carrying lantern. Hand sculpted, one of a kind. Introduced 2003. Mint condition. **$895–1,000**

Santa Pull Toy. 2001. 7½" × 19". Made of resin. *Courtesy of Bethany Lowe Designs, Inc.* $71.95–75.

Santa, Figure, Folk Art. "Children's Friend" by Bethany Lowe Designs, Inc. 28" × 14". Depicts Santa with red embroidered short jacket and hat and green velvet pants. Holds doll on one knee and teddy on other (he is seated). Hand sculpted, one of a kind. Introduced 2003. Mint condition.   **$2,495–2,700**

Santa, Figure, Folk Art. "Christmas Flight" by Bethany Lowe Designs, Inc. 34" × 20" × 36". Depicts Santa in carousel type of flying "plane." He is joined by stuffed animals and toys. Hand sculpted, one of a kind. Introduced 2004. Mint condition.   **$4,395–4,750**

Santa, Figure, Folk Art. "Santa on Antique Steamroller" by Bethany Lowe Designs, Inc. 25" × 24". Depicts Santa on old steamroller, holding teddie, wearing long tassled hat. Hand sculpted, one of a kind. Introduced 1999. Mint condition.   **$2,495–2,600**

Santas, Roly Poly. Group of various sizes. Reproduced from a vintage original. Courtesy of Jamieson Studios. New. Mint condition.   **4½" $11–15; 7½" $25–30; 9½" $38–42**

Scherenschnitte Art, Deco Deer with Flowers. Deco Christmas deer has a slightly 1920s feel, with a curving, smooth appearance. It measures 11" × 14", including mat. Photo and Copyright © Sharyn Sowell. All rights reserved. Mint and original condition.   **$45–55**

Scherenschnitte Art, Deco Deer with Stars. This deer is leaping through the starry night. The piece measures 11" × 14", including the mat. Photo and Copyright © Sharyn Sowell. All rights reserved. Mint and original condition.   **$40–50**

Scherenschnitte Art, Deer in Vintage Frame. These deer leap through the underbrush in a magical forest. The frame is an old farmhouse window and the piece measures 12" × 27". Photo and Copyright © Sharyn Sowell. All rights reserved. Mint and original condition.
        $195–225

Scherenschnitte Art, Reindeer, Stars, Moon. This piece has a Scandinavian feel, thanks to the artist's heritage, and measures 16" × 20", including the mat. Photo and Copyright © Sharyn Sowell. All rights reserved. Mint and original condition.   **$150–175**

Scherenschnitte Art, Santa's Parade. Incredibly detailed piece with Santa, wee gnomes, elves, and decorated with stars and birds. Measures 11" × 14", matted. Photo and Copyright © Sharyn Sowell. All rights reserved. Mint and original condition.　　**$165–180**

Scherenschnitte Art, Standing Art Deco-style Deer with Flowers. Black art, white background. 11" × 14", including the mat. Art deco feel with the classic deer/Christmas design. Photo and Copyright © Sharyn Sowell. All rights reserved. Mint and original condition.

$60–75

Scherenschnitte Art, Winter Play. One of recent Four Magical Seasons series. Winter Play measures 16" × 20", including the mat. Photo and Copyright © Sharyn Sowell. All rights reserved. Mint and original condition.　　**$165–180**

Snowman Tree, Lighted and Handpainted. Ceramic tree is one of a kind, painted and hand decorated with little snowmen scattered all about the branches. Contemporary. Mint condition.　　**$70–100**

Snowman, China. Made by Lenox. 4" tall and accented in 24 karat gold. Scarf around his neck personalized with name. Mint condition.　　**$25–35**

Stockings, Santa and Mrs. Claus. Christmas stockings with Santa and Mrs. Claus on them. 10" tall, made of cardboard, and have a paper candy bag on the back. Reproduced from Vintage Originals. Courtesy of Jamieson Studios. New. Mint condition.　　**$8–10/pair**

Toy, Stuffed Bear. "Christmas Red." 18" red mohair teddy, glass eyes, growler. Wears striped stocking cap and holds a real goose feather wreath. Original folk art creation by Baker & Co. Designs Ltd. New. Mint condition.　　**$295–325**

Toy, Stuffed Bear. "Lil Red." 13" red mohair teddy, has glass eyes, wool felt paw pads and a squeaker in his belly. Wears a stocking cap and holds Christmas goodies. Original folk art creation by Baker & Co. Designs Ltd. New. Mint condition.　　**$225–250**

Toy, Stuffed Bear. "Mr. Flakey." 18" mohair teddy with glass eyes and growler. He wears black socks and wool felt hat. He holds a vintage shovel. Original folk art creation by Baker & Co. Designs Ltd. New. Mint condition.　　**$295–345**

Toy, Stuffed Bear. "Sergeant Holiday." 22" red mohair teddy with glass eyes and a growler. He wears a vintage child's military coat and carries an antique horn and bottle brush tree. Original folk art creation by Baker & Co. Designs Ltd. New. Mint condition.　　**$525–575**

Toy, Stuffed Bear. "Victorian Make Do." Small mohair teddy sits atop a hand dyed wool "make-do" pincushion. Feather stitching and vintage buttons decorate the ball. Teddy holds a real goose feather sprig. Original folk art creation by Baker & Co. Designs Ltd. Mint condition.　　**$275–300**

Toy, Stuffed Bunny. "Angelica." 32" long beige bunny. Mohair head and hands, linen body and legs. She is wearing a vintage dress and shoes. Holding antique Christmas accessories, has a tinsel wreath and wooden wings. Original folk art creation by Baker & Co. Designs Ltd. New. Mint condition.　　**$595–625**

Toy, Stuffed Bunny. "Dolly Bunny in Pink." Mohair with a doll face. Has wool felt mittens and boots. Holds vintage goodies. Original folk art creation by Baker & Co. Designs Ltd. New. Mint condition.　　**$255–300**

Toy, Stuffed Bunny. "Dolly Bunny in Red." 13" red bunny with a doll face. Has wool felt mittens and boots and holds a vintage bottle brush tree. Original folk art creation by Baker & Co. Designs Ltd. New. Mint condition. **$255–300**

Toy, Stuffed Bunny. "Mr. S. Claws in Red." Standing Santa Rabbit. 24" tall, mohair and free standing. His coat and vest are made from vintage velvet and trimmed in antique tinsel. Holds a small feather tree in paw. Pack basket is filled with vintage accessories. Carries a vintage book under his arm. Original folk art creation by Baker & Co. Designs Ltd. New. Mint condition. **$725–775**

Toy, Stuffed Bunny. "Mr. S. Claws in Rose." Standing Santa Rabbit. 24" tall, mohair and free standing. His coat and vest are made from vintage velvet and trimmed in antique tinsel. Holds a small feather tree in upstretched paw. His pack basket is filled with vintage accessories. He carries a vintage book under his arm. Original folk art creation by Baker & Co. Designs Ltd. New. Mint condition. **$725–775**

Toy, Stuffed Bunny. "Skates Bunny." 12" beige mohair bunny in a vintage red skate. Wears a stocking cap and holds a vintage chenille candy cane. Original folk art by Baker & Co. Designs Ltd. New. Mint condition. **$265–300**

Toy, Stuffed Mouse. "Dickens Mouse." 10" beige mohair mouse, wool felt ears and tail. Wears a wool scarf and top hat. Original folk art creation by Baker & Co. Designs Ltd. New. Mint condition. **$185–215**

Toy, Stuffed Mouse. "Stockin Mouse." 10" dark grey mohair mouse. Wool felt ears and tail. Wears a striped stocking cap and holds a vintage ornament. Original folk art creation by Baker & Co. Designs Ltd. New. Mint condition. **$185–215**

Toy, Stuffed Panda. "Christmas Panda." 18" mohair panda wears a stocking cap and carries a ticking candy cane. Foot and paw pads are red wool felt. Original folk art creation by Baker & Co. Designs Ltd. New. Mint condition. **$295–345**

Toy, Stuffed Rabbit. "Holly Rabbit." 15" brown mohair rabbit with quite big feet. She wears a dress made from vintage fabric and holds a vintage bottle brush tree. Original folk art creation by Baker & Co. Designs Ltd. New. Mint condition. **$275–325**

Tree Topper, Champagne Finial. Department 56. #56.17624 Finial is a champagne color and features exquisite traditional gold, green, and red glitter detail. Made up of three round ornaments, sized 4½", 4", and 3½", respectively. Each of the round ornaments has very intricate glitter holly and ivy designs. Capped with textured spire about 10" long. Total length: 23½". Mint in box. **$40–75**

Trees, Bottle Brush, with Small Houses. All were introduced in 2004. Mint condition. 12" bottle brush tree set in small white house, **$21–25.** 9" bottle brush tree set in blue house, **$15.50–20.** 7" bottle brush tree set in pink house, **$11.50–15.**

Trinket Box, Disney, Donald Duck. Circa 1999. New. Mint in box condition. **$25–35**

Village Building, Blythe Pond Mill House, Department 56. Retired piece from Department 56. Issued in 1986 and retired in 1990. Lit from back. 7½" × 8¼" × 5¾". Marked "Dickens' Village Mill, Handpainted Porcelain, Made in Taiwan exclusively for Department 56, Minneapolis, MN." Bottom marked "Blythe Pond, Dickens' Series, 1986, Department 56." Has Department 56 sticker. Mint in box. **$230–275**

Village Building, Tuttle's Pub Building, Department 56. Retired piece from Dickens' Village Series. Issued 1986 and retired 1989. 6½" × 5¾". Marked "Dickens' Lane, Handpainted Porcelain, Made in Taiwan exclusively for Department 56, Minneapolis, MN." Bottom marked "Pub, Dickens' Series, 1986, Department 56." Department 56 sticker. Original box, some creases, minor tears and stains. Excellent condition.   **$200–250**

Village Building, Village Well and Holy Cross. Retired set from Department 56. Issued in 1987 and retired in 1989. Box marked "Heritage Village Collection, Village Well and Holy Cross, Set of 2, Handpainted Porcelain, Made in Taiwan exclusively for Department 56, Minneapolis, MN, 6547-1 USA." Bottom of well marked "1987, Department 56." Well has sticker but cross does not. Mint condition.   **$120–140**

Wood Fence. Nineteen pieces, in box. Eight long sections, two gates, and nine fence posts. Reproduced from a vintage original. Courtesy of Jamieson Studios. New. Mint condition.   **$58–64**

Wreaths, Bottle Brush. Three colors (red, green, and ivory). Courtesy of Jamieson Studios. New. Mint condition.   **$10–15**

Boxing Day (December 26)

Boxing Day, also called Saint Stephen's Day, is celebrated in England, Australia, New Zealand, and other places where people of English descent live. On this holiday, the day after Christmas, presents are given to those less fortunate. During earlier centuries, employers would give their employees gifts on Boxing Day, something akin to giving a tip. The needy would be given boxes of clothes or other durable goods. In fact, the term "boxing day" came from the boxes that donations might be left in, or the earthenware boxes that churches used to collect donations for the poor.

This holiday's collectibles include posters, stamps, figurines, and tickets or information about events held on that day.

PRICE LIST: BOXING DAY COLLECTIBLES

Figurine, Boxing Day Meet. Depicts rider in red riding clothes on grey horse with hounds at the horse's feet. Created by Border Fine Arts. Limited edition. Approximately 8" tall. Excellent condition.   **$500–550**

Figurine, Department 56, Dickens' Village. "A Boxing Day Tradition." #58595. Depicts a Victorian couple, father lifting child to place a package in large brown box. Approximately 3" tall. Excellent condition.   **$18–22**

Figurine, Peter Fagan Colour Box Bear. Called Boxing Day, XTC 313. Special Edition Christmas piece issued Christmas 1989 and retired in 1991. Features August String bear dressed for his Christmas Party. Excellent condition.   **$10–12**

Poster, 2003 Boxing Day Test. Commemorates the test match between Australia and India at the MCG in Melbourne, Australia on December 26, 2003. Drawn by artist Ivano. Approx. 25" × 17½". Excellent condition.   **$7–10**

Programme, Soccer Match, Wolves v. Villa, Boxing Day 1951. Programme has staples removed. Color depiction of team players in snowy conditions on cover. Good condition.
$50–55

Tickets, The Zutons, Boxing Day. Two tickets to see The Zutons at Carling Academy Liverpool on Boxing Day 2005. Mint condition.
$65–75

Kwanzaa (December 26-January 2)

The creator of this holiday, Dr. Maulana Karenga, states that it "brings a cultural message which speaks to the best of what it means to be African and human in the fullest sense." A Pan-American and African-American holiday, Kwanzaa celebrates family, community, and culture. People gather to affirm the natural bonds between them, either through blood or through cultural similarities.

Established in 1966, the holiday was a result of the Black Freedom Movement and was conceived to reaffirm social identity during the Black Liberation Movement. It is a time for people to recognize their roots in African culture and strengthen their communities. Finally, Kwanzaa was created to introduce and reinforce the *Nguzo Saba* (the Seven Principles.) These values are: *Umoja* (unity), *Kujichagulia* (self-determination), *Ujima* (collective work and responsibility), *Ujamaa* (cooperative economics), *Nia* (purpose), *Kuumba* (creativity), and *Imani* (faith).

Celebrants of the holiday greet each other in Swahili, exchange gifts (especially with children) like books and heritage symbols, and utilize the Kwanzaa colors of black, green, and red in their decorations. Homes are decorated in traditional African cloth and art, and fresh fruits and vegetables are part of the holiday meal. All of the foods and decorative accents are meant to embody African culture.

Kwanzaa collectibles include books, posters, figures, artwork, stamps, fabric, dolls, candles, jewelry, and ornaments.

PRICE LIST: KWANZAA COLLECTIBLES

Candleholder, Kinara. Kwanzaa candleholder depicts African woman whose hair spreads out and holds the seven candles that stand for the seven principles. 20¾" wide. Artist's mold has been broken, so this is a limited edition.
$85–100

Candleholder, Kwanzaa. Wood. Hand carved in Ghana. Gye Nyame design. 11½" × 6". Excellent condition.
$35–45

Doll, Madame Alexander. Kwanzaa doll (#10368) depicted in golden African robes and shoes to match. Created in 1996. 10" tall. Mint condition.
$50–60

Fabric, Kwanzaa. Four yards "Happy Kwanzaa" fabric. 45" wide cotton fabric, with Happy Kwanzaa, candles, red and green designed stripes all over. 100% cotton. Mint condition.
$25–30

Figurine, International Santa, Kwanzaa. SC15 Kwanzaa Africa. Part of The International Santa Claus Collection. An Exclusive Creation of International Resourcing, Inc. Depicts African gentleman holding aloft a plate of fruits with a basket of presents at his feet. Dressed in traditional African clothing. Comes with book about International Santas. Excellent condition. $75–85

Stamps, Kwanzaa. 32 cent stamps. Plate number pane from the press sheet of the Kwanzaa (Scott #3175) issue. Mint condition. $175–200

RESOURCES

Associations and Collector Groups

Coca-Cola Christmas Collectors Society
www.cavanaghgrp.com/ccccs

The Christopher Radko Starlight Family of Collectors
www.radkosales.com/JoinRadko Club.htm

Old World Christmas Collectors' Club
P.O. Box 8000, Department C, Spokane, WA 99203

Walt Disney Collectors Society
www.disney.go.com/DisneyArtClassics/collectorssociety

Swarovski Collectors Society
www.sparklingrose.net/scs.html

The Golden Glow of Christmas Past
www.goldenglow.org

CONTRIBUTORS

Lori Ann Baker-Corelis
Baker & Co. Designs Ltd.
614-865-0977
bakerdesigns@mac.com
www.bakercompanydesigns.com

Ginny Betourne
Trout Creek Folk Art
www.troutcreekfolkart.com

Gary Heidinger and Barbara Brunner
angel@christmas.li
www.christmas.li

Jamieson Studios
330-456-5593
fax: 330-452-9685
jjamieson@neo.rr.com
www.jamiesonstudios.com

Holly Knight, Collector
Florida

Jean Littlejohn
Clyde, North Carolina
ncsantamaker@brinet.com

Bethany Lowe
Bethany Lowe Designs, Inc.
16655 County Hwy 16
Osco, IL 61274
309-944-6213
fax: 309-944-3205
www.bethanylowe.com

Maison Russe
1720 Ogden Ave.
Lisle, IL 60532
800-778-9404
www.TheRussianShop.com

Nancy McJunkin
Nancy's Collectibles

281-350-3992
www.nancyscollectibles.com

Lori C. Mitchell
3309 Kensington Avenue,
Richmond, VA 23221
lori@ladeedahfolkart.com
La Dee Dah Folk Art
www.ladeedahfolkart.com

Jeff Ostroff
www.Sellerdropoff.com

Karen Pinckney
c/o Cocoa Village Antique Mall
105 Brevard Avenue, Cocoa, FL 32922
321-576-0393

C.S. Post & Co., A General Store
117 West 11th Street
Hays, KS 67601
785-628-3000
fax: 785-628-2228
www.cspost.com

Tom Pritchard
www.TomPritchard.com

Scott Smith
Rucus Studio/Rucus Graphics
P.O. Box 1872
Portage, MI 49081-1872
269-553-1852
www.rucusstudio.com

Sharyn Sowell Studio
www.sharynsowell.com

Museums and Auction Houses

The American Museum
Claverton Manor

Bath, BA2 7BD
England
01225 460503
Fax: 01225 469160
info@americanmuseum.org

Noel Barrett
P.O. Box 300
Carversville, PA 18913
215-297-5109
www.noelbarrett.com

Bonhams & Butterfields
220 San Bruno Avenue
San Francisco, CA 94103
www.butterfields.com

Christie's
London, +44 (0)20 7839 9060
New York, 212-492-5485
info@christies.com
www.christies.com

Christmas Museum
Deutsches Weihnachtsmuseum GmbH
Herrngasse 1
91541 Rothenburg ob der Tauber
Germany
weihnachtsmuseum@wohlfahrt.com

Doyle New York
175 East 87th Street
New York, NY 10128
212-427-2730
www.doylenewyork.com

Elmhurst Historical Museum
120 E. Park Avenue
Elmhurst, IL 60126
630-833-1457
www.www.elmhurst.org/

Garth's Auctions, Inc.
2690 Stratford Rd., P.O. Box 369
Delaware, OH 43015
740-362-4771
Fax: 740-363-0164
info@garths.com
www.garths.com

Morphy's Auction House
2000 North Reading Road
Denver, PA 17517
www.morphyauctions.com

National Christmas Center
3427 Lincoln Highway
Paradise, PA 17562
717-442-7950
Fax: 717-442-9304
info@nationalchristmascenter.com

Richard Opfer Auctioneering, Inc.
1919 Greenspring Drive
Timonium, MD 21093
410-252-5035
Fax: 410-252-5863
info@opferauction.com
www.opferauction.com

Skinner's Auction House
63 Park Plaza
Boston, MA
AND 357 Main Street
Bolton, Massachusetts
www.skinnerinc.com

Smithsonian Institution
Washington, D.C.
www.smithsonian.org

Sotheby's (locations worldwide)
1334 York Avenue at 72nd St.
New York, New York 10021
212-606-7000
Fax: 212-606-7107
www.sothebys.com

Theriault's
P.O. Box 151
Annapolis, MD 21404
410-224-3655
1-800-638-0422 (U.S. only)
Fax: 410-224-2515

BIBLIOGRAPHY

"About Lori Ann Baker." Baker and Company Designs. 5 October 2005.
www.bakerandcompany.com/about.html

"About the Publishers." 11 October 2005.
www.jewelspostcards.com/byp.htm

"About Us." Bethany Lowe Designs. 5 October 2005.
www.bethanylowe.com/about_us.php

"About Us." The Beistle Company. 13 October 2005.
www.beistle.com/aboutus.asp?User=consumer&ID=2yuTPjEmpb

"Adventskalender Museum." Richard Sellmer. 5 November 2005.

"The Advent Wreath." Latin Mass. 1 November 2005.
www.latin-mass.org/advent_wreath.htm

"All About the Christmas Tree." Religious Tolerance. 1 November 2005.
www.religioustolerance.org/xmas_tree.htm

"All Saints Day." Valuing Our Differences: Celebrating Diversity. 14 October 2005.
www3.kumc.edu/diversity/ethnic_relig/allsaint.html

"All Souls Day." Wikipedia. 14 October 2005.
www.en.wikipedia.org/wiki/All_Souls_Day

Almond, Steve. "The Kings of Candy." 16-23 March 2000. *Boston Phoenix*.
30 September 2005.

Althoff, K. W. *The Legend of the Nutcracker and Traditions of the Erzgebirge*. Midwest
Importers, Inc., 1983.

Alward, Mary M. "Valentine Card Challenge." Suite 101.com. 29 September 2005.
www.suite101.com/article.cfm/history_for_children/113528

"An American Christmas: Decade by Decade." Herbert Hoover Museum. 11 November 2005. *www.hoover.archives.gov/exhibits/AmChristmas/1970*

Angell, Carole S. *Celebrations Around the World: A Multicultural Handbook.* Golden, CO: Fulcrum Publishing, 1996.

Apkarian-Russell, Pamela E. *Postmarked Yesteryear: Art of the Holiday Postcard.* Portland: Collector Press, 2001.

Aurora, William. "History of Wind-up Toys." Bergen. 11 November 2005. *www.bergen.org/AAST/projects/Engineering_Graphics/johsch/page5.html*

Bear, David. "Travel: Giving Snow Globes a Fair Shake." *Post Gazette*, 08 October 2000.

Becket, James. *Christmas Collectibles.* Dallas: Beckett Publications, 1998.

"Bell Talk." American Bell Association. 2003–2005. 6 November 2006. *www.americanbell.org*

Black, Yuwanda. "History of the Christmas Stocking." 11 November 2005. *www.creativehomemaking.com*

"Black History Month." Black History. 17 September 2005. *www.blackhistory.com/cgi-bin/webc.cgi/home.html*

"Bobblehead Doll." Wikipedia. 7 November 2005. *www.en.wikipedia.org/wiki/Bobblehead_doll*

"Boxing Day." Snopes. 1 November 2005. *www.snopes.com/holidays/christmas/boxing.asp*

Bryan-Smith, Lissa and Richard Smith. *Holiday Collectibles: Vintage Flea Market Treasures Price Guide.* Iola, WI: Krause Publications, 1998.

"Captain Jack's Christmas Tree Farm." Christmas Tree. 11 November 2005. *www.christmas-tree.com/where.html*

"Christmas Designs." Hallmark. 5 November 2005. *www.pressroom.hallmark.com/christmas.html*

"The Christmas Tree." Biblical Quality. 5 November 2005. *www.biblicalquality.com/Christmas1.html*

"Christopher Radko Ornaments."
www.christopherradko.com/HowOrnamentsAreMade.aspx

"Christopher Radko." 2005. Radko.com 5 October 2005.
www.radko.com/PressRoomFacts.aspx

"The Chronological History of the Christmas Tree." *Christmas Archives.*
11 November 2005.
www.christmasarchives.com/trees.html

"Chronology of Events." 1999–2005. The Declaration of Independence. U.S. History.
7 October 2005.
www.ushistory.org/declaration/timeline.htm

"Cinco de Mayo History." 3 March 2005. Viva Cinco de Mayo. 7 October 2005.
www.vivacincodemayo.org/history.htm

"Clement Clarke Moore." New York Institution for the Blind. 5 November 2005.
www.nyise.org/moore/

"Clement Clarke Moore." Wikipedia. 5 November 2005.
www.en.wikipedia.org/wiki/Clement_Moore

"Clinking of Wine Glasses and Toasts." 11 September 2005. Wine Intro.
www.wineintro.com/champagne/clinkglass.html

Cohen, Hennig, and Tristram Potter Coffin, eds. *The Folklore of American Holidays,
Second Edition.* Detroit: Gale Research, Inc., 1991.

"Coke Lore." 5 November 2005.
www2.coca-cola.com/heritage/cokelore_santa.html

"The Cole Horsley Card." 2005. Scrap Album. 18 September 2005.
www.scrapalbum.com/xmashome.html

Dees, Beth. *Santa's Price Guide to Contemporary Christmas Collectibles.* Iola, WI: Krause
Publications, 1997.

"Earth Day 2005." Earth Day Network. 5 October 2005.
www.earthday.net/default.aspx

"Earth Day is Not April 22." Earthsite. 5 October 2005.
www.earthsite.org/origin.htm

"Easter Collectibles Signal Springtime." About Antiques. 5 October 2005.
www.antiques.about.com/library/weekly/aa032302.htm

"Easter Eggs." Holidays.Net. 5 October 2005.
www.holidays.net/easter/eggs.htm

"Easter on the Net." Holidays. 4 October 2005.
www.holidays.net/easter/story.htm

Elder, Bethany. "'Twas the Night Before Christmas Collection Reveals Santa's Many Images." Carnegie Mellon. 5 November 2005.
www.cmu.edu/cmnews/extra/031215_nitebeforexmas.html

Encyclopedia of Food and Culture. New York: Charles Scribner's Sons, 2003.

"Equality Day." 8 October 2005.
www.nwhp.org/events/equality-day/history-of-equality-day.html

Etter, Roberta B. *Tokens of Love.* New York: Abbeville Press, 1990.

Fendelman, Helaine, and Jeri Schwartz. *The Official Price Guide to Holiday Collectibles.* New York: House of Collectibles/Random House, 1991.

Festivals and Holidays. New York: Macmillan Library Reference USA, 1999.

"Flag Day." 2000-2005. Holiday Insights. 7 October 2005.
www.holidayinsights.com/other/flagday.htm

Glasell, Pamela. "Collector's Guide to Vintage Tablecloths." 11 November 2005.
www.forums.ebay.com/db2/thread.jspa?threadID=32885

Gregory, Ruth W. *Anniversaries and Holidays: Fourth Edition.* Chicago: American Library Association, 1983.

"Guy Fawkes and Bonfire Night." Bonefire. 14 October 2005.
www.bonefire.org/guy/bonfire.php

"Hallmark Corporate Timeline." 29 September 2005. Hallmark. *www.pressroom.hallmark.com/timeline_key_dates.html*

"Halloween." Religious Tolerance. 11 October 2005.
www.religioustolerance.org/hallo_np.htm

"Hanukkah." Wikipedia. 31 October 2005.
www.en.wikipedia.org/wiki/Hanukkah

"Happy New Year." 11 September 2005. Wilstar.
www.wilstar.com/holidays/newyear.htm

Hennigan, Linda Susan. "Recreator of Sailors Valentines." 29 September 2005.
www.lyndasusanhennigan.com/

"Herr Christian Steinbach, Nutcrackers." Christmas Treasures. 5 November 2005.
www.christmas-treasures.com/steinbac.htm

"The History of Arbor Day." The National Arbor Day Foundation. 6 October 2005.
www.arborday.org/arborday/history.cfm

"History of Christmas Bells." Holiday Insights. 6 November 2006.
www.holidayinsights.com/xmas/bells.htm

"History of Christmas Tree: Christmas Stocking." 11 November 2005.
www.siec.k12.in.us/~west/proj/claus/stocking.htm

"History of Dresden Ornaments." Elmhurst Museum. 11 November 2005.
www.elmhurst.org/elmhurst/museum/artifact2.asp

"History of Father's Day." 7 October 2005.
www.twilightbridge.com/hobbies/festivals/father/history.html

"The History of Flag Day."10 February 2005. U.S. Flag. 7 October 2005.
www.usflag.org/history/flagday.html

"The History of Halloween." History Channel. 11 October 2005.
www.historychannel.com/exhibits/halloween/?page=world

"History of Hanukkah." 1996–2005. The History Channel. 28 October 2005.
www.historychannel.com/exhibits/holidays/hanukkah/

"History of Holiday Ornaments." Christmas Decorations. 11 November 2005.
www.christmas-decorations-gifts-store.com/christmas_ornaments.htm

"The History of Labor Day." Department of Labor. 9 October 2005.
www.dol.gov/opa/aboutdol/laborday.htm

"History of Luciadagen." Bill Pietro. 31 October 2005.
www.billpetro.com/HolidayHistory/hol/xmas/lucia.html

"History of Mardi Gras." 1995–2005 Studio Melizio. 4 October 2005.
www.holidays.net/mardigras/story.htm

"The History of Martin Luther King Day." Info Please. 17 September 2005.
www.infoplease.com/spot/mlkhistory1.html

"The History of Memorial Day." 7 October 2005.
www.historychannel.com/exhibits/memorial/index.jsp?page=history

"History of New Year's Eve in Times Square." 11 September 2005. Times Square
Alliance.
www.timessquarenyc.org/nye/nye_history.html

"History of Nutcrackers." Magic of Nutcrackers. 5 November 2005.
www.magicofnutcrackers.com/Nutcrackers/CollectionFullSize.htm

"History of Passover." Wikipedia. 5 October 2005.
www.en.wikipedia.org/wiki/Passover_Seder

"The History of Snowglobes." Intimate Expression Gifts. 8 November 2005.
www.intimatexpressiongifts.com/snowglobe.history.html

"The History of Thanksgiving and Its Celebrations." 22 October 2005.
www.holidays.net/thanksgiving/story.htm

"The History of the Advent Calendar." About.com. 5 November 2005.
www.collectibles.about.com/library/weekly/aa120101a.htm

"History of the Bobblehead." Bill Bam. 7 November 2005.
www.billbam.com/hiofbo.html

"History of the Card." 8 May 2005. Penumbra. 29 September 2005.
www.novareinna.com/festive/valcard.html

"The History of the Christmas Tree." Suite 101. 11 November 2005.
www.suite101.com/article.cfm/perennials/13081

"History of the Original Austrian Snowglobe." Almost Europe. 2001–2005.
8 November 2005.
www.almosteurope.com/AAustrian/Products/Globes/snowglobehistory.htm

"History of the Wreath." Nanuke. 11 November 2005.
www.nanuke.net/mileaway/wreath_history.htm

"History of Valentine's Day." The History Channel. 28 September 2005.
www.historychannel.com/exhibits/valentine/

"History of Waterford." 11 September 2005. Waterford.
www.waterford.com/about/aboutus.asp

"History of Windup Toys." Antique Antiques. 11 November 2005.
www.antique-antiques.com/antique-wind-up-toys.shtml

Hooper, Andy. "The Agreeable World of Bobbin' Heads." 13 October 2005.
www.collectingchannel.com/cdsDetArt.asp?CID=&PID=1794

Howard, Vicky. *The Book of Santa Claus.* Kansas City: Andrews McMeel Publishing, 2002.

Hueston, Marie Proeller. "Collecting Children's Books." 1999–2005. *Country Living.* 6 November 2005.
www.magazines.ivillage.com/countryliving/collect/expert/qas/0,,284647_622435,00.html

"Images of Uncle Sam." 1996–1999. David R. Smith. 8 October 2005.
www.home.nycap.rr.com/content/us_contents.html

"International Friendship Day." Friendship. 8 October 2005.
www.friendship.com.au/friendday.html

"International Left-Handed Day." 8 October 2005.
www.lefthandzone.com/site/684713/page/228794

Johnson, George. *Pictorial Guide to Christmas Ornaments & Collectibles.* Paducah, KY: Collector Books, 2004.

Ketchum, William C., Jr. *Holiday Ornaments and Antiques.* New York: Alfred A. Knopf, 1990.

Kreider, Katherine. *Valentines with Values.* Atglen, PA: Schiffer Publishing, Ltd., 1996.

Kroma, Dawn and Lou. "Beistle: An American Halloween Giant." *Halloween Newsletter.* 13 October 2005.
www.spookshows.com/beistle/beistle.htm

"Kwanzaa: A Celebration of Family, Community and Culture." The Official Kwanzaa Website. 1 November 2005.
www.officialkwanzaawebsite.org/

"The Language of the Fan." Ideco. 30 September 2005.
www.ideco.com/fans

"Las Posadas." Mexico Connect. 1 November 2005.
www.mexconnect.com/MEX/austin/posadas.html

"Las Posadas: Christmas Celebrations in Mexico." Zuzu. 1 November 2005.
www.zuzu.org/mex.html

"Left-Handers Day." Left Handers Day. 8 October 2005.
www.lefthandersday.com/

"Lucia's Day in Sweden." Internet at Work. 31 October 2005.
www.internet-at-work.com/hos_mcgrane/holidays/nora.html

Macduff, Betty. "Classy and Colorful Candy Containers." Candy Container Collectors of America. 11 October 2005.
www.go-star.com/antiquing/candycontainers.htm

"Macy's Thanksgiving Day Parade History." New York City Tourism. 22 October 2005.
www.nyctourist.com/macys_history1.htm

"Making Valentines: A Tradition in America." 25 January 2001. American Antiquarian. 29 September 2005.
www.americanantiquarian.org/Exhibitions/Valentines/victorian.htm

"The Mark B. Ledenbach Halloween Connection." Halloween Collector. 11 October 2005.
www.halloweencollector.com/history/

"May Day Tradition." The Holiday Spot. 7 October 2005.
www.theholidayspot.com/mayday/history.htm

"The McDonald's History: 1954-2004." McDonald's.com. 5 November 2005.
www.mcdonalds.com/corp/about/mcd_history_pg1/mcd_history_pg4.html

"Memorial Day History." U.S. Memorial Day. 8 October 2005.
www.usmemorialday.org/backgrnd.html

"The Most Famous Poster." 9 April 2003. Library of Congress. 8 October 2005.
www.loc.gov/exhibits/treasures/trm015.html

"Mother's Day History." Mother's Day 123 holiday. 7 October 2005.
www.mothers-day.123holiday.net/

Moyer, Patsy. "The Real Snow Baby." 8 November 2005.
www.zianet.com/patsyandfriends/028%20article%20Snow%20Baby.htm

"National Grandparents Day." 1999-2004. Grandparents Day. 9 October 2005.
www.www.grandparents-day.com/short_ver.htm

"The Nativity." Livaudais Christmas Collection. 7 November 2005.
www.livaudaisnet.com/nativity/nativity.html

"Necco Chronology." Necco. 30 September 2005.
www.necco.com

"New Year." 17 September 2005. Japan Guide.
www.japan-guide.com/e/e2064.html

"New Year's Eve and New Year's Day: History." 11 September 2005. Brownie Locks.com
www.brownielocks.com/NewYears.html

"Old German Snow Babies." Mary Morrison. 8 November 2005.
www.marymorrison.org/OldGermanPieces.html

"Other Ringing Materials."
www.msu.edu/~carillon/batmbook/chapter6.htm

"Paper Preservation." Antique Web. 5 November 2005.
www.antiqueweb.com/articles/paperpreservation.html

"Pewter Figurines from Michael Anthony Ricker." Ricker. 2005. 6 November 2005.
www.ricker.com/index.cfm?fuseaction=page.display&page_id=23

Pinkerton, Charlene. *Holiday Plastic Novelties: The Styrene Toys.* Atglen, PA: Schiffer
Publishing, Ltd., 1999.

Pittsburgh-Post Gazette. 18 September 2005.
www.www.post-gazette.com/travel/20001008bear1.asp

"Poinsettias." 11 November 2005. Christmas Corner.
www.christmas-corner.com/pointsettia.cfm

"Pop Goes the Weasel." Worldwide Words. 13 October 2005.
www.worldwidewords.org/qa/qa-pop1.htm

"Preserving Ephemera." Ephemera Society. 5 November 2005.
www.ephemerasociety.org/

"Presidents' Day: History of the Holiday." Miami-Dade Public Schools. 29 September
2005.
www.patriotism.org/presidents%5Fday/

Reed, Robert. "Those Fancy Valentines." *Antiques Shoppe*. February 2005. 29 September 2005.
www.antiqueshoppefl.com/articles/feb05/valentine.htm

"Remembering Pearl Harbor." 2001. National Geographic Society. 28 October 2005.
www.plasma.nationalgeographic.com/pearlharbor/

"Remembering Romance: George Whitney Valentines." 2005. About Antiques. 29 September 2005.
www.antiques.about.com/library/weekly/aa020700.htm

"Rosh Hoshanah." Judaism 101. 9 October 2005.
www.jewfaq.org/holiday2.htm#Dates

"Saint Nicholas, Bishop." 1999–2004. Women for Faith and Family. 28 October 2005.
www.wf-f.org/st.nicholas.html

"Saint Nicholas." Culture, Government of France. 28 October 2005.
www.culture.gouv.fr/culture/noel/angl/stnico.htm

Santa Claus Collection. Des Moines, Iowa: Meredith Corporation, 2003.

Schiffer, Margaret. *Christmas Ornaments: A Festive Study.* Atglen, PA: Schiffer Publishing, 1995.

Schulman, Bruce. "The Fabergé Experience."
www.users.vnet.net/schulman/Faberge/bio.html

"Short History of Collectible Plates." World Collectors Net. 7 November 2005.
www.worldcollectorsnet.com/magazine/issue14/iss14p4.html

"Sisters' Day." Rumela. 8 October 2005.
www.rumela.com/events/events_august_sister.htm

Spicer, Dorothy Gladys. *The Book of Festivals.* Detroit: Gale Research Company, 1969.

"St. Boniface." 11 November 2005.
www.newadvent.org/cathen/02656a.htm

"St. Patrick." 24 August 2005. *Catholic Encyclopedia.* 2 October 2005.
www.newadvent.org/cathen/11554a.htm

"Statue of Liberty." 2 October 2005. The National Park Service. 8 October 2005.
www.nps.gov/stli/prod02.htm#Statue%20of

"Stimmung Stunde Christmas Page." Stimmung Stunde. 5 November 2005.
www.stimmungstunde.com/christmas/

"The Story of Mother's Day." Copyright 1995–2005. Holidays. 7 October 2005.
www.holidays.net/mother/story.htm

Sullo, Eleanor. "Mistletoe History." Essortment. 1 November 2005.
www.momo.essortment.com/mistletoehistor_rljx.htm

"The Symbols of Christmas." The Bestiary. 1 November 2005.
www.netnitco.net/users/legend01/xmas97.htm

"Symbols of Christmas: Origins of Christmas Symbols and Traditions." New York Times Company. 1 November 2005.
www.homeworktips.about.com/library/blxmasym

"Thanks-Giving Square." 22 October 2005.
www.thanksgiving.org/2us.html

"The Thanksgiving Story." Wilstar. 22 October 2005.
www. wilstar.com/holidays/thankstr.htm

Thompson, Sue Ellen, and Helene Henderson. *Holidays, Festivals, and Celebrations of the World Dictionary, Second Edition.* Detroit: Omnigraphics, 1997.

Thompson, Sue Ellen, ed. *Holiday Symbols 1998.* Detroit: Omnigraphics, 1998.

"Today in History: April 19, Yankee Doodle." The Library of Congress: American Memory. 8 October 2005.
www.memory.loc.gov/ammem/today/apr19.html

"Toy Banks." 5 November 2005.
www.pond.com/paris/docs/banks.html

"The Traditions of Easter." Wilstar. 5 October 2005.
www.wilstar.com/holidays/easter.htm

"Traditions: Vintage Christmas." Christmas Traditions. 5 November 2005.
www.christmastraditions.com/Themes/Xmas/XmasVin4.htm

Van Capelleveen, R. T. "Christmas Stamps." Fortune City. 1999. 8 November 2005.
www.fortunecity.com/marina/armada/367/christma.htm

"Veterans Day." Miami-Dade Public Schools. 22 October 2005.
www.patriotism.org/veterans%5Fday/

"Victorian Chocolate Molds." Wendy Mullen. 6 November 2005.
www.victorianchocolatemolds.com/index.htm

"Victorian Christmas Decorations." Miss Mary's Gazette. 5 November 2005.
www.missmary.com/gazette/1104-extra.html

"The Victorian Language of Flowers." 30 September 2005. Apocalypse.
www.apocalypse.org/pub/u/hilda/flang.html

"Vintage Holiday Creations by Jamieson Studios." Jamieson Studios. 5 October 2006.
www.jamiesonstudios.com/

Whitmyer, Margaret and Kenn. *Christmas Collectibles, 2nd Edition.* Paducah, KY:
Collector Books, 1996.

"Who Am I?" Trout Creek Folk Art. 5 October 2005.
www.troutcreekfolkart.com/wst_page6.php

Williams, Sue. "Tussie Mussies: Talking Bouquets." 30 September 2005. Emmitsburg.
www.emmitsburg.net/gardens/articles/adams/2002/tussie_mussies.htm

"Women Children's Book Illustrators." Ortakales. 6 November 2005.
www.ortakales.com/illustrators/

York-Cail, Cheryl. "Happy Hunting: Cookie Jars." 6 November 2005.
www.thegavel.net/2012.html

INDEX

Pages in italics indicate illustrations.

ABOUT THE AUTHOR

Dawn Reno (now Dawn Reno Langley) is the author of the Random House titles *The Official® Price Guide to Native American Art* (2003) and *American Indian Collectibles* (1989). She has written many other books, including *The Unofficial Guide to eBay and Online Auctions* (Wiley, 2001), *The Unofficial Guide to Managing Time* (Wiley, 2000), *American Country Collectibles* (1990), *Collecting Romance Novels* (Alliance Publishers, 1995), *Contemporary Native American Artists* (Chilton, 1995) *The Encyclopedia of Black Collectibles: A Value and Identification Guide* (Chilton, 1995), *Native American Collectibles* (Avon, 1994); *Advertising Identification and Price Guide* (Avon, 1993); and *Collecting Black Americana* (Crown, 1986). Langley is a nationally-known expert on antiques and collectibles who is well connected in the antiques and collectibles field. She is an avid collector, with a Christmas collection numbering thousands of items.

A former college dean and professor of creative writing and English, she lives in Raleigh, North Carolina, where she teaches British literature and writing at a college-prep high school.